*New Beacon Bible Commentary

JEREMIAH 1-25
A Commentary in the Wesleyan Tradition

Alex Varughese

BEACON HILL PRESS
OF KANSAS CITY

Copyright 2008
by Alex Varughese and Beacon Hill Press of Kansas City

ISBN 978-0-8341-2364-9

Unless otherwise indicated all Scripture quotations are from the *Holy Bible, New International Version*® (NIV®). Copyright © 1973, 1978, 1984 by International Bible Society. Used by permission of Zondervan Publishing House. All rights reserved.

King James Version (KJV).

The *New Revised Standard Version* (NRSV) of the Bible, copyright 1989 by the Division of Christian Education of the National Council of the Churches of Christ in the USA. Used by permission. All rights reserved.

The *Revised Standard Version* (RSV) of the Bible, copyright 1946, 1952, 1971 by the Division of Christian Education of the National Council of the Churches of Christ in the USA. Used by permission.

Library of Congress Cataloging-in-Publication Data

Varughese, Alex, 1945-
  Jeremiah 1-25 / Alex Varughese.
    p. cm. — (New Beacon Bible commentary)
  Includes bibliographical references (p.   ).
  ISBN 978-0-8341-2364-9 (pbk.)
  1. Bible. O.T. Jeremiah I-XXV—Commentaries. I. Title.

  BS1525.53.V37 2008
  224'.207—dc22

2008008240

DEDICATION

To my beloved wife, Marcia, and my dear children
Sarah, Jeremy, Timothy, and Rachel
with profound gratitude for their love and support.

COMMENTARY EDITORS

General Editors

Alex Varughese
    Ph.D., Drew University
    Professor of Biblical Literature
    Mount Vernon Nazarene University
    Mount Vernon, Ohio

Roger Hahn
    Ph.D., Duke University
    Dean of the Faculty
    Professor of New Testament
    Nazarene Theological Seminary
    Kansas City, Missouri

George Lyons
    Ph.D., Emory University
    Professor of New Testament
    Northwest Nazarene University
    Nampa, Idaho

Section Editors

Joseph Coleson
    Ph.D., Brandeis University
    Professor of Old Testament
    Nazarene Theological Seminary
    Kansas City, Missouri

Robert Branson
    Ph.D., Boston University
    Professor of Biblical Literature
    Olivet Nazarene University
    Bourbonnais, Illinois

Alex Varughese
    Ph.D., Drew University
    Professor of Biblical Literature
    Mount Vernon Nazarene University
    Mount Vernon, Ohio

Jim Edlin
    Ph.D., Southern Baptist Theological
        Seminary
    Professor of Biblical Literature and
        Languages
    Chair of the Division of Religion and
        Philosophy
    MidAmerica Nazarene University
    Olathe, Kansas

Kent Brower
    Ph.D., The University of Manchester
    Vice Principal
    Senior Lecturer in Biblical Studies
    Nazarene Theological College
    Manchester, England

George Lyons
    Ph.D., Emory University
    Professor of New Testament
    Northwest Nazarene University
    Nampa, Idaho

Jeanne Serrão
    Ph.D., Claremont Graduate University
    Dean of the School of Theology and
        Philosophy
    Professor of Biblical Literature
    Mount Vernon Nazarene University
    Mount Vernon, Ohio

CONTENTS

General Editors' Preface	9
Acknowledgments	11
Abbreviations	13
Bibliography	15

INTRODUCTION — 17
A. The Importance of the Book of Jeremiah — 17
B. Historical Setting — 18
C. Jeremiah the Prophet — 20
D. Content, Genre, and Structure — 22
E. Hebrew Text Traditions of Jeremiah — 26
F. Theological Themes — 27
  1. The Incomparable Creator — 27
  2. The Sovereign and Transcendent God — 28
  3. The Sovereign God's Special Relationship to Israel — 28
  4. The Sovereign God of the Nations — 29
  5. God the Sovereign Judge of Judah — 29
  6. God's Sovereignty and Freedom — 30
  7. The Sovereign God's Suffering Love — 31
  8. The Sovereign God of Hope, Healing, and Restoration — 31
  9. The Sovereign God's Sovereign Word — 32

COMMENTARY — 35

Superscription (1:1-3)
35

"Uproot and Tear Down": God Commissions Jeremiah (1:4-19) — 38

"Uproot and Tear Down": Judah's Idolatry and Infidelity (2:1—4:4) — 47

A. Yahweh's Lawsuit (2:1-37) — 48
  1. Sweet Memories (2:1-3) — 49
  2. Bartering for Junk (2:4-13) — 51
  3. Self-Imposed Slavery (2:14-19) — 55
  4. Self-Proclaimed Freedom (2:20-22) — 57
  5. Desperate for Love (2:23-25) — 59
  6. Yahweh or Baal? (2:26-28) — 61
  7. A Countersuit (2:29-32) — 62
  8. Shame and Humiliation (2:33-37) — 64

B. The Call to Return (3:1—4:4) — 66
  1. Return to Me (3:1-5) — 66

2. Return! (3:6-18)	69
3. Yahweh's Lament (3:19-22a)	72
4. A Model Liturgy of Repentance (3:22b-25)	74
5. Another Call to Return (4:1-4)	76

"Uproot and Tear Down": The Agency of the Enemy from the North (4:5—6:30) — 81

1. Disaster from the North (4:5-10)	83
2. This Is Your Punishment (4:11-18)	86
3. Oh, My Anguish! (4:19-22)	88
4. Cosmic Chaos (4:23-28)	90
5. A Woman in Scarlet Dress (4:29-31)	92
6. A Search and Rescue Mission (5:1-9)	94
7. The Sword of the Enemy (5:10-19)	96
8. A Foolish and Senseless People (5:20-31)	99
9. Flee for Safety (6:1-8)	102
10. The Wrath of God (6:9-15)	105
11. Ask for the Ancient Paths (6:16-21)	107
12. An Army Is Coming (6:22-26)	109
13. A New Task for Jeremiah (6:27-30)	110

"Uproot and Tear Down": Judah's False and Corrupt Worship (7:1—8:3) — 113

1. The Temple: A Den of Robbers (7:1-15)	114
2. Do Not Pray for This People (7:16-20)	119
3. A Deaf Society (7:21-29)	121
4. The Valley of Slaughter (7:30—8:3)	123

"Uproot and Tear Down": Judah's Deceit and Falsehood (8:4—10:25) 126

1. Even the Birds Know Better (8:4-13)	127
2. Not Enough Tears (8:14—9:1)	129
3. A Nation of Jacobs (9:2-11)	133
4. Let Me Tell You Why (9:12-16)	136
5. "How Ruined We Are!" (9:17-22)	138
6. A Little Sermon on Boasting (9:23-26)	140
7. Incomparable Yahweh (10:1-16)	142
8. The Inevitable Exile (10:17-25)	147

"Uproot and Tear Down": Judah's Covenant-Breaking (11:1—12:17) 151

1. The Broken Covenant (11:1-17)	152
2. Jeremiah's Lament and Yahweh's Response (11:18—12:6)	158
3. Yahweh's Lament (12:7-13)	164
4. A Call to Conversion (12:14-17)	168

"Uproot and Tear Down": Judah's Pride (13:1-27) — 171

1. The Ruined Loincloth (13:1-11)	172
2. Jars Filled with Wine (13:12-14)	175

3. Pride, Shame, and Humiliation (13:15-27)		177
a. The Disappearing Light (13:15-17)		177
b. A Lowly Place for the Royal Family (13:18-19)		178
c. How Long, O Jerusalem? (13:20-27)		179

"Uproot and Tear Down": No More Prophetic Mediation (14:1—15:21) 183

1. A Devastating Drought (14:1-9) 184
2. No Reprieve from Sword and Famine (14:10-16) 186
3. Yahweh Weeps (14:17-18) 190
4. Remember Your Covenant (14:19-22) 191
5. Judah's Fate Is Sealed (15:1-4) 193
6. No One Will Have Pity on Jerusalem (15:5-9) 196
7. Jeremiah's Lament (15:10-21) 198
   - a. The Prophet's Complaint and Yahweh's Response (15:10-14) 199
   - b. Jeremiah's Lament and Yahweh's Response (15:15-21) 202

"Uproot and Tear Down": Judah's Social World (16:1-21) 206

1. Do Not Marry (16:1-13) 207
2. Homecoming of the Exiled (16:14-15) 211
3. Judgment for Defiling the Land (16:16-18) 213
4. Confession of the Nations (16:19-21) 214

"Uproot and Tear Down": Judah's Self-Trust (17:1-27) 217

1. An Indelible Writing of Sin (17:1-4) 218
2. Two Ways of Life (17:5-13) 220
3. Heal Me! (17:14-18) 226
4. On Sabbath-Keeping (17:19-27) 228

"Uproot and Tear Down": Judah, a Vessel for Destruction (18:1—20:18) 233

1. Yahweh the Potter (18:1-12) 234
2. My People Have Forgotten Me (18:13-17) 237
3. The People's Plot and Jeremiah's Lament (18:18-23) 239
4. The Valley of Slaughter (19:1-13) 243
5. A Beaten but Bold Messenger (19:14—20:6) 247
6. Jeremiah: A Broken Vessel (20:7-18) 249

"Uproot and Tear Down": Judah's Political and Religious Leaders (21:1—23:40) 256

1. Death and Life Decisions (21:1-10) 257
2. Covenantal Duty of the Royal Family (21:11-14) 262
3. Another Sermon on Covenantal Duty (22:1-9) 264
4. Kings Under Judgment (22:10-30) 268
   - a. Shallum Shall Not Return (22:10-12) 268
   - b. Woe to the Oppressive and Unjust King (22:13-19) 269
   - c. The Fate of the Defiant City (22:20-23) 273
   - d. Coniah: A Despised, Broken Vessel (22:24-30) 275

	5. Woe to the Shepherds (23:1-8)	278
	6. Judgment on False Prophets (23:9-40)	284
	a. Indictment and Judgment (23:9-12)	285
	b. Prophets of Samaria and Jerusalem (23:13-15)	287
	c. True and False Prophets (23:16-22)	289
	d. Lying Prophets and Their Lying Dreams (23:23-32)	293
	e. The Burden of Yahweh (23:33-40)	297

"Uproot and Tear Down": Judah's Claim of the Land (24:1-10)   301
   The Good and the Bad Figs (24:1-10)   301

"Uproot and Tear Down": Judah and the Nations (25:1-38)   307
   1. Because You Have Not Obeyed (25:1-14)   308
   2. The Cup of Wrath and Yahweh's Universal Judgment (25:15-38)   313

GENERAL EDITORS' PREFACE

The purpose of the New Beacon Bible Commentary is to make available to pastors and students in the twenty-first century a biblical commentary that reflects the best scholarship in the Wesleyan theological tradition. The commentary project aims to make this scholarship accessible to a wider audience to assist them in their understanding and proclamation of Scripture as God's Word.

Writers of the volumes in this series not only are scholars within the Wesleyan theological tradition and experts in their field but also have special interest in the books assigned to them. Their task is to communicate clearly the critical consensus and the full range of other credible voices who have commented on the Scriptures. Though scholarship and scholarly contribution to the understanding of the Scriptures are key concerns of this series, it is not intended as an academic dialogue within the scholarly community. Commentators of this series constantly aim to demonstrate in their work the significance of the Bible as the church's book and the contemporary relevance and application of the biblical message. The project's overall goal is to make available to the church and for her service the fruits of the labors of scholars who are committed to their Christian faith.

The *New International Version* (NIV) is the reference version of the Bible used in this series; however, the focus of exegetical study and comments is the biblical text in its original language. When the commentary uses the NIV, it is printed in bold. The text printed in bold italics is the translation of the author. Commentators also refer to other translations where the text may be difficult or ambiguous.

The structure and organization of the commentaries in this series seeks to facilitate the study of the biblical text in a systematic and methodical way. Study of each biblical book begins with an **Introduction** section that gives an overview of authorship, date, provenance, audience, occasion, purpose, sociological/cultural issues, textual history, literary features, hermeneutical issues, and theological themes necessary to understand the book. This section also includes a brief outline of the book and a list of general works and standard commentaries.

The commentary section for each biblical book follows the outline of the book presented in the introduction. In some volumes, readers will find section ***overviews*** of large portions of scripture with general comments on their overall literary structure and other literary features. A consistent feature of the commentary is the paragraph-by-paragraph study of biblical texts. This section has three parts: **Behind the Text**, **In the Text**, and **From the Text**.

The goal of the **Behind the Text** section is to provide the reader with all the relevant information necessary to understand the text. This includes specific historical situations reflected in the text, the literary context of the text, sociological and cultural issues, and literary features of the text.

In the Text explores what the text says, following its verse-by-verse structure. This section includes a discussion of grammatical details, word studies, and the connectedness of the text to other biblical books/passages or other parts of the book being studied (the canonical relationship). This section provides transliterations of key words in Hebrew and Greek and their literal meanings. The goal here is to explain what the author would have meant and/or what the audience would have understood as the meaning of the text. This is the largest section of the commentary.

The ***From the Text*** section examines the text in relation to the following areas: theological significance, intertextuality, the history of interpretation, use of the Old Testament scriptures in the New Testament, interpretation in later church history, actualization, and application.

The commentary provides **sidebars** on topics of interest that are important but not necessarily part of an explanation of the biblical text. These topics are informational items and may cover archaeological, historical, literary, cultural, and theological matters that have relevance to the biblical text. Occasionally, longer detailed discussions of special topics are included as ***excurses.***

We offer this series with our hope and prayer that readers will find it a valuable resource for their understanding of God's Word and an indispensable tool for their critical engagement with the biblical texts.

Roger Hahn, Centennial Initiative General Editor
Alex Varughese, General Editor (Old Testament)
George Lyons, General Editor (New Testament)

ACKNOWLEDGMENTS

I was thrust into the world of Jeremiah during the course of a Ph.D. seminar directed by Herbert B. Huffmon at Drew University some thirty years ago. In the initial stages of my study of Jeremiah, the focus of my attention was on the shorter and longer Hebrew texts of the book. The outcome of this study was an unpublished dissertation on "The Hebrew *Vorlage* Underlying the Old Greek Translation of Jeremiah 1-20," under the direction of Herbert B. Huffmon and Paul A. Riemann in 1984. My interest in the book remained alive through an upper division undergraduate course on the seventh- and sixth-century prophets that I have regularly taught at Mount Vernon Nazarene University. This volume partially fulfills my dream that I had nurtured for several years to produce a commentary of Jeremiah from the perspective of the Wesleyan theological tradition.

Several people come to mind as the recipients of my gratitude for their role in helping this dream come true. Huffmon and Riemann, my professors at Drew University, deserve special recognition for their constant encouragement that motivated me to stay in the difficult world of Jeremiah during some of my own most difficult days.

This work began during a sabbatical granted to me by Mount Vernon Nazarene University in 2006. The administration of Mount Vernon Nazarene University continued to support me in this project by granting me a reduced teaching load during the 2006-7 academic year, for which I am deeply grateful.

Beacon Hill Press deserves special recognition for its vision, planning, and commitment to produce the New Beacon Bible Commentary series. There are not enough words to express my gratitude to Bonnie Perry, director of Beacon Hill Press, for being my cheerleader and trusted friend.

I am also thankful to Louis Stulman for reading portions of the manuscript of this volume and helping me with his insightful comments and encouragement. David Wilson read this volume from a pastoral perspective, and I am deeply in debt for his comments and suggestions for editorial changes.

Marcia, my wife, journeyed with me as I traveled once again through the difficult world of Jeremiah. Without her faithful and loving support, this work would not have been possible.

Finally, and most importantly, thanks be to God for his gracious presence and the guidance of his Holy Spirit that strengthened my feeble spirit during my journey through his Word.

—Alex Varughese

ABBREVIATIONS

With a few exceptions, these abbreviations follow those in *The SBL Handbook of Style* (Alexander 1999).

General

A.D.	anno Domini (precedes date) (equivalent to C.E.)
B.C.	before Christ (follows date) (equivalent to B.C.E.)
B.C.E.	before the Common Era
BDB	*Hebrew and English Lexicon of the Old Testament*
BHS	*Biblia Hebraica Stuttgartensia*
C.E.	Common Era
cf.	compare
ch	chapter
chs	chapters
e.g.	*exempli gratia*, for example
esp.	especially
etc.	*et cetera*, and the rest
f(f).	and the following one(s)
i.e.	*id est*, that is
lit.	literally
LXX	Septuagint
MS	manuscript
MSS	manuscripts
MT	Masoretic Text (of the OT)
n.	note
n.d.	no date
n.p.	no place; no publisher; no page
nn.	notes
NT	New Testament
OT	Old Testament
s.v.	*sub verbo*, under the word
v	verse
vv	verses

Modern English Versions

JPS	Hebrew-English Tanakh
KJV	King James Version
NIV	New International Version
NRSV	New Revised Standard Version
RSV	Revised Standard Version

Print Conventions for Translations

Bold font	NIV (bold without quotation marks in the text under study; elsewhere in the regular font, with quotation marks and no further identification)
Bold italic font	Author's translation (without quotation marks)

Behind the Text:	Literary or historical background information average readers might not know from reading the biblical text alone
In the Text:	Comments on the biblical text, words, phrases, grammar, and so forth
From the Text:	The use of the text by later interpreters, contemporary relevance, theological and ethical implications of the text, with particular emphasis on Wesleyan concerns

Greek Transliteration

Greek	Letter	English
α	alpha	a
β	bēta	b
γ	gamma	g
γ	gamma nasal	n (before γ, κ, ξ, χ)
δ	delta	d
ε	epsilon	e
ζ	zēta	z
η	ēta	ē
θ	thēta	th
ι	iōta	i
κ	kappa	k
λ	lambda	l
μ	my	m
ν	ny	n
ξ	xi	x
ο	omicron	o
π	pi	p
ρ	rhō	r
ρ	initial rhō	rh
σ/ς	sigma	s
τ	tau	t
υ	upsilon	y
υ	upsilon	u (in diphthongs: au, eu, ēu, ou, ui)
φ	phi	ph
χ	chi	ch
ψ	psi	ps
ω	ōmega	ō
ʽ	rough breathing	h (before initial vowels or diphthongs)

Hebrew Consonant Transliteration

Hebrew/Aramaic	Letter	English
א	alef	ʼ
ב	bet	b
ג	gimel	g
ד	dalet	d
ה	he	h
ו	vav	v or w
ז	zayin	z
ח	khet	ḥ
ט	tet	ṭ
י	yod	y
ך/כ	kaf	k
ל	lamed	l
ם/מ	mem	m
ן/נ	nun	n
ס	samek	s
ע	ayin	ʻ
ף/פ	pe	p
ץ/צ	tsade	ṣ
ק	qof	q
ר	resh	r
שׂ	sin	ś
שׁ	shin	š
ת	tav	t

BIBLIOGRAPHY

Bracke, John M. 2000a. *Jeremiah 1-29*. Louisville, Ky.: Westminster/John Knox.
———. 2000b. *Jeremiah 30-52 and Lamentations*. Louisville, Ky.: Westminster/John Knox.
Bright, John. 1965. *Jeremiah: A New Translation with Introduction and Commentary*. Anchor Bible 21. Garden City, N.Y.: Doubleday.
———. 2000. *A History of Israel*. Fourth Ed. Louisville, Ky.: Westminster/John Knox.
Brueggemann, Walter. 1983. "The Book of Jeremiah: Portrait of the Prophet." *Interpretation* 37:130-45.
———. 1998. *A Commentary on Jeremiah: Exile and Homecoming*. Grand Rapids: Eerdmans.
———. 2007. *Old Testament Theology: The Theology of the Book of Jeremiah*. Cambridge: Cambridge University Press.
Carroll, Robert P. 1986. *The Book of Jeremiah*. Old Testament Library. Philadelphia: Westminster.
Christensen, Duane L. 1975. *Transformations of the War Oracle in Old Testament Prophecy*. Missoula, Mont.: Scholars Press.
Clarke, Adam. N.d. *The Book of the Prophet Jeremiah*. *The Holy Bible: A Commentary and Critical Notes* IV, pp. 249-396. New York: Abingdon-Cokesbury Press.
Clements, Ronald E. 1988. *Jeremiah*. Interpretation. Atlanta: John Knox.
Craigie, Peter C., Page Kelley, Joel F. Drinkard Jr. 1991. *Jeremiah 1-25*. Word Biblical Commentary 26. Dallas: Word.
Duhm, B. 1901. *Das Buch Jeremia*. Tubingen: J.C.B. Mohr (P. Siebeck).
Fretheim, T. E. 2002. *Jeremiah*. Macon, Ga.: Smyth & Helwys.
Habel, Norman. 1965. "The Form and Significance of the Call Narratives." *Zeitschrift fur die alttestamentliche Wissenschaft* 77:297-323.
Heschel, Abraham J. 2001. *The Prophets*. New York: HarperPerennial.
Holladay, William L. 1986. *Jeremiah 1: A Commentary on the Book of the Prophet Jeremiah, Chapters 1-25*. Hermeneia. Philadelphia: Fortress.
———. 1989. *Jeremiah 2: A Commentary on the Book of the Prophet Jeremiah, Chapters 26-52*. Hermeneia. Philadelphia: Fortress.
Huffmon, Herbert. 1959. "The Covenant Lawsuit in the Prophets." *Journal of Biblical Literature* 78:290-95.
Lundbom, Jack R. 1999. *Jeremiah 1-20: A New Translation with Introduction and Commentary*. Anchor Bible 21A. New York: Doubleday.
———. 2004a. *Jeremiah 21-36: A New Translation with Introduction and Commentary*. Anchor Bible 21B. New York: Doubleday.
———. 2004b. *Jeremiah 37-52: A New Translation with Introduction and Commentary*. Anchor Bible 21C. New York: Doubleday.
Mays, James Luther. 1969. *Amos: A Commentary*. The Old Testament Library. Philadelphia: Westminster Press.
McKane, W. 1986. *A Critical and Exegetical Commentary on Jeremiah*. 2 vols. International Critical Commentary. Edinburgh: T & T Clark.
Miller, Patrick D. 2001. *The Book of Jeremiah*. New Interpreter's Bible 6, pp. 555-926. Nashville: Abingdon.
Mowinckel, Sigmund. 1914. *Zur Komposition des Buches Jeremia*. Kristiania: J. Dybwad.
O'Connor, Kathleen M. 1988. *The Confessions of Jeremiah: Their Interpretation and Role in Chapters 1-25*. Society of Biblical Literature Dissertation Series 94. Atlanta: Scholars.
Outler, Albert C. ed. 1984. *The Works of John Wesley. Volume 1. Sermons I:1-33*. Nashville: Abingdon Press.
Stulman, Louis. 1998. *Order Amid Chaos: Jeremiah as Symbolic Tapestry*. Sheffield: Sheffield Academic Press.
———. 2005. *Jeremiah*. Abingdon Old Testament Commentaries. Nashville: Abingdon.
Thompson, J. A. 1980. *The Book of Jeremiah*. New International Commentary on the Old Testament. Grand Rapids: Eerdmans.
Wesley, John. 1975. *Explanatory Notes upon the Old Testament*. Reprint. Salem, Ohio: Schmul Publishers.

INTRODUCTION

A. The Importance of the Book of Jeremiah

The book of Jeremiah occupies a prominent place in the Old Testament canon at least on three counts: (1) its massive size (the second longest book in the Bible and the longest prophetic book); (2) the complexity of its content and message; and (3) the towering prophetic figure behind the book that stands shoulder to shoulder with other great prophets such as Isaiah and Ezekiel. The tradition has placed this book between the scrolls of Isaiah and Ezekiel to highlight its significance as a major prophetic book. The theology of the book of Jeremiah is in direct contact with other Old Testament books such as Hosea and Deuteronomy, and it intersects with theological themes and ideas found in a number of other OT books, most notably Genesis, Exodus, Psalms, Job, Proverbs, Isaiah, and Ezekiel.

Jeremiah's influence is found in several New Testament

books, particularly in the Gospel of Matthew, Acts, several Pauline writings, Hebrews, and Revelation. Only the Gospel of Matthew preserves the name of Jeremiah in the response of the disciples to Jesus' question, "Who do people say the Son of Man is?" (Matt 16:13). Matthew also indicates that the massacre of infants in Bethlehem ordered by King Herod was a direct fulfillment of Jer 31:15 (Matt 2:17-18). All the Synoptic Gospels preserve Jeremiah's words "den of robbers" in Jesus' charge against the money changers and traders in the temple (Matt 21:13; Mark 11:17; Luke 19:46; see Jer 7:11). Jeremiah's new covenant message (31:31-34) is quoted almost verbatim in Heb 8:8-12.

B. Historical Setting

The opening statement of the book of Jeremiah (1:1-3) indicates that God's word came to Jeremiah in the thirteenth year of Josiah's reign (627 B.C.) and that it continued until the end of the eleventh year of Zedekiah's reign (587 B.C.). This statement thus locates the prophet's ministry during the late seventh and early sixth centuries B.C., a period that witnessed tumultuous change in the history of the ancient Near East (the political events outlined below follow the history of this period in Bright 2000, 313-47).

In 627 B.C.—the year of Jeremiah's call—Ashurbanipal (669-627 B.C.) the Assyrian king died, leaving the already weakening empire in the hands of rival political leaders. Judah was under the rule of a young king named Josiah (640-609 B.C.) who was placed on the throne at the age of eight. Josiah inherited a kingdom that was politically and religiously a vassal state of Assyria. His father Amon (642-640 B.C.) and his grandfather Manasseh (687-642 B.C.) promoted Assyrian forms of worship and other pagan religious practices in the land (2 Kgs 21:1-26). At the age of sixteen, Josiah "began to seek the God of his father David," and at the age of twenty (628 B.C.), "he began to purge Judah and Jerusalem of high places, Asherah poles, carved idols and cast images" (2 Chr 34:3; see vv 4-7). This religious reformation was aimed at restoring to Judah its national faith in God and liberating the nation from its political and religious loyalty to Assyria. Josiah's reform activities may have been prompted by the weakening of the Assyrian Empire during the final years of Ashurbanipal. During this religious reformation, the Book of the Law was found in the temple, which led Josiah to call the nation for the renewal of the covenant with God; the Book of the Law gave further impetus to Josiah to continue his reform activities (622 B.C.; 2 Kgs 22:3—23:14).

The Assyrian Empire continued to crumble in the next two decades. Babylon, led by Nabopolassar (626-605 B.C.), defeated Assyria and gained freedom in 626 B.C. A coalition of Babylonians and Medes brought Nineveh, the capital of the Assyrian Empire, to its end in 612 B.C. The coalition forces then moved to capture Haran, Assyria's last stronghold. In the meantime, Egypt decided to help its longtime rival Assyria to recapture Haran from the Babylonian-Mede forces.

As the Egyptian army led by Pharaoh Neco II was marching northward through Palestine, Josiah decided to stop them at Megiddo. In the battle that followed, Josiah was killed (609 B.C.). The Egyptians continued their march to Haran, but their attempt to help the Assyrians failed. The Babylonians established themselves as the new power broker in the ancient Near East.

It is not clear what prompted Josiah to get involved in international politics. Egypt's effort was clearly an attempt to exert its power during this critical period of geopolitical changes. Josiah may have foreseen the Egyptian ambition and perhaps decided to show support for Babylon, the emerging new world power. Whatever may have been Josiah's intentions, the tragic outcome of his effort to stop the Egyptians was Judah's loss of independence to Egypt. After Josiah's death the Judeans placed his son Jehoahaz on the throne (609 B.C.). But Pharaoh Neco deposed him and deported him to Egypt and placed his older brother Eliakim on the throne with the regnal name Jehoiakim. Jehoiakim remained a vassal of Egypt for the next four years (609-605 B.C.) and paid heavy tribute to Egypt with money and silver and gold he collected as taxes from the people (2 Kgs 23:31-35).

In the meantime, Egypt continued its attempt to gain control of the Syria-Palestine region. This led to a series of confrontations between the Egyptians and the Babylonians resulting in a decisive victory of Babylon over Egypt at Carchemish in 605 B.C. Nebuchadnezzar, who later took the throne of Babylon after the death of Nabopolassar in 605 B.C., led the Babylonian army in this battle. The Babylonian offensive continued southward into Palestine, which brought the Babylonian army to the Philistine Plain (604 B.C.). In that year, Jehoiakim decided to change his allegiance to Nebuchadnezzar, the new master of the region. Three years later in 601 B.C., Jehoiakim rebelled against Babylon (24:1); this may have been prompted by the withdrawal of the Babylonian army and its return home from the Egyptian border after suffering temporary setback in the battle against Egypt. In retaliation, the Babylonians sent bands of Syrians, Moabites, and Ammonites to destroy Judah (v 2). Second Kings reports the death of Jehoiakim (v 6), but the cause of death is not stated. According to the Chronicler's account, Nebuchadnezzar bound him in fetters to take him to Babylon (2 Chr 36:6). Scholars assume that he was assassinated during a palace revolt or he died on his way to Babylon as a prisoner in 598 B.C. His son Jehoiachin took the throne and ruled for three months. In 597 B.C. he surrendered to Nebuchadnezzar, who came to Jerusalem with his army. The Babylonian army took Jehoiachin, his mother, royal family members, high-ranking officials, and skilled workers to Babylon as prisoners along with treasures from the palace and the temple. Nebuchadnezzar placed on the throne Mattaniah, Jehoiachin's uncle, and gave him the regnal name Zedekiah (2 Kgs 24: 8-17).

Zedekiah's rule lasted for eleven years (597-587 B.C.). He made a trip to Babylon in the fourth year of his reign (Jer 51:59), perhaps to assure Nebuchadnezzar of his loyalty to Babylon. For reasons not clearly known, he rebelled against Babylon (2 Kgs 24:20). This may have been prompted by the message of the false prophets that God will soon bring Jehoiachin and the exiled people back to Judah and that God will break the yoke of Babylon (Jer 29:1-4). Nebuchadnezzar brought his army to Judah to put an end to Judah's rebellion. The Babylonians laid a siege against the city of Jerusalem; in 587 B.C., the city was taken by the Babylonians. Zedekiah, who attempted to escape, was captured and brought before Nebuchadnezzar at Riblah. He was blinded and taken as a prisoner to Babylon. The Babylonians destroyed the city and burned down the houses in the city, including the temple, and deported the population to Babylon. Only some of the poorest people were left in the land (2 Kgs 25:1-21).

Nebuchadnezzar appointed Gedaliah as governor over the population that was left in Judah. Under Gedaliah's leadership, those who were left in the land regrouped and Gedaliah challenged them to stay in the land and submit to the Babylonian rule. Even those Jews who escaped to Transjordan states returned to Judah, and there seems to have been a very brief period of peaceful life in the land (Jer 40:7-12). This came to an end and the nation was in turmoil again when a resistant group led by Ishmael, a royal family member, murdered Gedaliah around 582 B.C. Gedaliah's friends, led by Johanan, pursued Ishmael and the rebels, and the rebels escaped to the Ammonite territory. Fearing reprisal from Babylon, Johanan and his followers decided to leave Judah and escape to Egypt. They took with them Jeremiah as their hostage, without paying attention to his warning against going to Egypt (chs 41—43).

Jeremiah's ministry took place during this politically volatile period, which witnessed the rise and fall of major empires in the ancient Near East in the late seventh and early sixth centuries B.C. As the above outline of history indicates, Judah was caught in the middle of these geopolitical changes, and the impact of these events on Judah's political existence was disastrous. The book of Jeremiah gives witness to the crumbling political, social, moral, and religious conditions of Judah during this period. More than that, it gives witness to God's sovereign involvement in the historical process of this period. As God's spokesperson during this critical moment in the history of Judah and the nations of the world, it was Jeremiah's task to remind the covenant people of God that God's judgment on them for breaking their covenant with him was taking place through these historical events. The book indicates to us that his message to Judah, however, fell upon deaf ears.

C. Jeremiah the Prophet

The name Jeremiah, which is not an unusual name in the OT, more commonly appears in the book in the long form *yirmĕyāhû*, and nine times in the short form *yirmĕyâ* in 27:1—29:3 (Holladay 1986, 15). The meaning of the name is uncertain. Scholars suggest several possible meanings: "Yahweh exalts or lifts up" or "Yahweh casts or hurls" or "Yahweh loosens."

The book of Jeremiah does not contain any lengthy account of the personal life of the prophet. The biographical accounts in the book mostly sum up the prophet's actions and words. In the introductory statement of the book (1:1), Jeremiah is mentioned as the son of Hilkiah, a priestly resident in the village of Anathoth in the tribal territory of Benjamin. Hilkiah's identity is not known to us. An individual by the name Hilkiah served as high priest during the days of Josiah (2 Kgs 22:3-20). There is little evidence in the book that connects Jeremiah with Hilkiah the high priest of Josiah. Jeremiah's family association with Anathoth suggests that he may have been a descendant of Abiathar the priest, who in turn descended from the house of Eli (see 1 Sam 14:3; 22:20). He served as priest alongside Zadok during the days of David (2 Sam 15:24-29). Solomon exiled Abiathar to his family estate in Anathoth for giving support to Adonijah's claim to the throne after David's death. Solomon also made Zadok, who supported his kingship, as the priest in the place of Abiathar (1 Kgs 2:26-27, 35). It is very likely that the influential priests in Jerusalem who presided over the affairs of the temple belonged to the family of Zadok.

Jeremiah's prophetic ministry began in the thirteenth year of Josiah, in 627 B.C. (Jer 1:2). His call came while he was a young boy; his young age may have been the reason for his resistance to God's call (v 6). However, upon divine compulsion and reassurance, he accepted the task of the prophetic office (vv 7-10). His subsequent actions and words indicate that he constantly lived under this divine constraint to be Yahweh's spokesman to Judah.

Perhaps due to the conviction that Judah's destruction was near, and at the specific command of Yahweh, Jeremiah was never married (16:1-4). Yahweh's words, which Jeremiah spoke, made him more of an enemy than a friend of his nation. He was often denounced, pursued, and ostracized by his enemies. Even men of his own hometown of Anathoth wanted to put an end to his life (11:21-23). He was once barred from entering the temple (36:5) and a temple official had him beaten and put in stocks (20:2). The temple officials argued unsuccessfully before the royal officials that Jeremiah deserved the death penalty for announcing the destruction of the temple (26:1-9; cf. 7:1-15). His frequent calls to surrender to Babylon would have prompted the nation to view him as a traitor. After the Babylonian attack and deportation of the Judean citizens in 597 B.C., Jeremiah was thrown into a dungeon on charges of deserting to the enemy. Later he was transferred to a guardhouse where he remained until the destruction of Jerusalem in 587 B.C. (chs 37—38). The Babylonian army released him from the guardhouse and gave him the option either to stay in Judah or to go to Babylon as a royal guest, but he opted to stay in Judah (ch 40). Though Jeremiah was determined to stay in his ruined homeland, Johanan and his friends forcefully took him to Tahpanhes, a town within the Egyptian border (ch 43). The last known utterance of Jeremiah comes from this Egyptian locale (43:8—44:30), where presumably his life came to an end.

Recent scholarly assessment of the portrayal of Jeremiah in the book as a literary and theological product of the Deuteronomic traditions that gave shape to the book in the exilic/postexilic period greatly diminish and discount or even suppress the voice of the historical person of Jeremiah. Thus Carroll claims that the person of Jeremiah in the book is not a "real person" but the product of "various levels of tradition" making up the book (1986, 64). Brueggemann is more conciliatory than Carroll in his assessment of the person of Jeremiah. He does not think the book presents a "descriptive, biographical report" of the person of Jeremiah. He argues for the possibility that Jeremiah in the book is an "imaginative" and "theologically intentional" literary reconstruction of the "portrait" of the prophet governed by "a powerful person of memory." He also thinks that "the prophet himself was fully resonant" with the later portrayals of the prophet by the Deuteronomic tradition (1983, 131-32; also 2007, 27-28).

This commentary follows the trustworthiness of the historical reportage of Jeremiah in the book. The historical and biographical narratives in the book present the prophet as a person who was deeply aware of his calling to be a prophet of Yahweh at a critical time in Judah's history. He struggled with this call because it made him a person of intense conflict and dispute in the land, but he saw in the historical process the overwhelming display of Yahweh's sovereignty, which gave him the courage to speak with integrity about the coming death of Judah as well as its resurrection. The rejection of his message by the nation did not persuade him to withdraw from his ministry, but he remained a stubborn spokesperson for Yahweh. With stunning poetic imagination, he conveys in the book his (and Yahweh's) grief, agony, and suffering over a people who have stubbornly chosen for themselves the path of self-destruction. The book also portrays Jeremiah as a prophet of intense hope, who with passion and eloquence communicated to the nation Yahweh's gracious plans for its restoration and resettlement in the land after the days of its death and exile in a foreign land.

D. Content, Genre, and Structure

Materials in the book of Jeremiah seem to be organized into several literary blocks around the theme of judgment and salvation. However, the arrangement of these materials does not show any discernible chronological order or literary and theological coherence. Commentators generally divide the materials in the book into two sections: the first section (chs 1—25) centers on the message of judgment on Judah and Jerusalem and the second section (chs 26—52) centers on the theme of hope and salvation for Judah and Jerusalem. Most of the first section is in poetry; scattered here and there are prose materials mostly in the form of sermons. This section contains words of indictment against the social, political, and religious corruption of Judah and repeated threats and warnings of the nation's destruction through the agency of Babylon. This section also includes numerous calls for national repentance; these calls imply that the nation may avoid the impending judgment by giving heed to God's call for repentance.

The theme of salvation is sparsely found in a few isolated places in chs 1—25.

Biographical and historical narratives constitute the major part of the second section (chs 26—52). Chapter 26 narrates the events that followed Jeremiah's sermon in the temple (ch 7). This section also has large blocks of poetry (chs 30—33; 46—51). The theme of judgment is also found in chs 26—52 but is overshadowed by words of hope and salvation. Biographical materials are mostly accounts of events that happened during the reign of King Jehoiakim (chs 26, 35, 36) and King Zedekiah (chs 27—29, 34, 37—39) given without any chronological order. Judgment theme with repeated warnings of the coming exile appears in these chapters. The final days of Judah, the fall of Jerusalem, and the tragic fate of the Judeans are summarized in the biographical accounts in chs 40—44. An oracle addressed to Baruch constitutes chapter 45. Death of the nation, which is anticipated in chs 1—25, is taking place in these chapters as a historical reality. Scholars think that the biographical materials in chs 36—45 reflect the scribal activity of Baruch and hence describe these chapters as Baruch Narrative.

The book of consolation (chs 30—33), which contains hopeful words about restoration, is found before the narrative that deals with the destruction of Jerusalem and the exile of Judah to Babylon. Chapters 46—51, the Oracles Against the Nations, announce Yahweh's judgment of the surrounding nations. The book ends with an epilogue (ch 52), which corresponds to a great extent with the historical account of 2 Kgs 24:18—25:30.

Jeremiah 1—25 shows a variety of genre utilized by the prophet to convey Yahweh's message. Messenger-style speech is the most common genre in these chapters. Other genres include sermons, lawsuit, dialogue, symbolic acts, torah instruction, proverbial sayings, vision accounts, laments, prayers, and biographical reports. Scattered throughout chs 1—25 are recurring emotional outbursts of Jeremiah in the form complaints, laments, and prayers ("confessions").

The book of Jeremiah has generated considerable interest and speculation concerning its content and composition in the last one hundred years. Modern attempts to understand the book are usually traced to the studies of Duhm (1901) and Mowinckel (1914), who have identified in the book several literary strands or sources. Mowinckel described these as poetic oracles (source A), historical narratives (source B), and prose speeches (source C). He concluded that (1) the poetic oracles in chs 1—25 reflect Jeremiah's authentic words; (2) source B makes up the biographical materials in chs 26—44; and (3) prose sermons that are scattered throughout the book share the theological concerns and language of the book of Deuteronomy (1914, 21-38).

Though most recent scholars seldom describe the book in the categories employed by Duhm and Mowinckel, the debate over the content and composition of the book is alive and well. Two dominant and divergent views persist today. The first approach seeks to place the words of Jeremiah in the historical setting of the late seventh and early sixth centuries B.C. This view attributes all the poetic oracles and prose discourses to the prophet himself. The prose discourses may or may not contain theological expressions of later editors. This view attributes much of the so-called Deuteronomic words and phrases to the prophet himself. The historical and biographical materials come from Baruch the scribe, who was a trusted friend of the prophet. This view, with some variations, is reflected in the commentaries of William Holladay (1986, 1989) and Jack Lundbom (1999, 2004a, 2004b).

The second approach understands the book as a whole, particularly the prose sermons the result of the Deuteronomistic editing of the book (editors who were influenced by the theological concerns and language of Deuteronomy). Opinions of scholars on the extent of the Deuteronomic influence range from an overall editing of the book to an extensive Deuteronomistic redaction of the entire book. Carroll has suggested in his commentary that the book in its present form is the end product of the activities of various "redactional circles and levels of tradition" representing different social groups vying for power and position after the fall of Jerusalem. He suggests a long period for the formation of the book in its present form extending from the fall of Jerusalem into the Persian period (1986, 55-82). McKane also reaches a similar conclusion. He notices in the book a "long and complicated process of growth," "extending over a very long period . . . to which many people have contributed" (1986, xlviii).

This commentary approaches the study of the book of Jeremiah from the perspective that the book for the most part is made up of the words of Jeremiah, put together in the present form by compilers and editors of the words of Jeremiah during the Babylonian exile. As a book that has been through editorial hands during the exile, it is likely that the book in its present form may contain some of the theological perspectives and concerns of the community that gave the book its final shape. Nonetheless, it is difficult to isolate these additions from the original words of Jeremiah because the book lacks clear expressions of the conditions and the realities of the exile. There is no clear voice of the exilic community speaking in the book, as in Isa 40—55. Moreover, the exile of 587 B.C. is portrayed in chs 1—25 as an impending event; only in the historical accounts of chs 39—40 do we find references to the events of 587 B.C. Therefore, this commentary takes the seventh and sixth century B.C. historical context reflected in the book for its face value. Further, this commentary takes the view that the community that gave shape to the book's final form preserved the historical context of the late seventh and early sixth centuries B.C. and the voice of Jeremiah during this period to give recognition to the reality that its present suffering (the Babylonian exile) is the outcome of its rejection of God's words spoken through the prophet. From this perspective, one can also imagine that this community found the hope for its future in the words of the prophet who also spoke of its restoration and rebuilding.

Though there are two divergent positions on the content and composition of the book, modern commentators in general have followed the view that materials in the book lack a clear structure and organization and that the book shows no chronological order or literary and theological coherence. In response to this prevailing view, Stulman has recently shown theological and literary unity to the book from his perspective of the book as "a symbolic tapestry with narrative seams" in his *Order Amid Chaos: Jeremiah as Symbolic Tapestry* (1998, 17; 2005, 13). He finds five major units in each of the two sections of the book; the first section (chs 2—6; 7—10; 11—17; 18—20; 21—24) deals with the theme of "dismantling" and the second section (chs 27—29; 30—33; 34—35; 36—45; 46—51) deals with the theme of "rebuilding." Each section has an introduction and conclusion (chs 1, 25 and chs 26, 52 respectively). Stulman argues that the prose sermons "provide important rhetorical, literary, and theological clues for understanding the text" of Jeremiah (2005, 15).

The conventional division of the book into two major sections (chs 1—25 and 26—52) is based on the assumption of some thematic continuity within these sections. The common assumption is that chs 1—25 follow the theme of uprooting and chs 26—52 follow the theme of rebuilding. This is for the most part a reasonable understanding of the book and its content. However, we will see later as we work through the text that this line is not that clearly evident in the book; words of rebuilding are found in chs 1—25, and God's activity of uprooting is found in chs 26—52.

Approaching the book from a traditional historical perspective (an approach quite different from that of Stulman; see Stulman 1998, 2005 for his methodological and interpretive approach to the study of Jeremiah), this commentary aims to show that within these two major sections, there are smaller and larger literary blocks and that the various literary units within these blocks are linked together by common theological themes or some literary features. This commentary also aims to show that these smaller and larger literary blocks contribute to the overall structure of the book. In spite of the overall untidiness of the book, the book is thus readable; the common themes and literary features within these smaller and larger literary blocks contribute to the readability of the book. Thus we arrive at the same conclusion made by Stulman (i.e., that Jeremiah in its final form is readable and that it has literary and theological unity) from a different methodological and interpretive approach to the understanding of the book. Since the focus of this commentary is on chs 1—25, the following discussion does not include treatment of the structure of chs 26—52. This will be taken up in volume 2 of this commentary.

The materials in chs 1—25 declare the impending death of Judah's social, political, and religious world through Yahweh's uprooting and tearing down activity. This world that faces destruction is a world of idolatry, infidelity, corrupt worship, deceit and falsehood, pride, self-trust, covenant-breaking, corrupt and unfaithful political and religious leaders, and false hopes and false religious ideologies. This destruction will happen through the agency of an enemy from the north. No prophetic mediation will alter Yahweh's plans. Judah is a vessel being shaped by Yahweh for irreparable destruction. Its priests, prophets, and kings are corrupt, and they are responsible for the coming demise of the nation. Babylon is already on its way to act as God's agency of judgment. As the outline of chs 1—25 given below indicates, various literary blocks within chs 1—25 are organized around these theological issues and concerns (volume 2 will address the key theological concerns and literary structure of chs 26—52). The theme of "uproot and tear down" (1:10) provides an overall unity to the various literary blocks in chs 1—25.

In the commentary that follows later in this volume, an overview of each literary block is provided to show the literary and theological coherence of various literary units within these literary blocks. This does not, however, mean that the literary blocks themselves are arranged in any coherent order. Chapters 1—25 continue to have the appearance of an anthology of smaller blocks of materials arranged without any particular order.

"Uproot and Tear Down": God Commissions Jeremiah (1:4-19)
"Uproot and Tear Down": Judah's Idolatry and Infidelity (2:1—4:4)
"Uproot and Tear Down": The Agency of the Enemy from the North (4:5—6:30)
"Uproot and Tear Down": Judah's False and Corrupt Worship (7:1—8:3)
"Uproot and Tear Down": Judah's Deceit and Falsehood (8:4—10:25)
"Uproot and Tear Down": Judah's Covenant-Breaking (11:1—12:17)
"Uproot and Tear Down": Judah's Pride (13:1-27)
"Uproot and Tear Down": No More Prophetic Mediation (14:1—15:21)
"Uproot and Tear Down": Judah's Social World (16:1-21)
"Uproot and Tear Down": Judah's Self-Trust (17:1-27)
"Uproot and Tear Down": Judah, a Vessel for Destruction (18:1—20:18)
"Uproot and Tear Down": Judah's Political and Religious Leaders (21:1—23:40)
"Uproot and Tear Down": Judah's Claim of the Land (24:1-10)
"Uproot and Tear Down": Judah and the Nations (25:1-38)

E. Hebrew Text Traditions of Jeremiah

There is a substantial difference between the text preserved in the Hebrew Bible (MT) and the Greek translation (LXX) of the book of Jeremiah. Recent studies have shown that the LXX is a translation of a shorter Hebrew edition of the book of Jeremiah, which had about 3,000 fewer words than the text tradition preserved in the MT. This shorter Hebrew text of Jeremiah is not available to us, but it is believed to be the textual source for the Greek translation. Scholars regard the MT as an expanded edition of the book. Fragments of both of these Hebrew text traditions of Jeremiah have been found among the Dead Sea scrolls. A significant variation between the two text traditions (in addition to numerous missing words, phrases, or verses in the shorter edition) is the placement of the Oracles Against the Nations. In the MT, these are placed in chs 46—51.

In the LXX these oracles are placed in 25:14—31:44.

How and when the two divergent Hebrew text traditions of the book of Jeremiah were developed is not known. Scholarly speculation is that these two editions derive from a common source and that these two editions were nurtured and read as "scripture" by two separate Jewish communities. The MT is associated with the Jewish communities in Babylon or Palestine; the shorter text that underlies the LXX is associated with the Jewish communities in Egypt. The tradition assigns Tahpanhes in Egypt as the location of Jeremiah's last known oracles (43:8—44:14, 20-30). This leads to the possibility of tracing the shorter text to Jeremiah and/or Baruch who were taken to Egypt against their will by the Jewish group that escaped to Egypt (43:1-7).

F. Theological Themes

The theology of the book of Jeremiah is born out of the intense and painful historical crisis that Judah/Jerusalem experienced during the violent geopolitical power shift in the Euphrates-Tigris-Nile region in the late seventh and early sixth centuries B.C. The task of the theology of this book is essentially to make sense of the harsh and difficult historical realities of this period. The theology of this book addresses the historical, political, social, and religious conditions of Judah before the tragic events of 587 B.C.; it also speaks about Judah's future beyond the days of its tragic end. The book accomplishes this task by its portrait of God as the sovereign lord of history and particularly by linking contemporary historical events with God's purposive actions in history that display his sovereignty over Judah and the kingdoms of the world. This understanding of God provides the general theological framework for the vision of reality communicated through the various types of materials in the book. This theological framework is not developed in any systematic way in the book; however, it is possible to pull out various expressions of this unifying theology of the book through a careful reading of the book. In this volume, we will limit our observations to the theological expressions of God's sovereignty over Judah and the nations in the world found in Jer 1—25.

I. The Incomparable Creator

Jeremiah's claim of the sovereignty of God is linked essentially to his understanding of God as the incomparable Creator of the earth and the heavens, "the true God . . . the living God, the eternal King" (10:10). He is sovereign because he is the Creator. God's sovereignty is first and foremost evident in his creative power and wisdom through which he brought the earth and the heavens into existence. He not only "made the earth" and "stretched out the heavens" but also preserves and sustains his creation by giving it "autumn and spring rains in season" and by guaranteeing to its inhabitants "regular weeks of harvest" (10:12-13; 5:24). He is the Creator who "made the sand a boundary for the sea," so that the waters (chaos) that threaten his creation, though they "may roll, . . . cannot prevail" and cause his orderly creation to return to chaos (5:22). The sovereign Creator through his creative power thus guarantees the stability and the order of his creation. As the Creator of the universe, God's sovereignty extends over everything in the universe. The frequently found epithet for God "Yahweh of hosts" (*Yhwh Sebaoth*) in this book is a consistent reminder of the sovereignty and dominion of Yahweh over all the powers of the universe.

There is no comparison between this living God and the worthless idols of the nations, the work of human hands (10:1-6). As the sovereign Creator, he alone is the object of worship and fear (v 7). In vv 1-16 the prophet mockingly dismisses the claims of all other gods and their worshippers and warns Judah of the ineffectiveness and emptiness of idol worship that has infiltrated its religious life and changed its identity into an apostate nation. Israel's God—the living and true God who created the universe—is "the fountain of living water," the source of life, life that no idols (the "cracked cisterns") have the capacity to give (2:13 NRSV). Moreover, only this Creator God has the sovereign power to place before his creation "the way of life and the way of death" (21:8). Creation, in all of its aspects, thus belongs to the sovereign power of God.

2. The Sovereign and Transcendent God

An overemphasis of the temple ideology of the nearness of God led Judah to have a diminished understanding of the distance of God. The book presents the objective reality of God's distance by its claim that he is a *God far off* (23:23). The claim of the book is that God's sovereignty cannot be confined to earthly times and locations; his sovereignty is something that cannot be domesticated and controlled by his worshippers. Though through the covenant relationship with Israel, he is near and available in the temple, he is also the God who fills the heavens and the earth, who is in contact with every part of creation (v 24). Nothing in creation is hidden from him and nothing in creation is outside of his sovereignty.

3. The Sovereign God's Special Relationship to Israel

In the midst of a mocking and sarcastic rejection of idols, the book portrays God the Creator as "the Portion of Jacob," to whom belongs Israel, "the tribe of his inheritance" (10:16). The relationship between God and Israel is a covenant relationship; God has entered into a covenant with Israel and Israel is his special possession. The covenant has brought Israel to its peculiar status as a people "holy" to God or set apart for God (2:3). This relationship and God's undying faithfulness to Israel that attends to this relationship is the underlying theological basis for God's frequent address of Israel as "my people" even in the midst of Israel's senseless rejection of its covenant partner (vv 13, 31, 32, etc.). The covenant relationship is expressed variously in the book through the images of Israel as God's "bride" (v 2), and God as Israel's "father" (3:19) and the shepherd who gathers his flock (23:3).

4. The Sovereign God of the Nations

The sovereign Creator of the universe who has a special relationship with Israel is also the sovereign God of the nations. He determines and directs the destiny of the nations and uses them as agents of his sovereign plans and purposes. Both the nations of the world and the nation Israel with whom Yahweh has entered into a special covenantal relationship must acknowledge God's sovereignty over the universe and his moral order for the world. This acknowledgment or lack thereof is the basis of God's shaping of the destiny of a nation. The same theological principle is also at work in God's shaping of the destiny of individuals (18:1-12).

God appoints the prophet "over nations and kingdoms to uproot and tear down, to destroy and overthrow, to build and to plant" (1:10). He summons the kingdoms of the north to come and set up their throne in Jerusalem (v 15). More specifically, he intends to bring the king of Babylon against Judah (20:4); the mighty king of the great empire will serve God as his servant, a vassal who is not free to act on his will or freedom (25:9). Moreover, God will make all the nations drink from his cup of wrath, including Judah his covenant nation and Babylon the agent of his punishment of Judah (vv 15-29). In the first twenty-five chapters of the book, the theme of God's sovereignty over the nations intersects with his judgment of Judah and to a lesser extent with the judgment of all the nations. Judgment of the nations plays a larger role in the second part of the book.

5. God the Sovereign Judge of Judah

Jeremiah 1—25 clearly sees in the geopolitical events of the late seventh and early sixth centuries B.C. the clear display of God's sovereign power to shape history and direct its course to accomplish his plans and purposes. God's actions in history serve, first and foremost, the purpose of bringing his harsh judgment on Judah. The goal of judgment is "to uproot and tear down, to destroy and overthrow," to make the land and the city of Jerusalem desolate, because the people have rejected his *torah*—his gracious instructions for faithful covenant living (1:10; 6:19; 7:24; 8:9). From the outset, Judah is described as a forgetful nation that has no living memory of God's gracious dealings with it in the past and its covenant with him (2:4-13). The poetic imagery vividly describes the nation as an adulterous wife, a defiant servant, a nation that has sold its soul to serving foreign political powers and foreign gods (2:14—3:11). The sin of Judah is deeply ingrained in the heart of the nation (17:1). God offered Judah opportunities for repentance and faithfulness to the covenant, but this call only went into deaf ears (4:1-4). The nation broke its covenant with God by proclaiming, "I will not serve" (2:20). Judah's response to God's charges against it has been "I am not defiled" (v 23), "I have not sinned" (v 35). Judah is a nation that has "stubborn and rebellious hearts," hearts that are "uncircumcised," and "deceitful . . . and desperately corrupt" (5:23; 9:26; 17:9 RSV). When God invited Judah to walk in the good way, the response was "we will not walk in it" (6:16). When he appointed watchmen over them, the response was "we will not listen" (v 17; see also 11:8; 13:11; 22:21). Judah's response to God's call for repentance has been a defiant no (18:12).

Throughout chs 1—25, the book portrays Judah as a morally and socially bankrupt nation. The city of Jerusalem has no one left who does justice and seeks truth (5:1). The catalog of Judah's sins include shedding innocent blood (2:34), adultery and lust (5:7-8; 9:2), treachery, wickedness, and denial of justice to the orphan and the needy (5:27-28; 9:2), oppression and violence (6:6-7), greed, lying, and falsehood (6:13; 9:3-6). The temple sermon sums up these sins as the breaking of the covenant commandments (7:9).

The book also portrays God as the sovereign judge of Judah's spiritual and political leaders who have mismanaged and exploited his flock. Destruction is the fate of false prophets who have prophesied falsehood and assured peace to the people (5:12-14; 14:13-16; 23:9-40). The Davidic kings who reneged on their royal duty to do justice and righteousness receive a word of tragic death and the end of the royal line (21:1—22:30).

Chapters 1—25 portray God as a God who will punish Judah for its sin. The Babylonian invasion is God's holy war against his recalcitrant people (21:3-10). Using vivid imageries, chs 1—25 portray judgment as military invasion and God as the One who is sending the enemy nation against Judah (4:5-8, 13-18; 5:6, 14-17; 6:1-8, 22-25; 16:16-18; 21:1-10). What awaits the rebellious nation are sword, famine, pestilence, captivity, massive death, unburied dead bodies, and complete takeover of the land by the enemy (5:17; 7:32—8:3; 9:16; 10:17-18; 11:22-23; 14:11-16; 15:1-4; 20:4-6; 21:8-10; 23:39-40; 24:8-10; 25:8-12). The intensity of the judgment language conveys the massive force with which God will accomplish the uprooting and tearing down of Judah.

6. God's Sovereignty and Freedom

In several places in chs 1—25, the book holds God's sovereignty and his freedom in proper balance. These chapters make clear that God who determines the course of history is also open to changing his plans and purposes and that he indeed changes his mind according to human response. The decisions he makes are not inflexible and final. In ch 18 using the image of a potter, God makes known his sovereignty and freedom. He declares the uprooting and destruction of nations. He also declares the building and planting of nations, but he changes his mind about uprooting and destruction when the nation on which destruction is announced repents of its evil. In the same way he changes his mind about building and planting when the nation to which this word is spoken does evil in his sight.

God who is sovereign and free to change his mind also permits human beings to respond either positively or negatively to his demands. The numerous examples of Judah's stubborn rejection of God's call to repent illustrate the freedom of human beings (2:20; 6:16, 17; 11:8; 13:11; 18:12; 22:21). These examples show that God's word of judgment on Judah became a reality not because this word was spoken as an unalterable decree but precisely because Judah refused to give heed to God's repeated calls to repent and return to him.

7. The Sovereign God's Suffering Love

Though the judgment language occasionally describes God as withholding his pity and compassion for Judah (13:14) and withdrawing his "peace . . . , steadfast love and mercy" (16:5 NRSV), the overall attitude of God to Judah is his love. The opening words to Judah begin with a recital of the love relationship between God and his people (2:2). The rest of chs 1—25, particularly chs 2—3, shows how Judah's infidelity severely damaged this love relationship. Judah has become a nation with many lovers, but God holds fast to his love for Judah, his unfaithful wife. It is clear in chs 2—3 that God is deeply hurt by Judah's rejection of his love. His heart is broken; he suffers the agony of a scorned lover. His suffering love compels him to set aside his own law so that his wayward wife could return to him (3:1). The suffering God painfully wishes for the return of a loving and intimate relationship with his ungrateful daughter/unfaithful wife (v 19). The lament in v 19 is most likely God's lament for his wayward children. His suffering love prompts him to go to the places of Baal worship to rescue his children from their bondage to Baal. The deep pain and anguish the prophet experiences in chs 1—25 mirrors the suffering love of God (4:19-22; 8:18—9:1). The agony of the prophet is the agony of God; the lament of the prophet is the lament of God; the tears of the prophet are the tears of God.

8. The Sovereign God of Hope, Healing, and Restoration

The theme of judgment dominates the materials in chs 1—25. The deceased and dying nation has a physician; though he offers healing, the people refuse to come to him (8:18-22). So death and destruction and exile will come, but that is not the end. Scattered here and there we also find words of hope in chs 1—25. It is clear, as Brueggemann suggests, "the ground for hope" for the nation that is faced with death and destruction is "the suffering of (God) the wounded lover" (2007, 85). God's suffering love and his will to heal his people remain resolute even in the midst of judgment. The enemy will not show any mercy when they come, but God will not permit a "full end" of his people (4:27; 5:10, 18 NRSV). Judgment is not his final word; beyond death lies the days of the resurrection of the nation. The exiled nation will be brought back, and they will live once again in their own homeland. God will bring his people back to Zion and set over his people faithful shepherds (3:13b-18). Hope is extended to the nations also. In v 17, the prophet anticipates the nations gathering to God's throne in Jerusalem. The divided people of Judah and Israel will be reunited and return to the land that God has given to their ancestors (v 18). Though God will punish the nations and send them away from their lands, God will bring them back to their land (12:14-17). This text also includes a conditional promise that the nations will be built up in the midst of Israel. Restoration of Israel from the lands of its exile to the land of promise is stated again in 16:14-15. The theme of God setting over his people faithful shepherds (see 3:15) is elaborated in 23:1-9. This text anticipates the restoration from exile, the reign of a Davidic king who will rule his people with justice and righteousness, and the peaceful and secure dwelling of Israel in the land.

Hope is most clearly given to the people exiled to Babylon in 597 B.C. (24:4-7). Those who were taken out of the land in 597 are the object of God's favor. They were uprooted and their world was destroyed; however, God will bring them back to their land and plant them and build them. They will receive the gift of a (new) heart. They will enter into a (new) covenant with God. Exile is not the last word from Yahweh; it is the open door for people of God to enter into a new future with God.

9. The Sovereign God's Sovereign Word

Throughout the book of Jeremiah there is a focused attention on God's sovereign word. The introduction presents the words of Jeremiah as the "word of the LORD" (*děbar yhwh*) (1:1-2). The prophet's message is often introduced by phrases such as "the word of the LORD came to me," "the LORD said to me," "thus says the LORD," "oracle of the LORD," and "the word that came to Jeremiah from the LORD." The book is replete with the phrase "oracle of Yahweh" (168 times; Holladay 1986, 35). The Hebrew word *dābār* ("word") is found over ninety times, far more than any other OT book (Stulman 2005, 28).

The book, from the beginning to the end, aims to show how God's sovereign word is at work in Judah's national life, including the life of the prophet, as well as in the international scene. It is this sovereign word that calls and appoints Jeremiah to be a prophet to the nations (1:4-10). This word authorizes the uprooting and tearing down of Judah and the nations; it is also this word that authorizes the building and planting of Judah and the nations (v 10). Nothing in the land escapes the rigid scrutiny of the word in chs 1—25. Priests, prophets, people, kings, royal family, the temple worship, nations in the world—all come under the judgment of the word (2:4-13; 5:30-31; 7:1-15; 8:8-12; 20:1-6; 21:1—22:30; 25:1-38). Rejection of the word means tragic consequences. However, it is also the word that brings about restoration and rebuilding, covenant renewal, faithful leadership, and secure life in the land. The divine word, graciously spoken, is thus the hope of the nation under judgment.

The book also acknowledges the reality that God's word is often distorted and contradicted by (false) prophets who claim to have their authority to deliver the word from God. The true prophets are privileged to stand in the divine council; they receive the word directly from God. That word is "like fire," "like a hammer that breaks a rock in pieces" (23:29). The words of the false prophets are words that derive from the visions of their heart and words of falsehood; however, the people love to hear those words that offer them peace and well-being. They reject and ridicule the true words of God spoken by the true prophet. God's sovereign word ultimately triumphs and reveals the falsity of words spoken in his name by (false) prophets (6:13-15; 14:13-16; 23:9-40).

COMMENTARY

SUPERSCRIPTION (1:1-3)

Chapter 1 serves as the prologue to the book of Jeremiah. This chapter consists of the title (vv 1-3) and the call and commissioning of Jeremiah (vv 4-19). There are no prophetic speeches in this chapter. The title statement provides insight into the family background of Jeremiah prior to his call and the historical context of his ministry. The call and commission narrative establishes Jeremiah as an authentic and authorized voice of Yahweh. The commission narrative also provides in a nutshell the message of the book that Yahweh's impending actions in history would result in the dismantling of all the existing conditions and the establishment of new realities for Israel.

BEHIND THE TEXT

The introductory verses (vv 1-3) constitute the title statement of the book or its superscription (see similar title statements in Isa 1:1; Hos 1:1; Amos 1:1; Mic 1:1; Zeph 1:1). The title provides in a brief statement the identity of the prophet behind the book and the historical, geographical, and theological context of the book. It is likely that this heading was attached to the book by those who gave the book its final form during the exile of Judah in Babylon.

IN THE TEXT

■ **1-3** The heading (v 1) associates the content of the book with Jeremiah, who belonged to a priestly family in the village of Anathoth. **The words of Jeremiah** refer to the content of the entire book, which includes not only the spoken words but also the actions of the prophet. Verse 2 indicates the divine origin of the words of Jeremiah (***to whom the word of Yahweh came***). Jeremiah's words and actions echo the **word of the LORD** (*děbar yhwh*) that came (*hāyâ*, lit. happened) to him (v 2). Jeremiah is simply the messenger who communicates through words and actions Yahweh's words that came to him. The introduction also presents the coming of God's word to Jeremiah (revelation) as a historical reality, an event located within the framework of Judah's history. Yahweh's word came to Jeremiah for a period of forty years, from **the thirteenth year** (v 2; 627 B.C.) of Josiah's kingship ***until the captivity of Jerusalem*** (v 3; 587 B.C.).

Anathoth

> Anathoth was part of the inheritance of the tribe of Benjamin, but it was also a designated Levitical town for the priestly families (Josh 21:18). It was located about three miles north of Jerusalem in the tribal land of Benjamin. The modern Arab village of Anata preserves the ancient biblical name. Archaeologists think that the ancient village was located at a site very close to the modern village of Anata.

Though Jeremiah's call took place in 627 B.C., historical references in the book indicate a more active period of the prophet's ministry during the reign of **Jehoiakim** (609-598 B.C.) and **Zedekiah** (597-587 B.C.). **The eleventh year of Zedekiah** (587 B.C.) is a powerful reminder of the destruction of Jerusalem and the beginning of Judah's captivity in Babylon (see Historical Setting for details). The introduction places Jeremiah as a witness of Jerusalem's destruction and Judah's exile to Babylon. The special reference to the captivity of Jerusalem may have been intentional; it seems to direct the exilic audience to discover in the words of Jeremiah the answer to their "how" and "why" and "what next" questions about their captivity in Babylon. This community would have been the first recipients of the book of Jeremiah in its present shape.

FROM THE TEXT

The book of Jeremiah begins with the claim of the divine origin of the content of the book and the authenticity and legitimacy of the prophet. Words that originate with God invite our attention and faithful hearing. Such words are powerful and authoritative; they cannot be subverted, controlled, or manipulated. No social, political, or religious power can override the authentic voice of God. The exilic community had to come to accept and come to terms with the powerful reality of God's word that came to them through the words of Jeremiah.

The book provided a fresh hearing of the words of Jeremiah to the community in exile. Previous generations have failed to give heed to the prophet, but the present generation in exile has the opportunity to find their hope in the rejected and despised words of the prophet. For the readers of scripture the challenge then and now is to hear in new and refreshing ways the word of God. This word, when faithfully obeyed, remains as the source of hope for all who live through difficult and uncertain days.

The text suggests a powerful contrast between Anathoth and Jerusalem. Anathoth is a quiet village; Jerusalem is the capital city. Anathoth is a metaphor of the rejected and the banished. Jerusalem is where power resides. But from Anathoth comes a lonely voice that questions, challenges, and confronts with courage the Jerusalem establishment. This voice from Anathoth is the voice of the banished, the powerless, and the marginal that is speaking against the powerful and oppressive voices of the Jerusalem establishment. At the outset the book thus anticipates a conflict between "Jeremiah of Anathoth," the authentic voice of God, and the power brokers in Jerusalem. Seldom do voices of justice, liberty, and truth originate in the world capitals where power resides. The liberating power of the gospel was first heard not in the streets of Jerusalem but in the insignificant villages on the shores of the Sea of Galilee. The voice of Jeremiah of Anathoth is not unlike the voice of Jesus of Nazareth. Both voices critique, challenge, and confront the powerful religious and political establishment. Both Jeremiah and Jesus challenge us to be authentic and fearless voices of God in our world.

The phrases "the words of Jeremiah . . . the word of the LORD . . . captivity of Jerusalem" (vv 1-3 NRSV) all at the outset point to the message of the book that the exile was not the outcome of some unfortunate turn of political events but was a tragedy brought about by God's powerful words. The exiled people of God must come to terms with this reality, so that they can share in the hopes and dreams of this book. The reference to captivity is a challenge not to forget the past, while holding on to the hope for a better future. It is also a reminder of the truth that the God whom they experienced in judgment is also the God who will come with his power to heal and save them. Here we find hope for all who live in captivity because of sin and judgment.

"UPROOT AND TEAR DOWN"

GOD COMMISSIONS JEREMIAH (1:4-19)

BEHIND THE TEXT

Commentators read this text as a historical and autobiographical narrative (Bright 1965, 7; Holladay 1986, 45-46), or as a Deuteronomistic editorial construction patterned after the traditional commissioning narratives (Carroll 1986, 101). The text in its present form is a small literary block (1:4-19) that sums up the prophet's account of his call and commission to be Yahweh's prophet to Israel and the nations. This section has no clear thematic or literary continuity with the materials in ch 2. Three separate events constitute the call of Jeremiah. These events are described here in the form of conversations between Yahweh and Jeremiah in autobiographical form. The first conversation (1:4-10) preserves in poetry the call and commission of Jeremiah to be a prophet to the nations. Various elements of this call and commission reflect a pattern found in the call narratives of Moses, Isaiah, and Ezekiel (divine encounter, introductory word, commission, objection, reassurance, the sign; see Habel 1965, 297-323). The second (vv 11-12) and the third (vv 13-16) conversations take place in the setting of two separate visions. The narrative concludes with Yahweh's final charge and encouragement to Jeremiah (vv 17-19). It is not necessary to see these events as happening simultaneously or successively in the same setting, though that likelihood remains. Bright thinks that the two visions in verses 11-12 and 13-16 belong to an early part of Jeremiah's ministry, but not in the thirteenth year of Josiah, the year of Jeremiah's call (1965, 7). The visions and following conversations confirm Yahweh's call of Jeremiah and his intent to fulfill the words he has put in the mouth of Jeremiah.

IN THE TEXT

■ **4-5** The introductory statement (v 4) identifies the following conversation as Yahweh's word to Jeremiah, which happened as a revelatory event (*hāyâ*; see 1:2), and as such a historical reality experienced in person by Jeremiah. The first conversation focuses on Yahweh's involvement in the life of Jeremiah and his assignment as Yahweh's spokesperson even before his birth (v 5). Yahweh begins his speech by indicating that Yahweh **formed** Jeremiah in the womb of his mother (*yāṣār*, meaning "to form or fashion," conveys the idea of a potter shaping the clay into a vessel; see "The LORD God formed the man" in Gen 2:7). Verse 5 lists three divine actions of Yahweh **before** Jeremiah was formed in his mother's womb, and **before *(he) came forth from the womb.*** The twice-occurring phrase **before** (*bĕṭerem*) conveys the idea that Yahweh's decision to appoint Jeremiah to be his spokesperson took place "long before the present moment when Jeremiah is informed of the decision" (Lundbom 1999, 231). The first divine act (**I knew you**) shows Yahweh's personal knowledge and relationship with Jeremiah in an intimate way (*yāda'*, meaning "to know," conveys the sense of personal and intimate relationship, often used in the OT to describe sexual intimacy between a man and a woman). The verb *yāda'* also occurs in the context of ancient covenant relationships in both the OT (Gen 18:19; Amos 3:2) and nonbiblical sources (Huffmon 1959, 290-95). In the covenant context, the verb expresses the idea of the existence of a covenant between a suzerain and a vassal. It is thus likely that **I knew you** may refer to Yahweh's covenantal relationship with Jeremiah that he established with him even before Yahweh formed him in the womb. The second divine act (**I set you apart**; *qādaš*, meaning "to consecrate," "to set apart," or "to make holy") indicates that Yahweh consecrated Jeremiah for a particular divine purpose. This is similar to the OT idea of consecrating people, places, things, etc., for sacred purpose (see Paul's testimony in Gal 1:15). The third divine act (***I made you***; lit. "I gave you" from *nātan*) conveys the divine assignment of Jeremiah as a **prophet** (*nābî'* technically is a spokesperson for Yahweh) **to the nations.** At the outset it is clear that Jeremiah's calling is to be a prophet to the nations in the world (*gôyim*). Most commentators understand this commission to include both Israel and the nations in the world. This task is further elaborated in v 10.

God's Sovereignty and Human Freedom

Though the language of v 5 seem to suggest that Jeremiah's vocation was predetermined by Yahweh by some sort of predestination, Jeremiah's objection in v 6 indicates his freedom to resist and even reject the divine assignment by the exercise of his own will. Human freedom is most clearly found throughout the book, particularly in Israel's defiant resistance to God's word (see "I will not serve" [2:20], "we will not walk" [6:16], "we will not listen" [v 17], and "it's no use" [18:12]).

■ **6** Jeremiah's response to this divine announcement, **Ah, Lord Yahweh** (see also 4:10; 14:13; 32:17), conveys shock, alarm, or dismay (Holladay 1986, 34) and implies some hesitation or even objection on the part of Jeremiah (v 6). **I do not know how to speak** is parallel to Moses' words in Exod 4:10. **I am only a child** reflects Solomon's recognition of his young age and the need for wisdom to govern the people of Israel (1 Kgs 3:7). **Child** (*na'ar*) could also mean a boy or a young man; we cannot determine the specific age of Jeremiah at the time of this encounter with Yahweh. Jeremiah sees himself as inadequate, ill prepared, and without wisdom and maturity to be Yahweh's spokesperson.

■ **7** Yahweh responds to this resistance (v 7) using Jeremiah's own words (**Do not say, "I am only a child"**). Holladay refers to this as a "homely advice" (1986, 35); Lundbom labels it a "kindly rebuke" (1999, 233). Yahweh's reply seems to serve as a reminder to Jeremiah that his low self-image should not hinder him from obeying the call to be his prophet. Regardless of Jeremiah's low self-esteem, he should go to **all to whom** Yahweh sends him and speak **all that** Yahweh commands him to speak (v 7). This is precisely the function of the prophets who stood in the tradition of Moses as Yahweh's spokespersons (see Deut 18:18). Both the audience of Jeremiah and the words he must proclaim are to be determined by Yahweh and not by Jeremiah. The divine charge, **all that I command you, you shall speak,** does not leave any room for Jeremiah's own words.

■ **8** Yahweh challenged Jeremiah not to be **afraid** (v 8) of his audience. Jeremiah would face conflict and opposition when he delivers Yahweh's words to his audience. The audience is unspecified. Jeremiah need not fear his enemies because Yahweh will be with him. **I am with you** (see v 19; 15:20) is a frequently found promise of salvation in the Scriptures (see Gen 28:15; Exod 3:12; Josh 1:5; Judg 6:16; Isa 41:10; 43:5; Matt 28:20). The divine name Yahweh echoes this promise (Exod 3:14; 6:2). Yahweh's commitment to his prophet is to deliver or **rescue** him from his enemies (*nāṣal* conveys the idea of rescuing or snatching away someone from a dangerous situation, such as enemies, trouble, or even death). The reward for his faithfulness is his life. Yahweh will spare his life from his enemies and from the destruction that is coming upon the nation. Later biographical accounts show that Yahweh kept him safe from his enemies (see 11:21-23; 20:11-13) and from the catastrophe that happened in 587 B.C. (40:1-6). At the outset of his call, there is both the anticipation of opposition to Jeremiah's ministry and offer of help and deliverance from Yahweh. Verse 8 ends with an oracle concluding formula (*nĕ'um yhwh*, lit. "oracle of Yahweh") found 168 times in the book of Jeremiah (Holladay 1986, 35). It is parallel to the expression "says the LORD" often found at the conclusion of a prophetic speech.

■ **9** Following the words of assurance of his presence, Yahweh performed a symbolic act to give further assurance to Jeremiah that he was indeed his messenger (v 9). ***Yahweh stretched out his hand and touched my mouth*** is parallel to Isa 6:6-7. Yahweh's speech that followed this action (***behold, I have placed my words in your mouth***) echoes the words of Deut 18:18 ("I will put my words in his mouth"), which anticipate the establishment of the prophetic office after the days of Moses. These words indicate Jeremiah's legitimate standing in Israel's prophetic tradition. His later words about finding and eating Yahweh's words (Jer 15:16) reflect this initial experience, which inaugurated him into the prophetic office. This symbolic act also signals the ongoing revelation of Yahweh's words throughout his prophetic career. Yahweh did not give all his words in one instance at one decisive moment. Revelation continued to come to Jeremiah as an ongoing activity in his relationship with Yahweh. This announcement of Yahweh thus gives assurance to the one who did not know how to speak, that Yahweh will give him the appropriate words at the appropriate time. Jeremiah did not need to concern himself with what to say to his audience.

■ **10** Verse 10 elaborates the precise nature of the prophetic task of Jeremiah. Yahweh's appointment of Jeremiah (***I have appointed you*** from *pāqad*, which means "attend," "visit," "appoint," etc.) over nations and kingdoms signifies his installation into the prophetic office on that day of his encounter with Yahweh. **Nations** in 1:5 is expanded in v 10 to include **kingdoms;** however, no specific identity of the nations and kingdoms is given. Though specific reference to Judah/Jerusalem is lacking, it is obvious that Judah is the primary nation to which Yahweh is sending Jeremiah. Most of the oracles in the book are addressed to Judah, and oracles addressed to the nations are found primarily in chs 46—51. The reference to the nations, however, clearly implies Yahweh's sovereignty over the nations and particularly over Babylon, which plays a significant role in the historical events narrated in the book. Verse 10 elaborates on the task of Jeremiah the prophet. Using metaphors taken from agricultural, building construction, and military settings (**to uproot and tear down, to destroy and overthrow, to build and to plant**), Yahweh communicates to Jeremiah the destructive and the constructive power of his words that he has put in the mouth of his prophet. The apostle Paul responded to the charges of weakness with the claim that the weapons of his warfare (i.e., the word of God) have "divine power to demolish strongholds" (2 Cor 10:4).

The significance of v 10 to the message of the book cannot be underestimated (see the occurrence of "to uproot and tear down, to destroy and overthrow, to build and to plant" in different variations in 12:14-16; 18:7-9; 24:6; 31:28, 40; 42:10; and 45:4). Metaphors that deal with destruction indicate divine judgment; those that deal with construction indicate salvation. The order in which these verbs occur shows the reality of judgment preceding salvation. The outcome of Jeremiah's preaching is thus clear: bring judgment and destruction upon all corrupt and evil conditions that exist in the world of Jeremiah and then usher in a new era of Yahweh's sovereign work, which promises a new moral order in the world.

■ **11-12** The call and commission narrative is followed by two vision reports, which include a question-answer style dialogue between Yahweh and Jeremiah (1:11-12, 13-16). These vision accounts convey the trustworthiness of Yahweh and his words. The dialogue begins with Yahweh's question, **"What do you see, Jeremiah?"** (v 11; see also 24:3; Amos 7:8; 8:2; Zech 4:2; 5:2). Jeremiah's answer and Yahweh's response to Jeremiah contain a wordplay (*maqqēl šāqēd*, ***a branch of an almond tree*** in v 11, and *šoqēd*, **watching** or "wakeful" in v 12). Almond trees usually blossom in early February, a sure indication of the arrival of springtime in Palestine. Yahweh's reply, **"You have seen well"** indicates his acknowledgment of the accuracy of Jeremiah's visionary seeing. Yahweh is committed to his words, and he is **watching** over to fulfill his words of destruction as well as rebuilding. He will see to it that the words that come out of Jeremiah will come to fruition. Faithful speaking of the word is Jeremiah's task; faithful fulfillment of the word is Yahweh's promise.

■ **13-14** The vision of the boiling pot (vv 13-16) graphically describes the manner in which the word of judgment will be executed. This vision also begins with the question, **"What do you see?"** Jeremiah's vision involves a **boiling pot** with its *face* or the rim **turned away from the north,** thus its opening facing the south (v 13). Yahweh's explanation of the vision indicates the breaking loose of disaster, like the overflowing of boiling water from a tilted cooking pot (v 14).

■ **15** North is the direction from where the enemy will come. Enemy invasion of the land of Judah is clearly implied here. Yahweh will summon ***all the tribes of the kingdoms of the north*** and authorize the invasion of Judah (v 15). Though the invading power is not specifically identified here, but rather spoken of in general terms, Babylon is specifically identified as the enemy from the north in 25:9. The conquering kings will sit in judgment as rulers and judges and determine the destiny of Yahweh's people (v 15). **The gates of Jerusalem** is the traditional place for delivering judgment (see 39:3, which describes a scene like the one mentioned in v 15*a*). The second part of v 15 seems to convey the scene of siege against Jerusalem and other fortified cities of Judah (see also 4:5-8, 16-17; 6:1-8).

■ **16** Verse 16 shifts the subject of this judgment action from the kings of the northern tribes to Yahweh, thus making the kings his human instruments. The coming disaster is clearly Yahweh's judgment (*mišpāṭ*) upon his people who have forsaken their covenant with him and followed the path of idolatry. Judah's **wickedness** (*rāʿâ*, also "evil") is the direct cause for Yahweh's pouring out of evil (*rāʿâ*; v 14) from the north. **Burning incense to other gods** was a clear violation of the first commandment; the book contains several references to this sin of Judah (7:9; 11:12, 13, 17; 18:15; 19:4, 13; 44:3, 5, 8, 15, 17, 18, 19, 21, 23, 25). The covenant nation has broken the first commandment and practiced idolatry by participating in the religious rituals of Baal religion and worshipping the idols they have made as the object of their worship. The vision thus makes clear that Yahweh is shaping the geopolitical events to "uproot and tear down" Judah for breaking the covenant with him.

North in the OT

The OT makes frequent reference to the "north" (ṣāpôn); in the poetic language of Ps 48:2 Mount Zion is located in the far "north." In Jeremiah the enemy will come from the "north." In Ezek 38 and 39 Gog and his forces will come against Israel from the "north." In Canaanite mythology, Baal's mountain is called Zaphon (ṣāpôn). Here in Jeremiah the reference simply indicates the northern direction from which the Babylonians will arrive in Palestine from their location in Mesopotamia, since it would have been impossible for them to cross the desert and enter Palestine from the east.

■ **17** The vision reports conclude with Yahweh's words of reassurance to Jeremiah (vv 17-19). These verses convey what Yahweh had asked Jeremiah to do to prepare himself to be his spokesperson as well as what Yahweh had promised to do to make the mission of Jeremiah possible. ***Gird up your loins*** is a metaphor that conveys a call to get ready for action (v 17). This phrase indicates the act of tying up the long garment around the waist with a belt or waistband to free up a person to walk, work, run, engage in war, or prepare for a verbal confrontation (see Job 38:3; 40:7). Jeremiah must be prepared to meet whatever challenges—including conflict and confrontation—he may face during the course of his ministry. ***Rise and speak*** is the call to start his prophetic ministry at that particular moment. There is no waiting time between the call and its fulfillment. Jeremiah should deliver **whatever** Yahweh would **command** him to speak. This command to get his ministry started is followed by a stern warning that Jeremiah must not give up or give into the pressure, either physically or emotionally, or let his strength collapse before his enemies. This warning is followed by another warning that Yahweh himself will break Jeremiah before his enemies, if his strength breaks down before them.

■ **18** In v 18, Yahweh comforts Jeremiah with the announcement that he is acting decisively at that particular moment (**today**) to strengthen Jeremiah, like a city with a strong fortress, to defend himself from the enemies. But we need to consider this also as an ongoing promise from Yahweh to Jeremiah. The metaphors (**a fortified city, an iron pillar and a bronze wall**) all indicate Yahweh's powerful defense of his prophet to make him an unassailable target of his enemies. Yahweh also revealed to Jeremiah the strength of the opposition; he will be standing ***against the whole land, against the kings of Judah, against her officers, against her priests, and against the people of the land*** (v 18). All the religious and political power structures and dominant ideological forces and even the ordinary people of the land constitute the enemy. Jeremiah will be a one soldier army against a formidable enemy. (It is important to note that at critical times in his life, Jeremiah received help and support from some powerful people; see 26:16-19; 36:11-19; 38:7-13).

■ **19** However, in this holy war, victory is assured to Jeremiah. Yahweh will not allow the enemy to **overcome** his prophet (v 19; see 20:11). Yahweh promised to be with Jeremiah (**I am with you**) and **rescue** him from his enemies (see 1:8). What Jeremiah can count on as certainty in the midst of intense opposition is the faithful presence of Yahweh and the guarantee of salvation from enemies.

FROM THE TEXT

Jeremiah's call is a remarkable testimony to the biblical tradition of God's calling that comes to individuals to do special services for him. The autobiographical events associated with Jeremiah's calling, nonetheless, do not establish a pattern one should expect to find in our contemporary religious experience. What is important here is that people do not self-designate themselves for God's service. The privilege of designating a person to do God's work belongs to God. Moreover, God is personally and covenantally committed to those whom he calls to do his work. His words to Jeremiah concerning his knowledge, consecration, and appointment remind us of the faithfulness of the One "who began a good work" that he will "bring . . . to completion" (Phil 1:6 NRSV). The attention given to the personal details of the call, however, should not distract us from the basic objective of this call account. It is placed in the opening of the book to invite the readers to hear the words of Jeremiah as an authentic, God-called individual, who received revelation from God, the record of which is contained in the book that bears his name.

Jeremiah 1:4 has often been a scripture used in contemporary debate over the sanctity of life. This text, taken together with Job 10:8-12 and Ps 139:13-16, provides a scriptural basis for treating human life from the prebirth stage in the womb to death with dignity. Jeremiah's God was with him until the end, sustaining, preserving, and defending his prophet through all of life's circumstances, which for the most part was filled with disappointment, frustration, ridicule, opposition, and even death threat. The church must hear this text with the conviction and commitment to sustain, preserve, and treat with dignity and care all stages of human life.

By calling a young boy to be his prophet, God refutes the traditional notion that words of wisdom and power come only from the mouth of the aged and the experienced (see Matt 21:16; cf. Ps 8:2). As in the case of Moses, Gideon, and Saul (Exod 4:10-12; Judg 6:15 ff.; 1 Sam 9:21), he chooses an unlikely individual and offers to him the assurance of his presence (Jer 1:8). Age and maturity or even theological training do not necessarily make a person qualified or ready to proclaim God's word, which is often difficult and hard. Even the most experienced person needs to show humility and obedience when confronted with the reality of God's word.

Adam Clarke on the *Called of God*

> Those who are really called of God to the sacred ministry are such as have been brought to a deep acquaintance with themselves, feel their own ignorance, and know their own weakness. They know also the awful responsibility that attaches to the work; and nothing but the authority of God can induce such to undertake it. (254)

The divine act of placing the words in Jeremiah's mouth meant that he was to live a life shaped and nurtured by the word that was at work in his life. Fretheim observes that as the bearer of God's word "the prophet becomes the word of God," which at times in the book results in the "merging of prophetic acts and divine acts" (2002, 56-57). As the one who embodied God's word, Jeremiah often spoke words that were harsh and difficult, which for the most part made him an object of suspicion and hatred in the land. Prophets like Jeremiah have always been and always will be "prophets without honor," but the mark of their integrity is their commitment to continue to become the word of God through their faithful proclamation of the word that is placed in their mouths.

Jeremiah's call was to be Yahweh's spokesperson to the nations. The call of God erases geographical and cultural boundaries and sends the called person to the world, which becomes the parish, the setting of one's ministry. The task is specific, but the audience is general. In our contemporary hearing of this text, we need to recognize God's vision for the world, which in turn should become our vision. There is a link between Jeremiah's commission and the Great Commission, which mandates, "Go and make disciples of all nations" (Matt 28:19).

Uproot, tear down, destroy, and overthrow indeed are harsh words that vividly and colorfully portray the inevitable reality of a chaotic end without any possibility of escape. To the exilic audience who received the book in its final form, the memory of that destruction was still very fresh. However, for the original audience of Jeremiah's preaching, this word would have only signaled the coming end, but not without the possibility of escape through their faithful response of repentance. We should not hasten to conclude, as Brueggemann does, that the exile was an "inescapable reality," the evidence of "God's magisterial governance," a tragedy that God "ordained" for his people (1998, 26-27). The exile came upon a people who rejected time and time again the repeated calls from the prophets to return to God. We do not need to conclude that this tragedy had to happen and that the word of judgment placed in the mouth of Jeremiah at the time of his call remained static until its fulfillment. Jeremiah's frequent calls to repentance in the book clearly convey the possibility of a renewed relationship with God and escape from the reality of judgment. The exile simply reminds us that repeated rejection of the call to repentance may lead to that "point in the course of the lives of individuals or communities or nations when a certain kind of future does become inevitable, when it may be too late for repentance to shape the future in a positive way" (Fretheim 2002, 56). We should hear these words of judgment in the context of the gospel invitation to respond to the offer of the gift of salvation at the present moment (Rom 13:11; 2 Cor 6:2).

Build and **plant** are words that offer grace and hope to a nation already on a path of self-destruction. These words make clear that the threat of judgment was not God's final word. The community that experiences judgment because of its stubborn refusal to repent will once again encounter the surprising and amazing grace of God. The verbs **build** and **plant** contain the promise that "God can work newness, create historical possibilities *ex nihilo*, precisely in situations that seem hopeless and closed" (Brueggemann 1998, 25). Jeremiah's assertion about destruction and renewal has relevance not only for national and community history but also for individual lives shattered by the power of sin. We hear in this book reverberations of the dynamic optimism of grace that gives hope to the most hopeless sinner. The gospel clearly announces the power of God to make alive those who are "dead" in their "trespasses and sins" (Eph 2:1 NRSV; see vv 1-10).

The visions in Jer 1:11-16 affirm two things about God: first, God is faithful to fulfill his words. The words he placed in Jeremiah's mouth are not empty and vain words. His watching is his commitment to be prompt in fulfilling his threats and promises (Clarke, 254). The power of destruction and the power of renewal have already been unleashed by the placing of his words in Jeremiah's mouth. Here we find a hidden call to Jeremiah to be faithful to his calling just as God will be faithful to his words. Second, the visions affirm God's sovereignty over nations and his involvement in historical processes and geopolitical events. Historical and political changes and shifting political landscapes are not the work of some autonomous power brokers in the world. God is the sovereign Lord of history. He is the One who directs the destinies of nations. No one nation can determine its own destiny or the destiny of other nations. The focus of the second vision, however, is not the destiny of the kingdoms from the north, but that of Judah, God's covenant people. The collapse of Judah would not come as some accidental event in history, but as his judgment for its covenant-breaking and forsaking of God. The principle that sin will be judged is clearly emphasized in these vision accounts.

Finally, we must consider God's promise to be with Jeremiah to deliver him from his enemies as his faithful commitment to all his faithful followers (Exod 3:12; Matt 28:20*b*). "I am with you" is the classic and the persistent promise of God's presence in the Bible. Implied in this promise is the call to abandon self-reliance and self-sufficiency. In the context of Jeremiah's call, it is given specifically to those who are called into ministry. The call to ministry is a serious call; the decision to enter ministry is a serious decision. The context of ministry has always been and always will be difficult and hostile to those who faithfully proclaim God's word. However, those who remain faithful still hear these words: "I am with you to deliver you" (Jer 1:8 NRSV).

"UPROOT AND TEAR DOWN"

JUDAH'S IDOLATRY AND INFIDELITY (2:1—4:4)

Overview

Jeremiah 2:1—4:4 describes Judah as a nation of idolatry and covenant infidelity. There is no logical arrangement to the various literary units in this section. This section portrays Yahweh as a scorned lover who desperately seeks the return of his unfaithful wife. There are repeated calls for Judah's repentance in this section. There is only a hidden threat of judgment, and this is conveyed primarily by a reference to the fate that came upon the northern kingdom Israel. This section also includes the promise of the restoration of both Judah and Israel.

Poetry dominates in this section (2:2-3; 2:4—3:5; 3:12-14, 19-23; 4:1-4). Interspersed here and there are a few short prose statements (3:6-11, 15-18, 24-25). These prose statements demonstrate some inner linkage between the poetic and prose materials in this section. They function either as expansion and commentary of the poetic theme or as voice of hope in the midst of utter hopelessness produced by the poetic oracles. Thus 3:6-11 gives a historical illustration of Judah's/Israel's betrayal of God and covenant infidelity described in the preceding poetic oracle (vv 1-5). In vv 15-18 we find a detailed commentary on God's promise to bring his people back to Zion made in the preceding poetic oracle (v 14). The poetic confession of sin and idolatry in vv 22*b*-23 is continued in the prose statement in vv 24-25.

What may be a consistent feature of these oracles is their conversational style. However, discontinuity is evident even in these conversations. Questions are asked but no clear answers are given. In vv 1-5 a question is asked about the law of divorce and remarriage, but there is no divorce or remarriage. Yahweh shares with Jeremiah the story of two sisters in vv 6-10 and speaks to Israel with desperate longing for its return in vv 11-13. In another speech, Yahweh promises a bright future to Israel (vv 14-18). Yahweh speaks to himself in a lamenting tone in vv 19-20, where he is portrayed as a disappointed parent and a dejected lover. The people speak in vv 21-25 in a lamenting and weeping tone and confess their guilt. This section ends with another urgent appeal of Yahweh to Israel to return (4:1-4). What provides some coherence to these disjointed oracles is the consistent imagery of Israel as an unfaithful wife and children and Yahweh's appeal to Israel to return.

References to Jerusalem in 2:1 and 4:3 indicate that Judah/Jerusalem was the intended audience of 2:1—4:4, at least at the time of the final form of the book in the exilic setting. However, we also see in this section oracles addressed to the entire nation Israel (2:4, and specifically to the northern tribes in 3:12). In their original setting, the oracles in this section may have been directed to both Judah and the northern tribes left in their land (and/or those who may have escaped to Judah) after the Assyrian takeover of their land in 722 B.C.

A. Yahweh's Lawsuit (2:1-37)

BEHIND THE TEXT

Some formal elements of a lawsuit (*rîb*) that Yahweh brings against Judah are present in ch 2. The dispute pattern (accusations and counteraccusations in vv 5, 9, 13, 20, 23, 29, 31, 35) and the role of heavens as witness in v 12 suggest the lawsuit form of the oracles in this section. The elect people of Yahweh have acted in unfaithfulness and thus offended the covenant maker; therefore, they stand under the threat of judgment. Fretheim describes the oracles in this chapter as Yahweh's lament, though he recognizes some similarities to the lawsuit genre in this chapter (2002, 60).

There are eight literary units in ch 2 (vv 1-3, 4-13, 14-19, 20-22, 23-25, 26-28, 29-32, 33-37). Yahweh's lawsuit against Judah's covenant infidelity seems to be the connecting theme of these oracles.

Lawsuit Genre in the Prophets

The OT prophets have occasionally used the lawsuit genre to bring God's indictment against Israel. The assumed setting is that of a court in which God presides and functions as both plaintiff and judge. The key word in this genre is *rîb* (meaning "dispute," "argue," "contend," etc.), which conveys the idea of a lawsuit. In some cases God summons a witness (usually mountains or the earth or the heavens); the plaintiff presents the case and the defendants (Israel) speak. The verdict comes from God, who finds the people guilty of violating the covenant conditions. Micah 6 is perhaps the most clearly developed illustration of this genre of prophetic speech. God's covenant with Israel is the theological basis for God bringing a case against his people. The underlying assumption is that Israel violated the terms of its covenant relationship with God.

It is difficult to establish the setting of this chapter, in which there are no clear indications of any specific historical events. Commentators have attempted to place these oracles before 622 B.C. or to a period after 622 B.C. References to Egypt and Assyria in vv 18 and 36 suggest a date before the collapse of the Assyrian power in 612 B.C.

1. Sweet Memories (2:1-3)

IN THE TEXT

■ **1** This oracle is specifically addressed to the citizens of Jerusalem, which could be taken to mean the people of Judah. The oracle begins with the usual introductory formula (see 1:4, 11, 13). Yahweh commanded Jeremiah to **go** and deliver a message to Jerusalem, the center of Judah's political and religious power structures (2:1). **Proclaim in the hearing of Jerusalem** (or, "call out in the ears of Jerusalem;" Holladay 1986, 82) conveys the idea that the message was either to be proclaimed or read to an audience (Holladay 1986, 82).

■ **2** The message (vv 2-3) is intended to bring to the memory of the people something they have forgotten. **I remember** (*for you*) (*zākartî lāk*) conveys the act of remembering something that took place in the past that has consequence for the present, such as determining the course of action in the present (Holladay 1986, 82). The awkward expression *for you* (*lāk*) suggests Yahweh recalling for the people something they had forgotten. Verse 2 describes a special kind of relationship Yahweh once had with Israel, something like the honeymoon period in a bridegroom-bride relationship. What Yahweh remembers (and what the people have forgotten) is their **devotion** (*ḥesed*) to him when they were **youth,** or the earliest days of Israel's covenant relationship with him. There is a quality of permanence when *ḥesed* is the foundation of interpersonal relationships. What this memory of the past reveals is the reality that *ḥesed* is absent in Judah's present relationship with Yahweh. Though the call to remember and not to forget the past is very much a part of Israel's traditions (Deut 8:2, 11, 18), the text indicates that Judah existed without a living memory of its covenant relationship with Yahweh.

Ḥesed in the OT

The Hebrew word *ḥesed* has several shades of meaning. English translations translate this word as "steadfast love," "covenant love," "mercy," "grace," "favor," "kindness," "devotion," "unfailing love," "covenant loyalty," etc. God's covenant commitment and faithfulness to his people is the primary idea that this word seeks to convey. He remains faithful, loving, forgiving, trustworthy, merciful, and gracious in the midst of the total absence of these qualities among his people. So when we speak of God's *ḥesed*, we are speaking of his abounding grace that never fails.

Yahweh also remembers the **love** (*'ahăba*) Israel as a bride had for him during her **betrothal period.** *'Ahăba* in Hebrew conveys both divine love and love in human relationships. Yahweh's memory of the past also includes how Israel **followed** him in the wilderness, a land where there were no signs of life. This walk would have been a walk of trust and complete confidence in Yahweh, Israel's covenant partner, protector, and provider.

Israel's Wilderness Period

Jeremiah 2:2 presents an idealized picture of Israel's wilderness period (see also Hos 2:14-15; 9:10). The narratives in Exodus, Numbers, and Deuteronomy show that loyalty and faithfulness were qualities entirely lacking in Israel during the wilderness wandering period. Instead, these books present this period as a period of frequent complaint, murmuring, rebellion, and God's judgment.

Jeremiah 2:2 is a nostalgic visit to the past to bring to Judah's memory its covenant relationship with Yahweh. The purpose of this message was not to erase from Israel's memory the days of its rebellion. It was perhaps intended to show by comparison that Israel was far more faithful and devoted to Yahweh during the wilderness period than the present moment in its history. Indeed, now there is no relationship at all between Yahweh the husband and Israel his bride.

■ **3** Yahweh's memory also includes Israel's special relationship to him as his **holy** people (*qōdeš*; see 1:5), a nation set apart by him and for him. Yahweh had set apart Israel for the purpose of his service, and in that sense Israel was a holy people. Israel was Yahweh's **firstfruits,** like the gift a farmer brings from the harvest as an expression of gratitude for the gift of the land and good harvest. Since the firstfruits belonged to God, only the priests and their families were permitted to eat them. Verse 3 indicates that the nations that attempted to conquer Israel during this early period incurred guilt, and Yahweh's judgment came upon them for taking what belonged to him for his service.

Israel's Holiness

Israel is holy not in the sense that the people possessed some moral attributes or inherent purity, but in the sense that they belonged to God by virtue of their election at Mount Sinai (Exod 19:6). Israel's holiness is thus holiness in relationship to God. Israel is holy as it listens and obeys God's voice and lives in covenant faithfulness. This also means that Israel ceases to be holy the moment it departs from the covenant relationship with God.

FROM THE TEXT

The idealized portrait of the God-Israel relationship in this text takes us beyond the actual history of that period narrated in Numbers and presents a positive and affirming portrait of Israel. How did the days of rebellion and murmuring turn into days of devotion and love? Is it that Jeremiah is rewriting history and giving the negative past a positive spin? Or does Jeremiah see here a God who is fully capable of forgiving and forgetting the sins of his people? All that God remembers about Israel is its covenant loyalty, love, and devotion to him and his covenant commitment to protect and defend his holy people. In the forgiving and forgetting nature of God's relationship with his people, "I remember" is an act of grace, God's gracious overture of reconciliation to a sinful nation. This message would have been particularly comforting to its readers/hearers in the exilic setting. Though they are in exile, as their ancestors were in Egypt, there is yet another opportunity to encounter God in the wilderness and walk with him in devotion and love. In the gracious and grace-filled memory of God, he does not remember our sins (see 31:34), rather he sees us as his people who have the capacity to love and follow him again. It is this forgiving grace that is at the heart of the Christian gospel. Paul reminds us that "in Christ God was reconciling the world to himself, not counting their trespasses against them" (2 Cor 5:19 NRSV).

2. Bartering for Junk (2:4-13)

IN THE TEXT

■ **4-5** Yahweh's accusations in vv 4-13 suggest the lawsuit genre of this literary unit. The text focuses not only on the past but also on the present state of the relationship between Yahweh and his people. The oracle addresses the entire house of Israel (those of Judah and the surviving members of the northern tribes). The oracle begins with a rhetorical question, **"What injustice did your fathers find in me?"** (v 5). The answer is obvious. Yahweh is not a God who acts unjustly (*'āwel* conveys the idea of injustice) or does wrong. The present state of affairs has a long history, and that history goes back to the days when the ancestors of Israel (**your fathers**) began to distance themselves from Yahweh. The covenant nation distanced itself from Yahweh not because of Yahweh's injustice but because of its attraction to **vanity** or nothingness (*hahebel*; **worthless idols**), a pejorative epithet here for Baal (see the reference to Baal in v 8). Israel came under the seductive influences of Baal religion and went after a god who has no substance or power. Ironically and tragically, the nation became *vain* or nothing (*hebel*).

■ **6** Verse 6 describes the people's forgetfulness of Yahweh who brought them out of their slavery, led them through the wilderness, and gave them the gift of the land in which they lived. No one asks the question, **"Where is the LORD?"** The enemy may ask this question to challenge the faithful (Ps 42:3; 79:10), but the failure to ask this question by the covenant people means that they have no memory of Yahweh's saving deeds in the past. This question would have connected each new generation with the faith traditions of the past and with the saving deeds of Yahweh. The rest of v 6 describes the desert land through which Yahweh led Israel into the Promised Land. Words like **pit (rifts)**, **drought**, and **darkness** portray the impassability of the wilderness region through which Israel made the journey into the Promised Land. The **land of desert** and **pit** perhaps refer to the wilderness area of steep ravine, which is part of the geological depression that extends from the Dead Sea to the Gulf of Aqaba. The land through which Yahweh led his people is not only impassable but also entirely inhospitable to human existence, because it is a land of perpetual drought. It is a land of deep **darkness** (*ṣalmāwet*; "shadow of death" in Ps 23:4). Neither do people pass through this land nor does anyone dwell in this place.

Baal Worship

The Canaanite religion was a fertility religion; this religion revolved around the belief that Baal was the source of the productivity of human beings and the land. Baal literally means "lord" or "husband." The association of the name Baal to cities or towns indicates that each town or city had its own Baal, or the god that was worshipped as the primary god of that locality (see Baal of Peor in Num 25:3).

The Baal worship was grounded in a cyclic myth that connected drought and the lack of productivity of the ground to Baal's defeat by Mot, the god of death, and the descent of Baal into the underworld. The Canaanite religion also believed that Anat, Baal's consort, released him from the underworld and brought him back to life. Sacred prostitution was a part of the worship of Baal, which was thought to bring sexual vitality to Baal and to arouse him to engage in sexual activity with Anat. The devotees of Baal believed that the sexual union between Baal and Anat brought the rains and made the ground fertile and productive. Every year this cycle was repeated, and the worshippers participated in various rituals that were of sexual nature. When Israel came into the land of Canaan, the people incorporated this belief into their faith; the covenant people thus began to perceive Yahweh as the God who delivers his people from their enemies and Baal as the source of their material prosperity.

■ **7** Verse 7 addresses Jeremiah's audience (**you**), not the past generations. Each generation stands as a witness to the experiences of the previous generations (see Deut 5:2-4). Yahweh brought Israel through the difficult and life-threatening wilderness into the **garden land** (*karmel*). *Karmel* may be a reference to fruit-producing orchards (perhaps associated with *kerem*; vineyard) or fertile and productive farmland or even a forested place (see Isa 29:17; 37:24). Israel—not only the past generations but also the present generation—**defiled** Yahweh's land (**my land, my inheritance**) through idolatry and made it a loathsome place.

■ **8** The culprits responsible for Israel's forgetfulness of Yahweh are the very same people who were entrusted with the sacred task of guarding and preserving Israel's faith traditions (v 8). **Priests,** the custodians of the Law, failed to ask, **"Where is the LORD?"** and thus failed to bring Yahweh's memory to the people. The people went after Baal because of the priests' dereliction of duty to teach them the acceptable way of worship. **Those who** *handle* **the law** have failed to properly teach and interpret the Law. They were to be the repository of the knowledge of Yahweh in the land; ironically, they themselves did not know (*yāda'*; see 1:5) Yahweh. The **shepherds** or rulers (*rō'îm* is a common designation for political rulers in 3:13; 6:3; 12:10; 23:1, 4; 33:12) have **rebelled** against Yahweh (*pāšě'û* from *pāša'* is the act of rebellion, transgression, or revolt against God). **Prophets,** by assuming that title, were to function as faithful spokespersons of Yahweh. However, the prophets supported and promoted the Baal cult and became prophets of Baal. The followers of Baal *do not profit* anything from their devotion to it, because this god has no real existence, and therefore it is a worthless idol.

■ **9** Because of this systemic apostasy in the land, Yahweh will bring his **charges** (*'ārîb* from *rîb* is usually understood as a term that belongs to the legal context) not only against the present generation but also against their **children's children** (v 9). The case will continue as long as this apostasy continued among the covenant people.

■ **10-12** In vv 10-13 the prophet addresses Israel's betrayal of Yahweh for gods that have no substance. Such betrayals of gods do not take place anywhere else in the world, but only in Israel. The implied addressees of vv 10 and 11 seem to be those who witness the legal proceeding (Holladay 1986, 90), though one could arguably see the defendants themselves being addressed here. The identity of the addressees is not important. What is important is the answer to Yahweh's question: **Has a nation exchanged gods, though they are no-gods?** (v 11). Though **Kittim** (lit., islands of the Kittites) in the west and **Kedar** (the home of the Arab tribe) in the east are known for trade and commerce, one would not find "for sale" signs on their gods (v 10). The search for an answer in the farthest west or the farthest east would show that no one in the pagan world has done such a transaction of their gods. In Rom 1:23, Paul states that the Gentiles "exchanged the glory of the immortal God for images resembling a mortal human being or birds or four-footed animals or reptiles" (NRSV). Yahweh's accusation, *But my people have exchanged its glory for something that does not profit,* conveys the unthinkable and incredible conduct of his people (v 11). Though Yahweh is bringing his lawsuit, the defendants are still addressed as **my people,** the covenant nation. Israel traded Yahweh, its **glory** (*kabōd*; see Ps 106:20; Hos 4:7), for idols that have no life or worth (Jer 2:11). In v 12, Yahweh calls **heavens,** the eternal and faithful witnesses of the Sinai covenant, to be shocked and **appalled** at this incomprehensible conduct of Israel, Yahweh's covenant partner.

■ **13** Yahweh's accusation and indictment of Israel reaches its climax in v 13. The covenant nation (**my people**) has committed **two sins,** both of which have been clear sign of its determination to walk away from Yahweh and walk after other gods. The number **two** suggests that though Israel's evil was primarily trading Yahweh for Baal (and thus one evil), that secular and profane action also had a negative theological outcome (one evil act the outcome of which was also evil). The covenant people have **forsaken** Yahweh, **the spring of living water** (*mĕqôr mayim ḥayyîm*). **They have forsaken me** shows Israel's rejection and violation of the first commandment (see also 16:11; 17:13; 22:9). The evident outcome of forsaking Yahweh was the rejection of the spring of living water; see this metaphor again in 17:13. The metaphor could be traced to Israel's traditional understanding of Yahweh as a living God (Deut 5:26; 1 Sam 17:26, 36; Jer 10:10; 23:36; Hos 1:10). Yahweh is also the fountain of life (Ps 36:9). The covenant people rejected the living water, the fountain (source) of their life, and made for themselves **cisterns,** holes dug into the ground to collect rainwater. Such cisterns/holes were usually plastered inside to make them watertight. **Broken cisterns** perhaps mean cracks in the plaster of the inside walls of the cisterns. Verse 13 makes the contrast between Yahweh and Baal very clear; indeed, there is no comparison between Yahweh, the life-sustaining source for his people, and Baal who neither has life nor can sustain life.

FROM THE TEXT

The goal of Jeremiah in this text is to challenge his audience to "remember" and not to "forget" the saving deeds of God (Deut 8:2, 11). It is in this remembering that the covenant with God is kept alive and traditions are kept. The text also serves as an indictment against the leaders of Jeremiah's generation for their failure to shape and nurture a covenant-keeping community. This text would have challenged the people in exile to set an agenda for their renewed relationship with God as a covenant people. Their future rests on their commitment to become a remembering people, a people for whom God is the only source of life.

This text reminds the modern readers that a living memory of God is essential to faithful relationship with him. It also reminds us of the tragic outcome of pursuing other gods for good health, good fortune, and good life. Where the living God is traded for idols, worship reverts from an I-Thou relationship to a frantic exercise in self-gratification. "Becoming like the God we see" (Beatific vision) was a worthy goal promoted by many of the Eastern and Western church fathers. True worship begins with true perception of the God we worship. True worship is also grounded in the sacred memory of faith traditions that have sustained and nourished the faith community for generations. When that memory is gone, when that memory is not nurtured, the distinction between the living God and gods of this world disappears and faith becomes a commodity for sale in the marketplace for cheaper and glittery substitutes. The temptation to trade the living God for false gods is as powerful in our time as it was in the days of Jeremiah. The gospel invites us to drink the water that will never make us thirsty but will become in us "a spring of water gushing up to eternal life" (John 4:15 NRSV; see 7:37-38).

3. Self-Imposed Slavery (2:14-19)

IN THE TEXT

■ **14** This unit continues Yahweh's indictment of Israel and the charges of apostasy. Israel's contemporary political involvement is the focus of this unit. Yahweh's questions in vv 14, 17, and 18 indicate the futility and the disastrous outcome of Israel's political alliances with other nations. Answers to these questions are clear. Three metaphors in v 14 (**servant, slave,** a helpless **plunder** by invading armies) illustrate Israel's present predicament. The text seeks to explain why Israel, Yahweh's honored servant (see Isa 42:1; 49:3; also Jer 30:10) and treasured possession (Exod 19:6), is a slave to other nations, and why Israel is the booty of invading armies.

■ **15** Verse 15 expands the metaphor of Israel as a helpless prey being attacked by **young lions.** The military threat by a powerful nation is the thrust of this verse. Though Assyria is sometimes described by the lion metaphor (see Isa 5:29), it is very likely that young lions here refer to Babylon, which is already on the rise as the new political power. Verse 15b contains war imagery; Israel suffers the disastrous consequences of seeking alliances with the nations. Enemy invaders have destroyed the land and burned the cities of Judah. The text may be referring to an actual event, though a specific historical context cannot be determined.

■ **16-17** The Hebrew text of v 16 is difficult to translate. **Noph** is Memphis, the ancient capital of Egypt, located just south of Cairo. **Tahpanhes** (modern Tel Defneh) is located on Lake Menzaleh in northeast Egypt. Both of these cities became centers of Jewish refugees after the Babylonian destruction of Jerusalem in 587 B.C. (43:7-9; 44:1). This verse seems to indicate that humiliation and disgrace will be heaped upon Judah even by the Egyptians. Verse 17 conveys the idea that there is no one else to be blamed for the disastrous situation of the nation. The nation has brought this troublesome condition upon itself by its *forsaking* of Yahweh. This forsaking has happened while Yahweh was leading the nation *in the way.* It is not certain whether Jeremiah traces here the nation's forsaking of Yahweh on her way to the Promised Land or simply a reference to the apostasy of the nation throughout its history with Yahweh.

■ **18** Questions in v 18 suggest Israel's failed foreign policy. These questions indicate the politicians' decision to surrender Israel's freedom to foreign political powers in exchange for national security. The metaphors, **water of the Nile** (*mê šiḥôr*) and the **water of the Euphrates** (*mê nāhār*), expand on Israel's forsaking of the spring of living water in v 13.

Israel's Return to Egypt and Assyria

Egypt and Assyria have been rival political powers in the past, but they became allies when Babylon emerged as the new world power over the Fertile Crescent in the last quarter of the seventh century B.C. Egypt enslaved Israel in the earliest days of its history. Jeremiah describes Israel's returning to Egypt for political help as returning to the days of its slavery in Egypt. It is not only despicable but also a mockery of Yahweh who rescued Israel from Egypt. Assyria was the nation that wiped out the northern tribes of Israel from the political map of the world. Still, Judah trusts in these powers and makes alliances with them for political security. The exact date of these pro-Egyptian and pro-Assyrian overtures in Jerusalem cannot be determined. Events in the last quarter of the seventh century provide a general background of this text.

Verse 18 establishes a direct correlation between seeking alliances with political powers and going after other gods; neither other gods nor political powers are able to save Judah. The connection between 2:13 and 2:18 is clear. Verse 13 deals with Judah's false religious security; v 18 deals with its false political security. In both of these crucial areas, Judah has declared freedom from Yahweh and returned to slavery—a clear sign of the nation's lack of trust in Yahweh.

■ **19** Judah's acts of **wickedness** and **backsliding** (*mĕšubâ*, constant turning back and forth, from the root *šûb*, meaning "to turn, return, or repent") at the end will lead to **evil and bitter** experiences from Yahweh (v 19). **Your wickedness will *instruct* you** (punish you; verb form from *ysr*; the noun *mûsār* usually means "discipline" or "correction") indicates that Yahweh's teaching or disciplining actions are at work in Judah's history. **Backsliding** refers not only to unsteady and unfaithful relationship with Yahweh but also to political vacillation and changing loyalties to foreign powers. **Rebuke you** also conveys the idea of correction or chastening. The covenant people do not treat Yahweh with **awe;** they do not show respect for his authority over them. The unit ends with the assertion that the nation that pursues the path of evil can expect nothing but evil from Yahweh. Rejecting Yahweh will not lead to freedom but only lead to death.

FROM THE TEXT

The vivid and colorful images of destruction and devastation (v 15) in this text portray a furious and angry God who has given his people over to their enemies to bring upon them evil, disaster, shame, and humiliation because they have traded him for political security. Such is indeed the reality of divine judgment portrayed in this text. In the original setting of this text, the prophet's goal would have been to convince the people to return and realign themselves with God, the only way for them to avoid the coming exile. The text would have served as a reminder to the people in exile that they are in Babylon because they have sold themselves out to foreign gods and foreign political powers. They have received the wages of their sin and reaped what they have sown. Now they must answer God's rhetorical questions to find a way out of Babylon. The way out of Babylon rests on their decision to abandon loyalties to foreign gods and foreign political powers and to drink from the "spring of living water."

The rhetorical questions in this text also reflect a God who agonizes over the lost and surrendered freedom of his covenant people. The dominant metaphor in this text is that of a grieving and sorrowful God whose love is scorned by his people. Though they have once embraced his covenantal love for them, now they reject his love. Had God remained wrathful and destructive, he would have walked away from his people who have walked away from him. Only a God who grieves and experiences pain, a God who makes himself vulnerable before those who walk away from him, would dare to ask the kinds of questions we hear in this text. God's questions in this text indicate his longing to take back his prodigal children; they do not belong to the faraway lands of Assyria or Egypt. We find a marvelous display of God's grace in these questions; by asking these questions, he initiates the process of healing the broken relationship. These questions reflect the suffering love of God that compels and motivates him to do whatever he needs to do (including the threat of punishment) to bring home those who are on the path of self-destruction and ruin. God's resolve here is not to abandon those who have forsaken him. This reaching out of God to bring home the wayward and the lost is at the heart of the Christian gospel.

The text also invites us to reflect on the freedom that we enjoy through the liberating power of the gospel. There is a significant parallel between the freedom God brought to Israel and the freedom from the power of sin and death that comes through the gospel of Jesus Christ. The danger of freedom is that it is too easy to mistake it for license to sin and self-indulging actions. Also, if the purpose of freedom is not fully understood, then the temptation of those who are free would be to continue to live in slavery and bondage (as some Jewish Christians did in the first century). Paul's admonition to the Galatian churches not to "submit again to a yoke of slavery" and not to use their "freedom as an opportunity for self-indulgence" (Gal 5:1, 13 NRSV) echoes the thrust of Jeremiah's message.

4. Self-Proclaimed Freedom (2:20-22)

IN THE TEXT

■ **20** Three metaphors describe Israel's distorted relationship with Yahweh. Verse 20 paints the picture of a stubborn animal that refuses to remain under the yoke of its master, and a cheap prostitute who sells herself to anyone at any place. Verse 21 shifts the metaphor to a pure quality stock of vine that has become degenerate and worthless. **Your yoke** refers to Israel's submission to the Sinai covenant, which was done without any coercion from Yahweh. Though Israel's coming under this yoke was an act of free choice, Yahweh considered breaking the yoke an act of rebellion (see 5:5). But soon after the covenant was made (**long ago**), Israel broke the commitment. **I will not serve** indicates Israel's defiant and willful breaking of the Sinai covenant and its decision to renege on the commitments made at Sinai. The path Israel chose instead of serving Yahweh in freedom was the path of bondage to other gods on **every high hill and under every spreading tree** (see the same phrase in 1 Kgs 14:23; 2 Kgs 17:10; also see this phrase with some variation in Jer 3:6 and 17:2). These phrases identify the location of the Canaanite fertility cult. ***You stooped to be a harlot*** further conveys the idea of the Israelites' participation in the fertility cult of Baal. Israel the devoted and loving wife of Yahweh has cheapened herself by selling her body and soul to Baal wherever there was a place of Baal cult.

■ **21** Yahweh's lament and heartbreak is vividly expressed in v 21. The picture of Yahweh here is that of a frustrated and disappointed farmer who with all good intentions and plans, planted his vineyard with **choice vine** (*śōrēq*, a high-quality vine that produces dark red grapes). The text is closer to the language of Isaiah's parable of the vineyard (Isa 5:1-7). The vine that should have produced choicest grapes has turned out to be ***degenerate and strange.*** The Hebrew text of line 3 is not very clear; see Holladay for an emendation of the text to read something like "How have you become putrid?" (Holladay 1986, 98-99).

■ **22** No attempt on the part of Israel can remove the deep stains of its moral corruption (v 22). There are no detergents that can wash away the stain of the guilt of Israel. **Soda** and **soap** are rough equivalents of the detergents Jeremiah mentions here. They are potent detergents that can remove all types of dirt and stains from one's clothing. **Use an abundance of soap** suggests the idea of repeated use of the detergent to clean something unclean. **Wash** (*kbs*) here is a human activity, but in Ps 51:2 and 7 it refers to God's activity of cleansing a sinner from the stains of guilt. The **stain** is the stain of Israel's guilt (*'āwōn*), which is so deeply ingrained that it cannot be removed by any detergents. Neither are there any cultic rituals that will remove the guilt of Israel; it remains before Yahweh as evidence of the nation's covenant-breaking (see Isa 1:18 for Yahweh's offer to Israel for cleansing that will come from him; Ps 51:2, 7 also contain an appeal to God for washing and cleansing from sin).

FROM THE TEXT

The text invites its readers to reflect on serving God in joyful freedom. Freedom to serve God means participation in God's life-sustaining grace. Freedom to serve God also means producing fruit that reflects grace at work in our lives. The vine imagery suggests the kind of fruit God's people are to produce, fruit useful for God and for the world. This freedom is the opposite of self-proclaimed autonomy. Autonomy means rejection of grace and forfeiture of

God's call to participate in a meaningful and productive life. Though the text ends abruptly and without giving any hope to its ancient readers, it is clear in Jeremiah that God is the only hope for those who remain with the deep stains of sin and guilt. Jeremiah's audience, then and now, would find comfort in the words of Isaiah:

> Though your sins are like scarlet,
> They shall be like snow;
> Though they are red like crimson,
> They shall become like wool. (Isa 1:18 NRSV)

Here we find God extending grace even to the most wretched sinner.

5. Desperate for Love (2:23-25)

IN THE TEXT

■ **23** The text begins with a rhetorical question and then moves into a vivid description of Israel's misconduct and covenant-breaking, using imageries that are colorful, sarcastic, and filled with sexual overtones. Israel is a lying spouse, an unrestrained Baal devotee, a swift she-camel, and a wild donkey. Still Israel maintains innocence and emphatically rejects Yahweh's charges against it. Yahweh's question is not intended to solicit an answer, but rather to reject Israel's claim of innocence.

I am not defiled is an audacious claim by a nation that refuses to admit guilt (v 23). The charge against the covenant people is that they went after Baal; however, when the judge asks the question, "How do you plead?" their answer is "Not guilty." The issue seems to be on the defilement of the land by Israel's Baal worship (see 2:7).

I have not run after the Baals is an outright lie (v 23). It is ironic that the nation that claimed innocence is also the nation that admits its hopeless pursuit of "strangers" (see v 25 NRSV). How can the people deny their wayward conduct when they have left their footprints on their path to Baal? They will only need to take a **look at** their **(your) way** (*derek*) **in the valley,** or way of life in the past. *Way* also seems to have a double meaning, not only its ethical meaning (conduct) but also the path Israel has taken to follow Baal **in the valley.** Valley here is most likely the reference to places where Baal worship was carried out in Israel. Commentators follow the LXX and Vulgate reading and connect "the valley" to the Valley of Hinnom where Israel practiced child sacrifice (see 7:31-32).

Consider what you have done is a call to acknowledge guilt (v 23). The nation that denies its sin and claims innocence must come to a sober understanding of the seriousness of its covenant-breaking way of life. Then it will recognize that its conduct was like that of a **swift she-camel** *crisscrossing her*

tracks. The metaphor simply serves here to portray the restless and vacillating conduct of Israel, a nation that cannot make up its mind, a nation that is unrestrained and unreliable.

■ **24** The metaphor changes in v 24 to a **wild donkey** in the desert. The language of this verse is vivid and vulgar. The female donkey in heat vigorously and passionately pursues the male, by **sniffing the wind** to catch the scent of the male. The once devoted wife of Yahweh (see 2:2) has become like a sexually craved female donkey that no one can restrain when she is in heat.

■ **25** The animal imagery continues in v 25. Yahweh urges Israel to put an end to its frantic pursuit of Baal. Bright paraphrases v 25*a* as follows: "Do not run till your shoes wear out, and you faint with thirst, chasing false gods" (1965, 16). ***There is no hope*** is Israel's response to Yahweh's plea (see also 18:12 for the same response from the people). This response does not mean the hopelessness of the situation the nation is faced with but rather the attitude of indifference and determination of the people not to change the course of the path they have taken. This attitude is reflected in the next line, ***I love strangers,*** and ***I must go after them.*** ***Strangers*** (*zārîm*) could mean aliens or foreigners (as in Isa 1:7), but here the context favors the meaning "strange gods" or **foreign gods** (see Deut 32:16). Israel is determined to pursue other gods. No one and nothing could bring the nation back to Yahweh.

FROM THE TEXT

In this text we find two distinct images: a wife who claims innocence but admits that she is long gone from her husband, and a scorned lover who still speaks to his unfaithful wife. Israel in this text is a deeply disillusioned nation going through a critical identity crisis. The nation wants to be known as God's people, but its behavior testifies to its stubborn rejection of God. To whom do I belong? That seems to be the question Israel cannot truly answer. Jeremiah, through powerful metaphors, reminds his generation that its identity crisis is the outcome of its lack of commitment to its covenant with God. Israel's failed marriage, as in most failed marriages in our society, can be traced to the people's refusal to fully participate in their marriage to their covenant partner. This is the story of love received but never given back. For the covenant people to fully enjoy their relationship with God, they must return to him. False claims of innocence would not heal the pain they have inflicted on God. Repentance and return to a fully committed relationship is necessary to bring healing to the broken relationship. The fact that God speaks to Israel is evidence of his grace to his unfaithful covenant partner. The text reminds its listeners, then and now, that though our sins separate us from God, and though unfaithfulness is the way of life we have chosen for ourselves, God remains gracious and willing to be reconciled with us. There is more grace in God than sin in us. That seems to be Jeremiah's message in this text for its readers.

6. Yahweh or Baal? (2:26-28)

IN THE TEXT

■ **26** The theme of Israel's pursuit of Baal continues in vv 26-28. The imagery is more refined, however. The metaphor shifts from unrestrained animals to a **thief** in v 26. A thief caught in the act of stealing can expect nothing but disgrace (*bōšet*, lit. "shame"; see also *bōšet* as a contemptuous substitute for Baal in 3:24; 11:13; also Hos 9:10). Israel is caught in the act of its religious apostasy and political alliances. All the responsible parties—**kings, officials, priests, prophets**—will suffer shame and humiliation when Yahweh's judgment comes. The gods they worshipped and the nations they depended on for help and support will fail to come to their rescue.

Asherah and Massebah

In the Canaanite cult, a wooden pole represented Asherah, the consort of Baal, or the mother goddess, the symbol of female fertility. Massebah, an upright stone pillar, represented male fertility. These were set up near Canaanite altars usually located on "every high hill" and "under every green tree" (2:20; 3:13 NRSV).

■ **27** Yahweh mocks at Israel's confession of faith in Baal with sarcasm and humor (v 27). The people of Yahweh confess to a piece of **wood, "You are my father"** and to a pillar of **stone, "You gave me birth."** This is what they perceive as the truth about their origin. Israel does not remember that Yahweh is the One who gave birth to the nation (see Deut 32:6). They cannot even distinguish between their mother and father. They think a female goddess is their father and a male god is their mother! Moreover, **they have turned their backs** to Yahweh. This is a contemptuous act, the opposite of turning **their faces** to Yahweh as an act of worship. When distress and disaster come, they will turn their faces to Yahweh with the plea for help, *arise* **and save us** (see Ps 3:7 for the prayer of the psalmist). Though it has broken the covenant, the nation still maintains its traditional faith in Yahweh as a mighty warrior. However, they return to that faith only when they are in deep trouble.

■ **28** Verse 28 indicates that Yahweh is not easily persuaded by false religious pretensions. This verse begins with a mocking question, also rhetorical in nature. The gods whom the people made for themselves are nowhere to be found when they are in trouble. **Let them come** is a challenge to the nation as well as to its gods. Baal and his consort are totally helpless to do anything to save those who cry to them for help. The *time of your distress* could be any political threat Judah faced in the last twenty-five years before the end of statehood in

587 B.C. The focus of the verse shifts to the polytheistic nature of the Israelites' worship at the time of Jeremiah (see "your gods" at the beginning and at the end of the verse). The last two lines are hyperbole; these lines convey the idea that pagan gods have infiltrated every town and every segment of the Judean population (see 11:13; Hos 10:1). Ironically, however, Judah can expect no help at all from these home-made gods who are good at making promises but cannot be found when their devotees need help.

FROM THE TEXT

We find in this text a people who live in two worlds. One world belongs to God and the other world belongs to Baal. In the arena of their normal daily existence, they seek comfort in Baal's promises of prosperity and productivity, but in distressing life situations they call upon God for help. The devotion they show to God is like "the morning mist . . . the early dew that disappears" (Hos 6:4). Jeremiah warns them that when the judgment day comes, no one will come to their defense. The living God whom they denied and Baal whom they trusted for prosperity and life will be silent; the former will not hear their cry, and the latter cannot hear at all. The tragedy of 587 B.C. was a clear signal of the impotence of "other gods" on whom Judah depended for help.

The issue of turning to other gods is alive and well in our days as well. Often in our contemporary times, we witness deep spirituality during a national or local crisis, but then quickly we return to our consumerism and trust in our own capacity to make things work. This text urges us to reflect more seriously on the call to Christian discipleship. Following the gospel call means saying no to the gods of this world. Jesus says to his disciples, "No one can serve two masters; for either he will hate the one and love the other, or he will be devoted to the one and despise the other. You cannot serve God and mammon" (Matt 6:24 RSV).

7. A Countersuit (2:29-32)

IN THE TEXT

■ **29** As in several of the previous oracles, this text also includes a number of rhetorical questions (vv 29, 31, 32). Yahweh's first question, **"Why do you bring charges against me?"** (v 29), implies Israel's lawsuit (*rib*) against him. It is not clear what Israel's charges are against Yahweh. Perhaps the question reflects a popular sentiment that Yahweh does not help his people when they are in distress. The question also claims that the people who have broken the covenant have no legal basis for a lawsuit against Yahweh. Only Yahweh has a valid case, and his charge remains the same. The nation as a whole has **rebelled** against Yahweh. This is the same charge as in 2:4-13. Rebellion (*peša'*) against Yahweh and his covenant is the primary charge against Israel.

■ **30** Israel's defiance against Yahweh is also evident in its stubborn refusal to accept correction from him (v 30). Whatever actions Yahweh has taken to discipline the nation did not produce their intended outcome. ***I have stricken your children*** suggests foreign military invasion of the land that resulted in a painful and destructive outcome. The verb **stricken** (*hikkêtî*) implies severe beating, but Yahweh's children refuse to accept **correction** (*mûsār*; see also 5:3; 7:28; 17:23; 32:33). Commentators connect **Your sword has devoured your prophets** (v 30) to the murder of Uriah the prophet during the reign of Jehoiakim (26:20-23). Jeremiah himself narrowly escaped death during the trial following his temple sermon (see 26:1-24). **Like a ravening lion** (v 30) indicates that the martyred prophets of Israel suffered violent death by the hands of those who opposed them.

■ **31** Verse 31 addresses the present **generation**. Those who clearly perceive Yahweh's past and present relationship with Israel would know that he has not been like **a desert . . . a land of great darkness** to Israel. The rhetorical questions in this verse reflect the language of 2:6. Yahweh is indeed the One who brought Israel through the wilderness, a land of darkness. This verse seems to suggest that the people of Yahweh treat him like a dark and dangerous God with whom they should have no association at all. This may have been the popular perception of the people about Yahweh. The next question, **"Why do my people say . . . ?"** introduces another quotation, perhaps another popular sentiment in the land. Israel's claim, **we have roamed** (v 31), implies the nation's autonomy and exercise of freedom from Yahweh. The last line, **we will come to you no more,** seems to suggest Israel's firm rejection of Yahweh as the object of her worship. **Come to you** belongs to the language of worship (see Pss 5:7; 42:2 NRSV, etc., where "come" refers to one's entrance into the temple to worship God).

■ **32** Verse 32 also begins with a rhetorical question. The first part of this verse suggests the vivid memory of a woman who keeps her wedding day ornaments. How that imagery fits with the second part of this verse is not clear. One might associate the bridal ornaments with the pride and glory of a bride and thus something that cannot be forgotten by her. If so, the complaint of Yahweh could be that Israel has forgotten him, her precious ornament (see v 11). The text may not be intended to present a neat and exact comparison between the first and second part of this verse; the focus might be on the verb **forget**. Yahweh's bride (**my people**) has no memory of her husband or her wedding day, and her walk with him in the wilderness during their honeymoon days (see 2:2). The final phrase, **days without number,** indicates the long history of Israel's forgetfulness of Yahweh.

FROM THE TEXT

The central issue in this section is Israel's forgetfulness of God. This issue coupled with Israel's infidelity occupies the center stage of the oracles in ch 2. The counter lawsuit, the killing of prophets, self-proclaimed freedom—all suggest Israel's incredible capacity to forget the past, particularly God's gracious and faithful deeds on behalf of his covenant people. Jeremiah treats infidelity and forgetfulness on the same level; both bring pain and agony to God; both compel him to take action. Jeremiah once again reminds his audience of the impact of their sin on God's self. Though the covenant people have forgotten God, he remembers them. Had God forgotten Israel, it would have no hope. The exilic readers would have found God's address of Judah as "my people" a source of comfort and hope. They would also have been challenged to gain a new perspective of God as a God who remembers them even in their exile. It is in the remembering mercy of God we find grace here—grace that bids to remember and return, grace that urges to stop rebellion, and grace that invites God's wayward people to be reconciled with him.

8. Shame and Humiliation (2:33-37)

IN THE TEXT

■ **33** Verse 33 presents Israel as a people who are highly **skilled** in making and executing plans to seek **love** (*'ahābâ* in Hebrew denotes both pure and impure affection). Love here is not Israel's deep devotion to Yahweh, but its passionate pursuit of Baal, and thus illicit love and in the religious terms adulterous love or unfaithfulness to Yahweh. Commentators differ in their reading of the second part of v 33 (see Holladay, "In fact you have done ill; you have been trained in your ways"; 1986, 56; Lundbom, "So even you can teach your wicked ways"; 1999, 295). The reading adopted here, **so, even the evil (women) you have taught your ways,** conveys the idea that the people of Yahweh are the teachers from whom others learn their evil way of life.

■ **34** Verse 34 is another accusation of Yahweh that Israel is guilty of shedding innocent blood (see also 7:6; 22:17; 26:15). The blood stains of the **innocent poor** are found on Israel's **clothes** (lit. "skirts," meaning the outer garment). The innocent poor are the innocent and needy in the society. The second part of this verse indicates that the shedding of blood was acts of murder and not acts committed in self-defense or to protect one's house and property from thieves. The NIV correctly reads the last line (**Yet in spite of all this**) as a transition to the next verse (v 35).

■ **35** The first part of v 35 presents another response from Israel. The people claim innocence in spite of all the charges against them by Yahweh. *I have been innocent* (*niqqêtî*) could also be translated as "I have been acquitted" (JPS). This response may reflect Israel's false perception that Yahweh has accepted their claim of innocence. This fits well with the next line, **he is not angry with me.** The second claim may also be an assertion of the traditional idea that Yahweh will not hold his anger forever (see also 3:5; Pss 30:5; 103:9; Hos 11:9). However, Yahweh refutes all such false claims. Yahweh's anger has not turned away from his people. He is determined to render his judgment on Israel. Israel's claim, **I have not sinned** (*ḥāṭā'tî;* the verb *ḥāṭā'* means "miss a goal, go wrong, sin," etc.), directly contradicts the nation's assertion of its love for foreign gods (see 2:25). The legal language is clear in this verse. Yahweh will indeed take the guilty Israel into a court for **judgment.** No protestation of innocence will deter him from going through with this legal process to establish the guilt of Israel.

■ **36** The opening question of v 36, **how casually you go about** ("Why do you go about . . . ?" "How you cheapen yourself" JPS), conveys the nonchalant attitude with which the nation made decisions that were critical to its future. **Changing your ways** here is most likely changing of political loyalties. Israel has made a decision without any careful thinking or counting the cost and most importantly without consulting Yahweh. The text specifically deals with Israel's shifting political leaning in the direction of Egypt. The context of this text is not clear; it most likely belongs to the period of the Egyptian domination over Judah following the death of Josiah in Megiddo in 609 B.C. (see 2 Kgs 23:29-35). Israel will suffer shame and disgrace just as it suffered shame by the hands of the Assyrians (see 2 Kgs 16:7-18).

■ **37** The consequence of making unholy alliances with political powers is clear (v 37). As in the previous cases, when Israel suffered shame and humiliation at the hands of its political patrons, this time also, the people will **go out** with their **hands on** their **head.** Israel rejected Yahweh; therefore, he has rejected those whom they trust. The nation that had hoped to be prospered by its foreign political alliances will be utterly disappointed. None of the political allies of Israel will be able to help in the time of its need—when Yahweh brings his judgment on the nation (v 37).

FROM THE TEXT

This text is about Israel looking for love and security in all the wrong places. The kind of love the nation pursues is love that does not restrain, love that permits autonomy and self-determination. That kind of love Israel found in its pursuit of Baal. Israel's claim of innocence is perhaps an indication of its misguided theological thinking about God as a God who accommodates other gods in his people's religious life. Israel's political overtures and alliances with other nations for national security certainly attest to its newly found freedom in Baal. The text makes clear that God would not permit his people to have other gods; Israel's God does not stand on the sidelines and watch the parade of other gods pass by. He rejects his people who have broken the covenant and their gods, both in their religious and political life.

The text ends with the portrait of Israel without other lovers. The only one that remains now is God, whom she followed in the wilderness with the love and devotion of a newly married woman. Would Israel ever find true love? The answer to this question is in the opening oracle of ch 2 (vv 1-3), the message of which controls all other God-Israel interactions in this chapter. Israel's future hinges on its decision to return to the wilderness and start all over again its relationship with God. God is still the Husband and Redeemer of his covenant people. This is the thrust of Jeremiah's oracles in 3:1—4:4. The text would have confronted the exilic community with the message that their rejection by God and their shame and humiliation were by no means final. Those who have forsaken their first love only need to "repent" to find grace and mercy once again from God (Rev 2:4-5).

God's judgment is on Israel for its claim of innocence. Though the catalog of its sin is too long to enumerate, it refuses to confess and insists that it has not sinned ("I have not sinned" Jer. 2:35). Such claims of self-righteousness hinder any possibility of a restored relationship with God. First John describes such claims as self-deception and claiming fellowship with God while "we walk in darkness" (1:6). John also tells us that "if we confess our sins, he [God] who is faithful and just will forgive us our sins and cleanse us from all unrighteousness" (v 9 NRSV).

B. The Call to Return (3:1—4:4)

1. Return to Me (3:1-5)

BEHIND THE TEXT

The law of divorce and remarriage in Deut 24:1-4 provides the legal framework of Jer 3:1-5. However, Jeremiah does not make a direct application of the Deuteronomic law. The situation in Jeremiah differs from Deuteronomy in that the question in Jeremiah is about the legality of a husband returning to his divorced wife who married another man. The situation in Deuteronomy is about the first husband remarrying his divorced wife who has been divorced by another man or has become a widow. In the Deuteronomic law, the assumption is that the divorced wife takes the initiative to return to her first husband, who was not permitted to take her back as his wife again (Miller 2001, 603).

IN THE TEXT

■ 1 Yahweh asks two questions in v 1. Yahweh's first question reflects the legal procedure of divorce or "sending away" a woman with a bill of divorce. The question, **should he return to her again?** requires a negative answer on the basis of the popular understanding of the law of divorce and remarriage. Covenant infidelity on the part of Israel and Yahweh's lawsuit in the preceding oracles lead us to assume that the divorce proceeding is underway. Verse 8 makes reference to Yahweh's divorce of the northern kingdom Israel, but it is unlikely that this oracle is addressed to the northern kingdom. The key issue here is about a man who divorced his wife returning to her in order to take her back as his wife.

Yahweh's second question (**Would not the land be completely defiled?**)

indicates that taking back a divorced wife would indeed bring the defilement to the **land** (v 1). The land is Yahweh's property and therefore it is holy. Any breach of the covenant laws would result in the loss of the sanctity of Yahweh's land. The land is already defiled by Israel by its adultery **with many lovers.** Most translations take the last phrase, **return to me** (v 1), as a question (**Would you now return to me?**). But the interrogative particle is lacking in the Hebrew text. If it is taken as a question, then it implies that Israel's return to Yahweh is legally impossible since she has defiled the land with her adultery. The phrase also could be translated as an imperative, Yahweh's urgent appeal to his wayward and unfaithful wife to return to him (*šûb* conveys the idea of repentance and return), though his own law prohibits an adulterous wife to be reunited with her husband (Miller 2001, 603). Yahweh expresses here his willingness to take his unfaithful wife back at any cost, even if it means breaking his own law and bringing defilement to the land.

■ **2** Verses 2-5 expose Israel's dangerously depraved condition and its shallow religious commitment. The intent of these verses is to elicit the nation's repentance. True repentance can come only if the people come to terms with the reality of their depravity. They only need to lift their eyes to the **barren heights** (*šĕpāîm*) to recognize the perversity and depravity of their conduct (v 2). **Barren heights** indicates the cultic places of Baal worship (see "every high hill" 2:20). Israel has been **ravished** and violated by her lovers in the places she pursued them. The imagery in v 2 also compares Israel to an ***Arab*** (*'ārābî* perhaps means a caravan trader) waiting on the desert road to sell his merchandise to those who pass by. Verse 2 ends with Yahweh's complaint that his land has become unclean by the **prostitution and wickedness** of his people.

■ **3** Israel also needs to recognize the ecological consequence of her adulterous way of life (v 3). The natural calamities that came upon the land are a direct outcome of Israel's idolatry. The agricultural activities failed because Yahweh withheld the much-needed **showers** and **spring rains** or "latter rains" from the land. What Israel hoped to get from Baal was rain and fertility, but what the people experienced was drought. The text thus asserts that only Yahweh has the power to bring rain or withhold rain (see also 5:24; 14:22). Though Baal failed Israel, she refused to show shame or humiliation. Israel was resolute in its pursuit of Baal, who has no power over nature.

■ **4** Yahweh's question in v 4 seems to suggest that Israel has taken Yahweh for granted. The nation claims to have exclusive and personal relationship with Yahweh (see the use of **my** in these verses), though in reality the people do not call upon his name. The people call Yahweh **My Father** only when they are in trouble, such as drought or other calamities. The idea of Yahweh as Father stems from the covenant relationship (see Isa 1:2; Hos 11:1). Israel also claims that Yahweh is the **friend** (*'allûp* also means "companion," "confidant," etc.) ***of*** her **youth. Father** and **friend** are not parallel expressions. The latter fits better with the husband-wife imagery found in chs 2—3.

■ **5** Verse 5 begins with two rhetorical questions, both of which require a negative answer. These questions are placed in the mouth of Israel. The first question conveys the idea that Yahweh will not maintain wrath forever or bear a grudge against Israel forever. The second question conveys the same idea of Yahweh keeping his wrath only for a while. These questions are consistent with Israel's traditional faith. The covenant people claim this faith though they have broken the covenant and worshipped Baal. Verse 5*b* presents Yahweh's words. His assessment of Israel is that they have pious words in their mouth while they commit the worst kind of evil.

FROM THE TEXT

Tension between God's law and his will to extend grace (will to love) is clear in this text. The law demands God to remain impassionate toward a people who have acted unfaithfully in their relationship with him. However, his grace (love) compels him to permit the possibility of their return to him. We see a glimpse of this love that permits a sinner to return to God in the words of Hosea's wife: "I will go back to my husband as at first" (Hos 2:7). This grace is at the heart of Yahweh's command to Hosea, "Go, show your love to your wife again" (3:1). In both Hosea and Jeremiah, though deeply hurt by the infidelity of his covenant partner, God remains passionate and committed to his people. Both books show the love of a wounded lover, love that suffers pain but remains firm in the commitment to love. God's questions in this text imply his gracious overtures to an unworthy people. He takes the initiative for Israel to find a place again in his presence. The only thing the people need to do is to return, or repent of their waywardness. Such a return would have spared Judah from the tragedy of 587 B.C. The text also speaks to God's people about the possibility of their return to him even in their exile. Grace reaches out, then and now, to the wayward children of God who live in "a distant country" far from their father's home (Luke 15:13; see vv 11-32). Where the law says no, grace says yes; this is the hope for sinners who hear this text today.

There is yet another way this text speaks to us today. The people of Israel presume to have a personal and exclusive relationship with God, though their conduct contradicts their claims. Their language of piety reflects faith in Yahweh, but they practice a religion that has nothing to do with God. They claim grace but refuse to live in the experience of grace. They call God "my Father," but they are passionately devoted to Baal, their "owner." They claim God as the companion of their youth, but they have many gods in their life. Jeremiah here reiterates what Isaiah has said concerning the hypocritical piety of his audience, "These people draw near with their mouths and honor me with their lips, while their hearts are far from me" (Isa 29:13 NRSV; see also Mark 7:6). Any incongruity between one's religious claims and actions indicates hypocrisy and false piety. John puts it this way: "If we claim to have fellowship with him yet walk in the darkness, we lie and do not live by the truth" (1 John 1:6).

2. Return! (3:6-18)

BEHIND THE TEXT

There are three literary units in 3:6-18, all connected with the theme of apostasy and call to repentance. The first unit (vv 6-11) is in the form of a story that Yahweh is narrating to Jeremiah. The second unit contains a message that Yahweh commanded Jeremiah to proclaim to Israel (vv 12-13). The historical reference places the text during the reign of Josiah. The third unit (vv 14-18) anticipates the future return of Israel as a unified nation to Jerusalem; the city will take the place of the temple and the ark of the covenant.

The story in vv 6-11 is similar to Ezek 16:44-63 and 23:1-49 in that like the Ezekiel stories, this story also attempts to establish Judah as guiltier than the northern kingdom Israel. Commentators differ in their perspective on the relationship of this story to the stories in Ezekiel. Bright sees close relationship of words and phrases in this story to Jeremiah's poetry and suggests that the story is not dependent on Ezekiel (1965, 26). He places the story during the reign of Josiah, particularly in the context of Josiah's effort to incorporate the defunct northern kingdom into the Judean kingdom (1965, 26). Holladay labels this text as a midrash on 3:12-13, a later addition perhaps incorporated into the book in the Persian period. He also thinks that the allegories in Ezek. 16 and 23 may have influenced the shaping of this story (1986, 77, 81).

Verses 14-18 focus on future conditions. The promise of return to Zion, establishment of political leaders, and fulfillment of the ancestral promises indicate a period after the nation's exile.

IN THE TEXT

■ **6** The story in verses 6-11 begins with Yahweh's question to Jeremiah. The question focuses on the idolatrous and unfaithful history of Israel, the northern tribes (v 6). In this verse and throughout this section, Israel is called **backslider** (*mĕšûbâ*), a name that characterizes the northern tribes as a backsliding people, who have constantly turned away from Yahweh. The second part of v 6 describes Israel's participation in the fertility cult **on every high hill and under every spreading tree.** This is the accusation we also find in 2:20.

■ **7** Verse 7 conveys what Yahweh is saying to himself; he thought that Israel would recognize the folly of going after Baal and decide to **return** to him (*šûb*). However, Israel decided to remain devoted to Baal and live the adulterous way of life. Israel's apostasy was clearly known to Judah, her ***faithless*** sister. The adjective faithless (*bāgôdâ*) implies covenant betrayal, and thus is similar in meaning to Israel's name *mĕšûbâ*.

■ **8** Yahweh responded to *mĕšûbâ* Israel's adultery with a decree of divorce, following the Deuteronomic law (v 8; Deut 24:1-4). The reference here is to the destruction of the northern kingdom and the exile of the northern tribes in 722 B.C. However, *mešûbâ* Israel's history has not taught *bāgôdâ* Judah the lesson on faithfulness. Neither did she fear the outcome of her actions.

■ **9** Though Judah saw what Yahweh has done to her sister nation Israel, she followed her sister's path and brought defilement to the land (v 9). She committed adultery by worshipping **stone and wood** (symbols of male and female fertility in Canaanite religion; see 2:27), which was for her a casual matter.

■ **10** Judah did not make any attempt to **return** (*šûb*) to Yahweh with her whole heart (v 10). Verse 10 implies that there may have been some sort of an attempt to return to Yahweh worship, but it was not a wholehearted effort but only a **pretense.** Commentators connect this verse with the failure of Judah to return to Yahweh with **all her heart** during Josiah's religious reformation (see Lundbom 1999, 308; Miller 2001, 604).

■ **11** The story ends with a comparative assessment of *mešûbâ* Israel and *bāgôdâ* Judah. The exiled people of the northern kingdom are more **righteous** (v 11) than Judah. Israel is righteous not in terms of moral quality but in terms of relative innocence when compared to Judah. Judah is guiltier than Israel because she has not learned the lesson from the fate of Israel.

■ **12** The story is followed by a message to the people who once lived in the northern part of the land (vv 12-13). **North** here also could mean northern lands, or the Assyrian provinces where the Israelite tribes were living in exile. Though Yahweh divorced the northern people, now he initiates reconciliation. Yahweh sent them away from his land; now he invites them to **return** to him. In Hebrew **Return, backslider** Israel constitutes a wordplay (*šûbâ mešûbâ yiśrā'ēl*). The call to return, on the one hand, is a call to return home from the land of their exile and perhaps to be reunited with the people of Judah (see Josiah's effort to extend his religious reform into the northern tribal area; 2 Kgs 23:15-20). On the other hand, it is a call to repent of backsliding and make a commitment to return to Yahweh and return to proper Yahweh worship in Jerusalem. This call to return is followed by Yahweh's gracious words of compassion and forgiveness. Yahweh who invites his unfaithful people to return home is **merciful** (v 12). Yahweh is no longer angry because Israel has suffered punishment for her sins.

■ **13** The first step toward reconciliation and restoration comes from Yahweh, but for restoration to become a reality, steps need to be taken by Israel (v 13). These steps include admission of **guilt,** rebellion against Yahweh, worship of **foreign gods** (*zārîm*, lit. "strangers"), and failure to obey Yahweh. Mercy is freely offered here to Israel, but that offer comes with the call to repent. Without repentance, Israel cannot experience Yahweh's forgiving grace.

■ **14** The next oracle (vv 14-18) also continues the theme of return/repentance. The oracle begins with a wordplay with assonance (*šûbû bānîm šôbābîm*, lit. "return, apostate children"). Yahweh the **husband** (*'ānōkî bā'altî bākem*, lit. "I am *baʿal* over you"; *baʿal* means "lord" or "master" "owner," "husband," etc.) claims Israel as his possession; he is Israel true owner/*baʿal*. The second part of v 14 contains Yahweh's promise to bring his faithless children to **Zion,** to his home. He will take his unfaithful children from every family, clan, and tribe. **One from a town and two from a clan** does not indicate that only certain elect people will be brought back to Zion. Lundbom describes this as a "stereotyped" phrase that conveys the idea that "returnees will come from every city and every tribe" and "that their numbers will increase to a virtual swell" (1999, 313). This promise of Yahweh bringing his people back to Zion would have been good news to the Judeans who have heard this message in their exile in Babylon.

▪ **15** Yahweh will not only bring his children back to Zion but also place over them **shepherds** (*rōʿîm*, here and elsewhere in Jeremiah refers to political rulers) after his own heart (v 15), faithful kings like David who would seek Yahweh's will (see 1 Sam 13:14; 16:7). Like good shepherds they will feed and lead Yahweh's people by acknowledging Yahweh as sovereign Lord, and with discernment that comes from their obedience to his Torah. Wisdom that comes from the fear of Yahweh will be the characteristic quality of future Davidic rulers that Yahweh would place over his people.

▪ **16** Verse 16 anticipates a future era (**in those days**) of Israel's population growth in the land. By now, Israel would have known that the fulfillment of Yahweh's promise to Abraham did not require Israel to be living in the land of promise (see 29:6; also Exod 1:7). The future will usher in new conditions and new ways of relating to Yahweh. The old way of relating to Yahweh by taking an oath on the ark of the covenant will be discontinued. The memory of the ark, which symbolized Yahweh's presence, will be erased from Israel. Verse 16 seems to reflect the post-587 days when the ark and the temple did not exist.

▪ **17** Verse 17 extends the place of **Yahweh's throne,** which the Israelite tradition confined to the ark, to include the city of Jerusalem. The city of Jerusalem will be known as the throne of Yahweh. Not only Israel, but **all nations** will make pilgrimage to Jerusalem to worship Yahweh in his holy city. Nations will also abandon **the stubbornness of their evil hearts.** The universal perspective in this text anticipates that the nations will no longer exercise their stubborn human will and self-reliance. The call to return addressed to Israel in the beginning of this oracle suggests that for the nations to come to Yahweh, Israel must take the lead first by her own return to Yahweh.

▪ **18** The future Jeremiah anticipates for Israel includes the end of geographical divisions and religious claims that separated the two kingdoms; they will come together from a **northern land** (v 18) to the land of their inheritance. The northern land could be a reference to the lands of Assyria and Babylon, the lands where Israel and Judah lived in exile. The exile of both kingdoms will end; the people will return to their homeland. The text invites the audience of Jeremiah to participate in these promises by their response of "return" to Yahweh.

FROM THE TEXT

This text contains God's promises to his people who were in exile. These promises offer to Israel hope for a better future—return to the homeland, increase in population, faithful Davidic rulers, a city that would remind the nation of God's presence, a city to which the nations would come seeking God as the object of worship, and political and religious unity in the land. These promises represent the sum total of all of God's promises to Abraham and David. At the center of these promises is a God who remains faithful in the midst of the unfaithfulness of his people.

Though the call to return/repent is frequently heard in this text, the promises come without any conditions. Repentance is not a condition for the fulfillment of these promises. These promises will be fulfilled in the future not because of Israel's repentance, but because of God's faithfulness. The call to repent, however, is an important reminder to Israel and to us that the benefit of repentance far outweighs the conditions of life lived in exile, away from God. "The wonder of repentance" is "the open gateway" through which sinful humanity could enter to fully participate in the future God has prepared for them (Heschel 2001, 132).

What makes Israel's return to God a possibility is the grace of God (*ḥesed*), and the return of Israel is thus a grace-initiated event. The text also reminds that return is not a casual matter; return means claiming one's sins and taking responsibility for one's actions. Sins have to be acknowledged, confessions need to be made, and decisions to change need to be taken.

We hear in the promises of this text expressions of God's grace, which seek obedient response with genuine repentance. The gospel of Jesus Christ proclaims the good news of God's kingdom. Jesus' words, "The kingdom of God is near. Repent and believe the good news!" echo the words of this text (Mark 1:15).

3. Yahweh's Lament (3:19-22*a*)

BEHIND THE TEXT

Verses 19-20 express Yahweh's pathos; here Yahweh is speaking to himself. The text has no direct link to the preceding oracle, and it fits better in the context of the oracles of apostasy in 3:1-11. In its present position, the text seems to indicate that Israel rejected the call to return and the promise of future blessings.

Verses 21-22*a* begin with a lament and end with a call to return. It is likely that the lament expressed in v 21 is Yahweh's weeping over Israel (Holladay 1986, 123; Fretheim 2002, 86), although it could also be understood as Israel's lament before Baal in the setting of the fertility cult (Lundbom 1999, 321). This commentary connects this lament with the lament of Yahweh in the preceding verses (19-20). This lament is followed by another call to repent (v 22*a*).

IN THE TEXT

■ **19** Verse 19 begins with an emphatic *I said to myself,* which expresses Yahweh's inner thoughts. Yahweh's memory takes him back to the earliest days of his relationship with Israel. He recalls here his plan to **treat** Israel **like** (or, among) his **sons** (*'ăšîtēk babbānîm;* lit. "I will place you among sons") and give them a pleasant and beautiful land. The suffixes of the verbs **treat you** and **give you** are in feminine singular, which indicate Yahweh's treatment of Israel as his daughter. **Sons** here may be the nations (*gôyim*) referred to in the next line (Lundbom 1999, 318). If so, a daughter receives inheritance among sons, a custom usually practiced in ancient Israel only when a father died without any sons (Num 27:1-8; 36:1-12). The text thus suggests here the unusual custom of a father favoring his daughter and treating her like his sons. Yahweh sets aside his own inheritance law and chooses to give Israel a place among the nations in the world. If this interpretation is correct, then Israel receives the land as a gift, indeed an unmerited gift and thus an act of grace. Yahweh gave Israel the **most beautiful** (lit. "beauty of beauties"; see Ezek 20:6; Lam 2:15 for similar descriptions of the land) possession of the nations as an inheritance from him. Yahweh's hope in giving Israel the gift of the land was that she would call him **Father.** Yahweh thought that his daughter would respond to his generosity with love and gratitude and that she would not go after other gods.

■ **20** What Yahweh hoped would happen did not happen (v 20). Israel betrayed Yahweh like an unfaithful wife betraying her **husband** (*rē'âh,* "her companion," most likely refers to her husband). She showed no commitment to her relationship with him. This verse gives us a glimpse into Yahweh's suffering brought about by his recalcitrant daughter/wife.

■ **21** Yahweh's lament in vv 19-20 is followed by another lament in v 21. It is not clear whose *voice* is heard on the **barren heights.** The NIV reads the verse as the lament of the people of Israel. Most commentators relate this verse either to Israel's lament over its apostasy or to Israel's lament before Baal in the setting of the fertility cult. However, it is likely that this lament is linked to the preceding verses; if this is correct, here we find Yahweh's weeping *for* the children of Israel, his ungrateful daughter and unfaithful wife (see Holladay 1986, 123; Fretheim 2002, 86). It is likely that the text thus presents Yahweh at the cultic places of Baal (**barren heights**) pleading with his people to stop their apostasy and return to him. This text indicates Yahweh's self-humiliation and his self-emptying to rescue his people from their addiction to Baal. Yahweh pleads with his people who have changed their **ways,** or the covenant way of life, and have forsaken Yahweh with whom they have made the covenant.

■ **22a** Verse 22a is another call to repentance. This call is the same as in v 14.

The call to repentance comes with the promise of healing (see the theme of Yahweh the healer in 8:22; see also Hos 14:2). Yahweh reminds Israel that her hopeless addiction to Baal is not beyond his healing power.

FROM THE TEXT

The parental and spousal imagery in this text helps us understand the depth of God's pain and agony because of Israel's apostasy. God's heart is broken by an ungrateful daughter and unfaithful wife. Fretheim notes that in this text "God suffers the effects of a broken relationship at multiple levels of intimacy" (2002, 86). The situation of God here is that he suffers both as an agonizing parent and a deeply hurt spouse. God suffers here because Israel has spurned his love and responded to his grace with ingratitude. Only those parents who have experienced the stubborn rebellion of their children, and spouses who are hurt by the marital infidelity of their partners, could begin to grasp the intensity of God's sorrow and disappointment in this text. God who is brokenhearted in this text, however, continues to yearn for the love of his daughter and the love of his wife. The Johannine expression, "For God so loved the world" reflects this suffering love of God for sinful humanity (John 3:16).

The text also reflects the suffering God as a God who empties himself to the lowest level of divine deprivation to win his wayward people back to himself. Israel does not belong to the bare places of Baal; she belongs to God. It is the suffering love that compels him to go to his wayward wife and unfaithful daughter to plead with them to return to him. The promise to Israel is her healing, return to wholeness, and health. This text would have spoken powerfully to the exile people. They would have found in this text the portrait of a God who enters into the land of their exile with the offer of his healing love. There is a significant parallel between God who goes to the bare places of Baal seeking to redeem his lost children and the Lord Jesus Christ who makes himself "nothing" and humbles himself in the Kenosis text (Phil 2:5-11).

4. A Model Liturgy of Repentance (3:22b-25)

BEHIND THE TEXT

Most commentators understand the liturgy of repentance in 22b-25 as Israel's genuine or pretentious response to Yahweh's lament and call to return. It is difficult to imagine the stubborn and rebellious Israel making a genuine or pretentious response to Yahweh. What is more likely is that here we have what the prophet intended as a model prayer for the people, patterned after Hos 14:1-3. The call to return in v 22a is parallel to Hos 14:1. In both Hosea and Jeremiah, this call to return is followed by a liturgy of repentance. What is lacking in Jeremiah is the prophetic instruction found in Hos 14:2a ("Take words with you and return to the LORD. Say to him"). The language of this liturgy is clear; all the necessary areas of Israel's sins are covered by the language. The nation that has lost its vocabulary of faith, and was thoroughly immersed in the Baal cultic language, receives in this text an instruction in the traditional language of penitence. The first plural forms (we, us) indicate Jeremiah's self-identification with the apostate people. Another call to return in 4:1-4 would not have been needed, if this confession was Israel's sincere response to the call to return in 3:22a.

IN THE TEXT

■ **22b** The ritual of repentance begins with v 22b and continues through v 25. Israel's coming to Yahweh is the first step in this liturgy of repentance (v 22b). Coming to Yahweh is an act of worship (see Pss 42:2; 100:2; 132:7). The prayer thus instructs the people to reverse their stubborn refusal to come to Yahweh (see Jer 2:31). Israel's coming to Yahweh also means rejection of Baal. The next step in the liturgy is the confession of faith in Yahweh as Israel's God. This means a return to the traditional covenant faith that there are no other gods, but only Yahweh.

■ **23** The liturgy moves from confession of faith in Yahweh to a total renunciation of Baal and the places of fertility worship (v 23a). This includes the acknowledgment that **hills** and **mountains,** where Israel practiced fertility cult, are centers of falsehood (*laššeqer* means "the Lie," a demeaning term for Baal; Lundbom 1999, 322) and confusion (noise) created by the wild behavior of Baal worshippers (Holladay 1986, 125). The renunciation of Baal is followed by another confession of faith in Yahweh that he is the only source of Israel's **salvation** (v 23b). No other God can save Israel (see Hos 14:3).

■ **24** The next step in the liturgy is the recognition that following Baal has brought nothing but Yahweh's judgment in the form of agricultural and economic disaster throughout Israel's history (v 24). The reference is likely to military invasions that resulted in agricultural and economic loss. **Our youth** perhaps indicates the wilderness days when Israel encountered the Baal cult at Baal-Peor (Num 25:1-9). **Shame** (*bōšet,* meaning "shame" or "shameful thing") is another derogatory name for Baal. The ancestors of Israel worked hard for flocks, herds, sons, and daughters and gave credit to Baal as the source of these blessings. In the end they were all destroyed by the invaders. This is the judgment for rejecting Yahweh, the true source of Israel's blessings.

■ **25** In the final segment of this liturgy of repentance, Jeremiah instructs his audience to participate in a ritual to demonstrate their sin and guilt (v 25). **Let us lie down** suggests lying on the ground to express penitence and sorrow. They must recognize the truth that the "shame" they followed after (i.e., Baal) indeed became their **shame,** the cause of their humiliation. Covering with disgrace or dishonor may be the ritual of covering the face with the penitent's torn garment, another symbol of shame and disgrace. The liturgy of repentance concludes with another confession of sin. Jeremiah instructs the covenant people to acknowledge the truth that their sin against Yahweh extended over generations, from the earliest days of their existence to the present day. The specific sin of the people is that they have not obeyed Yahweh their God. This is precisely what Yahweh's lawsuit is all about (2:1 ff.). Jeremiah reminds Israel that this liturgy of repentance, not its countersuit or claims of innocence (see 2:23, 29, 35), is the proper response to Yahweh's lawsuit against his covenant people.

FROM THE TEXT

The events of 587 B.C. indicate that what Jeremiah had hoped to accomplish through this model prayer was not realized. The people continued in their idolatry and as a result the judgment of the exile came. The community in exile would have found in this prayer the language for prayer and confession, and hope for healing and restoration. The steps Jeremiah prescribes for healing and restoration are clear: confession of faith in God and commitment to return to him, renunciation of false gods, trust in the salvation that comes from God, recognition of the reality of God's judgment, and confession of sin. Jeremiah's liturgy of penitence reflects the words of the prodigal son: "Father, I have sinned against heaven and against you. I am no longer worthy to be called your son" (Luke 15:21). In the Christian tradition, confession, absolution, and the pronouncement of peace symbolize the healing of broken relationship between God and the worshipping community. John reminds us of this healing power of confession: "If we confess our sins, he [God] is faithful and just and will forgive us our sins and purify us from all unrighteousness" (1 John 1:9).

5. Another Call to Return (4:1-4)

BEHIND THE TEXT

Jeremiah 4:1-4 formally concludes the series of oracles that begin at 2:1. This larger block of materials (2:1—4:4) begins and ends with a message to the citizens of Jerusalem (2:2; 4:3). Various references to northern Israel in 2:1—4:4 indicate that the oracles in this section address the whole nation, both Judah and the remnant of the northern tribes. Jeremiah 4:1-4 has two parts; the first part (vv 1-2) is a call to return addressed to Israel. Jeremiah's oracles to the northern tribes probably end here. The focus seems to be on the conditions that need to be met by Israel in order for it to participate in the Abrahamic promise, particularly the promise of Israel becoming a blessing to the nations. The second part (vv 3-4) is a call to be circumcised to Yahweh, addressed to the people of Judah/Jerusalem. Thus, these verses are also linked to the Abrahamic tradition. The theme of repentance and inner transformation dominates vv 1-4.

Though this unit has a thematic continuity with the liturgy of repentance in the preceding section, its setting is not clear. Some commentators connect it to the reform of Josiah in 622 B.C., which extended into the northern territory (2 Kgs 23:19-20).

IN THE TEXT

Yahweh is the speaker in 4:1-2. Yahweh's instruction follows the prophet's model prayer of confession in the preceding unit. As children of Abraham, Israel's calling is to mediate God's blessing to the nations. To fulfill that calling, the wayward people of Israel must not only repent of their idolatry and return to God but also show evidence of true repentance. These verses indicate the actions the people must take to show the genuineness of their repentance.

■ **1** *First*, they must return to Yahweh (v 1a). The conditional clause (**If you will return**) indicates that repentance, in order to be genuine, must be a decision to return to Yahweh. **Return** (*šûb*) in these verses reinforces the repeated calls for repentance in ch 3. The second line of v 1 is most likely a "then" clause [*(then) to me you return*]. The text calls Israel to make a solemn commitment to seek Yahweh and put an end to its pursuit of Baal. *Second*, they must get rid of their **idols** (*šiqqûṣîm* means "detested things" or "pagan gods and idols"). Those who wish to return to Yahweh can no longer hold on to other gods. *Third*, they must not **go astray,** or resist the temptation to go after other gods.

■ **2a** *Fourth*, they must not take Yahweh's name in vain (v 2a). **As Yahweh lives** is a traditional oath taking expression in Yahweh's name (Exod 20:7). Repentance and return to Yahweh means oath taking in Yahweh's name with a commitment to **truth** (*'ĕmet*), **justice** (*mišpaṭ*), and **righteousness** (*ṣĕdāqâ*)—the qualities that best describe the character of Yahweh. The one who takes the oath in Yahweh's name must reflect the character of Yahweh who is trustworthy, just, and righteous.

■ **2b** The focus of v 2b is on **the nations.** The divine promises made to Abraham, which include a blessing to all the families of the earth, will be realized only if Abraham's descendants exemplified truth, justice, and righteousness in their relationship with Yahweh (see Gen 12:3; 18:18-19; 22:18; 26:4). Verse 2 ends with the claim that the nations will **boast** in him, or take pride in him. **In him** here most likely refers to Yahweh, though the context permits it to be understood as Abraham, since the text relates to the Abrahamic promise in Genesis.

■ **3** Verse 3 is another call to repentance, this time addressed to the people of Judah and Jerusalem. Yahweh's speech begins with a metaphor taken from the agricultural setting (**Break up *for yourselves* unplowed ground;** see also Hos 10:12). Tilling fallow ground before planting new seed is necessary not only to break up and soften the soil that has become hard due to inactivity but also to uproot and destroy weeds and thorns that have taken over the soil. **Do not sow among thorns** reinforces the idea of planting seed on carefully prepared soil by removing thorns and weeds from the soil. (In the parable of the sower, Jesus compares seeds sown among thorns to those who hear the word but fail to produce fruit because of the cares of the world and their delight in wealth; Matt 13:7, 23.) The metaphor clearly indicates long years of inactivity in Judah's relationship with Yahweh. The metaphor also calls for genuine repentance on the part of Judah. Yahweh invites those who have been "uncultivated in righteousness" to break up their "fruitless and hardened hearts" in repentance to allow the "seed of the word of life" to be sown in them (Clarke, 266). Repentance will lead Judah to be fruitful and productive for Yahweh. The text also suggests that thorough reform needs to take place along with repentance. Repentance without moral reform is tantamount to sowing on fallow soil or sowing among thorns.

■ **4** Verse 4 continues the speech addressed to the citizens of Judah. The metaphor moves from tilling unplowed ground to circumcision of the heart. Yahweh calls the citizens of Judah to **circumcise** themselves (or, **be circumcised**) to Yahweh. **Remove the foreskins of your heart** indicates that circumcision that Yahweh demands here is an internal act. The shift in emphasis of circumcision from an external act to an internal act suggests God's plan to create a community that is inclusive and open to all who would respond to God's call to repentance (Stulman 2005, 60). **Heart** (*lēb*) is the seat of human emotions, thinking, planning, and decision-making. Here again, the text focuses on the initiative of the people of Judah to Yahweh's call to return. Yahweh's speech ends with a stern warning that rejecting the call to repentance and inner transformation would lead to disastrous consequences. Those who refuse to recognize and respond to this call will face the **wrath** of Yahweh, which will **burn like fire** from which there will be no escape. The burning fire of Yahweh's anger is on Judah for all the evil it has committed; the text implies that repentance is the only way to escape judgment.

FROM THE TEXT

We find in this text a biblical theology of repentance. The message of this text may be outlined as follows:

i. Repentance involves *a turning away from* one's self-centered and self-directed way of life and *a turning to* a life instructed, guided, directed by God.

ii. Repentance involves *a turning away from* all other gods that compete for one's loyalty and *a turning to* God who alone is worthy of loyalty and devotion.

iii. Repentance involves *a turning away from* the kind of existence that has no fixed center, a life that wanders aimlessly and *a turning to* God's presence, which offers stability and security.

iv. Repentance involves *a turning away from* life without integrity and *a turning to* truthfulness, justice, and righteousness in one's relationship with God and the world.

v. Repentance involves *a turning away from* a useless and wasted existence and *a turning to* a life that is productive and useful to both God and the world.

vi. Repentance involves *a turning away from* a closed heart to God and *a turning to* God with an open heart.

vii. Repentance involves *a turning away from* God's wrath and *a turning to* God's grace and favor.

This kind of repentance is what enables a person to fully participate in mediating God's grace to the world, the goal of "the gospel [announced] in advance to Abraham" (Gal 3:8). Again, the promise of this text covers all—both Jews and Gentiles—and invites all to participate in mediating God's blessings to the world.

The text establishes a point of contact with the ritual of circumcision in the Abrahamic traditions in Gen 17, the Deuteronomic call to circumcision (Deut 10:16; see also 30:6), and Paul's description of circumcision as an inward act (Rom 2:28-29). Moses called the people to circumcise the foreskin of their heart (Deut 10:16), but he also said that God himself would circumcise the heart of his people (30:6). Jeremiah challenges here the already circumcised participants in the Abrahamic covenant to be circumcised again. The external sign of the covenant they already have through physical circumcision does not fulfill the call to repentance. Neither does the ritual of external circumcision meet the conditions of covenant with God, which requires one's total commitment to live on God's terms. Paul tells us that "real circumcision is a matter of the heart" (Rom 2:29 NRSV). God calls his people to bring their whole heart in conformity to his will. Clarke describes the call to circumcision as a call to "put away everything that has a tendency to grieve" God (266). Paul makes clear that this spiritual circumcision involves "the putting off of the sinful nature" ("the body of the flesh" NRSV) and that it is not a circumcision made by human hands but that it is "the circumcision done by Christ" (Col 2:11).

The spiritual circumcision that initiates believers into a life of holy living where the desire of our heart is to love God with all our heart, all our soul and all our strength (Deut 6:5; Matt 22:37) is a significant emphasis of Wesleyan theology. In his sermon on "The Circumcision of the Heart" John Wesley described "circumcision of the heart" (Rom 2:29) as the "habitual disposition of soul which in the Sacred Writings is termed 'holiness', . . . the being cleansed from sin, 'from all filthiness both of flesh and spirit', . . . the being endued with those virtues which were also in Christ Jesus, the being so 'renewed in the image of our mind' as to be 'perfect, as our Father in heaven is perfect'" (Outler 1984, 402-3).

JEREMIAH

4:1-4

"UPROOT AND TEAR DOWN"

THE AGENCY OF THE ENEMY FROM THE NORTH (4:5—6:30)

Overview

Announcement of judgment dominates the oracles in Jer 4:5—6:30. At several places the oracles indicate Yahweh's judgment coming through the agency of an enemy nation from the north or from a distant land (4:6, 16; 5:16; 6:1, 22, 25). Commentators do not agree on where "the enemy from the north" oracles end. Some think that the series end in 6:30; others extend the series to 10:25 because of the reference to the nation from the north in 10:22 (Holladay 1986, 133; Holladay considers not only the enemy from the north motif but also other literary connections between 4:5—6:30 and 8:4—10:25). Lundbom describes 4:5—10:25 as a "foe-lament" collection with the prose insertion of 7:1—8:3 (Lundbom 1999, 333). In 4:4—6:30 Jeremiah vividly portrays the coming judgment as the inevitable outcome of Israel's idolatry and infidelity.

Poetry is the predominant feature of this literary block (4:5-9, 13-26, 27-31; 5:1-17, 20—6:30). The poetic oracles in this section are not organized in any logical order. They are, however, connected together by the theme of judgment through the agency of an unnamed enemy from the north.

Oracles in this section contain various speakers. Though Yahweh is the primary speaker who announces the coming judgment, often the prophet interjects with his own indictment of Judah, expressions of his pain and agony, and intercessions and pleading with Yahweh on behalf of the people (4:8, 11-12, 14, 18, 19-21, 23-26, 31; 5:3-6, 12, 14a; 6:10-11a, 26, 28). Occasionally the people express their lament over their utter ruin and fear of the impending destruction (4:13b; 6:4, 24). The enemy also speaks twice with the call to prepare for war and invade Judah (vv 4-5). Some unspecified witnesses interject in vv 16b and 17b.

The poetic oracles in this section are interrupted by three prose units (4:10-12, 27; 5:18-19). The two prose statements in 4:10-12 seem to serve as a commentary on the poetic oracle in vv 5-8, which describes the evil that God is bringing from the north to make the land totally desolate. Verse 27 provides a little comfort ("I will not make a full end" NRSV) to the nation that is threatened with total devastation. Jeremiah 5:18-19 is another prose commentary aimed to ease the pain of judgment announced in vv 15-17. Though the enemy that God is bringing is a formidable power that will destroy everything in the land, God will not "make a full end" (NRSV) of Judah.

This section differs from the preceding section (2:1—4:4) in a number of different ways. Imageries of marriage and marital infidelity that dominate 2:1—4:4 are virtually lacking in 4:5—6:30. Yahweh is no longer a God who anguishes over his adulterous wife but is a divine warrior who prepares himself to wage war with Judah. He recruits a formidable enemy to be on his side to carry out Judah's total devastation. The sin of apostasy and idolatry that dominates the oracles in 2:1—4:4 is mentioned only once in this section (5:6-7). Sins of the people in this section are lack of justice, truth, knowledge of Yahweh, and greed.

The judgment language in this section utilizes a number of metaphors. Descriptions of war and the invading army come from the scene of wildlife (attack by lion, wolf, and leopard in 4:7 and 5:6) and destructive forces of nature (hot wind in 4:11). Metaphors taken from agricultural setting indicate the intensity of devastation (4:17; 5:10; 6:9). The language of 4:23-26 conveys cosmic chaos and destruction. Jeremiah also expresses the intensity of his own suffering as well as that of the people in imaginative ways (vv 19, 31). The metaphors in this section articulate a dreadful and devastating judgment; its effect will reach all the inhabitants of the land, including the prophet himself.

The oracles in 4:5—6:30 do not indicate a precise historical setting. The frequent reference to the enemy from the north suggests the impending Babylonian invasion. The rise of Babylon as a superpower in the political landscape of the ancient Near East in the last decade of the seventh century may have been the general setting of these oracles. Occasionally the prophet describes the enemy invasion as having already taken place; however, the oracles for the most part suggest a future event that would bring total chaos and desolation of the land.

The exiled community would have recognized the threat of judgment in these chapters, not as empty words but as a reality they have already reckoned with that is very much a part of their shattered existence away from their beloved homeland. They would also have been reminded by these chapters that there was no one to blame but themselves for their fragile existence in the land of their exile.

1. Disaster from the North (4:5-10)

BEHIND THE TEXT

The judgment oracles begin with an announcement from Yahweh. Yahweh is the speaker in vv 5-7. This oracle warns the people that the enemy is advancing toward Judah. Verse 8 is a response from the prophet, addressed to the people. This is followed by another announcement of judgment (v 9), which describes the effect of judgment on the leaders. The unit ends with Jeremiah's accusation that Yahweh has deceived the people (v 10).

IN THE TEXT

■ 5 The unit begins with Yahweh's announcement to proclaim to the people of Judah and Jerusalem the news of the war that is fast approaching (v 5). The imperatives **declare, proclaim,** and **say** indicate the sending of messengers throughout the land with an urgent message. This is followed by five more imperatives, **blow, call out, give in full,** say, **gather together,** all aimed to urge the people to escape and seek protection from the enemy attack. Blowing **the horn** (*šôpār*) gave the people warning about an imminent danger. The meaning of the imperative **give in full** (*mal'û* in the intensive form) is difficult to determine; most translations read it as a supporting verb of the preceding imperative (**call out**), and thus together both verb forms are translated as **cry aloud.** The people are urged to seek protection in the **fortified cities** that offered protection from enemy invasion (see the same call in 8:14). During the time of Jeremiah, in addition to Jerusalem, there were many other fortified cities in Judah (Lachish, Arad, etc.).

■ 6 The call to give warning continues in v 6. The imperative **raise a flag** (or signal pole or banner) could mean raising a "distress signal" to warn the people to escape to Zion, the principal fortified city in Judah (Lundbom 1999, 336). It is also possible to interpret this as a call to follow the signal bearer, march toward Zion, and seek refuge here. This is not the time to **stand around** and delay action or to wait it out to see if the threat is real; the imperative **take refuge** is a strong warning to get out and get going before the enemy comes to destroy the land. The real force behind the imminent danger is Yahweh, the One who is **bringing evil** against the land. The nation is under the serious threat of God's judgment that is coming through the agency of a nation **from the north** (see 1:15 for comments on the enemy from the north). The expression **great disaster** (*šeber gādôl*, also found in 6:1; 14:17; 48:3; 50:22; and 51:54) indicates that the enemy assault will result in the total devastation of Judah.

■ **7** Verse 7 utilizes the metaphor of a lion to describe the enemy, a common metaphor for the enemy in the prophets (see Isa 5:29; Ezek 32:2). In Hosea, Yahweh is the lion who attacks Israel (5:14). The identification of the enemy nation as destroyer parallels the lion imagery. The first part of this verse uses three expressions (**gone up,** set out, **gone out**) to convey the idea that the army of the enemy is already mobilized and on its way. The goal of the enemy is to make the land of Judah a desolate and ruined place. The massive assault of the enemy will result in the destruction of the cities, and the cities will be left **without inhabitant.**

■ **8** In v 8 the prophet calls the people to respond to this terrible news with the traditional ritual of mourning. Wearing sackcloth, lamenting, and wailing are signs of grief shown during times of calamity. The call to begin the ritual of mourning indicates that the threat is real and imminent. Typically these rituals are undertaken when disaster strikes; however, here the people are encouraged to do these rituals before the disaster has taken place. Though the enemy is a nation from the north, it is Yahweh who is mobilizing this enemy. What the nation is about to experience is the ***burning*** **anger of *Yahweh*.** Yahweh's wrath is upon Judah for its refusal to repent and return to him.

The Day of the Lord

4:6-10

The day of the Lord in ancient Israel originally meant the day when God will save Israel from its enemies, and thus the day of Israel's salvation. But beginning with Amos it has taken the negative meaning as the day of Yahweh's judgment. The OT prophets describe this day as a day of Yahweh's anger and wrath and the punishment of all who are his enemies.

■ **9** Verse 9 indicates that all the key leaders of Judah—**king, *princes*, priests,** and **prophets**—will find themselves helpless and ineffective to save the nation from the coming disaster. **That day** in the prophets typically is the Day of the Lord. That day is the day when Judah will experience the wrath of Yahweh. The **heart** of the kings and princes will ***fail*** or lose courage when they are faced with enemy. The priests and the prophets also will be dismayed by the coming disaster. The nation and its leaders who have presumed that Yahweh will not be angry forever will be totally disappointed (see 3:5).

■ **10** Verse 10 portrays Jeremiah as Yahweh's accuser and antagonist. The accusation, **you have deceived this people and Jerusalem,** seems to place full responsibility on Yahweh for the impending calamity and the failure of the leadership. Jeremiah also accuses Yahweh of giving the message of **peace** or total well-being (*šālôm*) to the people and thus deceiving them at a time when they were faced with the grave danger of being cut down by the **sword** of the enemy. Elsewhere Jeremiah also brings charges against the false prophets that they have misguided the nation with the proclamation of "peace, peace," a message that did not originate with Yahweh (see 6:14; 8:11; also 23:16-22). Jeremiah's complaint of Yahweh deceiving his people is parallel to his complaint that Yahweh deceived him (see 20:7 where a different verb form is used). Here this accusation may in reality be an indictment against Israel's leadership, particularly the false prophets who have given assurances of "peace" to the people in Yahweh's name. This message seems to have been the propaganda promoted by Judah's political and religious leaders. The unsuspecting people of Judah would have thought of this message as the true voice of God since it came from the leadership in Jerusalem.

FROM THE TEXT

This judgment oracle vividly and imaginatively portrays the reality of God's judgment on Judah. The text makes clear that this judgment comes from the pathos-filled God of the previous section (chs 2—3) who is the real enemy of the people who have refused his repeated calls for repentance and have presumed upon his enduring grace and mercy. However, the real irony in the text is that it is also a warning and a call to escape from the enemy and to seek refuge in Zion. Does Jeremiah intend to convey that Zion, the dwelling place of God, is the only real place for Judah's escape from his wrath? That likelihood cannot be ruled out, though Zion itself comes under the prophetic attack later in his oracles. We should also regard the call to put on sackcloth, weep, and lament as the prophet's "last minute plea for repentance" (Craigie 1991, 73). Genuine repentance and contrition may persuade God to halt the enemy march and spare Judah from total destruction. These warnings and call for grieving indicate a ray of hope for the nation's survival. The God of wrath who announces judgment is also the God of grace and mercy and the hope of sinners.

Jeremiah in this text is a one-person minority in Judah, a nation controlled by powerful political and religious leaders. He is an outsider to the political and religious establishment that promotes the ideology of "all is well" as an unconditional guarantee from God. Jeremiah, nonetheless, confronts the power structure with the message that it is not "peace" but "sword" that is at work in the nation. His commitment to truth telling indicates the character and function of a true leader. Ultimately, when all other leaders have failed, and all their voices were proved wrong, only his voice survived to remind what was left of Judah that truth telling is what matters the most. To the exilic community this would have meant acknowledging the exile as God's judgment. Their future now depends on their willingness to "flee" to Zion—God's presence—for safety, and on their trust in God's graciousness to restore them.

2. This Is Your Punishment (4:11-18)

BEHIND THE TEXT

Verses 11-18 continue the theme of the coming disaster that Yahweh is bringing upon Judah through an enemy nation from a distant land. This section begins with a prose statement (vv 11-12) from Yahweh, followed by a poetic oracle (vv 13-18) that describes the enemy as a swiftly moving force.

IN THE TEXT

■ **11** The message is for the people of Judah and Jerusalem, and it is about what will happen **at that time,** the day of Yahweh's judgment (v 11). The **scorching wind** indicates the intensity of the judgment. The reference may be to the sirocco, the dry, hot, and destructive east wind (see 18:17). The location of its origin is in the **bare** heights in the desert; east wind comes from the desert in the east. The wind is coming toward Yahweh's **dear** people (*bat 'ami*, lit. "daughter of my people"). This is the irony here; in spite of the severity of Yahweh's judgment, his relationship with his covenant people has not changed; he still regards them as his daughter, a people very dear to him. The goal of this wind is not winnowing or cleansing or sifting out the grain from the chaff, usually accomplished by milder and gentler winds. The agricultural metaphor suggests massive and indiscriminate destruction of the land and its inhabitants by the enemy nation.

■ **12** Verse 12 indicates that the wind that is moving toward Judah is **stronger than** the sirocco and that it will blow away everything in the land. The real destructive force behind this storm is Yahweh who speaks **judgments against** that sinful nation.

■ **13** Verse 13 is a continuation of Yahweh's speech, which utilizes imageries such as **clouds, whirlwind,** and **eagles** to portray the speed and the force of the enemy nation that is moving toward Judah (see Isa 5:28; Ezek 38:16; Hab 1:8). The enemy is addressed in third person (**he, his**), but no identity is given. This verse is somewhat parallel to Jer 4:7, and thus it is likely that the reference here is to Babylon or its king. The people (or, Jeremiah put the words in the mouth of the people) respond to this bad news with a **woe** statement that expresses their feeling of utter ruin and hopelessness.

■ **14** Verse 14 is a call for repentance and an end to evil so that the nation may be spared from the enemy attack. Holladay designates Jeremiah as the speaker here, although this could also be understood as Yahweh's call to repentance (Holladay 1986, 141). No external ritual of cleansing will **wash** (*kābas*) away the **evil** of Jerusalem (see 2:22). What is corrupt and in need of thorough cleansing is the **heart**—the seat of all ***evil* schemes** and evil **thoughts.** In Ps 51:2 and 7, the psalmist appeals to God to wash him from his iniquity; here God is asking the people to wash their heart. Holladay observes that it is only here in the OT we find "heart" as the object of the verb "wash" and that the text is parallel to the call to circumcise the heart in Jer 4:4. He aptly sums up the intent of 4:4 and v 14 this way: "Both expressions call for a radical renovation of character, the will, to render it fit for covenant with Yahweh" (Holladay 1986, 157). Verse 14 ends with the question, **How long will you harbor *within you your evil schemes?*** This question implies that the nation has been on the path of scheming and doing evil for a long time. The question also establishes the guilt of the nation. Its salvation from judgment now rests on its willingness to be thoroughly transformed and to live a life of covenantal faithfulness.

■ **15** Verse 15 relates how the enemy is moving faster and getting closer to Jerusalem. The announcement of **disaster** comes from **Dan,** the northern boundary of the land of Israel. The second line indicates that that announcement is now being heard from **Mount Ephraim,** most likely the hill country of Ephraim, north of the territory of Benjamin. Soon the enemy will arrive in Jerusalem.

■ **16** In v 16, Yahweh instructs his messengers to proclaim to the **nations** the message ***concerning*** the disaster that is approaching Jerusalem. The purpose of announcing this news to the neighboring nations is not clear. The phrase "behold" or "look" invites the attention of the nations to observe what is happening in the historical scene. The nations receive the word that ***watchers*** (a besieging army) are coming toward Jerusalem **from a distant land.** The meaning of the word ***watchers*** is not clear; the reference is to the army of the enemy (Holladay suggests the translation "shouters," meaning the scouts of the invading army who advance into the land with shout or raised voice; 1986, 159). Babylon is intended by the phrase **distant land.** The military metaphor is clear in the last line; the enemy soldiers have already ***raised their voices*** or **war cry against the cities of Judah.**

■ **17** The first line of v 17 completes the description of the advancing of the enemy. They are now in Jerusalem and have already taken their position around the city like the ***guards of* a field.** Guards of a field imply those who protect crop or animals in an open field. The scene is that of a siege, and the army of the enemy is now in control of the city. The second part of v 17 indicates that Jerusalem's rebellion against Yahweh is the cause of this precarious situation of his beloved city.

■ **18** In v 18 Yahweh makes it known to Judah that these calamitous conditions come because of its evil **conduct.** There is no one else to blame for the bitter experiences of war and destruction. This is ***evil*** being paid back for evil. ***It has reached your heart*** may mean that the calamity is fatal and that soon death would come upon Judah. The people with an evil heart are about to be struck at the very center of their being. The nation will reap evil because it has a long history of sowing evil.

FROM THE TEXT

It is too easy for us to miss v 14 and the hope it seeks to convey. This verse is almost buried under the language of war. When we strip away the war imagery in the surrounding verses, the promise of salvation emerges to give balance to this otherwise judgment heavy unit. The hope expressed here in the possibility of salvation is not wishful thinking on the part of Jeremiah. He rises above his own poetic and prophetic imagination of the approaching danger and imagines for God's people a future even on the brink of their imminent destruction. The possibility of salvation introduced in this verse is real. The external threat of the enemy can be averted; for that to happen there must be an internal change within Judah—a thorough washing of its heart from all evil—an intentional reordering of its social, political, and religious life. It must shape and order its existence using the standards of the covenant and become a covenant-keeping people.

The community in exile would have found in v 14 a continued call for a radical reordering of its inner life. This is the key for it to experience the saving power of God. Judgment is seldom the last word no matter how horrifying may be the language in which it is couched. Judgment is real; so is the offer of grace that leads to salvation. James admonishes us to "wash" our "hands," "purify" our "hearts," "grieve, mourn and wail," and "humble" ourselves before God (4:8-10). Both Jeremiah and James remind us that these actions are necessary for us to enjoy God's grace that comes through his offer of salvation.

3. Oh, My Anguish! (4:19-22)

BEHIND THE TEXT

Some commentators consider 4:19-21 to be the first of several so-called confessions of Jeremiah. These verses express the prophet's deep emotional anguish over the approaching enemy and the impending destruction of Judah. Most commentators keep v 22 as part of the literary unit and consider it as a response from Yahweh to the prophet's anguish and lament in vv 19-21.

Jeremiah's "Confessions"

In a number of places in chs 1—25 Jeremiah expresses his personal prayers and intense emotional feelings (4:19-21; 8:18—9:1; 11:18—12:6; 15:10-21; 17:14-18; 18:18-23; 20:7-18). Scholars have designated these texts as Jeremiah's "confessions." The label does not mean that the prophet is acknowledging his sins and seeking forgiveness from God. Recent scholars see these texts in many ways similar to the laments in the book of Psalms. The prophet's laments are addressed to God, and they often contain the prophet's conversation with God. Personal suffering is often a central issue in these laments.

In the past, scholars have thought of these laments as private prayers and not as a part of his public message. Recent scholarship, however, regards these laments as part of the prophet's public message. Scholars also think that these prayers have become model prayers for the faithful people of God during their exile and after their return to their homeland. O'Connor finds two levels of theological meaning in these texts. At a personal level, in the setting of the life of the prophet, these confessions present a unique meaning applicable only to the prophet. But in the literary setting of the entire book, she thinks these confessions serve the purpose of explaining why God's judgment came on Judah that rejected the prophetic word. These confessions in the setting of the entire book, according to O'Connor, "proclaim the justice of God in destroying the nation" (1988, 159-60).

IN THE TEXT

■ **19** Verse 19, though it sounds more metaphorical than real, expresses the actual physical experience of the prophet. The prophet who brings the dreadful words of judgment experiences the effect of judgment in his personal life, even before the judgment word is actualized in history. The first two lines indicate gut-wrenching **pain** that the prophet experiences in his physical being. The third line expresses the tearing of the **walls** (agony) of his **heart** like that of someone who suffers a massive heart attack. His **heart is roaring** like a turbulent and raging sea. The inner turbulence does not allow him to **keep silent**. What causes this physical, emotional, and psychological pain is the **sound of the horn, the alarm of war,** he hears in the land.

■ **20** Verse 20 conveys the sound of the war that is being heard in Judah. The enemy announces the crashing and shattering of one structure after another (**disaster follows disaster**; *šeber 'al šeber*, lit. "crash upon crash") in the land. The attack of the enemy has caused the total destruction of the land. **My tents** and **my tent-curtains** refer to the house of the prophet; this perhaps indicates destruction of the dwellings of the citizens of Judah when the judgment will come suddenly and in an instant. Some commentators think that the destruction of tents and curtains indicate the destruction of the Jerusalem temple (see Holladay 1986, 162). If the context of this verse is one of the Babylonian invasions (597 or 587 B.C.), then **my tents** could actually refer to Jeremiah's own house in Anathoth, which would have been destroyed by the invading army.

■ **21** The prophet's lament continues in v 21. The question **how long** indicates the prophet's total despair over the unbearable conditions that do not seem to go away. What he sees all around him is the *flag* or the distress signal raised by the helpless victims of the war, and what he hears all day is the **sound of the horn** as enemy soldiers move from one village to another.

■ **22** In v 22 Yahweh reminds the prophet the reason for this calamity, something the prophet already knows. Yahweh's people (**my people**) are suffering the consequence of their foolishness and their lack of knowledge of Yahweh.

4:19-22

A fool is a person without wisdom or the fear of Yahweh. Knowing Yahweh means to have a personal and covenantal relationship with him. Yahweh's people have lost all **understanding;** ironically, they have wisdom to do that which is evil. This wisdom does not originate with Yahweh but in their evil heart. Having been set in their foolish ways, they show no evidence of any knowledge of what it means to do good.

FROM THE TEXT

The text contrasts Jeremiah (who knows God) with Judah (who does not know God). Jeremiah knows God and so he has discernment of historical realities. He is a full participant in the covenant relationship with God. Judah does not know God. Though signs of the war are all around, the nation remains oblivious and obtuse about things that are critically important. In contrast, Jeremiah fully experiences the dreadful and devastating impact of the military invasion even before it takes place. He enters into the thick of life to experience pain and suffering. He suffers the agony and the anguish of the dying nation. He articulates for them the emotional distress they could not express. He cries out for the numb and the voiceless people of Judah. He becomes for them their voice in the hope of persuading God to show mercy to his people who do not know him and who are deep in their sinful way of life. In the weeping of Jesus over Jerusalem, we see a similar display of passion over a people and a city that refused to know God and to discern the truth that God's judgment was upon them. They, too, failed to do good by accepting God's offer of *shalom* for them (Luke 19:41-44). We learn from Jeremiah and Jesus what it means to know God and what it means to do good in the most distressing hour of the day.

4. Cosmic Chaos (4:23-28)

BEHIND THE TEXT

In vv 23-26 Jeremiah conveys the universal scope of the destruction. This is followed by a Yahweh speech (vv 27-28) that essentially agrees with the terrifying portrait of devastation that Jeremiah paints in his speech. The massive assault by the invading army, the agency of Yahweh's judgment, will dismantle all the secure and stable structures of creation. The language of these verses is reminiscent of the Day of the Lord descriptions in the prophets (Amos, Joel, and Zephaniah in particular); however, it lacks apocalyptic imagery. The fourfold repetition of the phrase **I looked** in vv 23, 24, 25, and 26, followed by the particle ***behold*** indicates the visionary character as well as the symmetrical structure of this unit. These verses draw from the language and imagery of Gen 1.

IN THE TEXT

■ **23** The effect of the enemy invasion is the return of the earth to its **formless and *void*** (*tōhû wābōhû*) condition (v 23; see Gen 1:2). Sun, moon, and stars that gave light in the sky disappeared. The universe returned to primordial darkness.

■ **24** In v 24, the impact of the enemy invasion is compared to that of a massive earthquake that moved the **mountains** and **hills,** the most stable and secured structures of the universe.

■ **25** Verse 25 paints the picture of the disappearance of human and animal life. ***Human*** beings who were created in God's image to rule over creation have vanished from the earth. "Birds" (NRSV) that were created to fill the sky fled their home. Disappearance of humans and birds is a theme in Zeph 1:3.

■ **26** Verse 26 describes the devastation of the ***garden*** land (*hakkarmel*; see 2:7) of Yahweh—i.e., the Promised Land, which is often described metaphorically as a land flowing with milk and honey and fruit trees and orchards (see Deut 8:7-8). The Promised Land has become a desert with ruined cities because of the ***hot*** anger of Yahweh. The gift of Yahweh is no longer a place suitable for human inhabitation.

■ **27** The vision is followed by a poetic oracle (vv 27-28) in which Yahweh affirms the authenticity of what Jeremiah saw. The **whole land** (v 27) could be a reference to the Promised Land in the previous verse, though some commentators see here a reference to the whole earth. The first part of this verse affirms the ***desolation*** of the land implied in v 26. The last line of v 27 (***I will not make a full end***) indicates Yahweh's resolve to be gracious in the midst of this devastating judgment. Judgment will not lead to total destruction.

■ **28** Yahweh's speech continues with another description of the devastating effect of the judgment on the whole universe (v 28); both the **earth** and the ***sky*** (the heavens and the earth in Gen 1:1) will suffer the ravaging consequence of the judgment that is coming upon Judah. **The earth will mourn** or wither away and will become a barren and unproductive place. The sky that provided light to the inhabitants of the earth shall become **dark.** Cosmic doom and gloom is vividly portrayed in the first part of v 28. The second part of v 28 indicates that this judgment is unavoidable because it has already been **spoken** and ***planned*** by Yahweh. The speech ends with Yahweh's resolve not to **relent** or **turn back** from his decision to bring judgment upon Judah.

FROM THE TEXT

Modern readers of this text may compare Jeremiah's portrait of the desolation of the earth to the frightening images of a nuclear holocaust. Why would God return his beautiful creation back into primordial chaos? Why would he undo what he created? Why would he turn his beautiful garden into a wasteland? The chilling description of the devastating and cataclysmic judgment that affects the whole universe warns us of the disastrous consequences of our covenant-breaking with God. The language of this text does not seem to give much hope because of the sense of finality it conveys through imageries of chaos and devastation. To Jeremiah's immediate audience this ominous word would have been a warning to escape this impending chaos by returning to God who threatens them with his unrelenting and uncompromising stand against them. The exilic readers of this text would have understood what this chaos meant because their world was suddenly dismantled in an instant with the onslaught of the Babylonian army. Their life in exile was indeed the experience of chaos described in this text.

Though the text does not ask, "What next?" it is clear that God's intent is not to leave this chaos a permanent condition. The survival of the exilic community is a remarkable testimony to God's resolve not to bring a complete end to his people though the judgment nearly annihilated every stable structure in the land. Judah brought this chaos not only upon itself but also on the whole creation. But the text gives hope to Judah that it can once again live in the **garden land.** If creation was reverted to chaos because of covenant-breaking by God's people, then it is certainly possible that their covenant fidelity would transform their present chaos into order, beauty, and symmetry. Covenant fidelity on the part of God's people is necessary for the coherent and orderly existence of the whole creation. Paul expresses a similar conviction about the liberating and transforming power of the gospel: "The creation waits with eager longing for the revealing of the children of God" (Rom 8:19 NRSV). He goes on to affirm his conviction that the freedom of the children of God from their bondage to sin is the hope for the liberation of the whole creation from its present state of decay brought about by sin (vv 20-23).

5. A Woman in Scarlet Dress (4:29-31)

BEHIND THE TEXT

Jeremiah's announcement of Judah's terrible and devastating destruction at the hand of a massive military power ends with another imagery of an abandoned city and of a woman writhing in pain as she delivers her first child. Verses 29 and 30 seem to be Yahweh's speech to Judah. Verse 31 is Jeremiah's speech that describes the agony of Judah, which concludes with a lament raised by the nation being attacked by the enemy.

IN THE TEXT

■ **29** Verse 29 describes the frantic attempt of the inhabitants of the city of Jerusalem to flee from the enemy as they hear the **sound** raised by the sentry who announces the coming of "horseman and archer" (NRSV) (the first line could also be read as **at the sound of,** thus the sound coming from horseman and archer). As the Babylonian soldiers approach the city, the frightened inhabitants flee to find a hideout in the **thickets** and **among the rocks.** The city is completely abandoned.

■ **30** Verse 30 is addressed to Jerusalem, personified as a street woman. Though the city is ruined and destroyed, she does not show signs of her distressful condition, nor does she acknowledge that Yahweh's judgment is upon her. Instead of wearing sackcloth and ashes and showing signs of mourning and sorrow, she remains fully decked with her costumes and ornaments hoping to attract and seduce her enemy. **Scarlet** dress, ***ornaments of* gold,** and painted **eyes** reflect the attire of a street woman. Jerusalem is doing everything to make herself look beautiful. Does she think that the enemy could be seduced by her beauty? Verse 30 ends with the description of the reality she faces; even her **lovers** have rejected her; they now seek to destroy her life.

■ **31** In v 31 Jeremiah compares the distress and anguish of Judah to that of a woman who is giving birth to her **first child.** Jerusalem, poetically called ***daughter Zion,*** is crying and ***panting,*** and **stretching out her hands** in deep anguish and pain. In unbearable pain, she screams a cry of despair (***woe to me!***). She admits that her life is under assault by the enemy and that she has no strength left in her. Her life is in the hands of those who are ***killers.***

FROM THE TEXT

Three different and totally unrelated imageries portray Judah under the sentence of destruction and death. The imagery of panicked and frightened citizens of a city desperately looking for a hideout under enemy assault makes sense. The imagery of Jerusalem as a street woman dressed in her costumes of harlotry trying to seduce the enemy does not make much sense but nonetheless conveys Judah's nonchalant response to the danger it faces. The imagery of a woman in labor and screaming with pain and anguish also makes sense because it conveys how victims of war respond to suffering and brutality. How these three contrasting imageries relate to each other is not clear; perhaps they convey in different ways Judah's scurried attempts to manage the crisis and its resistance to acknowledge God's judgment as the inevitable outcome of its wanton and adulterous way of life. Though not explicitly stated, the poem implies that neither God nor the prophet succeeded in eliciting repentance though judgment was announced in the harshest language possible. What else is there for God to do but to unleash the power of the enemy? The frightening certainty of destruction and death looms over Judah. The imageries of this text are about to become the real-life experience of the nation. Killers are on the doorstep of Judah because it has closed its ears to all warnings and pleading from God. That is alarming news, nonetheless a warning, for the modern readers of this text. Words of judgment, when not heeded to, may indeed become the last word from God.

6. A Search and Rescue Mission (5:1-9)

BEHIND THE TEXT

This unit has three parts. The unit begins with Yahweh's command to the prophet to search through the streets of Jerusalem for a person of integrity (v 1). In the second part (vv 2-6) the prophet gives his report (vv 2-3); this is followed by his inner thoughts about the depravity of both the small and great in Judah. The prophet then announces Yahweh's judgment (v 6). The third section (vv 7-9) may be taken as an independent unit. Yahweh speaks again. These verses could be linked to vv 1-6 because they indicate that Judah by its own wicked conduct has nullified Yahweh's offer of pardon (v 1).

IN THE TEXT

■ **1** Verse 1 begins with Yahweh's command to the prophet (or a search team?) to thoroughly investigate the **streets** and **squares** of Jerusalem to see if there is a single person of integrity in the city. Yahweh's command includes a series of four imperatives (**go, look, take note, seek**) that indicate the urgency of the situation. This command to search the city raises the possibility that Yahweh will forgive Jerusalem and Judah if one person who does **justice** (*mišpāṭ*) and seeks **faithfulness** (*'ĕmûnâ*) can be found in the streets of Jerusalem. Justice and faithfulness are essential qualities of the covenant way of life and marks of integrity in relationship with Yahweh and one's neighbor. The reference to one person is hyperbolic; it simply conveys the city's total moral bankruptcy. Obviously one would have to think that there were at least a few righteous left in the city including the prophet. Though the previous oracle (4:29-31) ends with the inevitable reality of judgment, this verse indicates Yahweh's willingness to spare the city from destruction. If we consider this verse as parallel to God's dialogue with Abraham in Gen 18 concerning the fate of Sodom and Gomorrah, then it is not difficult to find in this verse a sincere desire on Yahweh's part to withhold his judgment on account of the righteous in the city.

■ **2** The prophet knows the reality about the citizens of Jerusalem. He conveys to Yahweh that the people of the city live a life of lie and falsehood (v 2). They are quick to take an oath by Yahweh's name and thus show their religious piety, but swearing **falsely** is a way of life for them (*šeqer*, lit. "falsehood"; Lundbom translates *šeqer* as "the Lie" and thus sees this as a reference to Baal (1999, 377). The prophet's answer implies the futility of the search for the righteous in the city.

■ **3** Jeremiah affirms Yahweh's desire to find **faithfulness** among his people, though this quality is not found in Jerusalem (v 3). The rest of v 3 contains the prophet's evaluation that the people did not respond to the corrective measures that Yahweh had taken to prompt repentance from them. Judah **felt no pain** when it received severe beating. Even when judgment almost **consumed** the people, they remained stubborn and refused to accept it as Yahweh's **correction**. Judah responded to Yahweh's disciplinary actions with a stubborn face harder than *rock,* a strong determination not to show repentance.

■ **4** In v 4, Jeremiah's speech to Yahweh changes to his own inner thought. Though he agrees with Yahweh that lack of integrity is pervasive in Jerusalem/Judah, he thinks to himself that such moral degeneracy would be found only among **the poor** (*dallîm*) and senseless people in the land who are ignorant of **the way of** Yahweh (*derek yhwh* refers to the covenant way of life prescribed by the Torah) and the justice that Yahweh demands from them.

■ **5** Jeremiah's inner thoughts continue in v 5. He thought he would find among **the leaders** the covenant qualities of justice and faithfulness. Jeremiah is perhaps thinking about the religious and political leaders, the custodians of the Torah, who would be more knowledgeable about Yahweh's ordinances for his people. The prophet's search for integrity among the leaders, the prominent and powerful citizens of Jerusalem, resulted in the tragic discovery of their disregard for the Law and rebellion against Yahweh. The poor people and the leaders have all **broken off the yoke and** *snapped* **the bonds;** these metaphors describe the nation's stubborn refusal to live under the Torah requirements.

■ **6** Jeremiah's speech ends with the sentence that is already upon Judah (v 6). Jeremiah concludes that divine forgiveness cannot be extended to Judah. The people with their pervasive callousness toward Yahweh's moral and ethical demands are soon to become the helpless prey of wild and ferocious animals that tear and destroy their victim. The imagery of **lion, wolf,** and **leopard** intensifies the devastation that the invading army will inflict on Judah. It is interesting that the leopard *keeps watch over* (*šōqēd* in Hebrew; **lie in wait near**) the cities of Judah just the same way Yahweh is watching over (*šōqēd*) his word of judgment to fulfill it (see 1:12). All these imageries apply to Yahweh, who is the real adversary of Judah. Verse 6 ends with the theological rationale for this violent attack. The *transgressions* and **backslidings** are too many to count. Not forgiveness, but application of "the law of the jungle" is what awaits the people who have perverted the Torah and made Jerusalem a jungle-like place in the world (Brueggemann 1998, 63).

■ **7-8** It seems that Yahweh's question in v 7 (**Why should I forgive you?**) gives the guilty people one final chance to offer some evidence to compel Yahweh to extend forgiveness to them. This question could also be interpreted as Yahweh's resolve to uphold his verdict. The rest of vv 7-8 contain a catalog of Judah's sins; the people have violated and rejected the covenant way of life. They have **forsaken** Yahweh, **sworn by gods that are not gods, committed adultery,** went to **the houses of prostitutes** for sexual satisfaction, and lusted after their neighbor's wife. Judah's infidelity and apostasy are central issues in these verses. The metaphors of adultery, prostitution, and **lusty stallions** perhaps convey the moral depravity and sexual perversion of the citizens of the land. All of these sins the people committed while they were being *fed to the full* by Yahweh's gracious provisions.

■ **9** This unit begins with Yahweh's desire to forgive Israel for the sake of the righteous in the land (see v 1). However, v 9 indicates that the sins of the people have left Yahweh with no other option but to ***visit*** them (the Hebrew root *pqd* has several meanings, including "appoint," "attend to," and "visit"; "punish" is a common translation of this word). The question ***Shall I not vindicate myself*** conveys the idea of Yahweh taking actions to respond to the sins of his people and thereby to uphold his integrity as a God who established a moral order for the world. **Vindicate** (*nāqam*, often translated as "avenge") does not convey retaliatory action or revenge for wrong actions. The reference to Judah as a **nation** (*gôy*, a term usually reserved in the OT for pagan nations) suggests its place in the world no longer as a people set apart by Yahweh through a covenant. His justice demands action against those who have broken their covenant with him.

FROM THE TEXT

Divine forgiveness and divine justice are central issues in 5:1-9. God is willing and yearning to extend forgiveness to Judah, but there must be some evidence of justice and faithfulness in the land. The divine resolve, "that I may pardon Jerusalem" (NRSV) quickly changes to the question, **Why should I forgive you?** This question arises out of the deep dilemma of God, who wills to forgive but must remain true to his standards of justice and faithfulness. God's questions, ***Shall I not visit?*** and ***Shall I not vindicate?*** are asked, but they do not receive conclusive answers. On the one hand, they seem to reveal a "reluctant-to-judge God" (Fretheim 2002, 110). On the other hand, the rhetorical nature of these questions indicates that God holds Judah accountable for its actions and that he must punish the people for their sins. The open-ended nature of the questions in this text suggests the open-ended nature of God's offer of pardon and forgiveness. For Jeremiah's immediate audience that offer was the hope for their salvation until the judgment eventually came upon them. The exilic readers would have heard in this text a theological challenge to shape their future with covenant loyalty and justice and faithfulness in their relationships. The text reminds the modern readers that God's searching of our streets and cities and looking for those who do justice and practice faithfulness continues; God's offer of pardon also continues. No one can claim immunity from God's moral and ethical demands and standards for proper conduct. How we respond to this offer will determine the future of our individual and corporate existence.

7. The Sword of the Enemy (5:10-19)

BEHIND THE TEXT

This unit has three judgment speeches by Yahweh; the first two are in poetry (vv 10-11, 15-17), and the third speech is a prose oracle (vv 18-19). The speaker of vv 12-13 cannot be clearly identified; it is likely that Jeremiah is here denouncing the false prophets who have denied and rejected the judgment message. Some commentators attribute these words to the people; i.e., Jeremiah quoting the words of the people, which reflect their perception of all the prophets. Verse 14 is Yahweh's words directed to Jeremiah.

IN THE TEXT

■ **10** Yahweh's first speech begins with a command given to someone to **go through** (v 10) the land and ***destroy*** the ***vine rows*** (*šārôt* is found only here in the OT; though this word means "vine rows" or "vine terraces," the intent of this word may be to convey the common OT idea of Israel as Yahweh's vineyard). This command is parallel to the command given in v 1 to search the streets to look for the righteous so that Yahweh may pardon the city. Here clearly the intent is not Judah's rescue but its destruction. The command is most likely given to the army of the enemy nation. Though the destruction order is given, along with it also comes the command not to bring a ***full end*** to the vineyard (for a discussion of the grammatical possibility of reading the second line as a command to bring a full end, see Lundbom 1999, 388). The command is to **strip *away*** the ***trailing branches*** or cut down the branches that spread out, thus leaving only the main stem on the ground. Some commentators interpret this as a command given for a "thorough pruning" (Bright 1965, 40), though line one indicates that this is more than pruning, but a near destruction of the vineyard.

■ **11** Verse 11 gives the theological reason for Yahweh's command to destroy his vineyard. This verse also makes clear that the imagery applies to both the northern and southern kingdoms of Israel. The charge of unfaithfulness (see vv 1-10; also 3:6-11, 20) is again brought up here as the reason for this judgment. Though the judgment of destruction has already come upon the northern kingdom, the issue of its unfaithfulness is revisited here.

■ **12** Verses 12 and 13 seem to be Jeremiah's response to Yahweh's judgment, in which he holds the false prophets accountable to the calamity that is about to come upon the nation. The false prophets have **lied about Yahweh** and promised the people that Yahweh will not bring calamity or evil upon the nation. The phrase ***not He*** (*lō' hû'*; **He will do nothing**) is found only here in the OT; JPS translation reads this as "It is not so!" The NIV seems to convey the intent of this phrase. The second part of this verse expands the lie promoted by the false prophets. They confidently proclaimed to the people that no ***evil*** will come upon them (see 23:17) and that they will not see death and destruction by **sword or famine.**

■ **13** Verse 13 is a judgment speech directed against the prophets who have lied about Yahweh. It is likely a continuation of Jeremiah's response in v 12. Jeremiah describes the false prophets as **wind** (*rûaḥ* also means "spirit"), or people filled with meaningless and empty speech. Micah describes the true prophets as those who are filled with the "Spirit [*rûaḥ*] of the LORD" (Mic 3:8). The distinction between true and false prophets is that the **word** (*haddibbēr* here conveys the idea of "revelation"; Holladay 1986, 187) is not in the false prophets, or that

Yahweh has not given them his words. Elsewhere Jeremiah speaks of the false prophets as those who speak "visions from their own minds" (23:16). Verse 13 ends with the fate of the false prophets. They will face the same calamity that is coming upon the people. The evil they said will not come will indeed come upon both the people and the false prophets.

■ **14** Verse 14 is Yahweh's response to the prophet. The message is introduced as a speech from ***Yahweh God of Hosts.*** In contrast to the false prophets, Jeremiah has spoken the truth about Yahweh (***Because you have spoken this word;*** **Because the people have spoken these words**). The second line refers to Jeremiah's words, which truthfully portrayed Yahweh. Yahweh promises to continue to place his **words** in Jeremiah's **mouth** (see 1:9). Yahweh's words placed in the mouth of the prophet have the power to destroy the people like **fire** consumes **wood**. Yahweh is making the people like wood to be consumed by the fire of Yahweh's words. The destructive power of the prophetic speech alluded to in 1:10 is repeated here.

■ **15** Verses 15-17 contain Yahweh's second judgment speech directed to the people. Verse 15 describes the enemy nation that Yahweh is bringing against Judah. Again, it is clear that Yahweh is the real power behind the movement of this enemy toward Judah. This nation comes from a faraway place. The terms **enduring** and **ancient** refer to Babylon as a well-established nation with a long history. The last two lines of v 15 indicate the difficulty of any possible negotiation with the enemy because it speaks a language Judah does not understand. The people will be totally confused and lost because they would not understand the demands imposed upon them by the enemy. See the curse of Deut 28:49 for the description of the enemy as a "nation . . . far away . . . whose language you will not understand."

■ **16** Verse 16 describes the power of the enemy. The description of the ***quiver*** of the enemy as an **open *tomb*** is hyperbole; the precise meaning of this phrase is not clear. It perhaps conveys the idea that the arrows shot from the quiver are powerful, dangerous, and deadly. Its victims are destined to the grave. The army of the enemy is made up of **mighty warriors,** skilled in the art of war and trained to kill any opposition.

■ **17** The enemy will consume everything Judah needs for its existence (v 17). **Harvest,** **food, sons, daughters, flocks, herds, vines,** and **fig trees** are all essential for the survival of the people (see Hab 3:17 for similar description of the outcome of the enemy invasion; see also the curse of Deut 28:51). The enemy will destroy not only the essentials needed for the survival of the people but also the **fortified cities** they trusted in for their protection. **The sword** of the enemy will not spare anything in the land. The totality of destruction implied here reflects the language of v 10.

■ **18** Verse 18 gives some hope for the future of the people. The phrase **in those days** indicates that the day of judgment has not yet arrived. The goal of Yahweh's judgment is not to make ***a full end*** of Judah. Destruction will be catastrophic but not total (see v 10; 4:27).

■ **19** Verse 19 follows a question-answer style (see similar style in 9:12-14; 13:12-14; 15:1-4; 16:10-13; 22:8-9; 23:33). Here the question is about theodicy—question raised about the justification of the divine judgment. When judgment comes, the people will ask why Yahweh has brought this evil upon them. Yahweh instructs Jeremiah that he should then tell the people that this is the punishment for forsaking Yahweh and serving foreign gods. The destiny of those who forsake Yahweh and serve strange gods in the land of promise is serving **strangers** in a strange land. Serving strangers may mean both serving strange gods and foreigner overlords and masters in the land of exile (Holladay 1986, 191).

FROM THE TEXT

This text deals with God's judgment upon Judah, which is no longer his vineyard. Life as Judah has known it will come to an end. Every structure and institution will collapse at the attack of the enemy. The enemy will consume every life-sustaining source in the land. The nation that has trusted in its own power to shape and control its future is under the threat of annihilation. The only comfort for this nation is in God's gracious words, *I will not make a full end of you.* In the midst of a seeming end to everything, God pauses and admits his reluctance to totally annihilate his covenant nation. In the end what remains as good news in this text is God's sovereign freedom of grace that permits a future for his impudent nation. There is hope for the nation's future, but that hope does come with the word that the nation will serve its life in exile, a land that is not theirs, a land where autonomy cannot be exercised. God's covenant people who have forsaken him do not belong to him, but they belong to other gods; therefore, they cannot remain in his land, but they must go to the land of their gods. This text together with other biblical texts, beginning with Gen 3 and 4, reminds us of the connection between self-proclaimed freedom and exile. We are reminded here the truth that all history is shaped by God and that the history we shape for ourselves apart from God will certainly lead to exile. Exercise of autonomy brings the judgment of exile. We also hear in this text God's promise to be gracious and merciful to sinners; his sovereign will is not the total destruction of sinners. This in the end is the good news in this text.

8. A Foolish and Senseless People (5:20-31)

BEHIND THE TEXT

Yahweh's charges against Judah continue in this oracle. Yahweh is the speaker throughout this section. The goal of this speech is to justify Yahweh's judgment of Judah by giving a list of Judah's sins.

IN THE TEXT

■ **20-21** The oracle is addressed to **the house of Jacob**—all of Israel, though its immediate audience is **Judah** (v 20). Verse 21 begins with a call to **hear** (*šim'û*) and ends with the note that the people do not **hear** (*yišmā'û*). Using proverbial wisdom that defines and distinguishes the wise from the fool, Yahweh describes Judah as a ***stupid*** people ***without heart*** (v 21). The Hebrew word for heart (*lēb*) here means "understanding." The foolishness of the people is evident in the fact that they do not put into use their organs of perception (see Isa 6:9; Matt 13:14). Their blindness and dumbness are self-imposed; they stubbornly refuse to use their eyes and ears to see and hear what goes on around them. This is clearly a sign of their foolishness.

■ **22** Another evidence of Judah's lack of wisdom is in its lack of **fear** of Yahweh (v 22). The **fear** of Yahweh implies one's recognition of Yahweh as the Creator and sustainer of this universe, and his sovereign authority over creation. The opening rhetorical questions indicate what Judah does not do in contrast to the sea. The whole creation **trembles** (lit. "writhe") before Yahweh, but Judah does not. Yahweh's setting of **the sand** as **a boundary for the sea** (see Ps 104:9) reflects the ancient belief that the sea, the vestige of the primordial and turbulent waters, remains as a threat to the order and stability of the universe (see Ps 46:2-3 for similar expressions). The sea, the most unstable and unpredictable part of creation, recognizes its limit and remains within its boundary. But God's covenant people remain resistant and show no fear for his authority as Creator.

■ **23** Verse 23 connects Judah's lack of fear of Yahweh with its **stubborn and rebellious heart.** Judah is a nation that is rebellious and resistant to Yahweh at the core of its being—in its will, thinking, feeling, attitude, affection, and emotion. The people have ***turned and walked away*** from Yahweh because of their rebellious heart.

■ **24** Verse 24 indicates that Judah not only refused to acknowledge Yahweh's sovereign authority but also remained unresponsive and ungrateful to his gracious provisions. He provided for the nation all the rain in their due **season,** which it needed to harvest the crops at the designated **weeks.** ***Early rain*** falls in the autumn and winter months and ***latter rain*** falls in early spring. The weeks perhaps refer to the seven weeks between Passover and Pentecost (April-May). However, there was no national turning to Yahweh with **fear** and gratitude in their heart.

■ **25** Verse 25 describes the consequence of lack of fear and ingratitude. Judah's ***iniquities*** and **sins** are now working against it. Obviously this is also Yahweh's doing, his authority even over the power of sin to work its power against those who are sinners. The outcome of insolence and ingratitude is deprivation of the gifts of nature necessary for life's sustenance. Judah has been denied the fall and spring rain and the season of harvest because of its sin against Yahweh.

■ **26** In vv 26-28, Yahweh's indictment against his people catalogs their moral and ethical infractions and total disregard for the Torah requirements of justice and righteousness. Yahweh's people (**my people**) no longer make up a righteous and just society in the world, but a society that accommodates **criminals** who **set traps** to catch innocent and unsuspecting people (v 26).

■ **27** *Treachery* or deceit is a way of life for the criminal element among the covenant community (v 27). **Their houses** display evidence of their treacherous conduct and practices. Their wealth and greatness come not through fair and equitable business practices but through treachery and exploitation of the poor and the innocent in the society.

■ **28** Yahweh accuses these criminals of having exceeded all bounds of criminal behavior (v 28). They disregard the Torah requirements to execute justice to the *orphans* and the **poor** and needy in the society (v 28; see Exod 22:21-22; 23:6; Deut 10:18; 24:14, 17-18). They have abandoned the cause of the poor; they do not pursue justice for the poor by arguing their case in the court system.

■ **29** Verse 29 is a repetition of 5:9. See notes on 5:9 for the meaning of this verse.

■ **30** The oracle ends with Yahweh's accusation of the prophets and the priests as those who are responsible for the collapse of morality in the land (vv 30-31). The growth of violence and wickedness in the land, the total disregard for Yahweh's Torah, and the denial of justice to the orphans and the needy in the land all can be traced to the **horrible and shocking** example set by the religious leaders who have set a pattern of leadership based on false prophecy and abuse of power (v 30).

■ **31** False prophets and corrupt priests are indicted in v 31. Prophets who **prophesy lies** do not represent Yahweh. The source of their prophecy is not Yahweh's words. The accusation that *the priests rule by their hands* indicates misuse and abuse of power vested in the priestly leadership (v 31). The problem of wickedness in the land is systemic. The wicked among the people simply follow the failed morality of their religious leaders. The irony is that Yahweh's people (**my people**) **love** this way of life and leadership. Even the victims of violence do not speak up or raise a cry of protest. The whole nation is indicted for its complicity to the wickedness of the criminals and the corrupt leaders in the land. The oracle ends with the question, **"what will you do in the end?"** Certainly Judah cannot expect to go on with this systemic corruption forever. This question spoils the hope of the people who think that they could continue their wicked way of life unhindered and unquestioned by any moral authority. The question seems to invite Judah to ponder the options and consider the course of action it would take when it stands face-to-face with the reality of Yahweh's harsh judgment.

FROM THE TEXT

The text portrays Judah as a theologically and socially dysfunctional nation. The nation's theological disorientation is evident in its total lack of fear for God. In Israel's traditional faith, submission to the Torah requirements is the source of one's fear of God. Fear of God is the evidence of wisdom in personal and community life. Fear of God is expressed through the recognition of the sovereign authority of God as the Creator. When this theological foundation of covenant life is absent in the community, the consequence is total breakdown of all moral and ethical norms and disintegration of community life. Jeremiah locates the problem of Judah's theological dysfunction in the heart of the individual and the community—the inner core of humans where decisions are made and commitments are kept. Judah's heart refuses to hear and obey and remains stubborn and rebellious. The outcome of this rebellious heart shows up in its neglect of the legal rights of the orphan and the poor, its obsession with wealth and accumulation of riches at any cost, self-indulgent life, ingratitude to God's gracious provisions, practice of treachery and exploitation, and fraud and power politics of religious leaders.

God's word to Judah in this text begins with the call, **Hear** (see also Deut 6:4), which requires not only hearing but also appropriate response. Faithful hearing means faithful response, which in turn means faithful living. The text reminds us that the beginning point of faithful hearing and faithful living is a reorientation of the heart to God from our self-centered and self-indulgent life. This in the end is the antidote to our theological and social dysfunction. Both in Jeremiah's day and in our contemporary reading, the text demands an answer to God's question, **What will you do in the end?**

9. Flee for Safety (6:1-8)

BEHIND THE TEXT

This oracle is another dialogue in which the participants are Yahweh, the enemy, and the people. Yahweh speaks in vv 1-3 and 6-8. The first part of v 4 and v 5 contains words coming from the enemy. Verse 4b contains words spoken by the people. A number of words and phrases that appear in 4:5-6 also appear in 6:1 (**flee for safety, sound the trumpet, raise the signal,** and **disaster . . . out of the north**). The focus of the unit is on the enemy invasion of Jerusalem.

IN THE TEXT

■ **1** The oracle begins with a call to the people of Benjamin to **flee for safety** and take refuge elsewhere in the land (v 1). The imperative **take refuge** is similar to 4:6, where the call is to seek safety in fortified cities. **Jerusalem,** though it is a fortified city, is no longer a safe place. We do not know why the **people of Benjamin** are addressed here specifically. It is possible that this is a warning to the prophet's friends and relatives living in the city who would have considered it a safe place because of its fortifications. Warning is also given to the people of **Tekoa,** a fortified city, and **Beth Hakkerem** (lit. "house of the vineyard"), both of which are located south of Jerusalem, concerning the enemy that is coming from the **north. Disaster** *looks down from* the **north** suggests a "quasi personification" of evil (Holladay 1986, 206). The coming disaster is nothing like Judah has ever experienced.

■ **2-3** The exact meaning of v 2 is not clear. This verse seems to indicate how Yahweh once regarded the city (***Beautiful and dainty, I have likened Daughter Zion***). The NIV conveys the idea of Yahweh destroying the beautiful and delicate city. **Shepherds** and **flocks** in v 3 refer to the king and the commanders of the army of Babylon. The imagery of shepherds pitching their tents in the pasture and grazing their flock usually conveys the picture of an idyllic condition. In v 3, this imagery is inverted to convey the ominous message about the army encampment and the free movement and control of the Babylonian army in and around the city. The once delicate and beautiful city of Yahweh will be ravaged and destroyed by the ruthless and brutal forces of the enemy.

■ **4-5** In the first part of v 4, the shepherds give order to the army to **prepare for battle against** the city (*qaddĕšû milḥāmâ*, lit. ***sanctify war***). Jeremiah uses here the traditional holy war imagery. The enemy is preparing itself to fight a holy war in the same way Israel once fought holy war against its enemies (see Holladay 1986, 206). The enemy plans to attack at midday, the reason for which is not clear. Commentators give various explanations; the language might be poetic and it may simply mean that the enemy considers any time of the day as an advantage to them against Israel (Lundbom 1999, 418). The second part of v 4 contains the lament of the people. They express their frustration that the day is coming to an end. A nighttime battle against the enemy who could strike at any time means a sure defeat for Judah. The confident enemy again announces a nighttime attack against Judah (v 5). The object of the enemy destruction is the ***citadels*** or the fortified royal palaces, located within the city walls.

■ **6** Yahweh's speech resumes in v 6. The order is given by Yahweh to destroy the trees and begin the siege of Jerusalem. Timber from the trees would have been used to build **siege ramps.** The Mosaic law prohibited the destruction of the fruit trees when Israel waged war against enemies (Deut 20:19-20). Yahweh permits the enemy to destroy them and make the land a desolate place. The second part of v 6 is not very clear. The NIV seems to convey the thrust of v 6*b*. The city deserves this cruel and terrible punishment because it is a place filled with oppressive and violent people.

■ **7** Verse 7 utilizes the imagery of a well that keeps its water cool and fresh to convey the idea that Jerusalem keeps its evil fresh and readily available. The sound heard constantly in the city is the sound of violent and destructive actions of its citizens. What Yahweh hears and sees is the noise of violence and wounded people in the streets of Jerusalem. The scene is reminiscent of a violent city street where citizens are frequently awakened at night by the sound of gunshots and sirens of police.

■ **8** Yahweh's speech ends with a warning to Jerusalem (v 8). The Hebrew verb (*hiwwāsĕrî*; **Take warning**) suggests the idea of self-correction or self-discipline (thus it could mean "discipline yourself"). The warning also includes the threat that Yahweh will leave the city and will turn away from it in total "disgust" (see NRSV), if it fails to reform itself. Total desolation is what is in store for the city. The city will be an uninhabitable place when the judgment of Yahweh comes upon it. Verse 8 presents judgment not as an inevitable reality but as the outcome of Israel's failure to respond to Yahweh.

FROM THE TEXT

The text begins with a warning to the people of Benjamin to escape Jerusalem; it ends with a warning to Jerusalem to reform or face total destruction. There is no direct call for repentance, but only a serious warning. God does not speak here with his agonizing love, but as a military commander in chief who gives order to his army to get ready for battle. The war he intends to wage against Israel is a holy war; nothing will be spared from destruction. The beautiful and lovely city of Jerusalem, the idyllic pasture of God where he tended his flock, will become a killing field. The enemy will destroy the land completely. There will be no safe place for anyone in the land. What remains as hope for the people is the possibility that God would change his mind, if they would give heed to the warning. It is now in Judah's power to determine its future. Jerusalem could chose to remain as a city of never-ending violence or a city that responds to God's call for correction and discipline. The former option means catastrophic destruction; the latter option of a changed heart and changed way of life means withdrawal of God's judgment and experience of mercy. The events of 587 B.C. indicate that the people failed to respond and thus to avoid disaster.

This text would have reminded the people in exile the consequence of failure to **take warning**; it would also have served as a new call to them to regard their exile as correction because they have failed to take correction. There remains for them the possibility of experiencing God's favor once again, his turning toward them by their turning to him. We cannot read this text without paying attention to the words **take warning**. Our response will determine judgment or mercy from God, who punishes sin but remains gracious to sinners under judgment.

10. The Wrath of God (6:9-15)

BEHIND THE TEXT

This oracle reflects a dialogue between Yahweh and Jeremiah. Yahweh is the speaker of vv 9 and 11*b*-15. Verses 10-11*a* contain the words of the prophet. Verses 13-15 appear in a slightly different form in 8:10*b*-12. This unit continues the theme of Yahweh's judgment on Judah. This text gives the reasons for Yahweh's decision to pour out his wrath on Judah.

IN THE TEXT

■ **9** Verse 9 utilizes the imagery of grape gatherers going over every branch thoroughly to collect grapes that are left on the vine (**They shall glean thoroughly as a vine**). Gleaning is picking up what is left, which suggests the severity and the totality of judgment. **The remnant of Israel** means the Judean population that remains as the survivors of Israel after the Assyrians destroyed the northern tribes in 722 B.C. The imagery of grape pickers going over grape branches in the second part of v 10 indicates that no one will escape the coming judgment.

■ **10** In v 10 Jeremiah raises the complaint that the people have completely alienated themselves from Yahweh and his words. His opening question indicates that there is no one left who is willing to listen to the words of warning from Yahweh. The reason is that everyone has **closed** (lit. "uncircumcised") ears. The people of Judah have turned their ears off to Yahweh's voice and have refused to pay attention to his words. Yahweh's words, which for the psalmist were a delight (Pss 1:2; 19:8; 119:35), have become an object of ridicule and reproach to Jeremiah's contemporaries. (See Jeremiah's complaint that the Word that was a delight to his heart has also brought reproach to him [15:15-16].)

■ **11** Jeremiah's speech is continued in the first two lines of v 11. The prophet expresses here his agony because he is bottled up with the burning anger of Yahweh. The message that Yahweh has given him to preach is a message of his wrath against the violent and oppressive Israel. **I am weary of holding it in** is similar to the prophet's words of despair in 20:9. He is weary of being the only person in the land who bears the burden of the wrath of Yahweh. The response comes from Yahweh to **pour . . . out** the message of wrath indiscriminately in the streets of Jerusalem on all people—infants, young people, married people, and old people. (See 7:20, where Yahweh pours out his wrath on the people of Jerusalem.) Yahweh authorizes Jeremiah to unleash the power of judgment upon all the inhabitants of the land.

■ **12** Yahweh's wrath, when it is poured out, will lead to severe property and human loss (v 12). **Houses, fields,** and **wives**—all that is part of one's personal possession—will be taken over by the enemy. **Stretch out my hand** is another expression of the execution of Yahweh's judgment and the demonstration of his power.

■ **13** The reason for Yahweh's judgment is the systemic corruption in the land. The population as a whole is into illegal profit making (**greedy for gain** [v 13]). Religious leadership is no better than the people; they, too, are involved in the practice of falsehood. Lack of integrity has infected the covenant people from top to bottom.

■ **14** Verse 14 specifies the sin of the religious leaders. They have not given serious attention to the fractured condition of the nation. God's covenant people (**my people**) are living a broken and shattered life. The religious leaders do not make any attempt to diagnose and discover the root cause of the nation's brokenness, but they try to heal it as if it is a surface wound with their soothing words "**peace, peace**" (*šālôm* or well-being; see 4:10). When there is no sign of community or personal well-being in the land, they speak the message that all is well. They claim to be healers, but their patients remain broken and wounded.

■ **15** Verse 15 continues the indictment against the religious leaders. They do not feel **shame** even when they commit shameful and totally loathsome deeds. They are incapable of expressing normal human expressions of shame and guilt. When the enemy invades the land, the leaders will be among the fallen victims of war.

FROM THE TEXT

God's command to pour out his wrath indiscriminately on the entire population, including children, no doubt disturbs the modern readers of this text (v 11*b*). This command together with the metaphor of gleaning in v 9 does not seem to give much hope to Israel. A key objective of this harsh judgment was to penetrate deep into the **uncircumcised** ears (v 10) of the prophet's audience with the message that the Babylonian attack will be indiscriminate and that the collateral damage will be colossal. God's judgment is on the nation as a whole. Though children are not responsible for the sins of their parents, they, too, will suffer the effect of judgment. Innocent victims of modern-day wars remind us of the casualty of the Babylonian invasion portrayed in this text. The exiled Judeans would have witnessed this reality of war and destruction in 587 B.C.

The text conveys God's determination to unleash the power of judgment against Judah's systemic corruption. Only a communal decision to repent and reform, and open their ears to God, will persuade God to halt the enemy that is marching toward his beloved Zion to destroy it completely. We hear in this text the tragic consequence of rejecting God's word; the text also invites us to open our ears to God, the only sure way to receive his mercy and compassion.

We cannot escape the reality that the world of greed portrayed in this text is a reflection of the world in which we live today. Exploitation, greed, and deceitful conduct at every level of society are all too familiar to the modern readers of this text. The text specifically includes **prophets and priests,** the religious leaders of Jeremiah's day, among the greedy in the society. They, too, are involved in making a profit by selling their "make me feel good" religion to a deeply wounded people. Profit-making religion and the health and wealth gospel are alive and well in our day. The God of this text is a God who does not tolerate greed and deceit at any level, whether in government and politics, business, religion, or even in the ordinary lives of ordinary people. The text calls for reform in the way we do business, politics, and religion. The text also sternly warns of the wrath that will be poured out on all who defy that voice.

11. Ask for the Ancient Paths (6:16-21)

BEHIND THE TEXT

Jeremiah 6:16-21 is another judgment speech in which Yahweh is the main speaker. Verses 16 and 17 indicate a dialogue between Yahweh and the people. Yahweh's instruction is defiantly rejected by the people. The rejection of Yahweh's Torah compels Yahweh to take action. He calls upon the nations and the whole earth to witness the destruction he is bringing upon Judah.

IN THE TEXT

■ **16** Yahweh commands them to **stand** by the **roads** and **look** and **ask for the ancient paths** (v 16). The imagery of a traveler being called to decide between the right and the wrong path of journey is utilized here. Commentators associate **roads** with the wisdom tradition's emphasis on the two ways of life. Ancient paths most likely mean the Torah guidelines that Yahweh has established for Israel, the covenantal path on which Israel once walked. Yahweh offers the present generation that has wandered away from that ancient path an opportunity to return to the path of the Torah traditions of the past. The ancient path is the **good** path—the way that leads to life and covenantal relationship with Yahweh. This is the path of Moses, Samuel, and David. Yahweh's command ends with the promise of **rest** for his people, if they choose to walk on that good path. Rest is freedom from anxiety and fear— experience of *šālôm*—that one can have when traveling on the right path in the right direction. But the response of the people to Yahweh was no. They rejected Yahweh's call to reform their ways and follow the Torah requirements (see 2:20).

■ **17** Verse 17 describes another attempt by Yahweh to persuade his people to reform their ways. He appointed **watchmen**—his prophets—to **sound** the warning of judgment. The prophets that Yahweh appointed faithfully sounded the **horn,** but the people once again responded with no. They rejected not only Yahweh's wise counsel but also his warning signals.

■ **18-19** In vv 18-19, Yahweh calls the nations and the earth to **observe** Yahweh's **testimony** against Judah (v 18). The calling of the nations and the earth is parallel to the calling of heavens and earth as witnesses of Yahweh's lawsuit in Isa 2:2. Yahweh's testimony against Judah is his judgment word. He plans to bring **evil** upon his people for rejecting Yahweh's **law** (v 19). **My law** (*tôrātî*) refers to all the instructions that Yahweh has given to Israel. Evil that is coming upon the people is the **fruit of their** evil **schemes.** The evil they have sown is now ripe for harvest.

■ **20** In v 20 we find Yahweh's criticism of worship, its first occurrence in the book of Jeremiah. He rejects the offering of *frankincense* and *cane,* and **burnt offerings** and **sacrifices. Sheba** in southern Arabia is known for its aromatic frankincense. **Cane (calamus)** is the hollow stem of a certain type of tall grass, known for its aromatic scent. The identity of the distant land is not given. These imported products reflect the wealth and affluence of the worshipper. Burnt offerings and sacrifices were central to worship in Israel. In burnt offering, the sacrificial victim was completely consumed by the fire on the altar. In sacrifices, the choice portion was consumed on the altar, and the rest was consumed by the worshippers. Yahweh rejects all of these offerings and makes known his displeasure with the worshipping community (see Isa 1:11; Amos 5:22). The reason for his displeasure is clear in the preceding verse. Though they worship him with all the required sacrifices and even imported and expensive offerings, they refuse to listen to him or live by his Torah requirements.

■ **21** Verse 21 announces the judgment. Yahweh plans to set up ***stumbling blocks*** on the path of his people, which is not the good way ordered by the Torah but the evil way the nation has chosen for itself. These obstacles would cause the people to stumble and fall on the way. Judgment will affect everyone in the land; **fathers, sons, neighbors**—all will fall together and perish on their evil way.

FROM THE TEXT

The call to look for the ancient paths invites the modern readers of this text to reorient and refocus their priorities, values, beliefs, and practices. To Jeremiah's original audience, it was a call to a *torah*-centered life, to become once again God's covenant people. It also meant a life anchored in the great historical and theological traditions of the past, encapsulated in the stories that were handed down by the previous generations. They rejected that call and opted to travel on the wrong road in the wrong direction by stubbornly disregarding the signposts, markers, and warning signs. At the crossroads where they stood were paths with too many seductive attractions along the way. They chose to reject the way that led to life and opted for the path that led to their destruction.

God's people not only rejected the call to follow the ancient paths but also manufactured a self-serving religion with an extravagant display of wealth as a substitute for true obedience and faith. The text reminds us of the danger of mistaking affluent religious practices for true obedience. The former may make us feel good, but the latter is what truly pleases God (1 Sam 15:22).

The path that remains as the good path, then and now, is the path for life established by God. The ancient Torah requirements invited Israel to live as God's holy people in the world, to walk in the path of wholehearted love for

God and love for one's neighbor. This remains to be the path that leads to life. This remains to be the path that leads weary souls to their rest. Those who stand at the crossroads today hear the gracious invitation of Jesus, "Come to me, all you who are weary and burdened, and I will give you rest" (Matt 11:28).

12. An Army Is Coming (6:22-26)

BEHIND THE TEXT

Jeremiah 6:22-26 is another oracle on the enemy coming from the north. This oracle also is in the form of a dialogue. Yahweh speaks in vv 22-23 concerning the might and power of this cruel enemy ready for battle against Jerusalem. The people respond to Yahweh's speech with fear and panic (vv 24-25). Verse 26 seems to be Jeremiah's counsel to the people (see Holladay 1986, 219).

IN THE TEXT

■ **22** Yahweh's speech once again announces the direction from which the enemy nation will come (vv 22-23). Again, the identity of the enemy is not stated, except for its origins in a distant northern land. It is ironic that Yahweh's response to the people who bring the offering of frankincense imported from Sheba in the south is the announcement of his stirring up of a **great nation** from the north to punish them for their Torah violations. It is also ironic that the enemy is called "a people" (NRSV) (*'am*), a term usually reserved for Israel as a covenant people. It is also called a **nation** (*gôy*, the usual term for nations other than Israel) in the next line. Though the enemy is a nation among the nations in the world, it now has a special relationship with Yahweh as his instrument of judgment against his own covenant people who have broken the covenant. This enemy is coming from **the ends of the earth**—the farthest part of the known world for Jeremiah's audience (v 22).

■ **23** The enemy troops armed with **bow and spear,** powerful, sharp, and swift instruments of war (v 23). They are known for their cruelty and merciless treatment of their victims. The sound of the enemy as they march forward is like the sound of the roaring of the waves. The enemy has both cavalry and infantry forces, and they stand ready for the battle. Yahweh announces to **Daughter Zion** or Jerusalem that she is the target of their attack.

■ **24** Israel responds to this message with panic (v 24). The **reports** about the ruthless enemy are already heard in the land. This bad news has completely drained the strength of the people of Judah. Their **weakened hands** cannot lift up weapons to fight against the enemy. It is interesting to note that both v 23 and v 24 utilize the verb *ḥzq* with its meaning "grasp," or "seize." In the first instance, the enemy "grasps" bow and javelin as they advance toward Judah, whereas in v 24, anguish "grasps" the people. Their strength is replaced with anguish. The imagery of **a woman in labor** best illustrates the agony of the nation.

■ **25** Verse 25 continues the panicky response of the people. No place is safe from the enemy. The *field* where one works and the *road* where one walks are all controlled by the enemy. In other oracles, calls were made to "flee to the fortified cities" and "flee from Jerusalem" (4:5; 6:1); here the people decide to remain shut up in their homes because of the danger they perceive all around them. What causes fear among the people is the **sword** of the enemy. The verse ends with the expression **terror on every side,** a phrase found in 20:3, 10; 46:5; 49:29; also Ps 31:13; Lam 2:22). This expression here perhaps conveys the people's realization that they are surrounded by the enemy and that the threat of their destruction is imminent.

■ **26** The oracle ends with Jeremiah's call to do the customary mourning rituals (v 26; see 4:8). Sackcloth and ashes are also symbols of repentance. Here perhaps they express grief and loss. Jeremiah urges the people to carry out their own mourning rites in advance before their destruction comes because there will be none left to do these customary rituals in the land. They should weep and lament with the same intensity of those who weep at the loss of an only child. The reference to the loss of an only child perhaps also meant the end of any hope for Judah's future. The only thing that the nation can expect with any certainty is the swift and sudden attack of the land by a destroyer nation that Yahweh is sending against it.

FROM THE TEXT

The contrasting portraits of the ruthless and merciless enemy and the helpless and anguish-filled Judah evoke our sympathy for the nation that is in serious danger. These verses perhaps reflect the conditions just prior to the 587 B.C. disaster. Jeremiah counsels his audience to do what people normally do when they suffer great loss—put on sackcloth and observe mourning rituals and show their intense grief. Jeremiah's God cannot remain unmoved when his people express grief. This seems to be the hope that Jeremiah is giving to the people who are faced with the threat of destruction. The book of Lamentations indicates that it is in such expressions of profound grief that the exiled community eventually found confidence in the faithfulness, compassion, and covenant loyalty of God (Lam 3:21-33).

13. A New Task for Jeremiah (6:27-30)

BEHIND THE TEXT

This is the final unit of 4:5—6:30. The section as a whole clearly demonstrates the vulnerable place of Judah as a nation about to be devastated by an enemy that God is bringing from the north. This unit has the form of dialogue between Yahweh and Jeremiah. Jeremiah, who was appointed by God to be a prophet to the nation, receives a special task in this text. That assignment is the focus of v 27. Verses 28-30 contain the prophet's assessment of the people most likely after he has completed the task assigned to him.

IN THE TEXT

■ **27** The oracle begins with Yahweh's appointment of Jeremiah as an ***assayer*** and a **tester,** to test Judah, Yahweh's people (v 27). The task is like that of an assayer who extracts silver from lead by melting the ore at very high temperature. The Hebrew text ends the first line with the word *mibṣār*, meaning "fortress." Commentators emend the text to read *mĕbaṣṣēr* ("refiner" NRSV or **tester;** see NRSV "and a refiner among my people," a better reading than the NIV "and my people the ore"). The goal of this assignment is to make assessment of the ***way*** of the people, or their character and conduct, and to determine if there is anything of value left in the covenant people that would prompt Yahweh to save them from the coming judgment.

■ **28** The text does not say how Jeremiah carried out the task as an assayer and refiner. One would assume that the prophet was to make assessment of the people by the way they responded to his preaching. What Jeremiah found out about the conduct of the people is stated in vv 28-29. Rebelliousness is the basic characteristic of the people of Judah. It is a nation of **hardened rebels** who are set in their stubborn way of rebelling against Yahweh. Their life is totally immersed in malicious gossip. Jeremiah finds them hard and brazen, a nation of systemic corruption.

■ **29** Though the refining process was undertaken by the prophet to burn away the impurities of the people, it did not yield its intended outcome. Verse 29 perhaps refers to the fiery words of judgment spoken by the prophet aimed at reforming the nation. The refining words of Jeremiah have not been successful in removing wickedness from the land.

■ **30** Jeremiah's final assessment of the nation is that this nation is like impure silver, the impurity of which could not be removed by the refiner's work (v 30). ***They called them*** indicates the examination of Judah by some other group of people, the identity of which is not given. In v 30*b* the prophet gives the report of Yahweh's assaying of his people. Judah is a rejected nation. This is because Yahweh has found impurities in the nation that could not be removed by refining. A rejected nation has no worth and therefore is to be discarded. Yahweh's election of Israel is suspended here. They are no longer a privileged people, but a people destined for destruction.

FROM THE TEXT

This oracle declares in no uncertain terms God's rejection of his people. Jeremiah functions here as God's appointed assayer and reports that the people are corrupt through and through. The previous oracles have indicated the nature of the impurities that have made them worthless and thus a rejected people. These include idolatry, covenantal unfaithfulness, social injustice, deceit and fraud, corruption of political and religious leaders, stubbornness, and the list goes on. There is nothing that God wants to keep, and no hope is given for Judah that anything or anyone would survive the fire of judgment. There is no indication that the fire of judgment is for the purpose of refining the nation (see Zech 13:7-9 and Mal 3:1-4, where the goal of the refiner's fire is to purify the remnant or the nation as a whole). There is no possibility of salvation or future for the people rejected by God. This is the harsh word of judgment we find in this text. This is destiny of a people who have refused to "yield to either the *ordinary* or *extraordinary* means of salvation" (Clarke, 274). Any hope for the future depends solely on God's mercy and compassion. John the Baptist's statement, "every branch that does not produce good fruit will be cut down and thrown into the fire" is an appropriate reminder to the Christian readers of this text (Matt 3:10; see vv 10-12; also 1 Cor 3:13-15).

"UPROOT AND TEAR DOWN"

JUDAH'S FALSE AND CORRUPT WORSHIP (7:1—8:3)

Overview

There seems to be a general agreement among scholars that ch 7 introduces a new section in the book of Jeremiah. Jeremiah 7:1—8:3 demonstrates a clear thematic coherence with its critique of the temple ideology and indictment against Judah's false and corrupt worship. In its present form, 7:1—8:3 constitutes a long prose discourse, which seems to be made up of several smaller literary units (7:1-15, 16-20, 21-29 [v 29 in poetry in Hebrew], 7:30—8:3). There is no direct linkage between 7:1—8:3 and 8:4—10:25, which is mostly in poetry. However, oracles in 8:4—10:25 reiterate the themes of backsliding, idolatry, deceit and falsehood, forsaking of the Law, and the coming destruction that are also the focus of the sermon in 7:1—8:3.

Commentators approach the prose discourse 7:1—8:3 in two ways. Some view this discourse as the product of Deuteronomistic redaction and date it to the exilic or postexilic period. Others attribute the words and phraseology of this prose discourse to Jeremiah himself and date it to the last decade of the seventh century.

1. The Temple: A Den of Robbers (7:1-15)

BEHIND THE TEXT

Chapter 26, which provides a summary of the temple sermon, indicates that this sermon was delivered by the prophet "at the beginning" (26:1 NRSV) of Jehoiakim's reign (609 B.C.). Chapter 26 also gives us the report of the arrest and trial of Jeremiah for his scathing attack on the Jerusalem temple. The warning about the destruction of the temple clearly indicates a date prior to 587 B.C. Holladay analyzes the phrases and the construction of this sermon and concludes that the sermon is the work of Jeremiah and not the product of Deuteronomistic redaction (Holladay 1986, 240). The sermon portrays the religious fervor of the worshipping community. It also vividly describes the social context of the last decade of the seventh century B.C. The sermon draws its themes from two ancient traditions: the legal collection that preserves the Decalogue and the historical traditions surrounding the sanctuary at Shiloh. This text also makes reference to the destruction of northern Israel. The primary aim of this sermon is to denounce the temple ideology that promoted false confidence in the power of the temple to protect its worshipping community.

The sermon has three parts; each part conveys a message from Yahweh. The first part (vv 3-7) sets forth the conditions for the people's continued life in the land. The second part (vv 8-11) charges the people with converting the temple into a hideout for criminals. The third part (vv 12-15) announces the coming destruction of the temple.

IN THE TEXT

■ **1-2** The sermon begins with a customary introduction (***The word that came to Jeremiah from Yahweh;*** see also 11:1; 18:1). Yahweh's word begins with a command to deliver his message at the **gate** of the temple (v 2). The gate cannot be identified with certainty. It is likely that the gate may have been the entrance to the (inner?) court of the temple, the setting of some of Jeremiah's messages (see 19:14-15). The court is where Jeremiah would have met the worshippers. The message is addressed to the whole nation of Judah, the worshipping community in the temple.

■ **3** Jeremiah's sermon begins with Yahweh's call to **reform** or ***make good*** the ways and conduct of the worshipping community (v 3). The actions of the people must have their ultimate goal in producing good outcome. The call to reform suggests that the **ways and . . . actions** of the people were thoroughly evil; the people need to commit themselves to a radically new way of life. This command comes as the condition for Judah's continued existence in the Promised Land. **This place** refers most likely to the whole land and not just Judah or Jerusalem or even the temple. Some commentators translate the last part (**I will let you live in this place**) as "I will dwell with you" (see Holladay 1986, 241; also

NRSV). This reading suggests Yahweh's continued dwelling in the temple as a reward for the people's commitment to reform.

■ **4** Verse 4 calls for an end to the people's false trust and confidence in the temple. This verse critiques the ideology that the temple is an inviolable structure and that its security is part of Yahweh's covenantal commitment to his worshippers. Commentators are not clear about the three times repeated slogan, **They are (This is)** ***Yahweh's Temple, Yahweh's Temple, Yahweh's Temple.*** The meaning of ***they are*** in Hebrew is not clear. The view that this phrase refers to the temple complex with its many buildings is an attractive one. The repeated slogan evidently was part of the liturgy in the temple. We do not know the theological objective of this slogan. Commentators do not favor the view that this was some sort of a magical chant to ward off evil. This could also have been the chant of the pilgrims as they made their way to the Temple Mount (see these views in Lundbom 1999, 462). Miller thinks that this slogan was a popular "religio-political cliché" spoken against Jeremiah's warning about the impending danger to Jerusalem (2001, 636). Whatever this slogan meant, Yahweh demands an end to any claim the people made about his dwelling place.

■ **5** In vv 5-7 Yahweh establishes several conditions for the people's continued existence in the land. Conditions ("if" clauses) are set forth in vv 5 and 6; v 7 states the effect or outcome of the people's positive response to the conditions. The conditional clauses indicate what was lacking in Judah's community life. The first condition is the same as the command in v 3. It is likely that this is restated here as the primary command/condition. The rest of vv 5 and 6 elaborate the specific ways and areas of reform activities. The worshipping community must make a commitment to carry out ***justice*** (*mišpāṭ*) in the society. The reference here is particularly to justice toward one's ***neighbor*** (v 5). Justice calls for honesty and integrity in relationships and fulfillment of covenantal obligations.

■ **6-7** Emphasis on social relationship continues in v 6. The concern here is for the proper treatment of the weakest and the most helpless members of the society. Deuteronomy makes repeated calls to show care and concern to sojourners, orphans, and widows (10:18; 14:29; 16:11, 14; 24:17, 19-21). Reiteration of this theme in v 6 indicates that Judah has failed to keep the Deuteronomic instructions. The prophet gives similar admonitions to Jehoiakim in 22:3. This concern is also found in Isa 1:17, 23; 10:2; Ezek 22:7; Zech 7:10. The call to social justice also includes the call to put an end to shedding innocent blood (see Deut 19:10; see the charges against Jehoiakim in Jer 22:17). Verse 6 ends with a call to put an end to the worship of other gods. Absolute loyalty in its relationship to Yahweh is an essential condition for Judah's continued life in the land. Verse 7 reiterates the promise of continued life. **This place** is clearly identified in this verse as the land Yahweh has given to his people forever.

■ **8** The second part of the sermon (vv 8-11) challenges the audacious claim of a theologically and morally bankrupt people that they are safe in the temple of Yahweh. Verse 8 reminds them that their trust in the security of the temple is a delusion. What they trust cannot save them.

■ **9** The rhetorical questions in vv 9-10 function as indictment against Israel's violations of specific commandments in the Decalogue. The worshipping community has violated the commandments that were aimed to preserve social justice and theological integrity. Israel broke the eighth (stealing), the sixth (killing), the seventh (adultery), the third (swearing falsely), and the first (no other gods) commandments (v 9). Stealing denies the property owners the right to enjoy God's good gifts. Killing deprives the victims of the right to enjoy life, a gift from God. Adultery destroys the integrity of the marital covenant. Swearing falsely suggests the practice of dishonest oath-taking ("swear falsely" is literally "swear to the lie," which could mean swear by Baal). The charges of burning incense to Baal and walking after other gods indicate Judah's divided loyalty in the area of worship. Fidelity to Yahweh and neighbor has disappeared from the land.

■ **10** Though the people have violated the covenant stipulations, they still claim that they are **safe** in Yahweh's house (v 10). There is an incredible incongruity between Judah's way of life and its theological claims. The worshipping community without shame or guilt lives a life of crime, violence, dishonesty, and apostasy and considers the sacred dwelling of Yahweh as a place of safety and refuge.

■ **11** Verse 11 begins with a rhetorical question that establishes the reality that the temple worshipping community has converted the house of Yahweh into a **den of robbers. Den of robbers** means a cave where thieves hide themselves and their stolen properties from those who pursue them. Yahweh's name is associated with the temple; his name conveys his holy character, and as such the temple is his holy sanctuary. No evil is permitted there. The worshipping community has converted Yahweh's sacred sanctuary into a cave where they hide and seek safety for their life. This is a violent takeover of Yahweh's property, and he is well aware of what is going on in his temple. He has been **watching** the actions and words of his people, and nothing is hidden from his sight.

Shiloh

Shiloh was located in the tribal territory of Ephraim about 20 miles north of Jerusalem. Israel set up the tabernacle in Shiloh during the days of Joshua (Josh 18:1; 19:51). During the days of the judges Shiloh remained as the location of the house of God (Judg 18:31; 21:19). First Samuel 1—3 indicates that Eli served as priest at this sanctuary, which was also home to Samuel during his early childhood days. First Samuel 4 describes the capture of the ark by the Philistines and the death of the sons of Eli in the battle. Though the narrative in 1 Sam 4 does not say that this sanctuary was destroyed by the Philistines, its destruction may have been a known fact in the village of Anathoth, the home of Abiathar who continued the priestly line of Eli (1 Kgs 2:27).

■ **12** In the third part of the sermon, Yahweh announces the destruction of the temple and the exile of the worshipping community (vv 12-15). This section begins with a solemn reminder of the destruction of the sanctuary at **Shiloh,** where Yahweh made a **dwelling** for his **Name** in the earliest days of Israel. The present worshipping community is being asked to remember the fate of the sanctuary at Shiloh. This is a veiled threat against the temple, which is made explicit in v 14.

■ **13** Verse 13 states the reason for Yahweh's impending judgment. The people have not only broken the covenant and violated the commandments but also rejected and disregarded Yahweh's repeated calls for change and reform to their life.

■ **14** Yahweh's judgment on the people who trust in the temple for their security is announced in v 14. The temple in which they place their trust will be destroyed. The temple belongs to Yahweh; it is ***called*** by his holy **Name,** and it is a reflection of his character as a holy God. However, the wicked people of Judah no longer trust in the holy God who resides in the temple, but they **trust** in their false confidence about the temple. Therefore, he will bring upon his temple the same calamity that he brought upon Shiloh. Destruction will also be the fate of the land, which Yahweh has given as an inheritance to Judah's ancestors. Judgment is the means by which Yahweh will preserve the holiness of his name.

■ **15** Verse 15 announces the exile of Judah from Yahweh's presence; he will **thrust** the wicked people of Judah from his presence. Their fate will be the same as that of their **brothers,** members of the northern kingdom who were expelled from the land in 722 B.C. **The people of Ephraim** is a general reference to the northern tribes (Ephraim is frequently used by Hosea as a designation for the northern kingdom).

FROM THE TEXT

This sermon is a clarion call to Jeremiah's audience to repent and reform and thus to escape God's judgment. The events of 587 B.C. indicate that the people of Judah have failed to give heed to this call. The exilic community would have found in this text the theological rationale for the destruction of the temple, the land, and the exile of the nation. It would have also found in this sermon a proper theology of worship and its integral relation to social and community life.

The temple sermon of Jeremiah is the most powerful biblical response to fraudulent worship. Judah's worship was fraudulent because (a) it centered on the false claim that the temple offered well-being and protection to its worshippers; (b) it substituted repentance with religious fervor and slogans; and (c) it neglected the call to love God and love one's neighbor. The sermon, on a positive note, defines for us true worship. True worship is a display of total trust in God; it elicits genuine repentance; it engenders love for God and love for the neighbor.

The temple sermon reminds us that our places of worship symbolically represent the holiness of God who faithfully guides and sustains his people. Whatever takes place within these structures in the name of worship should be a reflection of the holiness of God. Moreover, though the places of our worship represent the holiness of God, they do not have any inherent power to save us. Neither do they provide immunity from judgment for our moral and ethical infractions.

Judah replaced repentance with its slogans, rituals, and religious fervor. The worshipping community showed no contriteness or commitment to change its sinful ways of life. Worship made the worshippers feel good inside but produced no change within. Encounter with the holy place does not lead to transformation; that can happen only when we encounter the Holy One. Worship that is transformative is worship that leads the community to recognize its sinfulness and to cry out for God's mercy. True worship leads to an encounter with the holy God, which in turn leads to life-transformation.

The temple sermon reminds us of the close connection between worship and common life. True worship calls for absolute loyalty to God. In true worship, there is no room for other gods. Also, true worship calls for true commitment to social justice. We have a tendency to think that breaking the Ten Commandments involves only flagrant and outright criminal behavior. Seldom do we think of the ethical and moral implications of the commandments. The second part of the commandments can be summed up in the law of "love thy neighbour as thyself" (Matt 19:19 KJV). Any action that betrays love means violation of the call to love our neighbor. In our social life, love for God is best displayed when we provide homes for the homeless, show care for the widows and orphans, and defend the rights of aliens in our lands. Our silence to these issues means a total disregard for the poor and the disenfranchised in the world. This sermon reminds us that the God we worship is indeed the God who is on the side of the widows, orphans, and aliens in the world. Worship that does not move us to be on the side of God on behalf of these defenseless poor is nothing more than a display of false religiosity.

Jesus' critique that the temple of his day has become a "den of robbers" (Matt 21:13; Mark 11:17; Luke 19:46) indicates that every generation needs to safeguard itself from the danger of self-serving religion. What Jesus observed in the temple of his day was not a strange coincidence with Jeremiah's assessment of the temple. The history of Christendom is filled with stories of tragic manipulation of the sacred sphere of God for self-serving religious, political, and economic agendas. This goes on in our world in the public and private lives of those who profess to be Christians. We immediately think of politicians who become very religious during election years, and business owners who peddle their Christianity to expand their business interest. Jeremiah and Jesus warn us that God is "watching" and that destruction is what is in store for those who exploit God's holy name for personal gain.

2. Do Not Pray for This People (7:16-20)

BEHIND THE TEXT

This unit contains two parts; in vv 16-19, Yahweh speaks to Jeremiah and forbids him to intercede for the people, who publicly display their devotion to other gods. This is followed by a judgment oracle (v 20), which announces the unquenchable fire of Yahweh's wrath upon everything in the land. Here we find the first of three places in the book where Yahweh commands the prophet not to pray for Judah (7:16; 11:14; 14:11; see also 15:1). This text has continuity with the temple sermon, which lists a number of violations of the Decalogue. Here the focus is on the violation of the first commandment. The scene of the sins of the people moves from the temple into the streets of Jerusalem. Commentators who view this text as authentic words of Jeremiah place this text in the days of Jehoiakim.

IN THE TEXT

■ **16** Yahweh begins his speech to Jeremiah by releasing him from his prophetic task of intercession (7:16). Three different commands are utilized in v 16 to emphasize the futility of intercession on behalf of Judah (**do not pray . . . do not lift on their behalf a cry . . . do not make intercession**). Israel's prophets inherited the task of intercession from Moses. It was their responsibility not only to warn the people of Yahweh's judgment but also to plead with him for mercy (see Amos 7:2, 5). Here Yahweh prohibits Jeremiah from carrying out this task on behalf of Judah. This is clearly a sign of the end of Yahweh's patience with a people who have consistently and stubbornly rejected his calls for repentance.

■ **17** The next three verses (17-19) contain a summary of Israel's pagan religious rituals, which were everyday practices in Judah and Jerusalem. The question in v 17 is not necessarily to make Jeremiah aware of these pagan practices but to suggest how common these activities were throughout the land.

■ **18** The first part of v 18 shows that everyone in the family was involved in the worship of **the Queen of Heaven.** The charge against Judah also includes its worship of **other gods** to whom the people offered **drink offerings** (see also 19:13; 32:29). Offering wine as a drink offering was part of Israel's worship of Yahweh (Exod 29:40), which the nation has incorporated into their pagan worship. These actions did not do any good except that they provoked Yahweh's anger against the people who have broken the prohibition against the worship of other gods.

■ **19** The first part of v 19 seems to negate the assertion made in v 18. Lundbom sees here a rhetorical device to emphasize the assertion that indeed the people have provoked Yahweh to anger (1999, 477). The second question in v 19 implies that what is more serious than provoking Yahweh's anger is that the people are bringing shame upon themselves by their participation in pagan worship.

■ **20** Yahweh's judgment is pronounced in v 20. Yahweh will pour out his wrath upon the nation that poured out drink offerings to other gods. Everything in the land will suffer the wrath of Yahweh. The effect of sin is widespread. It brings shame upon sinners and destruction of all creation.

The Queen of Heaven

The Queen of Heaven worship is mentioned only in 7:18 and in 44:15-25 in the OT. The Septuagint has here "the host of heaven." Scholars equate this goddess with the Assyrian-Babylonian goddess Ishtar, an astral deity of love, war, and fertility. Anat, Asherah, or Astarte may have been the local name for this goddess in Palestine. The worship of Ishtar included the offering of cakes made in the shape of stars (see 44:19). Ahaz (735-715 B.C.) may have introduced the worship of this goddess into Judah (see 2 Kgs 16:10-16). Manasseh (687-642 B.C.) is said to have "worshiped all the host of heaven" and built altars for "all the host of heaven in the two courts" of the temple (2 Kgs 21:3, 5 NRSV). Josiah's reform activities included the destruction of all the pagan places of worship. It is likely that worship of this and other pagan gods and goddesses was revived in Judah after Josiah's death.

FROM THE TEXT

God's command not to pray for the people is given to Jeremiah, and it concerns only the people of his day. We cannot establish a theological principle concerning how God may or may not act in other situations. Certainly, this is a harsh word, a word that gives no hope to the people. The end of prophetic mediation means the only source of hope for the people is their own cry before God, whom they have offended. Other similar prohibitions in the book indicate that though he was released of his duty as a mediator for the people, the prophet continued his ministry of intercession (11:14; 14:11; 15:1; see also 42:4). The point being made here is that the people have totally rejected God and that all the systems God has established for the people to maintain a healthy relationship with him, including prophetic mediation, have collapsed. The prohibition also suggests the end of God's patience with Judah.

The exilic community would have been reminded by this text that prophetic intercession alone would not bring reprieve to those under judgment for breaking the covenant with God. Indeed, prayer became for the people in exile an important way of communication with God. We hear in this text, on the one hand, a strong warning to the impenitent and stubborn sinners who gamble on God's never-ending mercy. On the other hand, Jeremiah's ministry of intercession throughout his career informs us that our intercession for others must continue even in the most hopeless conditions of their existence. The call of the gospel is to be fully engaged in reconciling the world to God (2 Cor 5:17-21).

3. A Deaf Society (7:21-29)

BEHIND THE TEXT

This unit has three parts: part one (vv 21-26) is an oracle addressed to the people; part two is Yahweh's speech to the prophet (vv 27-28); the unit ends with a lament of the prophet (v 29). Verse 29 stands alone, and it could be attached either to this unit or to the following unit. The unit as a whole is an attack on Judah's sacrificial worship in the temple and thus it is thematically connected to the subject of false worship in 7:1—8:3. The oracle seems to belong to the general setting of this larger unit; i.e., during the reign of Jehoiakim.

IN THE TEXT

■ **21** This unit begins with a sarcastic invitation to increase **burnt offerings** and **sacrifices,** above and beyond what the people are already doing in the name of Yahweh worship (7:21; see similar prophetic sarcasm in Amos 4:4-5). They have been busily involved in an elaborate worship that included worship not only of Yahweh but also of other gods. Since they have broken all the commandments, they are told to go ahead and **eat the meat,** the choice portion that belonged to Yahweh (see Lev 6—7).

■ **22** The traditions in the Pentateuch are clear on the fact that Yahweh required and established an elaborate pattern of offerings and sacrifices. Verse 22 seems to contradict those early traditions (***For I did not speak to your fathers nor did I command them, on the day I brought them from the land of Egypt, concerning burnt offering and sacrifice***). What does v 22 mean in light of the whole sacrificial system of worship, which was part of the Sinai covenant legislation?

■ **23** Verse 23 offers us the best solution to the problem of the meaning of v 22. The first and foremost requirement of Yahweh was obedience. The call to obedience came before the establishment of the sacrificial worship (see Exod 19:1-6). Obedience is the essential prerequisite to the ongoing covenant relationship (**I will be your God and you will be my people**). Long before the establishment of the sacrificial worship, Yahweh called Israel to listen, obey, and walk in his ways. Yahweh here reminds the people that obedience is a prerequisite to sacrifices and offerings.

■ **24** Yahweh also reminds the people that their history with him nonetheless was a history of their stubborn disregard for his call to listen and obey him (vv 24-26). They rejected Yahweh's voice and chose for themselves an autonomous way of life, following the directives of their **evil hearts.** There was no progress in their relationship, but only a steady increase in their rebellion and stubbornness.

■ **25-26** Verse 25 indicates that the people rejected Yahweh's voice, the words spoken by the prophets. **My servants the prophets** are the authorized spokespersons of Yahweh. He sent them from the time of Israel's departure from Egypt

until now with his words to remind the people to return to the covenant way of life (v 25). But the people **did not listen** or **pay attention** to Yahweh or to his prophets (v 26; see v 24). Each generation did worse than the previous generation. Stubbornness and self-will characterized the nation (v 26).

■ **27-28** Yahweh speaks to Jeremiah and reminds him that the people will reject his words just as they have rejected the voice of the prophets who came before him (v 27). Nonetheless, he must speak to them and make them aware of their moral and spiritual failure (v 28). Three things characterize the people: (a) they are a people who do not obey their God; (b) they have refused to accept discipline from Yahweh; (c) truth-telling is not a quality found among them (v 28). None of the fundamental qualities of the covenant relationship is found in Judah. This is clearly evident in the way they worship Yahweh.

■ **29** Verse 29 seems to be a lament of the prophet. Words of this lament are spoken most likely to Jerusalem, personified here as a woman. A woman cutting off her hair is a sign of mourning and showing grief. The people are urged to lament on the **barren heights,** the very same places they have frequented in their pursuit of Baal (see 3:2, 21). They have been **rejected** because they have rejected Yahweh. His **wrath** is upon **this generation** (Jeremiah's audience) for its participation in the covenant-breaking. The only recourse for the people is to return to the places of their idolatrous worship and lament before Baal, who could neither hear their lament nor do anything to save them from Yahweh's wrath.

FROM THE TEXT

God rejected Jeremiah's generation because they remained deaf to his voice while they were busy with their offerings and sacrifices. Doing worship became for God's people a substitute for being a worshipping community. The text reminds us that worship first and foremost is an act of faithful response to the voice of God. The context of worship sets the stage for and prepares the worshipping community to be addressed by God and to listen and respond to his voice. Listening to God means recognition of God's authority as the sovereign Lord. Listening to God means recognition of the covenantal relationship. Proper worship is a covenantal act, in which God speaks and the covenant community responds with gratitude and faithfulness. It is in worship that we yield and let God take control. The future of the covenant community is shaped by this covenantal speaking-listening mode of relationship. The covenant people of God stubbornly resisted the idea of listening to God. The path they have chosen instead was the path of self-determination and self-sufficiency, a life dictated by the directives from their own heart. As a result, rituals became a substitute for responsive listening and faithful obedience. This text serves as a warning against our modern tendency to be the dominant voice in our worship, where we are heard more often than the voice of God. It also reminds us that worship where

God's voice is muffled by human voices is not true worship.

4. The Valley of Slaughter (7:30—8:3)

BEHIND THE TEXT

This unit is made up of three oracles. The first oracle (vv 30-31) describes the defilement of the temple and Judah's engagement in child sacrifice. The second oracle (vv 32-34) is a judgment upon Judah for its worship in the Valley of Ben Hinnom. The third oracle (8:1-3) is another judgment word, which depicts the indignity that awaits the whole nation, both in life and in death. The first and second oracles are connected by the theme of worship in the Valley of Ben Hinnom. The second and the third oracles are connected by the theme of the dishonorable state of the dead. The unit as a whole is linked to 7:1-29 with its focus on Judah's corrupt worship. This unit may be assigned to the general setting of Jehoiakim's reign.

Child Sacrifice

Though the Mosaic law strictly prohibited child sacrifice (Lev 18:21; 20:2-5; Deut 12:31; 18:10), Judah's Kings Ahaz and Manasseh are said to have performed this abominable form of worship by burning their sons as offering to pagan gods and goddesses (2 Kgs 16:3; 21:6). This sacrifice was aimed to appease Molech or Baal (see Jer 19:5). Josiah's reform activities included the destruction of Topheth where children were sacrificed to Molech (2 Kgs 23:10). Jeremiah accuses the people of Judah that they have burned their sons and their daughters as offering in the Valley of Ben Hinnom (Jer 7:31). Obviously, the people regarded such practices in perfect conformity to their religious faith in Yahweh. It is likely that this perverted religious practice developed out of a misunderstanding of the commandment to consecrate the firstborn.

IN THE TEXT

■ **30** The temple discourse ends with a judgment word from Yahweh. Verses 30 and 31 indicate the reason for the coming judgment. Judah defiled the temple, the sacred sanctuary of Yahweh, by placing in its precincts pagan idols (v 30). The covenant people have replaced Yahweh with **detestable idols** and have thus brought defilement to the temple, Yahweh's house that bears his holy **Name**.

■ **31** Moreover, the people have made the place of abomination their holy place by building altars to pagan gods to offer their children as human sacrifice (v 31). They replaced the holy place with **high places of Topheth**. High places are pagan worship sites built on hills. Here their location is in the **Valley of Ben Hinnom** (*gê' ben-hinnôm* or simply *gê' hinnôm* or Gehenna) located southwest of Jerusalem. **Topheth** (*tōpet*; an Aramaic word vocalized with the vowels of the Hebrew word *bōšet*, meaning "shame") is commonly understood to be a place of fire or fire pit; it is associated with human sacrifice in the OT. Verse 31 ends with Yahweh's total abhorrence of human sacrifice. He rejects the notion that he would permit such atrocity committed in his name.

Commentators differ in their view of the date of the religious perversions described in vv 30-31. Some think that Jeremiah is referring to the days of Manasseh or Ahaz when pagan influences dominated the temple worship; others think that the text refers to the reintroduction of pagan practices after the days of Josiah who cleansed the temple and destroyed pagan idols. It is likely that during the days of Jehoiakim, the people reverted to child sacrifice in the Valley of Ben Hinnom.

■ **32** The judgment speech that follows (vv 32-34) is a condemnation of Topheth and the Valley of Ben Hinnom; this valley where the people offered their children to foreign gods will be known as **the Valley of Slaughter** (v 32). The people who have slaughtered their children in this valley will be slaughtered there. The place of their worship will become the place of their burial.

■ **33** Verse 33 indicates that the dead bodies of those who have worshipped other gods will be left unburied and that they will be food to carnivorous creatures. Those who polluted Yahweh's temple will be defiled, dishonored, and deprived of the normal funeral rites; their dead bodies will pollute the sanctuaries they have built for themselves.

■ **34** Judgment will bring an end to all social life in Judah and Jerusalem. The picture of the land and streets where **the voices of bride and bridegroom** are not heard (v 34) has apocalyptic overtones (Rev 18:23). The city where once songs of joy and gladness were heard will become a desolate and ruined place.

■ **8:1** The next judgment oracle (8:1-3) continues the theme of the dishonorable end of the idolatrous nation. The bones of the dead—of kings, princes, priests, prophets, and the prominent citizens of Jerusalem—will be removed from their graves (v 1). There will not be any rest to these people even in death.

■ **2-3** The bones of those who have loved and worshipped the astral bodies will be scattered and exposed to their gods whom they worshipped (v 2). The people loved, served, walked after, followed, and worshipped the sun, the moon, and all the heavenly bodies. Again, the judgment fittingly will bring the unfaithful and the idolatrous people before their gods who cannot do anything to restore their worshippers' dignity or honor or give them a proper burial. Those alive will find death preferable to life (v 3; see Rev 9:6). The surviving part of the nation will be driven out of the land, and death will be their choice rather than life under the miserable condition of the exile. They rejected the covenant offer of life; now they are faced with the destiny of death they have chosen for themselves.

FROM THE TEXT

The text shows how what was profane became sacred and what was sacred became profane. God's judgment is upon his people who have lost all sense of what is holy and what is profane. The text is a clear reminder to the reality that no human attempt to erase the boundary between the sacred and the profane can succeed; such attempts will come under the scrutiny and judgment of God. The text also makes clear that erasing such boundaries means choosing death instead of life that flows out of the holy presence of God. What we worship indeed will become our destiny. The ominous reality that the text reminds us is that judgment does not simply end with death. The choice of death leads to a permanent alienation from God. The terrible fate of the dead bodies and bones of the people of Judah reflects a "final discontinuity"—a permanent separation between God and those who have separated themselves from him through their unfaithful living (Brueggemann 1998, 85). This sharp and permanent discontinuity between the realm of life and that of death is addressed in Rev 21:7-8.

"UPROOT AND TEAR DOWN"

JUDAH'S DECEIT AND FALSEHOOD (8:4—10:25)

Overview

The oracles in 8:4—10:25, which are mostly in poetry with the exception of 9:12-15, 23-26 (prose in Hebrew), and 10:11 (an Aramaic verse), return to the general theme of sin and judgment, and thus maintain literary and theological continuity with the oracles in 4:5—6:30. This section also picks up the themes of the enemy from the north (8:16; 10:22), false prophets and their offer of peace (8:11), and the wholesale corruption and greed in the land (8:10), also found in 4:5—6:30. Miller observes in these oracles the same message of 4:5—6:30 "freshly and differently articulated . . . so that the reader gets a different slant, another image, a new vehicle for hearing more clearly the persistent word" of sin and judgment (2001, 643).

The oracles in this section are somewhat disjointed in the sense that they represent different voices with different concerns. There is neither logical sequencing of the oracles nor a single unifying theme in this section. Sin and judgment dominates in 8:4-13, 16-17; 9:4-9, 11, 12-16, 25-26; 10:17-18, 22. Backsliding, false claim of wisdom, corruption of religious leaders, idolatry, deceit and falsehood, and forsaking of the law are the key reasons for the coming judgment. Several oracles contain lament; they come from the people, the prophet, and Yahweh (8:14-15, 18—9:3, 10, 17-22; 10:19-21). This section also includes a *torah* instruction (9:23-24), an extended attack on idols mixed with a praise of the incomparable Yahweh (10:1-16), and a prophetic prayer (vv 23-25).

There seems to be some linkage between the poetic oracles and the prose materials in this section. Jeremiah 9:12-16 is a prose commentary that gives a theological rationale for the utter chaos and desolation of Judah and Jerusalem described in the preceding poetic oracle (vv 10-11). Verses 23-24, which describe wisdom with knowing Yahweh, does not have any direct link to the preceding or following oracles. Nonetheless, it responds to those who claim that they are "wise" (8:8-9). In the same way, 9:25-26 has no immediate literary or theological counterpart; the circumcision terminology in these verses could be linked to the call to circumcision in 4:4. Jeremiah 10:11 serves as a prose summary and commentary on the fate of the gods of the nations; this verse is clearly linked to vv 1-10 and 12-16, the poetic oracles that describe Yahweh as the incomparable God and Creator of the universe.

The oracles in this section do not indicate any particular historical setting; 10:22 seems to suggest a date before the arrival of the Babylonian army in 597 B.C., though 10:25 implies the destruction of Judah as an event that has already happened.

1. Even the Birds Know Better (8:4-13)

BEHIND THE TEXT

This oracle begins with two rhetorical questions taken from the proverbial wisdom tradition. These questions assert the lack of common wisdom among the people, even though they themselves claim to be wise. The text ends with a judgment word spoken against the unwise and unashamed people as well as their leaders. "Satirical disputation" may be the best description of the genre of this text (Stulman 2005, 96).

IN THE TEXT

■ **4-5** The oracle begins with two rhetorical questions (v 4) that assert the general observation that those who fall down get up and those who turn away return. Yahweh questions why this conventional and practical wisdom is not found among his people (v 5). Judah is a backslider nation that is set on its way of backsliding; the nation holds on to the deceitful way of life and refuses to repent. Verses 4 and 5 utilize the verb *šûb* ("return," "repent") five different times; twice in v 4 and three times in v 5. The repeated use of this verb indicates that repentance is a central issue in this unit. Yahweh's knowledge of Judah comes from his personal observation of the people.

■ **6** Though the people have not listened or been attentive to Yahweh, he has been attentive to the way they lived and conducted themselves in their daily life (v 6). What he finds among the people is speech that does not communicate truth, lack of remorse for the evil done (**no one who repents of his *evil***), and deliberate and untamed pursuit in the evil way of life. The metaphor of **horse charging into battle** suggests the abrasive and aggressive behavior of the people without giving any thought to the consequences of their action. The metaphor illustrates the lack of wisdom evident in their actions.

■ **7** Judah's lack of wisdom is further illustrated by an example taken from the world of birds (v 7). Migratory birds such as the stork, dove, swift, and crane recognize and follow their migratory path in their coming and going. It is clear to all who observe these birds that they follow a pattern that Yahweh has set for them as part of his created order. This verse contrasts the regular keeping of the time of migration by these birds with the dysfunctional behavior of Yahweh's covenant people with whom he has a special relationship. Yahweh's people (**my people**) ought to know better than these birds, but they do not. What they do not know, or what is not an internalized matter of their daily existence, is the **requirements** (*mišpāṭ*) of Yahweh. The most important requirement of Yahweh is the fulfillment of the covenantal obligation to love Yahweh and to love the neighbor.

■ **8** In vv 8-9 Yahweh directly engages the people, the scribes, and the wise. He disputes the claim of the people that they are **wise** and that Yahweh's **law** (*tôrâ*) is **with** them. The text implies that some form of the written Torah existed at the time of this oracle. The exact meaning of the second part of v 8 is not clear. The **scribes** were the copyists, interpreters, and teachers of the Law. One possibility is that here we have an accusation that the scribes have given false interpretation of the Torah and thus made it a *lie* and not the true word of Yahweh (**Surely, look, the lying pen of the scribe has made it into a lie**). Again, we do not know how the scribes would have falsified or misinterpreted the Law. As for the false prophets, we know that they preached a false message of peace. Lundbom suggests that *lie* (Hebrew *laššeqer*, lit. "the lie") here is a reference to Baal, and that the scribes were involved in making portions of the Law into a work to honor Baal (1999, 514).

■ **9** In v 9 Yahweh discredits the **wise,** the teachers and promoters of wisdom. Though they claim to have wisdom, in the end they will be put to shame. They will be **taken** away (**trapped**) by the enemy. This is their punishment for rejecting Yahweh's law, the foundation of their wisdom instructions. Since they have rejected the Law, the wisdom they claim is worth nothing.

■ **10-12** Verse 10*a* is a judgment word against all corrupt leaders. Verse 12*a* of ch 6 also expresses a similar judgment with some changes. The accusation and judgment in 8:10*b*-12 are also found in 6:13-15 with slight variation. See the commentary on 6:10-12.

■ **13** The oracle ends with a severe and harsh word of judgment against the unwise people and their unwise and renegade leaders (v 13). Verse 13 is difficult to translate. The NIV reads this as a judgment word (compare with NRSV). The text seems to imply the end of the nation. **No grapes on the vine** and **no figs on the tree** convey the reality that the judgment will result in the total annihilation of the people and their leaders. The end will not only be the end of the population but also be the end of all the blessings, including the fruitfulness of the land, that Yahweh has given as a gift to his people.

FROM THE TEXT

Jeremiah portrays in this text the complacent society of his day in which wisdom, repentance, guilt, integrity, shame, etc., were completely absent. The text also makes a clear connection between the sins of the people and the coming judgment.

This text addresses and clarifies several issues for its modern readers.

First, repentance is critically important to the covenant way of life. Repentance shows wisdom to recognize the God-ordered way of life and relationship with him and others. An unrepentant life means an autonomous existence without wisdom to handle individual and community affairs.

Second, the *Word in us* is more powerful than the *Word with us*. The former means submission, yielding, and respect for the Word; the latter means control, manipulation, and resistance to the Word. The former means transformation and change within that leads to obedient and faithful living. The latter means pride, complacency, and resistance to moral and ethical transformation. Possession of God's Word does not bring about change; real change can come only when we permit the Word to take hold of our lives.

Third, those who handle God's word should do so with integrity. The prophets preached peace and well-being when everything in their world was falling apart. What they wished to see around them was *shalom*, and so they preached *shalom* though in reality there was no *shalom* in the land, and thus made God's word into a lie. God's word, when faithfully proclaimed, will not cover up political, social, and economic ills of society but will expose them to public scrutiny.

Fourth, judgment is the inevitable reality that awaits those who refuse to follow the covenant way of life. The end that the text anticipates is a total withdrawal of all covenantal blessings. The people who have reneged on their covenant commitment do not receive here any hope for survival. There is no word of salvation in this text, but it ends with a judgment word. This word is as effective today as it was in the days of Jeremiah.

2. Not Enough Tears (8:14—9:1)

BEHIND THE TEXT

We hear in this text multiple voices; the language that dominates is that of lament. The reason for the lament is the impending destruction of land and its population by the invading army that is already in the land. The people lament in verses 14-15, 19*b*, 20; the prophet laments in 18-19*a*, 21, 22; 9:1 (8:23

in Hebrew); and Yahweh laments in 19c. The lament of the prophet is in reality the lament of Yahweh. In vv 16-17 Yahweh announces the judgment, which gives intensity to the laments in this unit.

IN THE TEXT

■ **14** In the first lament, the people ask why they should sit around and wait for their doom to come (vv 14-15). Instead, they decide to go to **fortified cities** (v 14). They think that they would be safe and alive for a little while in the fortified cities rather than in their unprotected towns. They know that their destruction is the judgment of Yahweh who has **doomed** them to **perish** and has given them **poisoned water to drink.** Drinking poisoned water is a metaphor for Yahweh's judgment of death upon the people (see 9:15; 23:15).

■ **15** The lament of the people includes an explicit acknowledgment of their destruction as a consequence of their sin against Yahweh. The false prophets have promised them **peace** and they hoped that peace and **healing** would indeed come (v 15). Now they are faced with the reality of evil conditions that threaten and terrify them.

■ **16** Yahweh's response to this lament is not comforting or reassuring, but a harsh reiteration of his judgment against the people (vv 16-17). Judgment is already set in motion; the enemy is moving southward from Dan with their snorting, fast-moving horses. The second part of v 16 conveys the terror being caused by the enemy. The quaking of the land and the devouring of everything in the land intensify the nature of the threat. The city of Jerusalem and its citizens are on the verge of being consumed by the power of the enemy.

■ **17** In v 17 the judgment metaphor changes to creeping poisonous snakes that cannot be tamed. The deadly poison of these snakes means sudden death. No lament, no confession, no grief on the part of the people will persuade Yahweh to suspend judgment.

■ **18-19a** In vv 18-19a the prophet expresses his agony and grief. The agony expressed in these verses is not just the agony of a suffering prophet but also of the suffering Yahweh (Fretheim 2002, 152). The NIV **O my comforter in sorrow** (v 18) is problematic. The Hebrew text is difficult to translate; "my joy is gone, grief is upon me" (NRSV) is a much better rendering. Harsh judgment does not bring joy but only pain and grief to both Yahweh and his prophet. Verse 19a indicates the cry of the people that is being heard **from a land far away** (see an alternate reading "from far and wide in the land" NRSV). **A land far away** suggests Babylon as the location of the cry of the nation, whereas the NRSV reading assumes the cry within the land of Israel.

■ **19b** The rhetorical questions in v 19b seem to be asked by the people (**Is Yahweh not in Zion? Is her King not in her?**). These questions on the one hand affirm Zion as the residence of Yahweh the King. On the other hand as part of the lament of the people, the questions imply that though Yahweh lives in Zion as their King, they have not received the help and protection that they expected to receive from him. Though kingship of Yahweh is a common theme in the Psalms (47—48; 93; 95—99), it is found only rarely in Jeremiah (see also 10:7, 10). Some commentators see these questions as Israel's continued insistence on Zion's inviolability because it is Yahweh's royal residence.

■ **19c** Yahweh interrupts the lament-questions of the people with his own lament-question (v 19c). If the people believe that Zion is Yahweh's residence, why did they provoke him with their idolatry? Though in theology the people claim Yahweh as their King, the real object of their worship is **worthless foreign idols**. The real cause of the present crisis is not Yahweh but the people who have broken their covenant with him. Yahweh's question not only traces the present crisis to the nation's idolatry but also reflects "divine suffering . . . *because* of what has happened" to his relationship with his people (Fretheim 2002, 152).

■ **20** The lament of the people is picked up again in v 20. Yahweh's lament does not give the people any more reason to complain, but their response is now a "pathetic mutter" (Holladay 1986, 293). Some commentators see the first two lines as a proverbial expression. **The harvest** refers to the grain harvest season in April-June and **the summer** refers to the summer months or the fruit-gathering season. Harvest seasons are seasons of joy and celebration. The proverb suggests that the deliverance the people expected at its appointed time has not come. The people lament because they realize that it is time for the harvest of Yahweh's judgment (see v 13). **We are not saved** is the cry of the community that is faced with the threat of total destruction.

■ **21** In 8:21—9:1 (8:21-23 in Hebrew) the prophet expresses his agony and laments over the sickness that is destroying the nation. Though we identify these verses as the lament of the prophet, it is difficult to separate them from Yahweh's lament. Fretheim thinks that Yahweh is the primary speaker in these verses (2002, 152). It is likely that the prophet is expressing his grief, which in reality is a reflection of Yahweh's grief. Both Yahweh and the prophet suffer because of Judah's sin and of the necessity of judgment. The prophet who speaks Yahweh's judgment word does not walk away but remains with the people and suffers with them. Their brokenness is his brokenness; their suffering is his suffering (v 21). Since the people refuse to repent and seek Yahweh's mercy, the prophet mourns and expresses his horror at the devastation that is coming upon them.

■ **22** The first two questions in v 22 affirm what is already a known truth. Certainly, there is **balm in Gilead**; certainly, there are healers known for their ability to heal in Gilead. Gilead, located in the northern part of Transjordan, was well-known for balm, a high-quality and aromatic resin from the balsam tree. The text indicates its medicinal use to heal wounds. Gilead also had its share of healers, the local practitioners of medicine. The intent of these questions is to assert the truth that just as Gilead is a dependable source of healing balm and physicians, so is Yahweh, the trustworthy healer of Israel (see Exod 15:16; Pss

103:3; 147:3; Jer 3:22; 17:14; 30:17; 33:6; Hos 6:1-3). The third question raises the issue of the continued sickness of Judah, though Yahweh is its healer. The text literally reads as follows: "why has new flesh not arisen on the daughter of my people?" The nation remains wounded and sick, though Yahweh is its healer. The reason for this is clear. Yahweh's people (see repeated reference **my dear people,** or "Daughter of my people" [bat 'ammi] four times in 8:19—9:1) refuse to turn to their healer for cure.

■ **9:1** Verse 23 in Hebrew is 9:1 in English translations. The text begins the prophet's desperate wish for an unceasing supply of tears (**Oh, that my head were . . . water and my eyes a fountain of tears**). The prophet's grief here cannot be separated from Yahweh's grief. What would enable him to express fully his grief and sorrow for the dying people of Judah is a head filled with water and eyes out of which tears will flow like a fountain. Perhaps then he can adequately express his grief and pour out tears **day and night** for the people who would soon face violent death by the enemy. We find in this verse human and divine grief expressed in the most distressing and hopeless manner.

The Suffering God

Fretheim helps us to understand the grieving heart of God and his suffering, which is a central issue in 8:4—9:1. He states:

The refrain-like use of the phrase "my (poor) people" (vv 19, 21, 22; 9:1, 2) is filled with pathos; the reader can almost envisage God uttering these words with "his head in his hands." To speak of judgment is no joy, for either God or prophet . . . the prophet here makes those divine feelings publicly available for all to see and hear. (2002, 156)

FROM THE TEXT

This text is one of the "most pathos-filled" poetic units in the book of Jeremiah (Brueggemann 1998, 91). One cannot read this text without feeling the intensity of the prophet's grief over Judah's stubborn determination to die rather than to seek healing from God. Jeremiah is not alone in grief here; the prophet's grief is an "embodiment of God's grief" (Fretheim 2002, 155). The mixture of divine anger and divine sorrow in this text indicates that in his anger God does not detach or disassociate himself from his people. The angry God does not walk away in his wrath. Brueggemann correctly points out that "God's anger . . . is largely subordinated to the hurt God experiences in the unnecessary death of God's people" (1998, 92). Life, and not death, is what God wills for sinners (Ezek 18:32). Judah, however, has chosen the path of death and rejected life. This brings intense hurt and heartache to God.

This biblical portrait of God who grieves over human sin and suffers with sinful humanity provides a corrective to the often misunderstood perception of God in the OT as a God of wrath and vengeance. The text also indicates that God grieves not only over human sin but also over human insistence to continue in the sickness of sin that leads to death. The implicit offer of the text is healing to the terminally ill. The text clearly portrays God as the healer of sin-sick souls. The text also recognizes the power of sin, which prevents sinners from coming to God for their healing. Death and destruction come to sinners not because there is a "deficiency of grace" but because they refuse to come to God for healing and life (Clarke, 280).

The exilic community would have heard in this text God's grieving over those whom he exiled into a foreign land. God's grief is not a one-time expression. His "day and night" weeping indicates that he remains passionate, grieving, and heartbroken even after judgment. The exilic community would also have been reminded by this text that God is their healer and the One who would bring them back to their homeland (see this hope expressed in Ps 147:2-3).

In our hearing of this text focus should be given to both of these aspects: God who grieves and God who heals. Divine pathos we find in this text finds another poignant expression in the weeping of Jesus over Jerusalem (Luke 19:41-44). As the Gospels indicate, grief moved Jesus to action, to his death on the cross, which in the Christian understanding is the symbol of God's healing love for the sin-sick world (see 1 Pet 2:24; Isa 53:5).

3. A Nation of Jacobs (9:2-11)

BEHIND THE TEXT

Some commentators treat 9:2 as a continuation of v 1. Some extend the previous oracle to v 3 because of the formal ending, **declares the LORD**. However, it is possible to treat vv 2-11 as a literary unit. Verse 2 begins the same way as v 1 does (see "Oh, that . . .").

This unit is made up of four speeches of Yahweh (vv 2-3, 4-6, 7-8, 9-11). The first two units conclude with the customary formula "oracle of Yahweh." The third and the fourth units begin as Yahweh's words. In the first speech Yahweh laments and expresses his deep desire to go away from the midst of Judah, followed by the reason for such a wish. The second speech gives a catalog of Judah's sins. The third speech is an announcement of judgment. The final speech begins with Yahweh's lament followed by an announcement of the desolation of Jerusalem.

IN THE TEXT

■ **2** The unit begins with Yahweh's painful desire to **leave** the people who have forsaken him. Some commentators view 9:2 as a lament of the prophet. It is possible to see here both Yahweh and Jeremiah joining together to express their deep desire to remove themselves from the midst of Judah. A **lodging place** in the wilderness is an overnight resting place for desert travelers. The wish being expressed here is not for a permanent relocation but for a temporary withdrawal from the covenant community. The reason for this wish is expressed in vv 2b-3; the community is no longer a hospitable place, a place of covenantal living, but a place filled with **adulterers** and **unfaithful people** (v 2b).

■ **3** Verse 3 continues the description of the sins of Judah. With the **tongue** as a weapon (**bow**), the people promote lies. What prevails in the land is not **truth** but **lies** (šeqer). Life moves **from one evil to another evil.** Every aspect of life—social, moral, religious, ethical, economic, judicial—all have been overtaken by the spreading lie. They have no concern for promoting truth because they do not have covenantal relationship with Yahweh, who looks for truth among his covenant people. **They do not** *know* **me** is the lament of the One who has been forgotten and replaced with false gods.

■ **4** In the next speech, Yahweh gives warning to the citizens of Judah to be on guard, to put no trust in brothers, friends, and neighbors (v 4). This verse indicates the disappearance of truth from social relationships and community life. **Every brother** *a deceiving Jacob* (Hebrew wordplay 'āqôb ya'qōb) seems to convey deception as the inherited trait of the covenant community.

■ **5-6** The disintegration of the fabric of social relations is continued in vv 5 and 6. Deception is what one can expect even from friends. The tongue is trained to speak lie and not truth. They are worn out because of their **iniquity,** but they still continue in their iniquity. In v 6, Yahweh reminds Jeremiah that his dwelling is in the midst of a people who heap **deceit upon deceit.** Deception is the way of life for the people of Judah because **they refuse to** *know* Yahweh. This means that they have rejected the covenant way of life.

The intent of vv 4-6 is not to present a negative portrait of Jacob but to draw a parallel between Judah's deception and Jacob's deceitful dealings before his face-to-face encounter with God and his name change to Israel (Gen 32:22-32). Israel is only a name the people carry as their national identity; in reality they are *Jacobs*—a nation of lying, slandering, and deceiving people.

■ **7** What is left for Yahweh to do with his people, who have disregarded faithfulness, truth, and integrity in their community life, but to enter into the judgment of refining and testing (v 7)? Earlier in 6:27-30, Jeremiah was appointed as an assayer and tester; the prophet found Israel "rejected silver" (v 30). The goal of divine testing is not necessarily to see if Jeremiah's assessment of the people is correct but to affirm what is already a known truth about Judah.

■ **8** Yahweh's finding is stated in 9:8. The refining and testing reveals that deceitful speech and the use of the tongue as a deadly weapon are indeed the characteristics of the people. Friends may speak **peace** (šālôm) to each other, but deep inside they are at war.

■ **9** The rhetorical questions in v 9 show Yahweh's determination to **visit** (pāqad here conveys the idea of visiting in judgment or to **punish**) the nation that has violated the terms of their covenant with him. Deceitful speech is highlighted here as an illustration of Judah's total disregard for the covenant.

Disregard for the covenant way of life is disregard for the covenant maker. This disregard for Yahweh is the basis for the judgment in v 9. Verse 9 repeats 5:29. (See comments on 5:29.)

■ **10** Verse 10 is a lament; this lament comes from Yahweh, who is deeply grieved by the covenant-breaking of Judah (***Over the mountains I will weep and lament, / Over the pastures in the wilderness a dirge . . .***). **Mountains** and **pastures** in the wilderness have become uninhabited places; the sound of the **cattle** is not heard; **birds** and **animals** have disappeared from creation. The language is hyperbole, and it is reminiscent of 4:24-26. Yahweh laments here because of the total devastation of his creation. What he created has been undone by Judah's covenant-breaking.

■ **11** Yahweh's lament is followed by another judgment word. The focus of v 11 is on the desolation of the city of **Jerusalem** and **the towns of Judah.** The verdict of turning Jerusalem into **a heap of ruins, a haunt of jackals** is shocking as well as bold. This judgment word stands counter to all the theological and political assessment of Jerusalem by the covenant community. The coming invasion of the city by the enemy is Yahweh's doing. The city that has become unfaithful will be made desolate by the enemy. The same fate will come upon the smaller towns of Judah.

FROM THE TEXT

The text portrays the crumbling social world of Jeremiah's audience and the total breakdown of community relations. The fabric of Israel's community life has disintegrated because truth-telling is no longer what governs neighbor relations or any other aspect of social interaction. Israel, the covenant community, has reverted back to being "Jacobs" by its deceitful patterns of behavior, which their ancestor had long ago abandoned when he encountered God face-to-face and received a new identity. This text is a powerful reminder and invitation to Judah to abandon its present social identity as "Jacobs" and to follow the model of their ancestor who saw God's face and was transformed to Israel (Gen 32:22-32). This transformation and the receiving of a new identity as a people who live in the experience of seeing God daily in their lives is what makes a community a truth-telling community.

The problem that confronts any society where truth-telling is rarely practiced is the breeding of suspicion and cynicism, which in turn leads to social breakdown. The text aptly reminds the modern readers that the power of speech, when it is exploited in any sphere of human life, can only lead to the collapse of social and communal life. "No one speaks the truth" (Jer 9:5) is an alarming assessment of the prophet's audience. It sounds cynical, yet a reality that we confront in our own time, in our marketplace, politics, media, family and social relations, and even in religious life. This concern is found in a number of psalms (Pss 12:2-4; 41:6; 52:2; 55:21). The concern over the power of the tongue is a clear issue in Jas 3:1-12. Jeremiah also reminds us that the root cause of this social malady is the community's refusal to **know**—to enter into a covenantal relationship with—God. Knowing God means commitment to follow a new way of life, a life not only of knowing God but also of being known by him. This alternative to a fraudulent and deceitful way of life requires us to "put off" our "old self" and to "put on the new self" as God creates us to be like him "in true righteousness and holiness." Paul reminds us that an important outcome of this transformed life is truth-speaking to our neighbors, which is essential to unity and community well-being (Eph 4:22-25).

The text also reminds us that God does not remain blind and deaf to the disintegration of social and communal life. God responds to the assault on integrity and truth-telling with grief and judgment. The text treats God's grief and judgment as inseparable realities. God, who laments over the desolation of creation, is also the One who is bringing the desolation. The theological necessity of judgment brings greater agony to God. See the relationship between grief and judgment in Gen 6:6-7. The death verdict on his beloved city does not come from an impassionate and unfeeling God, but a God who is brokenhearted at the disappearance of truth-telling in the city. As Fretheim points out, "God mediates judgment so that sin and evil do not go unchecked in the life of the world. But God does so at great cost to the divine life" (2002, 165). God's grief, here and elsewhere in the Bible, is not just an emotional display but a genuine expression of love. Genuine love is what makes genuine grief possible. "God so loved the world" is the best NT expression of divine grief; it is this love/grief that is manifested in God's self-giving on the cross for the sake of the world, not only to bring his judgment on sin but also to give hope and salvation to sinners (John 3:16; Phil 2:5-8).

4. Let Me Tell You Why (9:12-16)

BEHIND THE TEXT

This unit is in prose and has three parts: in the first part a threefold question is asked to make sense of the cause of what has happened to the land (v 12); the second part explains the reasons for the desolation (vv 13-14); the third part is an announcement of judgment (vv 15-16). In v 12 the desolation of the land has already taken place, but in vv 15-16, judgment is yet to come. The usual accusation-judgment pattern of Jeremiah's speech shifts here to a question-accusation-judgment pattern.

IN THE TEXT

■ **12** It is not clear who is asking the questions in v 12. The questions assume that the devastation announced in vv 10-11 has taken place. Some commentators attribute these questions to Jeremiah; others to Yahweh or to the community in exile for whom the tragedy of 587 B.C. remains as an enigma (see this third possibility in Stulman 2005, 103; Fretheim 2002 160). These are the questions the people will ask when the land will be made desolate by the invading army. They come from the people who were confident in the inviolability of Jerusalem. These questions assert that neither the wise nor the false prophets among the people can understand or explain what has happened, because they lack the wisdom to perceive Yahweh's involvement in the historical realities of their day. Those who have common wisdom would know that destruction and desolation of the land like a wilderness did not happen without Yahweh's involvement.

■ **13-14** Yahweh, knowing that common wisdom is lacking among his people (cf. 8:7), once again states the reason for their impending destruction (vv 13-14). The people have broken their covenant with Yahweh by forsaking the Law, by refusing to obey his voice and to live by the Law, by walking after their own self-determined ways, and by worshipping other gods. Rejection of the **law** (*tôrâ*) and disobedience to Yahweh's voice are signs of self-proclaimed freedom from Yahweh and any obligation to the covenantal way of life. For those who have rejected the covenant, the alternative is idolatry or worshipping whatever gods came by. Jeremiah deals with idolatry as something that bridged the generation gap—children learned idolatry from their fathers.

■ **15-16** The dire consequences of covenant-breaking (**therefore**) are stated in vv 15-16. The text refers to future events, which for the exilic community were past and present realities. The repeated first person reference in these verses indicates Yahweh's direct involvement in executing judgment. The judgment word utilizes the imagery of eating **bitter food** ("wormwood" NRSV) and drinking poisonous water. These provisions from God are not meant to sustain life, but to destroy it. Wormwood is a shrub that has a bitter taste. Wormwood and poisonous water suggest intense suffering and death (8:14; Lam 3:15, 19). The judgment also includes the exile of the nation among the peoples of the world (see this curse in Deut 28:64). Divine judgment will lead to the loss of any special privileges and the loss of the homeland. The exiled community will live among people who have strange customs and speak a strange language (see Jer 5:15). The **sword** of judgment will pursue Judah until the nation is brought to an end. Verse 16 portrays Yahweh as a relentless pursuer who will not stop until the judgment is fully carried out.

FROM THE TEXT

The text clearly suggests the close connection between autonomy-idolatry and God's judgment. The covenant people rejected the Torah, followed their stubborn heart, and worshipped other gods. Autonomy coexists with idolatry as conjoined offspring of human sin. Removing God from the center of existence means filling the vacuum it creates with oneself or other gods. The text also indicates that those who exempt themselves from obedience to the covenant live without the promise of life found in the Torah. The text informs the covenant people, who are perplexed and dismayed at their calamity, that they themselves are the real cause of death and destruction that came upon them. Those who relentlessly rejected the relentless call to *torah*-obedience are faced with the reality of the relentless pursuit of God to bring them to judgment. This theme of autonomy-idolatry-judgment is taken up by the apostle Paul in Rom 1—2.

The text instructs the exilic community that its future rests in its *torah*-obedience. Christian readers will recognize in this text that "obedience that comes from faith" in Christ is the real source of life, and the only alternative to death-filled existence and the only way to escape the reality of judgment (Rom 1:5).

5. "How Ruined We Are!" (9:17-22)

BEHIND THE TEXT

This poetic unit continues the lament theme of the previous poetic oracle (vv 10-11), which was interrupted by the prose material in vv 12-16. This unit contains a public ritual of mourning. Yahweh is the speaker in this unit. In vv 17-18, he summons the people to send for skillful mourners. In v 19 Yahweh gives the words of the lament to the professional mourners. He then summons the women to teach their daughters how to weep and lament (v 20). In v 21 Yahweh gives all the mourners the words of the lament. The unit ends with a word of judgment that Yahweh gives Jeremiah to proclaim (v 22). The alternate arrangement of summons and lament and the final word of judgment express the finality that death brings upon the nation.

IN THE TEXT

■ **17** The unit begins with Yahweh's summons to the people to call professional mourners, women skilled in weeping and lamenting for the dead (v 17). The text indicates the ancient custom of mourning rituals led by women who sing dirges and weep loudly to express public grief and sorrow (see the laments in 2 Sam 1:17-27; 2 Chr 35:24-25).

■ **18** Yahweh's summons continues in v 18; he urges professional mourners to hurry up and lament with such intensity of grief and sorrow over the nation's loss that would move everyone in the nation, including Jeremiah and Yahweh, to flood their eyes with tears (see **us, our** in v 18).

■ **19** Yahweh gives the language of the lament that is heard in Zion (v 19). It acknowledges that the nation suffered destruction and shame. It is forced to forsake its land and go into exile, because the enemy has destroyed the land. The lament makes clear that Yahweh and his prophet also participate in this national expression of grief. They are not some detached spectators, but full participants in the loss of the nation. The grief of the people is their grief. The loss of the nation is their loss. The exile of the nation is their exile. Dirges like these usually mean destruction has already come and there is no circumventing of the power of death. What prompted this lament is not clear. Perhaps the lament anticipates the end of the whole nation without leaving anyone to lament over the dead or bury their dead bodies (see vv 21-22). If so, this lament fulfills the public mourning rites customarily given to the dead, before death actually takes place (see Amos's dirge song in Amos 5:2).

■ **20** Verse 20 is Yahweh's speech to all the women in the land. Yahweh asks them to teach their daughters and neighbors the art of wailing and singing dirge songs. The intent of this call is to recruit and train every woman in the land in dirge songs so that lament will be heard throughout the land.

■ **21** The reason for the lament and the language of lament is found in v 21. The language of v 19 becomes more specific in v 21. The lament here is over death that intrudes and invades the land. **Death** is personified as a thief that comes up through the windows and sneaks upon unsuspecting victims. Ordinary houses and royal residences are all invaded and taken over by death. Death rules everywhere, including the streets and squares of the cities, the playground of little children and young men. Reference to **children** and **young men** indicates that death has nullified the future of the nation.

■ **22** The unit ends with a word from Yahweh, which adds to the grim and horrifying reality of death that has come upon the nation (v 22). The command ***speak thus*** is in masculine singular, which indicates that this word is addressed to Jeremiah. Verse 22 portrays vividly the horrible scene of a military strike against Judah. Death will invade the land and leave its victims like dung on the ground, like sheaves left in the field after harvest. **No one to gather them** indicates that when judgment comes, it will be so massive that there will be no one to bury the dead.

FROM THE TEXT

This lament reveals the destructive power of death. Death is everywhere; it invades homes and streets; it brings an end to everything in the land. It brings grief and sorrow to the whole land and everyone connected with it, including God. Though the text does not link death with sin, it is obvious from the surrounding texts that death in this text is the tragic outcome of Judah's covenant-breaking and its persistent rejection of God. Death comes upon a nation that was self-confident and presumptuous about its future. Death comes upon a people who thought life was a fixed reality and that they will live forever. Death comes upon Zion, which they thought was inviolable. The text shatters all ill-conceived hopes and claims of an overly confident people and asserts the truth that "the wages of sin is death" (Rom 6:23).

Public expression of grief we find in this text is alien to modern thinking.

We attempt to contain our grief, cover it up, or make it a private affair. Lament like this in the OT—particularly the lament psalms—shows that grief expressed and articulated with profound sorrow initiates the process of healing and brings hope to the grieving individual or the community (see especially the hope and trust statements in lament psalms; for example, see Ps 6:8-10). God is lamenting with the people who are under the judgment of death for their sin against him. This means that he does not leave them to the power of death. Genesis 6—9 tell us that God who brought the judgment of flood in grief initiated new possibilities for the human community. In the same way, God's grief in this text is the hope for a new future for the community that lives under God's judgment. The book reminds us that the grieving nation also heard the promise of life from the God who grieved with them (see chs 30—33).

6. A Little Sermon on Boasting (9:23-26)

BEHIND THE TEXT

This unit is made up of a short poetic oracle on boasting (vv 23-24) followed by a prose section that deals with the issue of circumcision (vv 25-26). Most commentators treat the two oracles together as one literary unit. A possible connection between the two parts is the issue of boasting or misplaced trust. The first part deals with misplaced trust in wisdom. The second part deals with Israel's misplaced trust in circumcision. The text has no thematic continuity with the preceding lament unit, but it presents life lived in true wisdom and knowledge of Yahweh as the alternative to death-lament filled life.

IN THE TEXT

■ **23** Verse 23 begins with a reference to the wise and thus it may be linked to the rhetorical questions in v 12. This verse also seems to function as a response to those who claim to be wise in 8:8. Verses 23-24 contrast **wisdom, strength,** and **riches** of the self-sufficient and self-reliant people with the covenant life of those who understand Yahweh and know his requirements. The text admonishes those who take pride in their possession of wisdom, strength, and riches to seek the path of true wisdom.

■ **24** True wisdom means understanding and knowing Yahweh as the God who practices **covenant faithfulness** (*ḥesed*), **justice** (*mišpāṭ*), and **righteousness** (*ṣĕdāqâ*) (v 24). Yahweh's *ḥesed* is his covenant commitment to love and be faithful and gracious regardless of changing circumstances and human responses. Justice and righteousness often appear together in the OT; Yahweh is committed to doing what is just and right. These are fundamental qualities with which Yahweh relates not only to his covenant people but also to the whole creation. These terms express his commitment to make things right and to defend and protect the poor and the oppressed in the society. ***In the earth*** could also mean "in the land" and if this is the meaning intended, the text may be referring specifically to Yahweh's covenant commitment to Judah despite the present circumstances of the nation (Stulman 2005, 106). Yahweh delights in exercising faithfulness, justice, and righteousness because these qualities represent his true character. Those who know him this way should then imitate these virtues in their life (see 4:2).

■ **25-26** The second part of this unit (9:25-26) is a judgment word and the issue of circumcision in these verses brings this text into contact with 4:4 and 6:10. The opening phrase (**the days are coming**) indicates the judgment as a future event. The nations listed among the **circumcised** are Judah's neighboring people. Except for **Egypt,** the other nations (**Edom, Ammon,** and **Moab**) shared a common ancestry with Israel (v 26). The list includes some desert dwellers (Arab tribes) that followed the custom of shaving the head as a religious ritual. It is not altogether clear the connection between the circumcision of Judah and that of the neighboring nations. **Judah** is simply listed with other nations without giving it any special status. The claim of circumcision by any of these nations, including the covenant people, does not exempt them from judgment; they all must face Yahweh's judgment. Though these nations are physically circumcised, Yahweh counts them as uncircumcised in their hearts. The circumcision that matters is the circumcision of the heart. The text concludes with special reference to **the whole house of Israel** as a people who are **uncircumcised in heart** (v 26). Israel is mentioned in particular because of its failure to pay attention to the call to the circumcision of the heart (see 4:4; also Deut 10:16).

FROM THE TEXT

The text reveals the human tendency to place trust in human values and resources. One's ancestry, religious heritage and customs, intellectual capacity, physical strength, wealth, education, race—all are potential sources of boasting, pride, and self-acclaim. The text does not devalue these things that are important to one's self-understanding and personal well-being. Rather, it clearly rejects human trust and confidence in these values and calls for our trust in God and our commitment to know him and to live by his values. These human values are worth nothing where there is no true personal relationship with God and where there is no commitment to promote faithfulness, justice, and righteousness in the community.

The text also links boasting in self-centered values to an uncircumcised heart—a heart that is turned toward oneself and not toward God. Misplaced trust in human values is a concern found in Paul's writings (see 1 Cor 1:26-31; 2 Cor 10:7-18). Though Paul had every reason to boast about his race, circumcision, education and training, and religious values and commitments, he counted all these as "rubbish." The most important aim in his life was to "gain Christ, and be found in him . . . to know Christ and the power of his resurrection . . .

becoming like him in his death . . . to attain to the resurrection from the dead" (Phil 3:8-11). Here we find the Christian alternative to vain boasting.

7. Incomparable Yahweh (10:1-16)

BEHIND THE TEXT

Scholars have raised questions about the authenticity of this poem largely due to its resemblance to the polemic against idols in Isa 40:18-20 and 41:7, 29; 44:9-20. One cannot with certainty argue for or against the authenticity of the text. The resemblance of this text to the Isaiah passages does not necessarily place it in the exilic setting; one could also argue that the passages in Isaiah may have been inspired by Jeremiah's words about the idols of the nations. Holladay, who argues for the authenticity of this text as a Jeremianic composition, thinks that the prophet sent this word to those who were exiled to Babylon in 597 B.C. (Holladay 1986, 329-30).

The poem as a whole aims to accomplish two things: to castigate idols of the nations as worthless human-made objects and to extol Yahweh as the incomparable God. The text would have thus served as a taunt and a strong rejection of the Babylonian claim of the superiority of their gods. The poem begins with a command to Israel not to learn the way of the nations (vv 1-2). In the rest of the unit, the themes of mockery/judgment of the idols (vv 3-5, 8-9, 11, 14-15) and the praise of Yahweh (vv 6-7, 10, 12-13, 16) alternate; this alternate arrangement intensifies the contrast between the idols and Yahweh.

Verse 11 is in Aramaic. This is in prose though words in this verse follow a chiastic arrangement (see Lundbom 1999, 593); Holladay thinks that this verse is original to the poem and not a later insertion. He also considers this verse as "the climax of the poem" (Holladay 1986, 325). Lundbom divides verses 1-16 into two "liturgies" with v 11 as the "centerpiece" (Lundbom 1999, 577). Another uniqueness of this poem is that verses 12-16 are also found in 51:15-19. The Septuagint shows significant variation after v 4. The Hebrew text of vv 6, 7, 8, and 10 are not in the Greek translation. The first part of v 5 in Hebrew also seems to be lacking in Greek. After v 4, the Greek translation reads, "It is embossed silver; they cannot walk." The second part of v 5 (**They must be carried . . . nor can they do any good**) appears in Greek after the content of v 9.

The Hebrew text of this poem shows frequent shift between singular and plural forms. In v 3, the antecedent of **it** is **customs;** the antecedent of **they** in v 4 is **craftsman** in v 3; the antecedent of **them** in v 4 (*they secure them*) is **it**. These variations may have been the result of careless transmission of the text, or as Holladay suggests, an intentional literary device utilized by the prophet to ridicule idols, which no one cares whether they are "one or many" (1986, 325).

IN THE TEXT

■ **1-2** The poem begins with an introductory formula that presents the content of this poem as Yahweh's word to the **house of Israel** (v 1). This reference seems to include not only Judah but also the scattered people of the northern kingdom. In v 2 Yahweh tells Israel not to follow the religious customs and habits of the nations in the world. The *way* **of the nations** is elaborated in the rest of the text as idol making and idol worshipping. Israel is also warned in this text not to be afraid of the *signs of the heavens.* Signs of the heavens are astrological speculations based on close observation of the movements and patterns of celestial bodies.

Astrology in Ancient Near East

According to the ancient Mesopotamian belief system, signs of the heavens conveyed the power of their deities over human affairs. Such signs induced a great deal of fear in the ancient people because they considered them as indications of some impending calamity.

■ **3-4** Verses 3-5 contain the first mockery of pagan gods. **Customs of the peoples** (*huqqôt* is usually translated as "statutes") here perhaps refers to idols (v 3). They are ***nothing*** (*hebel*, lit. "vapor," "breath," or "vanity") or powerless to do anything. They are made of wood cut down from the trees in the forest; they are given shape by skilled craftsmen; they are decorated with silver and gold and fastened with nails on a pedestal so that they will not wobble (v 4).

■ **5** In v 5, idols are compared to scarecrows in a field. They are worthless because they do not communicate or do anything to show their independent existence. Those who make and worship them must carry them. Unlike the idols, Yahweh speaks to his people and carries them (Exod 19:4; Isa 40:11; 63:9). Yahweh warns his people not to be afraid of the idols of the nations because they do not have any power in them, either to do any good or to bring any evil. Yahweh alone has the power to "make weal and create woe" (Isa 45:7 NRSV).

■ **6** The mockery of the idols is followed by a hymn-like praise of Yahweh and his incomparable greatness (vv 6-7). The second person address of Yahweh suggests that the praise comes from the prophet as the liturgical response to Yahweh's mockery of idols (or the intended response of the worshipping community). ***There is none like you*** affirms the answer implied in the question "Who is like you?" in other OT texts (see Pss 35:10; 71:19; 89:8; also Mic 7:18). This affirmation is also found at the end of this hymn (v 7). Twice in v 6 the word ***great*** (*gādôl*) is used. Greatness of Yahweh is a frequent theme in the psalms (40:16; 48:1; 135:5; 147:5, etc.). In v 6, focus is also given to the greatness of Yahweh's name and its power. Yahweh's name essentially conveys his character. There is no one who could be compared with Yahweh. In the preceding section, Yahweh reminded his people that they do not need to fear the idols because they cannot do any harm.

■ **7** Verse 7 affirms the conviction that Yahweh is the object of "fear" (NRSV) of all the nations. Fear in this context is not the fear of evil that Yahweh may bring but the recognition of his sovereign authority as Creator. Jeremiah addresses Yahweh as **King of the nations,** which conveys the sovereignty of Yahweh over kings and kingdoms of the world. This idea is also reflected in many of the psalms that celebrate Yahweh's universal kingship (see Pss 93, 96, for example). The hymn ends with another affirmation about the incomparability of Yahweh. **Wise men of the nations** may refer to the skilled craftsmen who make the idols (Holladay 1986, 332). In idol making, craftsmen become creators of their gods by giving size, shape, and beauty to the idols. Neither among these skilled god-makers nor in **their kingdoms** is there anyone who has the creative power of Yahweh.

■ **8** The praise of Yahweh is followed by another mockery of idols (vv 8-9). **They** in v 8 most likely refer to the idols and not to the wise men of v 7. Those who make the idols are the skilled craftsmen—the wise men of the nations. However, the idols do not have any wisdom, not even the wisdom of their makers. The second line of v 8 (*the instruction of nothings, it is wood*) asserts that the idols cannot give any instruction or correction to their worshippers because they are objects made out of wood. This is in sharp contrast to Israel's confession of Yahweh the Creator as the source of wisdom and his ability to grant wisdom and instruction to his creation.

■ **9** Verse 9 describes the process of making idols from expensive metals imported from faraway places such as **Tarshish** and **Uphaz.** Tarshish is presumably a port city in the western Mediterranean region. The location of Uphaz is not known; some scholars identify it with Ophir, presumably a location in the northeast coast of Africa. The makers of gold and silver idols are human craftsmen and metalsmiths. These workers do everything to decorate their handiwork and make them beautiful and costly. Idols makers clothe them with **blue and purple** clothing, colors of royalty, to bestow upon them the powers of royalty. However, like wooden idols, these idols of silver and gold remain worthless, senseless, powerless, and of no use to their worshippers.

■ **10** The praise in v 10 proclaims Yahweh as the **true God.** The first line also could be translated to read as follows: "But Yahweh is God—he is true." In contrast to the idols that are vapor, Yahweh is an enduring "reality" (Holladay 1986, 323, 333). In contrast to the idols of wood, Yahweh is the **living God.** He is not only the author of life but also the God who has life (see 23:36; Deut 5:23; 1 Sam 17:26, 36). Yahweh is also the *everlasting* **King;** in contrast to human kingship that is limited by time and the extent of life, Yahweh's kingship is eternal, and it extends throughout the course of history. The last part of v 10 focuses on Yahweh's **wrath.** The poem makes the connection between the phenomenon of earthquake and the wrath of God. Neither nature nor the nations can withstand the intensity of the wrath of Yahweh.

■ **11** The Aramaic verse (v 11) continues the thought of the wrath and fury of Yahweh. Yahweh is directing a group of people to speak his judgment word to another group. The identity of *you* (plural) and *them* is not clear (***Thus you shall say to them***). It is possible that Yahweh is sending a message to the gods of Babylon and the makers of these gods through the Judeans exiled in 597 B.C. in their own language. The message is that Yahweh's judgment is on the idols and that their destruction is certain. The only true God is the One who made the heavens and the earth. Idols that are worshipped as gods who had no role in creating the heavens and the earth must face the judgment of the true Creator God; they do not belong anywhere in his creation, so they will be destroyed.

■ **12-13** The judgment on the idols is followed by another hymn-like praise of Yahweh, the maker of **earth** and **heavens** (vv 12-13). The **power** of the Creator and his **wisdom** and **understanding** are extolled in v 12. The language of this praise reflects Israel's creation theology. Verse 13 gives more specific attention to the power of the Creator manifested in natural phenomena such as **rain, clouds, lightning,** and **wind.** Utterance of Yahweh's voice implies thunder (***When he utters his voice***), which accompanies rain or the ***tumult* of waters in the heavens.** The idols have no power to create any of these natural phenomena; it is Yahweh who makes rain necessary for the productivity of the earth. Verse 13 rejects the pagan claim that their gods control the natural phenomena and bring fertility to the ground.

■ **14** The final mockery of idols sums up the previously stated descriptions of the idols (vv 14-15). The first line of v 14 is not very clear. **Everyone** seems to refer to the whole humanity (*kol 'ādām*), though it is parallel to **every *smith*** in the next line. The mockery seems to begin with a general evaluation of all humanity as people without wisdom and knowledge. This line thus contrasts humanity with the Creator who alone has wisdom and knowledge. In Israel's thinking, wisdom is a gift given to those who have the fear of Yahweh, the recognition of Yahweh as the sovereign Creator. Idolatry indicates not only the lack of fear of Yahweh but also humanity's lack of wisdom as creatures. The second line of v 14 focuses on the smiths or the craftsmen—people with wisdom according to human standards—who are skilled in idol making. Their handiwork will bring no honor but only shame to them because the idols they make are a ***lie*** (*šeqer*), and they have no life in them. The usefulness of their product is a source of pride for artisans.

■ **15** Idol makers will be put to shame by their own handiwork because what they make are ***nothing,*** worthless **objects of mockery.** They are not objects of worship, rather objects to be mocked because of their utter uselessness to anyone. Verse 15 ends with an announcement that idols and their makers will be destroyed when Yahweh brings his judgment on the nations.

■ **16** The text concludes with a final statement of praise (v 16). Once again,

Yahweh is affirmed as **the Maker of all things.** He is not like the idols of the nations. **Portion** (or "possession") **of Jacob** is a name given to Yahweh to indicate his special relationship to Jacob/Israel. Just as Yahweh belongs to Israel, Israel belongs to Yahweh as **the tribe of his inheritance.** The text thus highlights the covenant relationship between Yahweh and Israel. Israel's covenant maker is the Creator of the universe. The phrase ***Yahweh of hosts* is his name** conveys the idea of the sovereignty and dominion of Yahweh over all the powers of the universe. Yahweh's name exemplifies his character and strength. This phrase constitutes the final confessional statement of the poem. Though variations of this phrase are found elsewhere in the OT, the phrase in this form is unique to Jeremiah, found 12 times in the book (Lundbom 1999, 599).

FROM THE TEXT

This text calls the people of God to reject idolatry, the making and worshipping of gods that worshippers can design, arrange, and manipulate to meet their individual needs. Idolatry is the worship of "created things rather than the Creator" (Rom 1:25). Idolatry promotes the "worship of what was meant to be used and the use of what was meant to be worshipped" (Augustine). The text would have reminded the exilic audience of Jeremiah that no matter what claims the Babylonians may make about the power of their gods over the God of Israel, these gods are of no value and they have no power to do any harm or good. The point that Jeremiah is making here is that there is no comparison between the God of Israel who is the Creator, Sustainer, and the source of wisdom and life and human-made gods in whatever form they come.

When idols take the place of the living God, human perceptions about realities change, because such perceptions are no longer grounded in the intent and purpose of the Creator but in the self-will of those who make such idols. Idolatry thus means a self-determined, self-centered, and self-reliant life. Idols of wood, silver, and gold in this text remind us that idols come in all sorts of forms and shapes. Gods we make in our world today are not always of wood and metal, but of our physical strength, intellectual capacity, work, wealth, material possessions, etc. Our trust in our capacity to make these things work for us and our claim that these things exist for us and that we exist for these things are subtle forms of idolatry. In such thinking, we lose sight of the world that God created for us to live, the world that is sustained and preserved and provided for by the Creator. Instead, we become preoccupied by the world that we are creating for ourselves, a world that we control for our self-interest. In this kind of world, there is no covenant way of life, no trust in the Creator, and no concern for others. The text reminds us that there is no enduring quality to this way of life and that shame and ruin is what awaits all who create and live in their own self-created world.

Paul describes idolatry as exchanging the "truth of God for a lie" (Rom 1:25). The alternative to idolatry, which the text connects with learning the ways of the nations, is commitment to live a life that is "holy and pleasing to God," a life that does not permit itself to be conformed to "the pattern of this world" (12:1-2).

8. The Inevitable Exile (10:17-25)

BEHIND THE TEXT

This unit appears to be made up of words from the prophet and Yahweh, though it is difficult to identify the speakers with certainty. The words assigned to the prophet may indeed be words spoken on behalf of the people. The prophet seems to be the speaker in v 17; the addressees are those who dwell under siege, most likely the inhabitants of Jerusalem. Yahweh then speaks a word of judgment (v 18). Verses 19-21 constitute a lament, most likely spoken by the prophet. In vv 19-20, he expresses the grief and the loss of the people, and in v 21 he places the blame for this tragedy on the leaders of the nation. These verses have some similarity to the content of 4:19-21 and 8:21—9:1. Verse 22 of ch 10 seems to be a word from Yahweh about the approach of the enemy form the north. This is followed by a confession of the prophet (vv 23-24). The unit concludes with a prayer of the prophet calling for Yahweh's judgment on the enemy (v 25). Verses 23-25 reflect the language of Pss 6:2; 79:6-7; Prov 16:9; 20:24. Some commentators treat v 25 as a later addition; it is likely that the prophet is utilizing the traditional language to invoke God's judgment upon the enemy on behalf of the people. The language of v 25 suggests the events of 597 or 587 B.C. as the possible setting of this text.

IN THE TEXT

■ **17** Verse 17 begins with an imperative in feminine; the addressee is personified Jerusalem, which is under siege by the enemy. The city is told to **gather up** its **bundle.** The reference may be to the exile's shoulder bag (see 46:19; Ezek 12:3-7), which contained a person's most valuable possessions. The people who would soon be exiled are being called here to collect their belongings from **the land** (*'ereṣ* could mean "land" or "earth" or "ground") and get ready for their exile. It is ironic that the city that was called "fortified" (*hammibṣār*; 4:5; 8:14) is now called a city **under siege** (*bammāṣôr*).

■ **18** Verse 18 is a word from Yahweh. The reason for the call to get ready for the exile is made clear here. The coming exile is not the work of an enemy nation, but it is the work of Yahweh. Like a stone is hurled out of a sling, Yahweh is about to thrust the people out of the land. The exile will be a violent event, and it will cast the people off into a distant land. The exile will be a time of great **distress** brought upon the people by Yahweh. The meaning of the last phrase of this verse is not clear. The verb *yimṣā'û* means **they will find out** (from *māṣā'* "to find"; **so that they may be captured;** "so that they shall feel it" NRSV). The text does not say what they will find out. A good possibility is that the exiled people will find out that their exile is Yahweh's judgment upon them.

■ **19** Verses 19-21 contain the words of lament spoken by the prophet; these words reflect the pain and agony of the nation. The prophet may very well be speaking for Jerusalem, the city that has lost its children to the Babylonians who have taken them into captivity. The lament contains expressions of intense suffering. It begins with a cry of despair and hopelessness (**woe**); what brings agony and anguish to the prophet is the reality that there is no healing in sight for the **wound** that is inflicted by the enemy. In the second part of v 19, the prophet speaks to himself and accepts the reality of his brokenness and determines to go through with it and endure it rather than to seek a way out of it. Perhaps the implied message is that Jerusalem should accept this tragedy as divine punishment and endure the present sufferings.

■ **20** Verse 20 makes clear that the people are included in this lament. The personified city is lamenting in this verse about the abrupt dismantling of its structures that provided home to its inhabitants. **Tent** and "cords" (NRSV) perhaps do not have any specific meaning, though some commentators associate them with the temple and the surrounding buildings. The second part of v 20 portrays the image of a mother grieving over the loss of her children. Her children are either taken away from her into exile or are killed. There is no one left to rebuild and restore her home.

■ **21** The reason for the brokenness and suffering is stated in v 21. The present calamity is brought upon the nation by foolish and **senseless shepherds** or leaders of the nation. The reference is to the kings who have failed to lead the nation with wisdom and understanding that they should have sought from Yahweh. Their senselessness is evident in their refusal to *seek* Yahweh's counsel. Because of their unwise rule and strategies and plans made without consulting Yahweh, these rulers have not enjoyed success as leaders of the nation; also because of their failed leadership, their **flock,** the people over whom Yahweh has placed them as shepherds, is **scattered** or driven out from its pasture.

■ **22** Yahweh's response to the lament of the prophet (and that of the people) is not words of comfort, but a solemn announcement of the destruction of Judah by the enemy (v 22). The first part of v 22 announces the coming of the enemy from the land of the north; it is presented as a rumor or report from a watchman. It is quite clear that the Babylonians are the enemy in this verse. The Babylonian army is already on the way to Judah; the report announces that the sound of the advancing army is already heard in the land. The language of the second part of this verse is similar to that of 9:11. The goal of the enemy is to bring total destruction to Judah, to make it a place uninhabitable for humans, to make it a wasted land, home for the jackals and other wild animals.

■ **23** The prophet responds to Yahweh's word with a confession, a prayer that recognizes the human inability to establish or shape one's own destiny (v 23). The finitude of humanity is clearly expressed here; humanity lacks wisdom to dictate its own future. Verse 23 clearly reflects the wisdom tradition's understanding of humanity (Prov 16:9; 20:24). Implied in v 23 is the recognition that Yahweh directs and shapes human destiny. Some commentators see in this verse the prophet's reflection of how the people justify their irresponsible behavior by citing traditional statements about human beings' lack of wisdom to direct their future (Holladay takes vv 23-25 as the people's attempt to justify their irresponsibility; 1986, 343-44). This verse together with v 24 make much better sense as the prophet's confession, an intercessory prayer for the people who have failed miserably to follow Yahweh or seek wisdom from him.

■ **24** Jeremiah recognizes the failure of the people and then appeals to Yahweh to be just and merciful in carrying out his disciplinary action against him (v 24). The prayer includes the people. The present crisis is Yahweh's disciplining of his people. His prayer **correct me** (*yassĕrēnî* from *mûsar*, meaning "correct," "discipline," "chastise," etc.) is an appeal on behalf of the nation. The nation's future depends on Yahweh's treatment of his people with justice and mercy. Disciplining the nation in anger and wrath means no future for Judah.

■ **25** The unit ends with a prayer in which the prophet appeals to Yahweh to carry out his judgment against his enemies and the enemies of Israel (v 25). Reference to **the nations** indicates that this prayer is directed against all the enemies of **Jacob** (i.e., Israel as a nation), not just the Babylonians. Yahweh disciplined his people using the nations as his instrument of judgment. Now it is time for his judgment of the nations. The reason for this appeal is clear: these nations do not **acknowledge** Yahweh as the sovereign Lord of history and Creator of the universe. They do not **call on** his **name** in worship and praise. They have destroyed the people of Israel and brought them to an end; they have destroyed the land of Israel. Some commentators think v 25 was added during the exile; the exilic community may have included in its worship an appeal to God for his judgment of the nations responsible for the downfall of Israel (see Pss 79:6-7; 137:7-9).

FROM THE TEXT

The text is for the most part a prayer in the form of the prophet's speeches directed to God. This prayer reveals a range of emotions that human beings usually display at the sudden loss of everything in life. There is a cry of anguish, pain, hopelessness, despair, grief, resignation, blame, confession, anger—all of which we witness when terrible tragedies take place in our world. The prophet expresses these emotions not only for himself but also for a community that is being hurled out of its homeland, a community that has become numb to the harsh realities of God's judgment. The language of this text would have given the community in exile the appropriate language to express its innermost feelings to God. The text would also have challenged the exiled people to confess their faith in God, who directs and shapes the future of his people even in the land of exile.

There is a close connection between Judah's sin and God's judgment of the nation in this text. However, we cannot conclude that this principle is applicable to every individual situation of tragedy and suffering. Whatever may be the cause of human suffering, the text gives us the language to speak to God. The prophet models for us how to speak to God in the midst of our deepest distress, how to express our pain and anguish, how to confess our inadequacy and failure, how to accept discipline from God, and how to let God be the judge of our enemies. Such openness with God is somewhat alien to our modern practice of prayer. Prayers such as these in the OT teach us that it is precisely in this way of prayer that we find it possible to imagine God's presence in the midst of our trouble-filled life. The experience of the reality of his presence gives us hope and turns our mourning into joy.

"UPROOT AND TEAR DOWN"

JUDAH'S COVENANT-BREAKING (11:1—12:17)

Overview

Chapter 11 introduces a new section in the book of Jeremiah. This section begins with a sermon addressed to the people of Judah/Jerusalem (11:1-17). The sermon begins with an announcement of Yahweh's curse on those who do not pay attention to **this covenant** and proceeds to describe the covenant violation of the past and present generations. The sermon ends with a harsh word of judgment that seems to give no hope to the nation. This is followed by a poetic lament or "confession" (vv 18-20) that reveals a plot against the prophet. This seems to provide a specific illustration of Judah's covenant-breaking activities (vv 1-17). Yahweh's speech in vv 21-23 is a response to the lament of the prophet. Jeremiah's lament ("confession") in 12:1-4 is most likely prompted by the plot against his life (11:18-20). Yahweh speaks again (12:5-6) in response to the prophet's lament. The poetic unit in vv 7-13 describes Yahweh's abandoning of his heritage and the enemies of Judah making the land a desolate place. The following prose unit (vv 14-17) balances the harsh words of judgment in the preceding unit with an announcement of Yahweh's judgment on the enemies that destroy his heritage. This speech, however, also makes a conditional promise that Yahweh will build up these nations if they would seek his ways.

1. The Broken Covenant (11:1-17)

BEHIND THE TEXT

This prose unit (with the exception of poetry in vv 15-16), which has the form of a sermon, focuses on the theme of covenant-breaking by Judah, and thus preserves a thematic continuity with the preceding chapters where Judah's unfaithfulness to Yahweh is a dominant concern. As in the previous chapters, here also we find the pronouncement of Yahweh's judgment upon Judah for breaking the covenant with him. This sermon shows several links to the language and theology of the book of Deuteronomy. Perhaps the most obvious relationship is the invoking of the covenant curse in Jer 11:3 following the pattern of the covenant curses in Deut 27—28.

Some commentators see this sermon as the work of Deuteronomistic redactors of the book and place it in the exilic/postexilic setting. Others, though they recognize similarities between this text and Deuteronomy, consider this text as a sermon that Jeremiah preached during the period of Josiah's religious reformation (Lundbom 1999, 615). Some earlier commentators have taken v 6 as an indication of Jeremiah as an itinerant preacher traveling throughout Judah and preaching this sermon in support of Josiah's reform activities. Bright identifies **this covenant** with the ratification of the Sinai covenant by Josiah but places the preaching of Jeremiah during the days of Jehoiakim (1965, 89; see also Thompson 1980, 343). He also thinks that the text in its present form belongs to the exilic setting, since v 8 seems to imply the destruction of Jerusalem (1965, 89). Holladay gives an extensive analysis of words and phrases in this sermon that show variation from Deuteronomistic phraseology and maintains the authenticity of the sermon as the words of Jeremiah (1986, 350-51). Holladay, however, places the sermon in the context of the recitation of Deuteronomy in the festival of booths in 594 B.C., and understands **this covenant** as a reference to the Sinai covenant (1986, 351-52). The repeated occurrence of **this covenant** may refer to the covenant renewed during the days of Josiah (see 2 Kgs 23:1-3), but there is no clear evidence that this was preached in support of the reform. The sermon implies that the reform activities did not accomplish long-lasting result and that the nation reverted to idolatry (Jer 11:9-11). It seems likely that the sermon was delivered in the years immediately following the religious revival when the spiritual fervor subsided in the land; the sermon aims to warn the people of the curses of the covenant. The people who have reneged on their covenant commitment are thus given a fair warning of the consequences of their action.

Influence of Deuteronomy in the Book of Jeremiah

Listed below are passages in Jer 1—25 that show significant similarities to themes and ideas in the book of Deuteronomy:

7:1—8:3	18:1-12
11:1-14	19:2-9, 11-13
13:1-14	21:1-10
16:1-15	22:1-5
17:19-27	25:1-14

The text of the sermon may be divided into at least four parts: vv 1-5, 6-8, 9-14, and 15-17. The first three parts are introduced with an introductory formula. The covenant is summarized in the first part of the sermon. The second part also contains a summary of the covenant with an added word that Judah has disobeyed Yahweh and therefore Yahweh has brought upon them the curses of the covenant. The third part relates Judah's disobedience to a conspiracy among the people. The warning of judgment is also given in this part. In the last part the judgment theme is dominant; serious disaster will come upon Judah for following other gods and worshipping Baal.

IN THE TEXT

■ **1-2** The sermon begins with the same introductory formula of 7:1 (see similar introductions in 18:1; 21:1; 30:1). Verse 2 begins with a summons to "hear the words of this covenant" (NRSV). The summons is given to **the people of Judah** and **the *citizens of* Jerusalem.** The citizens of Jerusalem receive special attention in this sermon, since the city and its leading citizens played a critical role in the leadership of Judah. The phrase **this covenant** is also found in vv 3, 6, and 8 (see also 2 Kgs 23:3). The goal of v 2 is to challenge the people to enter into a living relationship with Yahweh by reconnecting with the covenant made by their ancestors.

Covenant Theme in Jeremiah

Covenant is a recurring theme in Jeremiah. In 11:1-17 the focus is on fidelity to the covenant renewed by the people during the days of Josiah. The book also refers to Yahweh's covenant with Israel/Sinai covenant (14:21; 22:9; 34:13), the covenant with David and the Levites (33:20-22), the covenant with day and night (33:25), the covenant with the patriarchs (implied in 33:26), and the new covenant (31:31-34; see also reference to an everlasting covenant in 32:40; 50:5).

■ **3** Verse 3 identifies Yahweh **the God of Israel** as the One who is speaking to the people. He is the covenant God and what follows is the essence of the covenant he made with Israel at Mount Sinai. The sermon begins with a curse pronouncement, identical to the curse statements in Deut 27:15-26 (see also Gal 3:10). Obedience to the covenant is the basis for covenantal blessings; disobedience brings upon a person the curses of the covenant. This pronouncement implies that the people are already under the curse for breaking the covenant. The sermon also reminds the people that the **terms of this covenant** are not some new demands from Yahweh; they have always been a part of their history with

Yahweh. He gave these terms initially to the ancestors of the present generation when he **brought them out of** their bondage in **Egypt**. The sermon also reminds the people that their deliverance from Egypt was a mighty and gracious act. The phrase **iron . . . furnace** indicates the intensity of suffering Israel experienced when they were in Egypt.

■ **4** Verse 4 sums up the condition of the covenant. What was central to the Sinai covenant and the reenactment of it in this text is the call to **obey** and **do** everything Yahweh commanded his people to do. Fulfillment of this condition is essential to the fulfillment of Yahweh's promise, **you will be my people, and I will be your God**. The Yahweh-Israel relationship depends on Israel's commitment to live by the commandments and terms of the Sinai covenant.

■ **5** Israel's commitment to the covenant is essential to Yahweh's fulfillment of the **oath** he has made to its ancestors concerning the gift of **a land flowing with milk and honey** (v 5). The text implies the necessity of ongoing obedience in action for Judah's continued life in the land and enjoyment of the fruitfulness of the land. Jeremiah's response **Amen, Yahweh** is a personal recognition and acknowledgment of Yahweh's curse on those who refuse to live by the terms of the covenant. In Deut 27:15-26, this response comes from the people.

■ **6** In the second part of the sermon, we find a summary of the history of Israel (vv 6-8). Yahweh summons Jeremiah to speak the words of the covenant and admonish the people to **hear** and **do** the words of the covenant throughout Judah and Jerusalem (v 6). Verses 6-7 contain some of the elements of the first part, such as summons to speak to the people of Judah and Jerusalem, command to listen and obey the terms of the covenant, and reference to Yahweh's deliverance of Israel from Egypt.

■ **7** Verse 7 focuses on Yahweh's repeated warning from the beginning days of Israel's history until the present day to **obey** his *voice*. The past and present generations have been privileged to hear Yahweh's words (see 7:25).

■ **8** Verse 8 indicates that the response of the people to the consistent and repeated warnings of Yahweh was a deliberate decision to pay no attention to his words (see 7:23-26). The critical problem that Jeremiah sees in the history of Israel is summed up by the phrase **stubbornness of their evil *heart*.** What the people possess is not a pure, willing, obedient, submissive, responsive, and yielding heart, but a heart that is self-directed, autonomous, and thoroughly infected by evil. Judah's disobedience to Yahweh is an internal issue, an action that originates in its evil heart. Verse 8 concludes with the word about the unleashing of the power of the curse. **All the *words* of the covenant** are the curses pronounced upon those who violate the terms of the covenant. The Hebrew text implies Yahweh's judgment that came upon Israel in the past. Some commentators see here the destruction of Jerusalem (Carroll 1986, 269). The reference may be to all the past calamities that have come upon Israel and not necessarily the disaster of 587 B.C. In the Greek translation, most of vv 7 and 8 are lacking, and the Greek text reads here the failure of the present generation to hear and do the words of the covenant (the Greek translation has only the phrase "but they did not do" for v 8).

■ **9-10** The third part connects the present generation with those in the past who have violated the terms of the Sinai covenant (vv 9-14). Yahweh announces to Jeremiah that he has found a **conspiracy among the people of Judah and the citizens of Jerusalem** (v 9). Verse 10 indicates that this conspiracy is against Yahweh. The conspiracy involves the following: (1) they have made the decision to return to the lifestyle of iniquity and ignore Yahweh's words, which was characteristic of their ancestors; (2) they have followed after and served other gods; (3) they have broken the covenant that Yahweh had made with the ancestors. The reference to Judah along with Israel probably means here that Judah is now engaged in the covenant-breaking, the same sin committed by the northern kingdom people. The breaking of the Sinai covenant is clearly implied here. This is the first in a series of five instances where the language to "break covenant" occurs in Jeremiah (see also 14:21; 31:32; 33:20; 33:21; Stulman 2005, 123). Verses 9-10 together make clear that covenant-breaking on the part of Judah was not something that just happened by accident but was rather the result of a deliberate conspiracy, an outright revolt against Yahweh the covenant maker.

■ **11** Verse 11 vividly portrays the tragic consequence of covenant-breaking. The curses of the covenant are at work against the people who have broken the covenant. There will be no **escape** for Judah from the *evil* that Yahweh is about to bring upon those who have plotted to commit iniquity and violate the terms of the covenant. The broken covenant means nullification of protection and safety and all other promises of well-being guaranteed under the terms of the covenant. When disaster comes, the covenant breakers will naturally turn to Yahweh with their cry for help, in the hopes of being heard by the covenant maker. Yahweh's resolve is not to pay any attention to those who have refused to pay attention to him.

■ **12** When Yahweh rejects their cry, then the people will turn to their gods whom they served and worshipped for help (v 12). The gods whom they have trusted will not answer because they have no power to help or save their worshippers.

■ **13-14** Verse 13 indicates the proliferation of illegitimate places of worship that the people of Judah have set up to worship Baal. **Baal** is called here ***Shame*** (*bōšet*), a derogatory epithet also found in 3:24. Verses 12-13 contain language very similar to 2:27-28. Verse 14 is parallel to 7:16 where the prophet is forbidden to intercede for the people who have trusted in the temple and violated the terms of the covenant. Covenant-breaking nullified every aspect of the covenant protection, including the mediation and intercession of the prophets. There stands nothing and no one between Yahweh and those who have broken their covenant with him except the pronouncement of calamity.

■ **15** The final part of this sermon has two poetic verses (vv 15-16) and a concluding prose statement (v 17). Verses 15 and 16 are extremely difficult to make sense of (consult various translations for a reconstructed reading of the difficult Hebrew text, or translation based on the Greek text). A tentative translation of verse 15, following the breakdown of poetic lines in the JPS translation, is given below:

> *What is my beloved (doing) in my house?*
> *Her doing the plot—the many,*
> *Holy meat will pass away from you,*
> *because of your evil, then you will exult.*

The irony in v 15 is that Yahweh still refers to Israel as his beloved (*lîdîdî*; see the same word in the song of the vineyard in Isa 5:1). Yahweh questions what his people who have broken the covenant are doing in his temple. The question seems to have a sarcastic tone. This verse implies the illegitimate ways of worship in the temple as a **plot** or conspiracy against Yahweh in his own **house.** The relationship of the word **the many** (masculine plural) to the preceding word (**plot,** which is feminine singular) is not clear. Another difficulty is that the verb in the third line (**pass away**) is plural whereas the subject **holy meat** is singular. Lundbom thinks that "the many" is the primary subject, and he connects it with the verb and reads sacred meat as a secondary subject (thus "The many—also sacrificial flesh—will cease" [Lundbom 1999, 627-28]). Line 3 seems to be a judgment word; when judgment comes, worship will cease in the temple. **Holy** meat may simply refer to sacrifices of animals or the sacred portion of the meat that the worshipper was allowed to consume (see Hag 2:12 for the same phrase). Worship will cease in the temple because of the evil people committed there. **Then you will exult** is a difficult phrase; it does not make any sense in the context. Does it mean that the people will rejoice when the sacrificial worship ceases in the temple, or does it mean that they will rejoice in their evil deeds? The answer is not clear. The NIV reading seems to suggest that the sacrificial worship will not provide an escape to the people from the judgment and that the people rejoice when they are involved in their wicked deeds.

■ **16** Verse 16 is a judgment word that begins with a description of what Israel meant to Yahweh. Yahweh once called his people a **luxuriant olive tree** (see Hos 14:6 for the metaphor "olive tree" for Israel), beautiful of **fruit** and beautiful of **form.** Judgment will bring an end to Yahweh's relationship with Judah; this verse in Hebrew describes judgment as having already taken place (the use of perfect tense to indicate the certainty of the coming judgment). The nation that was once a source of joy and delight soon will be destroyed by the fire of judgment. The phrase **with a great roaring sound** indicates the shock and awe effect of the judgment.

■ **17** Verse 17 relates the judgment as Yahweh's doing; the one who **planted** Israel to be a "luxuriant olive tree" is the one who will set it on fire. Though the nation Babylon is the instrument of judgment, it is in reality **evil** (*rā'â*) that Yahweh brings against the nation that has committed **evil** (*rā'â*) against him.

The evil that Israel committed is its idolatry, the worship of Baal.

FROM THE TEXT

Fractured relationship with God is a key concern in this text. The text clearly presents the critical importance of hearing and doing the terms of the covenant to the relationship between God and his people. The text also makes clear that God's people failed to live by the terms of the covenant and thus forfeited the privileges inherent in the covenant relationship. The text describes Judah's covenant-breaking as a deliberate act, an intergenerational affair, and God as the humiliated covenant partner who is left with no choice but to impose upon his people the curses of the covenant. The once-beloved people of God whom he planted in the world to mediate grace to the world are threatened with destruction. The God whom they rejected will not hear their cry; the gods whom they served will not be able to help. Even the prophet is helpless to do anything to save them from destruction. The text is thus a stern warning to Jeremiah's audience that they are faced with a dangerous situation because of their long history of following other gods. The hidden assertion is that only a commitment to "hear" and "do" the terms of the covenant would avert the impending disaster.

The curses of the covenant at work remind us that God keeps the moral order he established for his people and that he holds them accountable for their actions. Moral conduct of the covenant community is a matter of deep concern to God. Though it may sound rigid and unloving, the truth is that the loving God will punish the unrighteous in the world. Israel's history in this text powerfully reminds us of the integral connection between our covenant with God and our moral and ethical responsibilities. Just as there are promises for faithful living, there are also stern reminders in the Bible about the severity of punishment for our moral and ethical infractions. This text warns us that "everyone to whom much has been given, much will be required" (Luke 12:48 NRSV). The text also reminds us that the call to covenant living is a call not only to "hear" the voice of God but also to "do" it. James admonishes his readers: "Do not merely listen to the word, and so deceive yourselves. Do what it says" (Jas 1:22). This hearing and doing is what in the end will lead to the realization of the promise of life, the alternative to the portrait of death in Jer 11:1-17.

The audience of this text in the exile would have found here the theological rationale for their exile and the destruction of their land. The text would also have reminded the people that they exist simply because of God's grace. Twice in the text we find reference to the gracious activity of God bringing Israel out of Egypt (vv 4, 7). Judah's future now depends on a second "exodus," God's gracious redemption of the exiled people from the land of their exile. This theme along with the establishment of a new covenant is the focus of the oracles in chs 30—31. Oracles in these chapters show that covenant-breaking on the part of Judah did not mean nullification of God's covenant with his people. In our hearing of this text today, we also need to hear the promises of the oracles in chs 30—31, particularly the new covenant promise in 31:31-34. In the midst of our unfaithfulness, God remains faithful to his covenant and initiates new possibilities for us to enter into a new covenant relationship with him. This is the good news we find in Jesus the mediator of the new covenant.

2. Jeremiah's Lament and Yahweh's Response (11:18—12:6)

BEHIND THE TEXT

Jeremiah 11:18—12:6 is mainly a conversation between Jeremiah and Yahweh. In this text we find Jeremiah's laments or "confessions" (11:18-20; 12:1-4), an oracle of judgment against the men of Anathoth (11:21-23), and Yahweh's word to Jeremiah about more difficult days to come (12:5-6). Jeremiah 12:1-6 does not flow smoothly with the preceding section; for this reason some commentators separate 11:18—12:6 into two distinct units (11:18-23 and 12:1-6). Jeremiah 11:18-23 most likely once existed as an independent unit. However, the following words and phrases and themes connect the two sections together: Yahweh's righteous judgment in 11:20 and Yahweh as righteous in 12:1; Yahweh testing the heart and inner parts in 11:20 and testing the heart in 12:3; prayer for Yahweh's vengeance in 11:20 and judgment of the enemy in 12:3; and the plot of the family against Jeremiah in 11:21 and 12:6; sheep to the slaughter in 11:18 and 12:3, the tree and its fruit in 11:19 and 12:2, the use of the word "cause" or "case," or *rib* in Hebrew in 11:22 and 12:1. These parallel expressions and themes justify the linking of these two passages together with its major emphasis on the plot against Jeremiah's life.

Because of the seemingly illogical order of the arrangement of the text (see 12:6 where the plot is revealed and 11:18 where Jeremiah is already aware of the plot), Bright places 12:1-6 before 11:18-23 (1965, 83-84). It is difficult to determine the date of this prophetic lament and Yahweh's response. Some commentators assume that the plot to kill Jeremiah by the people of Anathoth developed in the context of Josiah's reform activities (Lundbom 1999, 639). Other possible contexts that could have contributed to the plot against the prophet's life include his temple sermon in 609 B.C. (26:1) or the burning of the scroll by Jehoiakim in 605 B.C. (36:1). One should also remember that Jeremiah remained as a traitor to the whole nation and an embarrassment to his own family throughout his life. The placement of this lament in the literary and theological context of 11:1-17 seems to suggest that the proclamation of the covenant curse on the nation as a whole would have infuriated some of his family members to the point of taking action to silence the traitor among them.

IN THE TEXT

■ **18** Jeremiah's speech in vv 18-20 reveals that his life was in danger for speaking Yahweh's words. Verse 18 is difficult in that we are not told what Yahweh made known to Jeremiah; we assume that it is the plot of the people against his life given in v 19 (compare the NIV with the literal reading: ***Yahweh made me know and I knew; then you made me see their practices***). The identity of "you" in v 18*b* is not clear. Lundbom understands "you" to be another person, "a confidant" of the prophet "who told him of the plot after Yahweh made him aware of it" (1999, 636). It is likely that since the speech as a whole is addressed to Yahweh, "you" here refers to Yahweh. This verse conveys the general idea that Yahweh revealed to Jeremiah the ***practices*** or the "evil deeds" (NRSV) of the people against him.

■ **19** In v 19 the prophet indicates his total unawareness of the danger he was in, and that he did not know that the people had made a plot (lit. "they schemed schemes") against him. He was like a **gentle** or trusting **lamb led to the slaughter.** The imagery here is that of a sacrificial lamb that trustingly follows those who take it to be slaughtered as a sacrifice (see Isa 53:7). The imagery, however, does not quite fit the portrait of the prophet in the book, who fearlessly and passionately spoke against the evil in the land. The second part of v 19 sums up the plot. We assume that the words quoted here are the words of those who have made the plot against the prophet. The plot against Jeremiah is clear; what the enemy wants is his death. The imagery of destroying a tree with **its fruit** (lit. "bread") conveys the idea of destroying someone who is effective and prosperous in life. The goal of the enemies is to **cut** him down like a tree and make him disappear from **the land of the living** and together with it any memory of him so that no one would remember the prophet ever again (see Ps 83:4; Isa 53:8). One wonders how Jeremiah could have been completely oblivious to such a serious threat against his life before Yahweh revealed it to him.

■ **20** Like the conclusion of many of the lament psalms, the prophet ends his speech to Yahweh with an appeal to bring his enemies to his righteous judgment (v 20). The lament concludes with the confession that Yahweh has the power to bring proper judgment; the One to whom the prophet appeals is Yahweh, who is sovereign over the "hosts" (NRSV) of heaven and earth. Yahweh is also the righteous Judge, the One who will serve justice impartially to make things right (see Pss 7:11; 9:4; Zeph 3:4). Yahweh being the righteous judge determines the guilt and innocence not by the human standards but by **test**ing (*bōḥēn* means to "try" or "test"; see 6:27) the **mind** (*kĕlāyôt*, lit. "kidneys" or the most hidden part of a person's character, often translated as "mind") and **heart** (*lēb*, the seat of human emotions, thoughts, and feelings) of people. The prophet's conviction here is that Yahweh knows what is in the deepest part of his being concealed from others as well as what is in the inner being of his enemies (see Pss 7:9; 17:3; 26:2). The first part of v 20 is thus a claim of innocence by the prophet. If our assumption that the pronouncement of the curses of the covenant is the reason for the plot against his life, then the crime that he committed is his faithful proclamation of Yahweh's words. The hearts and minds of the people on the other hand are filled with evil plots and schemes. The appeal to Yahweh to carry out his **vengeance** upon his enemies is parallel to the psalmists' prayer to bring dishonor and shame to the enemy (Pss 35:4; 40:14; 70:2; 71:13). Yahweh's vengeance in the OT is not an act of revenge, rather the action by which the innocent is vindicated and the wicked is punished; Miller describes it as an "act of divine sovereignty and righteousness" (2001, 675). The appeal ends with the prophet confiding and committing his **cause** to Yahweh (see Ps 22:8). The prophet remains true to the tradition of the righteous to appeal to Yahweh for help rather than taking matters into his own hands.

■ **21** In vv 21-23, Yahweh responds to the prophet and identifies the men of Anathoth as those who are plotting to kill him, and pronounces his judgment against them. The text is not clear on the specific issue that brought antagonism from the town of Anathoth to Jeremiah's preaching. Some commentators assume that Jeremiah's support for the reform, which included the centralization of worship and the destruction of illegitimate sanctuaries, may have been the reason for the plot against his life. This would have included the cultic places in Anathoth where his family members may have served as priests. What is clear is their ban on the prophet's preaching in Yahweh's name. The preceding unit (11:1-17) strongly suggests that Jeremiah's pronouncement of the covenant curses may very well have been the issue here. **Do not prophesy in the name of Yahweh** is a stern warning and prohibition. The authorized prophet and even Yahweh come under the censure of the people of Anathoth.

■ **22-23** Yahweh has heard the prophet's appeal for his righteous judgment and vengeance on his enemies (vv 22-23). The divine name **Yahweh of hosts** indicates that the one who pronounces judgment has the resources to carry out his word; no power in the world can stop him from fulfilling the judgment word against the men of Anathoth. Those who plotted to cut Jeremiah off from the land of the living are faced with the same fate. Yahweh's judgment is coming upon them, which will bring an end to the whole town of Anathoth. Enemy invasion will kill its young men; the famine that follows the siege of the town will kill its young women. The evil they have plotted against Jeremiah will come upon them; this **disaster** will leave no **remnant** for the people of Anathoth.

■ **12:1** The second part of the confession begins with Jeremiah's speech to Yahweh (12:1-4). Jeremiah affirms that Yahweh is righteous [*ṣaddîq*; see Yahweh who judges "righteously" (*šōpēṭ ṣedeq*) in 11:20]. Verse 1 presents the speech as a dispute with Yahweh (the clause **when I make a case to you** has a judicial tone; see *rîbî* or "my case" in 11:20 and *'ārîb* or **I make a case** here). In the second part of 12:1, the prophet confronts Yahweh with his own ***judgments*** about the way in which Yahweh's justice works in the world. The prophets' judgments begin with a question, which asserts that the wicked prosper and the evildoers enjoy peace and rest in the world. The charge being made here is that what he observes in the world is contrary to the expectation of the righteous. What he expects to find in the world is the prosperity of the righteous and the suffering of the wicked, but it is simply not the case (see Job 12:6; 21:7-16). It is unlikely that Jeremiah had some particular people or group in mind; the reference to the **wicked** and those ***who deal treacherously*** may be applied to all the unfaithful people in the land.

■ **2** The prophet's judgments become more serious and direct in v 2. He charges Yahweh with the responsibility for planting the wicked and allowing them to establish themselves and **grow and bear fruit.** Here he traces the prosperity of the wicked to Yahweh's direct or indirect involvement. The second part of v 2 conveys the dishonest relationship the wicked maintain with Yahweh. Their words give all the appearance of their devotion to Yahweh and their proximity to him; yet they remain at a great distance away from him in their inner being. Yahweh makes a similar assessment of the contemporaries of Isaiah for whom religion meant external formalities without any internal commitment and devotion to him (Isa 29:13).

■ **3** The prophet claims that everything about him has been openly known to Yahweh (v 3*a*). The goal here is to contrast himself with the wicked who act deceitfully in their relationship with Yahweh. Unlike the wicked that are known for duplicity in their relation to Yahweh, he stands in a close relationship with Yahweh, a person known (*yādaʿ*; see 1:5) and seen by him. The second line of v 3 in Hebrew reads: **you have tested my heart with you** (see 11:20 on Yahweh testing the heart). The goal of Yahweh's testing is to clear the prophet of any guilt or to determine if his heart is right with Yahweh. The claim of being known, seen, and tested by Yahweh indicates total transparency and integrity on the part of the prophet; he is innocent of any wrongdoing. Underlying this claim of innocence is the protestation that in spite of his integrity, there is a plot against him. Verse 3*b* is an appeal to Yahweh to deal with the wicked in the same way they have planned to bring Jeremiah's life to an end. He urges Yahweh to **pull them out** or separate them **like sheep . . . to the slaughter.** The plot of the wicked is to kill him; therefore, they should be treated with the same fate. The last line (**set them apart for the day of slaughter**) repeats the same idea; the verb "set apart" is usually found in a cultic context, but here there is no cultic association. Holladay notes that the only other occurrence of the causative form of *qādaš* ("set apart") is in 1:5 where the verb is used to announce Yahweh's consecration of Jeremiah. Jeremiah may be suggesting that in the same way Yahweh consecrated him for his service, now he must consecrate the wicked for the day of their destruction (Holladay 1986, 378). Sanctifying the wicked for destruction reflects the ancient idea of *cherem* that Israel was commanded to follow in their war against the Canaanites (Deut 7:2). Calling for Yahweh's just retribution is a part of laments in the psalms (see Pss 10:15; 17:13-14; 109:6-20). Jeremiah borrows the judgment language from the judgment words of Yahweh (see 7:32; 19:6); the prophet agrees with Yahweh on the matter of the fate of the wicked (Fretheim 2002, 193).

■ **4** In v 4 the prophet sums up the impact of the sin of the wicked on the land, vegetation, animals, and birds. He begins with the question **how long,** which is often an expression of frustration, hopelessness, and impatience in the lament psalms (see 4:21; Pss 6:3; 74:10). Because of the evil committed by the wicked and because of their pride and self-confidence in their future, the whole land and everything in it face serious danger (see Hos 4:1-3). Drought and destruction of vegetation is most likely the subject of the first two lines. Even the animal world is threatened with extinction. Jeremiah ends his lament with the claim of the people that **he** (Yahweh) **will not see** their **end.** This is the arrogant thinking of the wicked that Yahweh pays no attention to their actions; they reject the traditional claim of Yahweh's punishment of the wicked. The aim of this lament is to urge Yahweh to take action against the wicked for the sake of the land and the animals that inhabit the land.

■ **5** Yahweh's response to Jeremiah is not at all assuring or comforting, but rather alarming (vv 5-6). Yahweh responds with two questions, each of which is aimed to portray a future that will be extremely difficult and troublesome for the prophet (v 5). The questions contain metaphors that compare the present with what lies ahead. Life now is like a footrace, and living in a land of peace; in both instances the prophet shows signs of weariness and weakness. What awaits him is a future where he will be faced with harsher realities of life; he will encounter severe opposition that is much harder to handle. Life will be like racing with horses or trying to get through the **thickets of the Jordan** ($g\check{e}$'$\hat{o}n$, translated here as "thickets," lit. "pride"; earlier commentators understood the word to mean "swelling"; see the NIV footnote that gives the alternate reading "the floods of"). The phrase refers to an area along the Jordan River where there is a thick growth of trees, bushes, and reeds due to the overflow of the river during winter and spring; this jungle-like region would have been home for different wild animals (Holladay 1986, 382). This verse reminds the prophet that things will get really worse and that he must prepare himself for dangerous days that are yet to come.

■ **6** Verse 6 identifies the prophet's immediate family members among those who are involved in the plot against his life. The previously mentioned "men of Anathoth" may have been just his family members. His **brothers** may have been part of a larger group that included others from the village. The very same people who should have protected the prophet from his enemies have become his enemies. They have turned against him and are in pursuit of him with a **loud cry.** He should not hope for help from his brothers; neither should he **trust them** when they speak good words. Treachery is found all over the nation, even within his own family. They will talk to him the way they relate to Yahweh, with words of praise in their mouth but with a heart that is far removed from him.

FROM THE TEXT

The laments of the prophet in this section reveal the traditional Israelite response to suffering. The language of the laments here reflects the language of the laments in the book of Psalms. The text relates the lament and questions of not only the prophet but also of the people in exile and all who confront the reality of evil in the world.

The prophet's laments come to us as prayers of a troubled soul, prayers that express a variety of human emotions. The prophet who is too preoccupied with God's word does not recognize the dangerous outcome of his preaching. He compares himself to a lamb led to the slaughter, a description that conveys the attitude and conduct of God's servants who are willing to risk their lives for obedience (see Isa 53:7; Acts 8:32-35). In the context of threat against his life, he does two things: first, he affirms his innocence; and second, he calls upon God to act according to his righteousness and bring judgment upon those who are seeking his life. Jeremiah's prayer is specific and to the point. What is at stake is his life, and he commits his case to God. There is no anger or vendetta expressed here, but only an earnest prayer for God's righteous judgment upon those who are seeking to destroy an innocent life. Jeremiah's laments in this text show us how to pray when we are victims of harassment and persecution.

Suffering of the innocent, particularly suffering for the sake of God, is a key issue in these laments. Jeremiah's life is in danger because of his call, his commitment to the prophetic ministry, and his faithfulness to God. Throughout the Bible we find persecution and death threat almost as a natural response of the world to those who are faithful to God. In Christian theology, suffering is often understood as the way of discipleship (Mark 8:34-38). Paul considered "the fellowship of sharing in his [Christ's] sufferings" as one of his primary goals of life (Phil 3:10). Proclaiming the message of Christ meant hardship for the apostle throughout his life, including life in prison in the final years of his life (2 Cor 11:24-28; Col 4:2). Christians in countries where freedom and democracy prevail may not fully grasp the connection between suffering and the call to Christian discipleship, but it is a reality that thousands of Christians encounter in their everyday life in many parts of our world. Even in countries where there is religious freedom, Christians often suffer indignity and ridicule for bearing Christ's name. The innocent suffering of Jeremiah, Jesus Christ, Paul, and others in the Bible is a pattern and comfort to all who suffer for the sake of the gospel in the world, particularly in world areas where preaching the gospel is met with great opposition and often the threat of death.

Jeremiah raises the question of God's justice, but the issue is not resolved in this lament. God does not even address the issue, but rather leaves the question unanswered as he does in Job. The prophet recognizes God as a righteous God, but he is puzzled by the prosperity of the wicked. This theological ambiguity is never resolved in the Bible. We continue to live in the tension between faith in God's righteousness and the alarming growth of evil in the world. For Jeremiah this tension was very real. God's word did not give him any comfort, but it only made things look worse. God's challenge to Jeremiah was that he must continue to face evil. What is important here is that God responds to the prophet's troubling questions, perhaps not with the answer the prophet had hoped to hear but with an answer that conveyed to the prophet the reality of God's presence with him every step of the way. What would make it possible for the prophet to survive the jungles of the Jordan is not his own strength but the strength that comes from God. He cannot trust his human brothers, but he can certainly trust God. Sometimes a different answer from God to our specific prayers may be what we need to hear to face difficult challenges in life and to gain new perspectives about life. In a strange way God gave these words to Paul, who made repeated requests to take away from him a thorn that was tormenting him, "My grace is sufficient for you, for my power is made perfect in weakness" (2 Cor 12:9). This in the end is the best answer and the best response to the problem of evil in the world.

3. Yahweh's Lament (12:7-13)

BEHIND THE TEXT

Jeremiah 12:7-13 is a divine soliloquy, a lament that depicts Yahweh's personal loss, somewhat akin to Jeremiah's lament in 10:19-22. The repeated occurrences of "my" (eight times) show the intense emotional connection that Yahweh has with his people and thus the intensity of his personal loss. The NIV uses the future tense throughout, though the Hebrew verbs in perfect tense indicate events that have already happened (see NRSV). The text indicates the desolation of the land by an enemy invasion. It is very likely that an actual situation is reflected in the text, though it is difficult to give a precise date. Lundbom and Bright place the text in the years 598-597 B.C. Holladay assigns the text to 605 B.C. or immediately thereafter (Lundbom 1999, 660; Bright 1965, 88; Holladay 1986, 386). The opening phrase "I have forsaken my house" (NRSV) seems to indicate the events of 587 B.C. Those who view "my house" as a reference to the temple date the text to a date after 587 B.C.

IN THE TEXT

■ **7** Verse 7 is both a lament and a judgment word that reflects Yahweh's mixed emotions. On the one hand, the text conveys sorrow and grief over the loss of that which is near and dear to Yahweh; on the other hand, it is clear that what has happened to the people is the result of his judgment upon them. Three times the text refers to Yahweh's judgment (**forsaken, abandoned, given**); three times the text refers to the object of the judgment as something very close to Yahweh (**my house,** *my heritage, the beloved of my soul*). Taken separately these three phrases have different meanings; **house** refers to the temple, *heritage* refers to the land, and *the beloved of my soul* refers to the people. **Heritage** sometimes also refers to Yahweh's people as in vv 8-9. Taken together, these phrases refer to the entirety of the land and the people, including the Jerusalem temple. What was once Yahweh's own is now in the ***hand*** of **enemies.** It is not that the enemy overpowered Yahweh and forcefully took what belonged to him, but rather he handed it over to the enemy. Yahweh has forsaken his people and everything that stood as symbols of his relationship with them. Forsaking, abandoning, and giving into the hand of the enemy all indicate the fate of those who have forsaken and abandoned Yahweh and followed other gods.

Heschel on God's Homelessness

> The Lord Who had dwelt in the midst of Israel was abandoning His dwelling place. But should Israel cease to be His home, then God, we might say, would be without a home in the world. (2001, 143)

■ **8** Verse 8 gives the reason for Yahweh's decision to hand his people over to the enemy. The people of Yahweh have become **like a lion.** The metaphor of lion is used in various ways in the OT; sometimes to describe the enemy (2:15), sometimes to describe Yahweh (Hos 5:14), and sometimes to describe the people, as in this text (see also Jer 2:30). In 2:30 the people have attacked the prophets like a "ravening lion." Yahweh is the prey in this text. The people have raised their voice or roared against Yahweh, a defiant act that brings his condemnation and hatred toward them. The accusation is perhaps about the defiant attitude of the people toward Yahweh through their outright and rebellious acts of covenant-breaking. The "beloved" people of Yahweh have thus become the hated people, the object of Yahweh's displeasure (see Hos 9:15 for a much stronger expression, "I will no longer love them" following the words "I hated them"). In Hosea and in Jeremiah, it is clear that Yahweh's love for his people does not come to an end, though he hates them (see Hos 11:8-9; Jer 31:3). Fretheim explains divine hate here as his treatment of the people as his enemy and not as his beloved (2002, 196).

■ **9** Verse 9 begins with two rhetorical questions that imply that Judah has become to Yahweh like a bird of prey and that he is using other nations to attack and destroy it. Some commentators translate the word $ṣābûa'$ to mean "hyena" based on the Greek translation. The NIV **speckled** follows the traditional translation and treats $ṣābûa'$ as a passive participle, which we prefer in this context. This verse ends with the command given by Yahweh to all the animals of the field to come and take part in the destruction of his people. The animal metaphors suggest that various nations will participate in bringing the downfall of Judah. The people who have been hostile to Yahweh will face intense hostility—not of one nation but of many nations. The final line of the verse indicates total destruction.

■ **10** The imagery shifts from wild animals to shepherds as instruments of judgment in v 10. Most commentators understand **shepherds** as a reference to foreign rulers, though the likelihood of Judah's kings cannot be ruled out. If the latter group is intended, then the verse holds the kings of Judah accountable for trampling and destroying the land. The context seems to prefer the foreign rulers and their army commanders. This verse conveys the deep sense of Yahweh's personal loss (use of **my** three times). Yahweh's **vineyard**, his ***portion***, his **pleasant *portion*** all refer to the land. The ruthless forces of the enemy by their trampling of the land and destruction of crops have turned the beautiful and productive property of Yahweh into a **desolate *desert***. This was done at the command of Yahweh, and yet he still suffers and mourns the loss.

■ **11** Verse 11 continues the theme of the desolation of the land brought upon by the invading armies. The repeated use of the word **desolate** (šĕmēmâ in v 10, and three times in v 11) suggests finality—total ruin of the land as an uninhabitable place. In Hebrew, v 11 expresses the intensity of Yahweh's grief over the desolation of the land with a series of similar-sounding words (śāmāh lišmāmâ . . . šĕmēmâ, nāšammâ . . . 'îš śām—"he made it desolate . . . desolate, made desolate . . . he lays"). The subject of the first verb is singular (śāmāh, lit. "he made it," which most translations change into plural ("he" to "they"; the NIV preserves the singular but gives the verb in the active a passive meaning). The subject of the verb in the first line is thus understood as the "shepherds" mentioned in the previous verse. If the singular subject is maintained, then the reference could be to Nebuchadnezzar (Lundbom 1999, 657). The second line seems to suggest that the land mourns to Yahweh concerning its desolate condition (see NRSV). This verse ends with Yahweh's lament over the fact that no one in the land seems to care about the totally desolate condition of the land.

■ **12** Verse 12 indicates that the enemy that is ravaging and making the land a desolate place is Yahweh's sword, the instrument of divine judgment. **Bare heights** in 3:2 refer to places of idolatry, but here and in 4:11 this phrase refers to the direction from which the enemy comes. Destroyer forces are marching throughout the land, from one end to the other, inflicting serious injury to the people of the land with the **sword** of Yahweh. The enemy invasion has brought not only destruction but also an end to **peace** or well-being (šālôm) to everyone (***there is no peace to anyone***) in the land.

■ **13** The agricultural imagery in v 13 further illustrates the desolation of the land. All human work to bring about a good harvest will end in failure because of the desolate and unproductive condition of the land. Those who plant **wheat** will end up harvesting **thorns**. Failed harvest means the people are reaping the consequence of their evil actions. Thorns and thistles is what the land will produce when the people will break their covenant with Yahweh (see Gen 3:18). The whole land and the people are faced with Yahweh's **fierce anger** because of the evil they have committed against him. The second part of the verse is a direct speech to the people. Yahweh tells the people to **be ashamed** of their failed **harvest**. The harvest failure is directly linked to the anger of Yahweh, which is not an emotional reaction, but Yahweh's just and righteous response to those who have violated the covenant. The people have brought this shame upon themselves by their evil deeds. There will be no šālôm to the people (v 12); neither will there be šālôm to the land.

FROM THE TEXT

The text focuses on two key issues: God's abandonment of his home, land, and people, and the desolation of the land. Both of these issues bring grief to God. God not only grieves but also recognizes the realities that the land faces—utter desolation, killing, and failed harvest, which no one in the land seems to care about.

The text raises the serious question of why God gave up his home, land, and people for the exilic audience. It may be difficult for us to assume how God could have given up his possession. The God of Jeremiah and the God in this text is a God who owns everything—everything belongs to him, yet he does not tightly hold on to them, but gives them up. He does not "micromanage" or "intervene" in "every little thing" to hold his control over the affairs of the land, but he "delegates responsibility for the land" to the people with whom he has made a covenant (Fretheim 2002, 199). God's forsaking of everything stems not from the fact that he was impotent to keep the ownership of his property, but from the failure of the covenant people to manage things as faithful custodians of God's land. The text tells us that the custodians of the land have turned against God like roaring lions and thus brought upon the land the present crisis. Desolation of the land is God's doing, but it is the direct consequence of the people's rejection of their responsibility to be caretakers of the land that God has given to them. Jeremiah's contemporaries as well as the exilic community would have seen in this text the terrible hurt their actions have brought not only upon themselves and their land but also upon God. The community in exile that was grieving over the loss of everything would have found in this text a fellow sufferer, a God who, like themselves, is afflicted, displaced, and homeless in the world (Heschel 2001, 142). The presence of their displaced God would have given them comfort and hope for the restoration of all that was lost.

The text speaks to the modern readers in several ways. The thought of God abandoning the beautiful houses we have built for him, our lands, and us is an uncomfortable one. Yet the reality is that the "household of God" does not have immunity from judgment (1 Pet 4:17 NRSV). In Christian theology, God's forsaking of his Son is the ultimate expression of divine displacement (Matt 27:46; Mark 15:34). The Gospels also present the displaced and forsaken God on the cross as the source of comfort and hope and peace to all who are forgotten, forsaken, exiled, and displaced in the world. God's personal loss is thus indeed a great gain for the sinful world.

4. A Call to Conversion (12:14-17)

BEHIND THE TEXT

Jeremiah 12:14-17 is a prose unit. The text speaks about the fate of the nations and Israel both in terms of their uprooting and building up again. Commentators disagree on the question of the authenticity of these verses. Most commentators attribute these verses to later editors, though there is support for authenticity in the commentaries of Thompson, Holladay, and Lundbom. A key issue is the theme of the nations coming to the faith of Israel, which according to some commentators reflects a postexilic development. The text seems to show these verses as authentic to Jeremiah. There are a number of words and phrases ("uproot," "build," "heritage," "As Yahweh lives") that are part of Jeremiah's vocabulary. The theme of Judah's restoration is also central to the book in chs 30—33. Restoration of other nations is a theme found in the Oracles Against the Foreign Nations (see 46:26; 48:47; 49:6, 39). In 3:16, the prophet speaks of the nations gathering in Jerusalem to honor the name of Yahweh (see also 16:19-21; Isa 2:2-4; Mic 4:1-3). There seems to be no compelling reason to treat these verses as a later addition to the book. The text anticipates future events, and it could be placed in the period between 597 and 587 B.C. (see Holladay 1986, 391).

IN THE TEXT

■ **14** The oracle is about the evil neighbors of Israel whom Yahweh calls **my evil neighbors** (v 14). Yahweh regards Israel's neighbors as "my neighbors" because Israel is "my heritage," "my vineyard," and "my portion" to Yahweh (see 12:7-10 NRSV). The identity of the neighboring countries is not given; perhaps the reference is to all the surrounding countries that were allies or supporters of Babylon in its campaign against Judah. The lack of reference to particular nations makes it difficult to say whether Babylon is among the evil neighbors; however, the geographical distance of Babylon from Judah does not necessarily exclude Babylon from the group. All who **attack** the land of Israel are included here. The land is Yahweh's **heritage,** which he has given to his people as a **heritage.** Yahweh announces his plan to uproot his enemies from their land. The verb form of **uproot** (*ntš*) occurs five different times in vv 14-17. This verb form is part of the call and commission of Jeremiah (see 1:10). Yahweh is active in the history of the nations in and through the prophetic ministry of Jeremiah. The uprooting in this verse is his judgment upon the evil conduct of Judah's neighboring nations. Though Yahweh is the One who is calling the nations to attack Judah elsewhere in the book, here the text affirms that the nations themselves will be judged by Yahweh, the righteous judge and the sovereign Lord of the nations. The uprooting of the nations implies the exile of the people from their lands (see the exile of the nations as a theme in chs 46—51). The word about the uprooting of **the house of Judah** is difficult to interpret; most commentators see Judah's uprooting from the midst of the nations as an announcement of Yahweh's rescue of the Jews from the lands of their exile. The verb **uproot,** which has a negative connotation in Jeremiah, is used in a positive sense in reference to Judah in this verse.

■ **15** Verse 15 announces Yahweh's intention to show grace and compassion to the nations he uprooted from their lands. Yahweh will show **compassion** (*rḥm*, a characteristic quality of Yahweh; see Judah's restoration as an act of compassion in Isa 54:7-8) to the nations and bring the exiled people back to their homelands. No particular reason is given for Yahweh's compassion to the nations; no call for repentance is found either. The nations with whom Yahweh does not have a covenant relationship are also given the promise of restoration simply as an act of grace. Chapters 46—51 reiterate this theme.

■ **16** Verses 16 and 17 are conditional in nature. Yahweh announces that the nations will be *built up* and will have a future if they will take part in the covenant way of the life of his people (v 16). The theme of "building up" is the opposite of "uprooting" introduced in 1:10. If this condition is met, then the nations will have a future and they will enjoy prosperity. The specific call is to adopt the covenant faith of Israel. The people who have led Israel to become Baal worshippers are called here to make a radical departure from their idolatrous way of life and to learn from Israel the ways of Yahweh. The underlying hope expressed here is that the restored Israel will establish itself as a faithful community.

■ **17** Verse 17 introduces the second "if" statement, the alternative to the choice of obedience and faithfulness to Yahweh. This verse announces the uprooting and destruction of the nations if they fail to respond to the call to follow the covenant way of life. This text thus ends with the threat of the destruction of the nations that do not recognize the sovereignty of Yahweh. The nations thus receive here a gracious invitation as well as a solemn warning.

FROM THE TEXT

The text speaks judgment against the enemies of God and the enemies of his people. We should not hasten to think that Israel somehow receives special treatment when God deals with its neighbors. It is very clear in Jeremiah and in other prophets that judgment of the nations come after God's judgment of Israel. The message of this text is that the nations that God used as instruments of his judgment against Israel are not immune or safe or exempt from the exercise of God's sovereign judgment. All the nations that fail to acknowledge him as God will be judged. However, the good news to the nations is that they also stand to receive his compassion. He will be compassionate to the nations just as he is compassionate to Israel. Judgment and compassion are served equally to both Israel and the nations. Just as he will bring Israel back to its homeland, he will bring the exiled nations back to their homelands. The goal of God is not to keep Israel and the nations apart from each other but to bring them together as a community of faith—teaching and learning the ways of God—his Torah, his gracious will for their life. Everyone who is willing to obey the ways of God is given the opportunity to experience God's compassion. There is only one standard with which God will deal with both Israel and the nations—that is the standard of covenant living.

The exilic community would have heard in this text the promise of its restoration and the role it was destined to play in reorienting the nations to covenant faith in God and in creating a common community of faith with shared promises from God. To what extent the postexilic Israel appropriated and advanced this message is not clear, though we know that the door was open for non-Jews to be admitted into the faith of Israel later in Israel's history. The future envisioned and promised in this text is the goal of the preaching of the Christian gospel. Paul makes clear in Gal 3:28-29 that all who "belong to Christ" are "Abraham's offspring, heirs according to the promise" (NRSV).

"UPROOT AND TEAR DOWN"

JUDAH'S PRIDE (13:1-27)

Overview

The prose and poetic materials in ch 13 are linked together by the theme of Judah's pride and Yahweh's plan to bring humiliation to Judah. The symbolic act in 13:1-7 and Yahweh's subsequent judgment word (vv 8-11) vividly portray Judah as a nation of great pride that stubbornly follows the path of idolatry. The prose speech in vv 12-14 announces Yahweh's destruction of Judah without showing any pity or compassion. The theme of "ruin" (Hebrew *šaḥ at*) in vv 7, 9, and 14 connects these units together. There are three poetic oracles in the second part of this chapter (vv 15-17, 18-19, 20-27). The first oracle is an appeal to the nation to abandon its pride and give glory to Yahweh before the judgment comes. The second oracle conveys the humiliation of the royal family and exile of the nation. The third oracle also focuses on the shame and humiliation of the nation because of its pride and persistent evil conduct.

Prophets and Symbolic Actions

The OT prophets occasionally delivered messages from Yahweh to Israel through symbolic acts, dramatic actions performed to give a visual presentation of the message being communicated (see Isa 20; Ezek 4; 12; Hos 1; 3; etc., for some well-known examples). It is likely that in most cases the performances were observed by an audience, but in some cases they may have been private deeds. Usually the narrative of the symbolic act will contain Yahweh's command to perform a deed, a report of the act, and an interpretation of the symbolic act in the form of an oracle from Yahweh.

1. The Ruined Loincloth (13:1-11)

BEHIND THE TEXT

Jeremiah 13:1-11 is the first in the series of several symbolic actions in Jeremiah (see 18:1-12; 19:1-13; 27:2-11; 28:1-11; 32:1-44). Verses 1-7 of ch 13 contain a series of three commands (vv 1, 4, 6) followed by a report of the prophet's obedience to Yahweh's commands (vv 2, 5, 7). Verses 1-7 are in autobiographical form. Yahweh speaks in vv 8-11 and gives the interpretation and meaning of the symbolic act. The text does not make clear that this symbolic act was observed by an audience (see the symbolic act in 19:1-13 where Yahweh instructs the prophet to take "some of the elders of the people and of the priests" [19:1] to go with him to watch his action). It is difficult to place the text in a specific historical setting. Holladay locates the text around 605 B.C. (Holladay 1986, 395-96); Lundbom places the original setting of this narrative in the early part of the prophet's ministry, during the reign of Josiah (Lundbom 1999, 671). This act was probably performed sometime around 597 B.C. to warn the people about the ruin of their pride.

IN THE TEXT

■ 1 The text begins with Yahweh's command to Jeremiah to buy and wear a **linen *loincloth*,** a garment piece that is worn on the loins. The interpretation of the symbolic act in v 11 describes the loincloth as clinging to the loins, which means that this was an undergarment that touched the skin of the prophet. The importance of linen is not clear; leather or wool also could have been used for undergarments (see 2 Kgs 1:8; Hos 2:9). Linen garments were part of the priestly attire (Exod 28:39). Some commentators see here an indication of Israel's vocation in the world as a kingdom of priests. The linen garment may have been a prized possession of an individual because it is made of expensive and fine-quality material. The interpretation of the analogy in v 11 seems to support the idea that Israel was Yahweh's prized possession. Heschel suggests that the central meaning of this symbolic act is in Yahweh's command to Jeremiah to put the loincloth on his loins. "The prophet must learn to feel for himself God's intimate attachment to Israel; he must not only know about it, but experience it from within" (2001, 149). Yahweh also commanded Jeremiah not to **dip it in water.** The command is not to wash and make the loincloth clean after wearing it, so that it will remain on the prophet's loins as a dirty garment.

■ **2-4** Verse 2 reports the prophet's obedience to Yahweh's command. Verse 3 reports Yahweh's word coming a second time; we assume a considerable amount of time elapsed between the first and second encounters with Yahweh. The command this time is to take the loincloth and go to **Perath** and **hide it** in a **crevice in the** *rock* (v 4).

Perath in the OT

Perath is usually found in the OT with the word "river," and it is understood to mean the Euphrates; this text is the only place in the OT where the word occurs without "river" or reference to a geographical location (Lundbom 1999, 668). The lack of reference to "river" together with the distance from Judah to Euphrates and the time it would have taken Jeremiah to make two journeys to Euphrates have prompted commentators to identify Perath in this text with *Khirbet fāra* (ancient Parah; Josh 18:23), three miles northeast of Anathoth (Lundbom 1999, 669). The location, however, creates problems for commentators who think that Jeremiah traveled to Perath/Euphrates to dramatically convey to Judah the message of the Babylonian exile. But the interpretation of this act does not include any reference to the coming exile, but only the ruining of the pride of Judah.

■ **5-7** Verse 5 is a report of the prophet's obedience to Yahweh's command. The act of hiding perhaps indicates burying it in the ground, since in the next verse he reports about digging out the loincloth. Verse 6 contains another command from Yahweh in which Jeremiah was commanded to go to Perath again and retrieve the loincloth. The time lapsed between the second and the third command from Yahweh is not specified; **many days** could mean a long period of time. Jeremiah did as he was commanded, and retrieved the ruined and totally useless loincloth, which was perhaps starting to disintegrate and break up (v 7). His prized possession has no longer any value or use for him or anyone else.

■ **8-9** As usual, the symbolic action is followed by a word from Yahweh (vv 8-11). Verse 8 is the usual introductory formula. Verses 9-11 contain the message from Yahweh. Just as the linen loincloth was ruined, Yahweh makes it known that he will **ruin the pride** of his people (v 9). The people of Yahweh will suffer utter humiliation. Whatever Judah took pride in—its religious and political claims—will be taken away from the people, resulting in shame and disgrace. How and when this will come upon the nation is not clear. Some commentators see here an indication of the judgment of the exile.

■ **10** Verse 10 makes clear the reason for the judgment. The nation of Judah is made up of **wicked people who refuse** to hear Yahweh's **words.** Instead, they have taken a path according to the dictates of their stubborn **hearts,** resulting in their pursuit of **other gods.** They have offered themselves as servants and worshippers of these gods and have thus violated the covenant with Yahweh. Therefore, their destiny will be like that of the ruined linen loincloth. Yahweh indicates that this people will be of no use to anyone.

■ **11** The message from Yahweh ends with a reminder of his past relation to Israel and Israel's refusal to live by the terms of the covenant (v 11). He kept the people of both kingdoms—the whole nation—***close*** to him in an intimate relationship with him. The Hebrew verb used here (*dbq*) is also found in Gen 2:24, which speaks of a man leaving his parents and clinging to his wife. Holladay puts it this way: "Yahweh intended Israel to be as close to him as wife to husband" (Holladay 1986, 397). The theological significance of the loincloth is clear in this verse. It simply conveys the inseparable and intimate relationship Yahweh once had with Israel through the covenant relationship. He called Israel to be a **people** who would reveal his ***name***—his character and power—to the world (see Deut 28:10). Israel was to be the object of Yahweh's **praise** and ***glory***. Israel ruined itself and became useless to Yahweh by their habitual rejection of his voice. It no longer clings to Yahweh in a covenant relationship.

FROM THE TEXT

This symbolic act would have reminded its first audience of Yahweh's assessment of the ruined condition of their relationship with him. The long history of the nation's covenant-breaking has disrupted and ruined the relationship between God and Israel. The exilic community would have heard in this narrative the theological rationale for the national ruin and disintegration of its religious and political system. Though the exiled people would have seen themselves as the ruined loincloth hidden in Babylon, the text would also have suggested to them that their future depends on their willingness to cling to God—to reenter into a relationship with God characterized by loyalty and devotion to him. Both its first audience and the exilic audience would have also sensed in the text God's disappointment with the way his relationship with Israel has turned out. There is nothing in this text that brings joy to God, but it conveys only the sadness he experiences because of Israel's failure to *cling* to him in a relationship of intimacy and inseparableness.

The text speaks to its modern readers in several ways. First, the loincloth analogy makes clear that God's relationship with his people is inseparable and intimate; they are highly valued by him. The language of *clinging* calls for love, loyalty, devotion, faithfulness, and commitment to our relationship with him. The text also indicates that the people of God are the object of his pride; he is the object of their praise. Second, the emphasis on "ruin" in this text indicates the possibility of a "ruined relationship" with God. No matter what religious or theological or cultural claims we make, our sins will ruin our relationship with God, resulting in our own ruin—a life without God and without hope in the world.

Our obedience, on the other hand, will bring praise and honor to God's name in the world, as well as an honored place for us in God's sight. Third, sins of God's people adversely affect the glory of God. The ruined loincloth also implies the ruined reputation of God in the world because of the sins of his people. Miller puts it this way: "God's glory depends in some fashion on what the community of faith does. How the Lord is perceived and responded to by the world is determined in no small measure by how the Lord's way is revealed through the life and work of those people who bear the Lord's name" (Miller 2001, 686).

2. Jars Filled with Wine (13:12-14)

BEHIND THE TEXT

This text seems to utilize a popular saying to convey a severe word of judgment. Lundbom regards it as another symbolic act under the assumption that the prophet may have been at a gathering where there were jars filled with wine (Lundbom 1999, 671, 673); however, this text lacks a specific act performed by the prophet. The text imagines a situation where there will be an exchange between the prophet and the people (v 12). The judgment anticipates the Babylonian destruction of Jerusalem; however, a specific date cannot be given for this text. The early or latter part of Jehoiakim's reign is a good possibility (see Lundbom 1999, 674; Holladay 1986, 402).

IN THE TEXT

■ **12** The text begins with Yahweh's instruction to the prophet to address the people of Judah with the saying **every *jar* should be filled with wine** (v 12). The Hebrew word for *jar* (*nēbel*) is interchangeable with "wineskin" as in the NIV. This saying conveys the idea that wine jars are supposed to be filled with wine. Yahweh sets up the potential response of the people as the context for the message that follows. The people may respond to the prophet's announcement with a sarcastic statement that there is nothing new in what the prophet has said. It is a matter of common knowledge that wine jars when empty are supposed to be filled with wine. If the setting of this text is a festival or some other celebration, it would have been unthinkable to display empty wine jars.

■ **13** In v 13 Yahweh gives the prophet the message he should give as reply to the condescending response of the people. The message extends the metaphor of wine jar and wine and interprets for the people what was actually intended by the prophet's saying. The application of the metaphor of the jar to the people raises the possibility that the metaphor of wine in v 12 may have meant blessings from Yahweh (Fretheim 2002, 206-7). If the people actually expected Yahweh's blessings to fill them, then Jeremiah informs them what is coming from Yahweh is a severe judgment. Whether or not this interpretation is correct, v 13 makes clear to the people that Yahweh intends to fill everyone in Judah, including **kings, prophets,** and **priests,** with **drunkenness** and intoxicate them not with wine but with his wrath. The imagery here reflects the "cup of the wine of wrath" (25:15 NRSV; see vv 15-29) given to all the nations including Judah to drink.

■ **14** Verse 14 expands the word of judgment. The relationship between Yahweh filling the nation with drunkenness and then dashing the people against each other is not clear. This perhaps indicates the continuation of the metaphor of the jars in v 14; if so, the smashing of the people **one against the other** implies the image of the smashing of the jars filled with wine. At any rate, this verse suggests a violent end for the nation. When the judgment comes, the wrath of Yahweh will be unleashed against the people and it will be experienced by all. The reference to brother against ***brother,*** **fathers,** and **sons** indicates the destruction of entire families. The end of Yahweh's mercy is intensified by the use of three words—***spare,*** **pity, compassion**—all essentially convey the same meaning. Total destruction of Judah is thus anticipated here.

FROM THE TEXT

The language of this text is harsh, and it does not seem to give much hope to Judah. Jeremiah's original audience would have heard in this text a clear warning to escape God's judgment of total destruction that is coming through the agency of Babylon. The enemy would treat Judah without pity or compassion. The people in exile have gone through the tragedy announced in this verse. Every drop of blessing has been squeezed out of them by the judgment; they are like empty wine jars and what they hope for is a refilling by God's compassion and pity.

We cannot read this text without being reminded, on the one hand, that God's judgment of sin is a reality and that it will be harsh and severe. But on the other hand, the end of mercy displayed through judgment means only the end of his patience with those who reject repeated calls for repentance and continue in their sinful way of life. This does not, however, mean that God empties himself of his love and compassion. If that were the case, there would be no hope for those who have heard this word in their exile. However, there is ample evidence in the book that God who threatened to destroy his people without mercy and compassion returned to them with the promise of their restoration and healing (chs 30—31). The good news of the gospel is that "where sin increased, grace abounded all the more, so that, just as sin exercised dominion in death, so grace might also exercise dominion through justification leading to eternal life through Jesus Christ our Lord" (Rom 5:20-21 NRSV).

3. Pride, Shame, and Humiliation (13:15-27)

BEHIND THE TEXT

The rest of ch 13 is made up of three poetic oracles (vv 15-17, 18-19, 20-27). Holladay suggests that the commonly shared words (*yārad*, "run down" in v 17 [NRSV] and **come down** in v 18; *tip'eret*, "beautiful" in vv 18, 20 [NRSV], and *'ēder*, **flock,** in vv 17, 20) unite these poems into a "small collection" in this chapter (Holladay 1986, 405). The theme of pride and judgment in the previous units (vv 1-11, 12-14) is continued in these poetic units. The language of these poems implies that the Babylonian invasion is imminent (see reference to those who are coming from the north in v 20). It is likely that the text belongs to a period immediately before the first wave of the Babylonian invasion in 597 B.C. The prophet returns to the theme of weeping and grief over the nation's impending destruction in vv 15-17. Verses 18-19 clearly anticipate the removal of Jehoiachin from the throne and the exile of the king and his queen mother in 597 B.C. Verses 20-27 announce the Babylonian takeover of Judah's political affairs and the scattering of the population of Judah.

a. The Disappearing Light (13:15-17)

IN THE TEXT

■ **15** The prophet begins this short oracle with a double imperative (**hear, give ear**), an urgent appeal to the people to listen carefully to Yahweh's words and to put an end to their arrogant and prideful attitude and conduct (v 15). The people who think of themselves too highly and exalt themselves before Yahweh and others hear a strong warning that it is time to take the path of humility.

■ **16** The imperative continues in v 16; now the prophet urges the people to **give** Yahweh their God the **glory** that he deserves. He alone is worthy of praise and worship. The call here is similar to the idea expressed in Ps 29:1. Giving Yahweh glory is Israel's duty, which the nation has neglected to do for a long period of time. Fretheim suggests an interesting possibility that the call to give glory is extended to the faithful in the land in the midst of the judgment that is inevitable and unavoidable (2002, 209). It is more likely that the imperatives in vv 15-16 convey one final chance to Judah to escape the judgment. The rest of v 16 indicates the perilous times that are ahead; before those days come, the people must give glory to Yahweh. Yahweh is about to bring **darkness** upon the people; the disappearance of **light** means life lived in danger and uncertainty. The people who wait for light are threatened with darkness descending upon them. The metaphor of light and darkness is clearly associated with the concept of the Day of the Lord (see Amos 5:18-20). Listening to Yahweh and giving him glory are the conditions the people should meet to escape the shadow of death that is about to cover the nation. This is a last-minute appeal for repentance and return to Yahweh.

■ **17** Verse 17 outlines the consequence of not listening and responding to the call to give glory to Yahweh. The only thing the prophet could do in response to the people's refusal to his appeal is to weep bitterly and let tears overflow in his eyes for the people who remain proud and arrogant. The prophet expresses his personal agony here because he is intensely aware of the destruction that awaits a defiant and self-sufficient people. As in other texts (see 9:1) the anguish of the prophet is also the anguish of Yahweh. He sees the captivity of the ***flock of Yahweh*** as the consequence of the nation's refusal to listen to Yahweh's words. The captivity of Yahweh's flock will deeply hurt both Yahweh and the prophet. The announcement of the captivity (perfect tense in Hebrew) presents a future event as having already taken place. The certainty of exile as the consequence of the nation's refusal to listen to Yahweh and its effect on both Yahweh and the prophet seem to be the intent of this announcement.

FROM THE TEXT

This text provides the necessary theological corrective to the harsh words of judgment in vv 12-14. On the one hand, God offers the people faced with the threat of an imminent destruction, the opportunity to be spared if they would listen and recognize God as the only God who is worthy of their praise. On the other hand, the text indicates that captivity will come if the nation rejects this offer. Judah refused this last-minute chance to escape the Babylonian invasion of 597 B.C. Now what remains for the community in exile is to rehear the words of Jeremiah and come to terms with the reality that even in exile, in a land of idols and other gods, only God is worthy of praise. The community's future rests on this confession of faith.

We also find in this text contrasting portraits of the nation and the prophet. The text portrays the nation as proud—self-sufficient, self-trusting, and self-exalting. On the other hand, the faithful prophet of God is brokenhearted and willing to be drowned in his own tears because of the pride and the ruin of his people. This self-humiliating act is the context for the prophet to share in the grief and pathos of God. Pride alienates us from God, but humility brings us closer to the heart of God (Phil 2:5-8).

b. A Lowly Place for the Royal Family (13:18-19)

IN THE TEXT

Most commentators view this oracle as Yahweh's word to Jehoiachin and his queen mother Nehushta (2 Kgs 24:8, 12, 15). The text is thematically connected to vv 15-17. The fall of the royal family signals the fall of the proud and arrogant nation. This text identifies Judah as the "flock" of Yahweh that will be taken into exile (see vv 17, 19). It is likely that the text belongs to the troublesome days following Jehoiakim's death. The text anticipates the removal of Jehoiachin from the throne by the Babylonians. According to 2 Kgs 24:8,

Jehoiachin's kingship lasted only for three months.

■ **18** The oracle begins with Yahweh's command to the prophet to speak to the king and the queen mother (v 18); the instruction (**say** in singular) is given to a single individual, most likely to Jeremiah. Lundbom, by taking into account Jeremiah's rather precarious relationship with the royal family, thinks that a messenger may have been used by the prophet to convey this message (1999, 680). However, it is also possible that here we have a command from Yahweh to the prophet to speak directly to the royal family (Fretheim 2002, 210). Jehoiachin was only 18 when he became king, so his mother would have held considerable power in the palace and in political decision-making. The message to the king and the queen mother is to ***step down*** from their seat of royal privilege and power and ***take a seat*** with the rest of the people. The reason for this call to consider themselves as commoners is the impending removal of their ***beautiful crown*** from their heads. The text anticipates the deposing of the queen mother and her son by the Babylonians.

■ **19** Verse 19 indicates that even **the cities in the Negev,** the southern border of Judah, will experience the impact of the Babylonian invasion. From the north to the south, the whole land will come under the control of Babylon. Moreover, the entire population of Judah will be **carried into exile**. The twice-occurring reference to being taken into exile in this verse implies the certainty of the Babylonian exile.

FROM THE TEXT

History has taught us the valuable lesson of the rise and fall of great empires and political structures. We also learn from history that human pride was the root cause of the fall of many great empires and kingdoms and governments. From a biblical perspective, God is involved in removing kingdoms and kings and political leaders who become proud and arrogant. As sovereign Lord of history, he is intent on removing any and all political powers that refuse to govern according to the standards of justice and righteousness. This text speaks not only to political governments of our day but also to all who claim power. Exile is the judgment on arrogance at any level and at any place, whether in politics, business, or religion. The God who speaks in this text is the God who indeed brings down "the powerful from their thrones" and lifts up "the lowly" and the poor in the world (Luke 1:52 NRSV; cf. 1 Sam 2:3-8).

c. How Long, O Jerusalem? (13:20-27)

BEHIND THE TEXT

This last oracle seems to address several issues. The text begins with an announcement of the enemy coming from the north (v 20). The scattering of the flock is a theme in vv 20 and 24. Shame and humiliation of Judah by foreign political powers is another theme in the text. The text also visits the issue of

Judah's idolatry and Yahweh's judgment. The imperatives in v 20 and the second person reference throughout this text are in feminine singular (except **your eyes** in v 20, and **you** in v 23 in masculine plural). It is likely that the oracle is addressed to Jerusalem. Lundbom connects v 20 with the previous oracle and assumes that this verse addresses the queen mother (1999, 682). Most commentators treat v 20 as the beginning of a new unit.

IN THE TEXT

■ **20** The text begins with a call to Jerusalem to lift up its eyes and see the Babylonian army coming from the **north** (v 20). The problem of masculine plural (**your eyes**) cannot be solved. BHS suggests reading it as feminine singular, following the Greek translation, which adds "Jerusalem" in this verse, thus suggesting Jerusalem as the addressee. The second part of v 20 is a rhetorical question, which indicates the scattering of the flock that has been charged under the care of the political and religious establishment of Jerusalem. The **flock** that is scattered and lost is the "flock of Yahweh" (see v 17). The question is thus more than a question about the scattering of the flock of Yahweh. It conveys, on the one hand, Yahweh's "anger and heartache" over his lost flock; but on the other hand, Yahweh blames the city's leadership that has reneged on its duty to preserve and protect his flock (Stulman 2005, 138). The reference to the people as *beautiful flock* perhaps suggests Jerusalem's pride over the inhabitants of the city.

■ **21** The Hebrew text of v 21 does not make much sense. The text seems to refer to the shame and agony that Jerusalem will experience because Yahweh is about to place over the city new leaders who were once its allies. Babylon with whom Jerusalem once maintained political alliance will be appointed by Yahweh as its new ruler. The covenant people who became proud will be thus put to shame because their allies will become their enemy. The result will be intense suffering. The metaphor of a woman in labor indicates the severe and wrenching pain the enemy will inflict on Jerusalem.

■ **22** In v 22 Yahweh responds to a question that Jerusalem may ask itself when calamity comes upon it. The city does not need to look elsewhere for the cause of its destruction, but it needs to reflect on its *great iniquity*. The lifting of **skirts** and the violating of **heels** indicate the exposure of nakedness (Lundbom 1999, 686). Rape and other sexual violence were part of the enemy's tactics to bring dishonor, shame, and terror in ancient war activities (unfortunately, this continues to be the case in ethnic and tribal conflicts in our civilized world also). The sexual imagery here suggests how ruthlessly the city will be violated by the invading army.

■ **23** In v 23, the text shifts focus to Jerusalem's deeply rooted depravity and deeply stained moral character. Using a proverbial statement, Yahweh asserts that the inhabitants of Jerusalem (**you**, masculine plural), set on their evil ways of life, cannot bring themselves to doing any good. The dark color of the skin of a **Cushite** (or Ethiopian; inhabitant of the region south of Egypt) and the spots on the skin of a **leopard** cannot be changed because these are inherent traits. Yahweh applies this generally known truth to the citizens of Jerusalem to indicate the unlikelihood of their capacity to change their evil practices and do that which is good. Jerusalem of Jeremiah's day has become a difficult place to be transformed because sin has penetrated deeply into the inner core of its existence.

■ **24** Verses 24-27 make clear that it is Yahweh who is bringing the judgment upon Jerusalem. The enemy from the north is Yahweh's instrument of judgment, and the coming political disaster is not the result of any geopolitical developments. Yahweh will **scatter** those responsible for the scattering of the "flock of Yahweh" like **chaff** is blown away by the **desert wind** (v 24). The metaphor suggests the worthlessness of Jerusalem and its exile. Judgment will come like a hot and devastating desert wind that will take the citizens of Jerusalem to a faraway place.

■ **25** In the same way Yahweh allotted parcels of land to the various tribes of Israel, he has allotted for the present generation their **lot** from him—the judgment of exile (v 25). This is the **portion** from Yahweh for those who have forgotten their covenant with him and put their trust in *falsehood* (šeqer), or **false gods**.

■ **26-27** In v 26, it is Yahweh, and not the enemy, who brings shame and humiliation to Jerusalem, which again indicates his direct involvement in the changing political circumstances (see v 22). Verse 27 returns to the earlier themes of adultery and idolatry (see chs 2—5). This verse again utilizes the language of sexual violence to show the total shame and humiliation of Jerusalem. The reason for this violence done against Jerusalem is the city's shameless practice of adultery and idolatry. Lady Jerusalem who left her husband, Yahweh, receives the word that he will humiliate her by exposing her as an adulterous woman. Verse 27 ends with a **woe** statement. Jerusalem, the **unclean** city, is destined for destruction. This woe statement ends with a question phrased with an awkward expression, which literally reads, *after how long?* The question could be read as a "rebuke" (so Lundbom 1999, 690; **How long will you be unclean?**). Or, as the NRSV suggests ("How long will it be before you are made clean?"), this question could be an indication of Jerusalem being made clean again in the future. If this reading is correct, then Yahweh who brings the harsh word of judgment remains hopeful that his beloved city will one day become clean again.

FROM THE TEXT

The community in exile would have found in this text the answer to their perplexing question, **Why has this happened to me?** Their shame and humiliation, their scattering, the violent and ruthless treatment of them by the invading army of Babylon—all are traced in this text to their **many sins**. The people who have made themselves unclean by their sins are living in an unclean land.

The final question, **How long** calls for a proper response then and now. God's desperate hope for his people to acknowledge their uncleanness is powerfully expressed in this question. The people of God in exile can hope for the end to their exile only when they recognize the reality of their sins that separate them from God.

Verse 23 does not convey a general truth about the inherent nature of human sin from which there is no escape or about the inability of human beings to do any good or to repent of their sin. The text needs to be understood in its context. It addresses the long history of Israel's stubborn resistance to God. The people of Judah of Jeremiah's day were so deeply immersed in sin that doing evil instead of doing good was their natural response to God. What the text affirms here is the damaging power of sin and its capacity to hold as "slaves" those who yield to sin (Rom 6:16). The final question, **How long,** indicates not only the possibility of a transformation from the state of sin to the state of holy obedience to God, but also the promise of this transformation to those who positively respond to God's question. Only an "obstinate refusal of the grace of God" would make this transformation impossible (Clarke, 291). Paul reminded his readers that they have an "obligation" to "put to death the misdeeds of the body" by the help of the Holy Spirit, so that they may live as God's children, "heirs of God and co-heirs with Christ" (Rom 8:12-13, 17).

"UPROOT AND TEAR DOWN"

NO MORE PROPHETIC MEDIATION (14:1—15:21)

Overview

Commentators recognize in chs 14 and 15 a series of dialogues in which Yahweh (14:1-6, 10-12, 14-18; 15:1-9, 11-14, 19-21), the prophet (14:13; 15:10, 15-18), and the people (14:7-9, 19-22) participate. These chapters contain two major literary units (14:1—15:9; 15:10-21). These units are mostly in poetry mixed with some prose statements (14:11-16; 15:1-2*a*, 3-4). The theme of drought sets the stage for the dialogues (see 14:2-6; 15:18*b*). The dialogue form contributes to the literary unity of these chapters.

Jeremiah 14:2—15:4 (or 14:2—15:9) has the form of a liturgy in response to a national disaster. The speeches of the people reflect a liturgy of repentance and confession; the confessions of the people in this unit (14:7-9, 19-22) are similar to the liturgy of repentance in 3:22*b*-25. If we assume that the speeches of the people are essentially the speeches of the prophet (the prophet putting words in the mouth of the people), then it is possible to see in these chapters essentially a two-way conversation—Yahweh's judgment speeches (14:1-6, 10-12, 14-18; 15:1-9, 11-14, 19-21) and the prophet's lament/confession (14:7-9, 13, 19-22; 15:10, 15-18).

Jeremiah 14:7—15:4 may also be understood as the prophet's intercession (14:7-9, 13, and 19-22) and Yahweh's rejection of the prophet's intercession (14:10-12, 14-18; and 15:1-4). The emphatic rejection of any prophetic mediation in 15:1-4 seems to support this view. Again, these oracles may have once existed independently of each other but were placed together here in this literary scheme by a later editor.

There is no indication of the setting of these dialogues, and therefore a precise date cannot be given to these chapters. The "drought" seems to be a memorable event, though we cannot give a date for this calamity. Holladay makes several arguments in favor of 601 as the date of the drought and the fast mentioned in 14:11 (1986, 427-29). The conflict with the false prophets suggests a date during the reign of Jehoiakim or Zedekiah.

1. A Devastating Drought (14:1-9)

BEHIND THE TEXT

Jeremiah 14:1-9 has two clearly identifiable parts: description of the devastating effects of a severe drought (vv 2-6), and a communal lament (vv 7-9). The introductory verse (v 1) could be taken as a superscription not only for this unit but also for chs 14—15 (Lundbom 1999, 695). The speaker of vv 2-6 is not identified, though we assume that Yahweh is depicting here the effect of the judgment (v 1). The words of the communal lament in vv 7-9 are perhaps words spoken by the prophet; it is likely that here the prophet is making another attempt to intercede for the nation by utilizing the language of lament.

IN THE TEXT

■ **1-2** The **drought** (*habbaṣṣārôt*; plural in Hebrew; v 1) may be understood as an abstract singular, and thus seasons without rain. Since Israel's theology confesses faith in God as the One who brings rain (v 22), this drought may be understood as an indication of divine judgment. Verse 2 indicates the terrible effects of the drought. **Judah** and **her** *gates* (reference could be to the gates of the **cities** of Judah) represent those who mourn because of the intensity of the drought. The gates of the cities (**they**) personify the people sitting on the ground wearing black clothes (***they are dark to the earth***), a common custom associated with mourning rituals (Lundbom 1999, 695). Jerusalem and its citizens join with the rest of the nation in the cry of distress caused by the drought.

■ **3** Verse 3 indicates that no one has any advantage or access to water; even the **nobles** in the city who have special access to limited resources suffer with the common folk because of the drought. Their **servants** go out to search for water and return with empty jars. Instead of water, what they bring with them is shame, dismay, despair, and grief (symbolized by the covering of head) because all the cisterns in the land are dry.

■ **4-6** The farmers also are filled with dismay and grief because of the dry and cracked ground, which is unsuitable for planting crops (v 4). It is not only the people and the land that suffer but also the animal world (vv 5-6). Without rain, water, grass, and herbage, both human and animal life faces the threat of extinction. The drought has brought all creatures to the same social level; suffering does not offer any special advantage to anyone.

■ **7** Verses 7-9 contain a communal lament. However, it is difficult to assume that a stubborn nation that has a long history of covenant-breaking could come up with such sincere words, unless one would take this as an insincere foxhole prayer by an unrepentant people seeking deliverance from an immediate danger. An alternative approach is to see the prophet as the intercessor, identifying himself with the sinful people (hence, the first person plural forms). The nation that has lost the vocabulary of prayer and the capacity to pray receives here an instruction in the traditional language of lament and confession of sin. There is an explicit confession of sin and admission of guilt in v 7. The prayer to act **for the sake of your name** indicates Israel's traditional conviction that the people depend solely on Yahweh's mercy and not in any merit of their own for their salvation (see Pss 25:11; 79:9; 106:8). In the midst of the guilt and sin of the people, Yahweh's will to act to preserve the honor of his name is the only source of hope for the people. The confession also includes the admission that the people have backslidden and sinned against Yahweh. **We have sinned against you** is the open admission of sin, which reflects the confession of truly penitent sinners (see Ps 51:6).

■ **8** The prayer affirms faith in Yahweh as the **Hope** and **Savior** of the people (v 8). Holladay thinks that hope (*miqwēh*, which also means "pool" of water) has a double meaning here, particularly in the context of the drought (1986, 433). Savior (*mōšîaʻ*) is another traditional name for Yahweh, rooted in his deliverance of Israel from Egypt and in the subsequent deliverances from various political powers (Isa 43:3; Hos 13:4). Israel's future depends on Yahweh who has been its Savior throughout the course of its history.

The prayer raises two questions (**why** in vv 8-9); such questions are frequently found in personal and community laments in the Psalms. The first question asks why Yahweh acts like a ***sojourner***, like a **traveler**, who has no permanent association with the place of sojourning or travel (v 8). This question is thus an appeal to Yahweh to be faithful to his covenant promises, for his faithful and abiding presence with his people, though they are sinners.

■ **9** The second question (v 9) asks why Yahweh is like a person **taken by surprise** or a **warrior** who has lost his strength. Again as part of a lament, this question is an earnest appeal to Yahweh to show himself once again to his people as their mighty deliverer, and thus be faithful to his covenant promises. These questions arise out of the desperate conditions of the people that the prophet sees as a sign of their abandonment by Yahweh. Though the present realities compel the prophet to raise questions about the power of Yahweh, he, nonetheless, confesses faith in Yahweh as the God who is **among** his people, and the people as those who are known by his **name** (v 9). In the end, the hope of the nation rests in the covenantal relationship between Yahweh and his people. If Yahweh would abandon his people, then there would be no future for them; so, the prayer concludes with an appeal not to **forsake** the community under judgment.

FROM THE TEXT

A significant issue in 14:1—15:4 is God's determination to rule out the possibility of prophetic intercession on behalf of the nation under judgment. The communal lament form of this text (vv 7-9) is a daring attempt on the part of the prophet to disregard God's command, which forbids intercession for the people (7:16; 11:14). Here the prophet speaks not for himself but for the community in the hope of persuading God to show mercy to those under judgment.

The lament also highlights the necessity of confession and recognition of sinfulness by the people of God. It provides the language of prayer for an unfaithful people who seek God's mercy. The physical calamity of the drought was a theological issue for the people in exile. For them, the drought in this text would have been a symbol of their abandonment by God. Along with their confession of sin, they would have been challenged by this text to raise their own questions about their abandonment by God.

The conflicting thought about God as a God who acts like a stranger and a God who is with his people is not strange to those who experience crisis in their life (Job represents an excellent example of this paradoxical thought). The lament raises serious doubts about God but still conveys strong faith in him as well as faith in the people as God's people. As I was writing this, I received an e-mail from a pastor friend in Jerusalem asking for prayer for the little Christian community in Gaza that is caught in the middle of the conflict between the Palestinian militia groups and the Israeli army. Israel's military attempt to rescue its kidnapped soldier has escalated the tension between Israel and the militia groups in Gaza. The small Christian community in Gaza may have been asking the question, "Where is God in the midst of death and destruction?" Christian communities like those in Gaza and in similar war-torn areas of our world do not seem to give up hope, though they have been living in the midst of violence and political conflict for several decades or centuries. For those who live in a less violent world, the issues of life may be a tragic accident or the news of terminal illness or some other human crisis. The text assures all the people of God that he is in the midst of our human troubles as the source of our hope and our "savior in time of trouble" (NRSV).

2. No Reprieve from Sword and Famine (14:10-16)

BEHIND THE TEXT

This section is in prose though some commentators and translations, including the NIV, treat v 10 as poetry. One would have expected Yahweh's favorable response to the prophet's prayer on behalf of the nation in the preceding unit. Typically laments in the OT are followed by oracles of deliverance and salvation. Instead, the response from Yahweh is a rejection of the prophetic prayer as well as the ritual performances of the people. Yahweh's response is given as a message to the people (see v 10). The message includes an indictment (v 10*a*) and two judgment statements (vv 10*b*, 15-16). Verses 11-14 constitute a dialogue between Yahweh and Jeremiah. This section has two parts: in the first part Yahweh commands the prophet not to pray for the people and announces the full end of the people (vv 11-12); in the second part, Jeremiah speaks to Yahweh concerning the false prophets who have misguided the people by giving them false hopes of peace (vv 13-14).

IN THE TEXT

■ **10** Yahweh's indictment of the people is that they have wandered away from him and that they have not applied any restraint to their idolatrous behavior (v 10). ***They loved to wander*** indicates that the people have replaced their love for Yahweh with love for other gods, whom they have pursued with greater loyalty and affection. Yahweh seems to be responding to the complaint in v 8 that he is behaving like a sojourner. It is not Yahweh who wandered away from his people, but rather it is his people who have wandered from Yahweh. Therefore, his judgment is upon them. The last three lines of v 10 are also found in Hos 8:13. He is displeased with their infidelity and **does not accept them** as his people. **Now,** therefore, is the time for Yahweh to **remember** and ***visit*** his people, not to bring salvation to them but to execute his judgment on their ***iniquity*** and ***sin***. So, the present devastating conditions are in reality the judgment upon a people who have drifted away from Yahweh.

■ **11** In v 11, Yahweh forbids the prophet to intercede for the people for the third time (see 7:16; 11:14). Though Yahweh prohibits the prophet from praying for the **well-being** of the people, as in the other two instances, the prophet does not yield, because yielding to the demand of Yahweh would mean a vocation that does not encompass the full scope of the prophet's call. It is also interesting to note that there is no indictment against the prophet for disobeying Yahweh's previous demands.

■ **12** This prohibition is followed by Yahweh's announcement that he will not **listen** to the prayers of the people or **accept** any of their liturgical actions aimed to solicit his favor toward them (v 12). The conjunction (**although**) seems to indicate that the people have responded to the national tragedy with the ritual of **fast,** the giving up of food and drink accompanied by various actions, to display grief and to solicit Yahweh's favor. The response of the people also included **burnt offering** and ***cereal offering*** required by the Law to show faithful relationship with Yahweh. Yahweh announces his rejection of the fast and disapproval of the offerings; instead he announces his decision to bring the people to their ***full end*** by **sword, famine,** and ***pestilence*** (see 5:12; also the repetition of **sword** and **famine** in 14:13, 15, 16, 18; 15:2). Yahweh has already unleashed upon the sinful nation the power of both the enemy nation (Babylon) and nature (famine and pestilence). Divine judgment is thus taking place through political and natural processes. The goal of judgment is the destruction of the sinful people.

■ 13 Verse 13 indicates a bold move on the part of the prophet to continue his intercessory function, though Yahweh commanded him not to pray for the people. The opening phrase **Ah Lord Yahweh** (see also 1:6) introduces a counterclaim or an argument against the divine response in 14:11-12. He points out that the real blame for the misguided theological perception and self-righteous ritual performances of the people belongs to the false prophets who have promoted *true* peace as a promise from Yahweh and have discredited the true prophet's message of sword and famine in the land (v 13; see 4:10; 5:12; 6:14; 8:11; 23:17). Jeremiah thus circumvents the divine command without actually disregarding or disobeying it and continues his intercessory role. He makes it known that the people subscribe to a theology that essentially conforms to their traditional understanding of Yahweh as the One who is the source of their well-being and blessings. The people have been caught between two ideologies, and they have yielded to the majority voice. How could they have known that the ideology of true peace in the land has not been a word from Yahweh? Jeremiah's bold assertion seems to imply that if the people have been misled by the prophets, then Yahweh must assume some responsibility for the national tragedy (Stulman 2005, 141-42).

■ 14-15 Yahweh's response indicates that the prophet succeeded at least for the moment to turn Yahweh's attention from the people to the false prophets (vv 14-15). Yahweh refutes and rejects the notion that he might in some way be responsible for the current crisis and totally disassociates himself from the false prophets (v 14). He asserts that what the prophets promote is *falsehood.* The emphatic statements, *I did not send them nor did I command them, nor did I speak to them,* portray the false prophets as unauthorized and illegitimate voices. They are not speaking visions from Yahweh but **false visions** of their own heart. What they practice is **divination, *worthlessness,*** and ***treachery***—all stem from their corrupt heart. Divination is a practice condemned by the Law (Deut 18:10). The unauthorized prophets who speak in the name of Yahweh will die by **sword and famine,** the very same fate that they said would not come upon the nation (v 15).

■ 16 The people who have rejected the true voice of Yahweh and have followed the prophets who promised well-being and immunity from judgment will also suffer the same fate (v 16). Ultimately, the people themselves are responsible for their actions. Famine and sword are realities from which there is no escape for the people. The streets of Jerusalem will be strewn with dead bodies of entire families. No one will receive any customary funeral rites. Verse 16 ends with the note that judgment is Yahweh's work of pouring out upon the people their own *evil.*

FROM THE TEXT

The text presents God's determination to punish the people who have not taken the steps to put an end to their pursuit of other gods. They do not live in obedience to the covenant way of life, but they claim righteous relationship with God through religious rituals. The certainty of judgment in this text is clearly connected to the lack of genuine repentance on the part of the people. The verdict of death is given to a people who think they can manipulate God with their religious performances. God forbids the prophet from praying for the people who remain unrepentant and practice a religion that does not promote obedience. Death is God's final word to those who presume upon his endless mercy and forgiveness. The only way out for the people from the verdict of death is their repentance. Without repentance, the people are destined for death.

The prophet's repeated attempts to intercede for the people indicate his commitment to his call and commission. It is God's prerogative to say no to prophetic intercession, but it is the prophet's task to do exactly what God had called him to do, which includes the ministry of intercession. He does not give up on praying for the people, though God forbids him to do so (see his intercession in v 13 and in vv 19-22). Jeremiah models for us the necessity to do our part regardless of what actions God may or may not take with regard to a particular issue. The text reminds the community of faith to be what God has called them to be in our world—"a royal priesthood"—without which the world has no hope (1 Pet 2:9).

The text presents Jeremiah's attempt to mitigate the sins of the people by placing the blame for their theological error on the prophets who were proponents of lasting *shalom* in the land. The false prophets assumed that God would not violate his covenantal arrangements with Israel. However, they have failed to take an inventory of the realities—the sins of the people and their covenant-breaking, the curses of the covenant, and the necessity of judgment. Their one-sided approach to theology portrayed a tamed and nationalistic God who will not nullify the covenant. They believed and promoted a message, which was subjective and only partially true. Falsehood, when recited often, can take the appearance of truth and be accepted as truth by an unsuspecting and vulnerable community. The text is unrelenting in its announcement of death to the false prophets and their naive victims.

The conflict between authentic spokespersons of God and those who presume to have authority because of some religious claims is attested in several places in the Bible (Jesus vs. the scribes and Pharisees in the Gospels, Paul vs. his opponents in 2 Cor 11. See also 1 Tim 6:3-5; 2 Tim 3:1-9). Unfortunately, this continues to be a problem even in our own day. Those who peddle the Christian faith in our day as a pill to cure the troubles and trials of life and a ticket to prosperity distort the message of the cross and preach visions and dreams of their own heart. Jeremiah reminds us here that ultimately it is the community's responsibility to discern and distinguish between those who speak authentically for God and those who promote visions of their heart.

3. Yahweh Weeps (14:17-18)

BEHIND THE TEXT

Verses 17-18 display a remarkably different attitude of Yahweh to his people. Yahweh, who is stubbornly resistant to any prophetic mediation or ritual performances of the people but stands firm with his words of "sword and famine," is portrayed in these verses as heartbroken and weeping for his ruined people. There is a shift in the way this unit begins. In contrast to the speech *about* the people in the previous unit (see v 10), now Yahweh asks Jeremiah to speak directly *to* the people (v 17). The intent of this direct speech is perhaps to share with the people a glimpse of Yahweh's grief. As in other laments in the book, the voice of Jeremiah and the voice of Yahweh are the same. The prophet is not a dispassionate spokesperson, but he is fully engaged with Yahweh in the sharing of his grief.

IN THE TEXT

■ **17** What the prophet must convey to the people is not words of judgment but words about the **tears** that pour down from his eyes **night and day** because of the terrible devastation he sees in the land (v 17; see 9:1). The second part of v 17 indicates the cause of Yahweh's lament. He weeps unceasingly for his people who have suffered a severe and fatal wound. The description of the people as the **virgin daughter—my people** indicates his deep affection and emotional attachment to the suffering nation.

■ **18** No matter where Yahweh looks, in the country or in the city, the land is filled with the victims of **sword** and **famine** (v 18). The reason for this devastation is stated in the last two lines of v 18. **Prophet and priest**—those who are responsible for the welfare of the people—have abandoned their responsibility. They ***wander around the land*** selling their message of health and wealth to a dying people without coming to terms with the realities of sin and judgment. ***They do not acknowledge*** that Yahweh's judgment is upon them and upon the people to whom they have sold the message of good health and good fortune. The meaning of **have gone to a land they know not** is not clear, though this translation is a possible reading of the Hebrew text. These two verses seem to belong to the context of the Babylonian invasion, either the events of 597 or 587 B.C.

FROM THE TEXT

This text is similar to various expressions of God's pathos elsewhere in the book. This text once again reiterates the theme that God's judgment does not mean an end to his relationship with his people. Judgment is a necessity because of sin and because of his commitment to do justice in the world. He does not remain unaffected by his actions of judgment but enters into solidarity with those who suffer because of his judgment. His unending tears evidence his deep grief and agony. This is further evidence of his commitment to the covenant with his people. So their hurt, even though it is inflicted upon them by his blow, becomes his hurt. This OT portrait of God is seldom understood by those who think of the God of Israel only in terms of his wrath and judgment. God's grief also moves him to act with compassion. So Israel hears again yet another word from this God: "I will turn their mourning into gladness; I will give them comfort and joy instead of sorrow" (31:13*b*).

4. Remember Your Covenant (14:19-22)

BEHIND THE TEXT

Chapter 14 ends with another lament and confession (vv 19-22). The first person plural forms in these verses have led most commentators to view this as the prayer of the community. However, we must also consider the possibility that the prophet, as an intercessor for the nation, may be offering this prayer on behalf of the sinful nation. This prayer is very similar to the lament in 14:7-9. A key issue that emerges in this chapter is the prophet's stubborn resistance to Yahweh's command not to intercede for the people. As we have seen in vv 7-9, here also the prophet may be interceding for the nation by utilizing the lament language. In the midst of Yahweh's stubborn determination to bring an end to the nation through sword and famine, the prophet remains stubborn in his commitment to be an intercessor and thus to continue his prophetic vocation. The prophet who weeps with God also confesses the sins of the people among whom he lives. Thus, he participates not only with God's suffering but also with the suffering of his people. These laments portray the prophet as a Moses-like figure who though always on Yahweh's side never detaches himself from the plight of the people.

IN THE TEXT

■ **19** The lament begins with three questions, all of which raise important theological issues (v 19). Does judgment and destruction mean that Yahweh rejected **Judah**? Does judgment and destruction mean **Zion** is no longer the delight of Yahweh and his dwelling place? Does judgment and destruction mean that

Yahweh no longer offers **healing** to the wound he inflicts upon his people (Isa 30:26)? The historical realities seem to suggest the possibility of Yahweh's utter rejection of Judah and Zion, which would mean no hope for the people. These questions convey the prophet's hidden fear that Yahweh has taken the steps to nullify his covenant commitment to his people. By asking these questions, the prophet hopes to persuade Yahweh to withdraw or suspend judgment and to begin the time of healing and thus to remain faithful to his covenant. The prophet does not deny the necessity of judgment; however, he intercedes with Yahweh not to prolong it to the point of total destruction. The present reality of judgment does not seem to give any hope for **peace** (***To hope for peace and there is no good***) and **healing** to the nation (v 19). Instead, they see a future filled with **terror.** The prophet convincingly argues that Yahweh's mercy and compassion is the only source for the nation's future and well-being.

■ **20** Verses 20-22 contain confession of sin and affirmation of faith in Yahweh. The language of vv 20-21 reflects Ps 79:8-9. The prophet recognizes the sins of the nation—not only that of the present generation but also of the past generations—as the reason for Yahweh's judgment (v 20). **The *iniquity* of our fathers** most likely means Israel's long history of idolatry. **We have indeed sinned against you** (see also v 7) is not only a strong admission of guilt but also an appeal for forgiveness.

■ **21** On behalf of the people, the prophet pleads with Yahweh not to treat Zion, his **glorious throne,** with contempt (v 21; most translations add "us," which is lacking in Hebrew). If he would abandon Zion, then there would be no hope for the people. The prophet reminds Yahweh that he must act in order to preserve the integrity and honor of his **name** (see also v 7). The question of covenant fidelity, which is implied earlier (v 19), is made explicit in the last two lines of v 21. While carrying out judgment, the prophet reminds Yahweh that he has an obligation to **remember** the **covenant** with those being judged. The covenant may refer to all the covenants Yahweh has made with Israel (Abraham, Sinai, and David). Israel's future rests on Yahweh honoring all the promises conveyed through these covenants. The present suffering means the curses of the covenant are at work; Yahweh remembers the sins of the people (see v 10). It can have a future only if he would remember his covenant fidelity.

■ **22** The final verse returns to the theme of drought. The prophet confesses faith in Yahweh as the only God who is able to bring rain from the heavens and thus end the calamity with which this dialogue started (v 22). The rhetorical questions in this verse give an affirmative answer. There are no **idols** among the nations that have the power to make **rain;** neither do the heavens send showers by its own power. The only rainmaker in the universe is Yahweh, the God of Israel. This confession leads to hope and expectation (***We wait for you***). The lament ends with another confession that it is Yahweh who does **all this**—drought and rain as well as judgment and salvation. Brueggemann calls this verse a "doxology" that "summons God to do what God characteristically and faithfully does" (1998, 140-41). The lament thus turns to praise and leaves the matter of "sword and famine" into Yahweh's hands with hopeful expectation in his covenant fidelity to Israel.

FROM THE TEXT

Jeremiah begins this lament with questions that acknowledge the reality of God's judgment on Judah. Judgment is already at work. The stable and secure structures of Judah and its religious ideology do not provide any hope for the people. The nation does not experience *shalom*. But there is a sense of optimism in this text, which comes not out of theological speculations or religious claims but from the prophet's perspective of God as the God who is ultimately the source of hope for his people. He admits the necessity of God's harsh judgment; however, he is also fearful that this judgment may lead to God's ultimate rejection of his people. So he appeals to "God's soul and pathos" to consider his "stake in the life of Israel" (Heschel 2001, 155). He recognizes the truth that any future for Judah rests on God's mercy that may come through the confession of sin. Key elements of this lament include the following: admission of sin and guilt, appeal to God to act not because of any merit of the people but to preserve his reputation and glory, appeal to God's faithfulness to his covenant, and finally the acknowledgment that God the sovereign Creator is the only hope for the people.

It is likely that this lament gave the people in exile an alternative way to perceive the realities around them. They would have been prompted to share this lament, not only in the expression of sorrow and confession but also in the hope it anticipates for healing and well-being. Confession of sin such as we find in this text initiates the process of healing. In the end the prophet's prayer for forgiveness and healing is answered, and we hear this answer later in the book: "I will forgive their wickedness and will remember their sins no more" (31:34). "I will bring health and healing . . . ; I will heal my people and will let them enjoy abundant peace and security" (33:6). This remains to be God's promise to those who recognize the depth of their sin and seek God's mercy through repentance and confession.

5. Judah's Fate Is Sealed (15:1-4)

BEHIND THE TEXT

Jeremiah 15:1-4 continues the dialogue between Yahweh and Jeremiah. Here we find Yahweh's response to the prophet's lament and confession of sin on behalf of the people. Yahweh's response seems to be a final no to the prophet's continued attempts to intercede for the people, though he was clearly forbidden to do so. Otherwise, a word about the futility of mediation even by Moses and Samuel would have been unnecessary (v 1).

Prophets as Intercessors

The prophetic ministry in the OT included standing before God to intercede for the people, and Jeremiah fulfilled that task, according to ch 14. He did this task as the representative of his great predecessors Moses and Samuel. Moses was able to persuade God to be gracious and merciful to Israel in the context of the apostasy of the golden calf and God's judgment on the nation (Exod 32:7-14; see also Num 14:13-19). Likewise, Samuel interceded for Israel in the midst of the Philistine attack and committed himself to be the nation's intercessor all his life though it has committed wickedness by asking for a king (1 Sam 7:5-11; 12:16-25). Stories of Moses and Samuel show that prophetic intercession often succeeded in winning God's favor on behalf of Israel. The rejection of Jeremiah as a mediator in ch 15 is only a temporary suspension of that role of the prophets. Jeremiah's persistent intercession for the people indicates that he remained faithful to that role of his prophetic ministry.

IN THE TEXT

15:1-3

■ 1 Yahweh's speech begins with the firm announcement that not even **Moses** and **Samuel** will be able to persuade Yahweh to ***turn*** his ***soul*** **to this people**, those who have broken their covenant with him (v 1). Yahweh's announcement also implies that the decision to bring judgment is final and that any further attempt by Jeremiah to intercede for Judah would be of no use.

Yahweh then proceeds to tell the prophet what his prophetic ministry is at this hour. He must **send** out Yahweh's people and **let them go** (v 1). There is a parallel between the command to send (them) and let them go and the Exodus tradition of Yahweh sending Moses to Pharaoh with the command "let my people go" (Exod 5:1-2). In the Exodus tradition, Moses leads the people to Sinai, to Yahweh's presence, and from there to the Promised Land. Here Jeremiah is commanded a reverse action—to send the people away from the **presence** of Yahweh and let them go out of the Promised Land. Judgment here is the reversal of the going **out** from Egypt, the reversal of Moses' work, and the reversal of all the covenantal blessings. This command reflects the final rejection of any covenantal mediation.

■ 2 The people may respond to this harsh word of judgment with the despairing question, **Where shall we go?** The answer contains the fourfold fate (**death, sword,** *famine,* and **captivity**) of the nation (v 2). Sword and famine would bring the nation to its death; death and captivity is the ultimate destiny that faces the nation.

■ 3 Verse 3 intensifies the judgment language by introducing four types of **destroyers** as the agents of judgment when Yahweh visits his people to punish them. The four types of punishment and the four types of destroyers perhaps reflect the idea of the finality and the totality of judgment (see Ezek 14:21; Rev 6:8). No one will escape the reality of judgment. The reference to **the sword, the dogs, the birds, and the beasts** indicates that both human and nonhuman agencies will participate in carrying out Yahweh's judgment. The dead will not receive proper burial but will become food for animals. The devastating impact of the Babylonian invasion is clearly projected in this verse.

■ **4** The judgment will make Judah an object of horror to the neighboring kingdoms; these nations will be horrified by the terrible reversal of Judah's fortune (v 4). Verse 4a implies that the covenant curses are unleashed against the people who have broken the covenant (Deut 28:37). However, in v 4b Yahweh holds **Manasseh son of Hezekiah** as the person responsible for the death and captivity of Judah. Some commentators think that v 4b is a later addition. In the Deuteronomistic history, Judah's downfall is attributed to Manasseh's apostasy (2 Kgs 21:1-18; 23:26-27; 24:3-4), which is supported by this text. Throughout the book, though the sins of the people and the sins of the leaders are treated as important reasons of judgment, the prophet points his finger at the royal family as the primary culprits responsible for Judah's downfall.

FROM THE TEXT

God's no to any prophetic mediation, including that of Moses and Samuel and the final words of judgment, do not seem to give any hope for Judah. The only option left is the direct appeal of the people for God's mercy. They can no longer depend on the covenant mediators for immunity from judgment. This text raises the question of the efficacy of intercessory prayers for those who persistently reject the call to repentance. Some have assumed from texts like this that at a certain point, intercession begins to lose its effect because judgment has begun its work. They may be right in thinking so. However, the overall evidence in the book suggests that God has left the door open for the people to repent and thus avert judgment until the end. The ongoing interaction between God and Jeremiah and Jeremiah and the people suggest that even this seemingly final word was after all not a final word. God's desire would have been to spare the people from sword, famine, death, and exile. Intercession alone could not have persuaded God to change his mind because God is bound in a relation not only to his faithful intercessors but also to a people for whom intercession is being made. God's decision to act or not to act in response to intercessory prayer may also have something to do with factors such as the response of the people. It is the resistance of the people that compels God to say no to intercession. So, it is appropriate to think that no to intercession in this text does not mean no to Judah's repentance, which would have spared the nation from sword, famine, death, and exile.

6. No One Will Have Pity on Jerusalem (15:5-9)

BEHIND THE TEXT

After a brief prose unit the text returns to poetry again, which is continued through v 21. Commentators treat vv 5-9 as a single unit. Yahweh seems to be the speaker throughout this unit. The judgment-lament scheme of the previous units is continued here. Yahweh's judgment in vv 1-4 is followed by a lament (v 5), which is again followed by words of judgment (vv 6-9). The Hebrew text of vv 6-9 describes Yahweh's actions in vv 6-9 in the past tense, except v 9c, which indicates a future action. The past tense verb forms suggest actions that Yahweh has already undertaken or actions being perceived as having already taken place because they are set in motion by Yahweh. Verse 9c describes the final stage of the divine judgment. The Babylonian invasion of 597 B.C. may have been the setting of this lament-judgment speech.

IN THE TEXT

■ **5** In v 5 Yahweh responds to the finality of judgment he announced against Judah with a lament of his own, which is structured in the form of three rhetorical questions. The questions are addressed to Jerusalem; the city represents the nation. The feminine figure in this verse is picked up again in vv 8-9. Jerusalem is portrayed here as a lonely and forsaken woman. The questions affirm the reality that no one will show **compassion,** no one will **lament,** and no one will **turn aside** to ask about Jerusalem's **peace** (*šālôm*). Jerusalem ("the city of peace") that represents *shalom* for the nation itself will be deprived of *shalom*. Jerusalem's loss of well-being indicates the loss of well-being of the whole nation. The questions imply that others will recognize the calamity of the nation as well-deserved judgment and therefore the nation is undeserving of any comfort.

■ **6** Yahweh's lament is followed by his direct speech to Jerusalem (v 6), which provides the theological reason for the lonely and forsaken condition of the city (and the nation). The city is forsaken by others because it has **forsaken** Yahweh. Instead of walking forward with Yahweh, it has **walked backward,** or walked away from him, and thus totally alienated itself from Yahweh. Verses 6-9 list a series of actions in the first person that Yahweh has undertaken to carry out his judgment. These verses indicate Yahweh's intense determination to bring judgment upon Judah. Yahweh's hand, which he **stretched out** once to save the nation from Egypt (v 6; see Exod 6:6; 7:5; Deut 4:34), has been stretched against it to destroy it because of its apostasy. The fate suffered by the enemies of Israel is now its fate. The final phrase *I am weary of relenting* (v 6) indicates that Yahweh's patience, which the people have experienced time and time again in their past history, has come to an end. Fretheim relates Yahweh's "weariness" to the "expending of the divine life" "by bearing the sins of the people over a long period of time." This "entails a self-giving for the sake of the continuing relationship" with those who have continually rejected him (2002, 232-33). The text here clearly indicates the end of Yahweh's gracious dealing with his people. Divine forgiveness at this point in the covenant nation's history is out of the question.

■ **7** Verse 7 indicates the effect of judgment. The imagery of v 7a is taken from the agricultural setting. ***I have scattered them*** indicates the judgment of the exile. Like a farmer who uses the **winnowing fork** to throw the mixture of grain and chaff into the air so that the chaff will be blown away by wind, Yahweh will scatter the people. The phrase ***in the gates of the land*** refers to Yahweh's judgment of exile pronounced and carried out in the gates of the cities throughout the land (Lundbom 1999, 728). In addition to exile, Yahweh has also ***bereaved*** (or, lit. "made childless") ***and destroyed*** his people (**my people**). Divine judgment has made Jerusalem childless. Destruction and death by the enemy's sword is implied here. Verse 7 ends with the note that the divine judgment did not lead the people to ***turn back*** from their wicked way of life (see Amos 4:6-11 for similar evaluation of the people's failure to repent when Yahweh sent a series of calamities against Israel). The people are determined to stay the course of apostasy in spite of Yahweh's serious attempts to bring them back to him through devastating judgment.

■ **8** Yahweh's judgment has nullified the promise that God had made to Abraham that his descendants will be as numerous as the "sand on the seashore" (Gen 22:17; 32:12). Jeremiah describes that war and destruction has increased the number of widows in the land; they are **more numerous than the sand of the sea** (v 8). Women who have lost their children and husbands symbolize the nation without the promise of life and posterity. Verse 8 also describes the **anguish and terror** being experienced by Jerusalem, the mother who was made childless and a widow; she is under a sudden and unexpected attack by a **destroyer.** She is without the protection of her young son or her husband because both of them have been victims of the war.

■ **9** Verse 9 continues the imagery of Jerusalem as a forsaken woman under attack. The woman who bore **seven** children, a woman of great strength, blessedness, and security, has lost all her strength and remains fragile, weak, and lifeless. Though her days were bright and prosperous, they have suddenly become dark. She is a ***shamed and disgraced*** woman because of her widowhood and childlessness. Verse 9 ends with more devastating news. Those that remain in the land, those who have survived previous calamities have no hope; Yahweh intends to hand them over to the **sword** of the enemy. Yahweh's previous judgment actions were aimed to lead the people to repentance, but they have failed. Total destruction by the enemy is what is in store for the recalcitrant people of Judah.

FROM THE TEXT

This text is filled with mixed emotions; God expresses his grief and anger to his people who have rejected him and walked away from him. We find in this text a people without anyone to show pity to them or lament for them or seek their peace (*shalom*). Exile, death, and total annihilation are written all over the text. These harsh words of judgment together with God's rejection of any prophetic mediation in the preceding unit seem to give no hope to the people. However, the text also suggests that God kept the door of repentance that leads to salvation open for Jeremiah's immediate audience. Judah suffered the tragic events of 587 B.C. because it refused to repent before destruction and death finally came.

This text would have reminded the community in exile that if rejecting God and walking away from him have brought exile and disruption to the Abrahamic covenant, then certainly returning to God would reverse the conditions of judgment in which they lived. God addresses the people who are under judgment as "my people." This means that even in judgment God does not abandon his people. "My people" in this context of judgment expresses God's grief and agony over the terrible fate of the nation. This divine grief and God's concern for his people provide the answer for the questions asked in v 5. When no one else would show pity, when no one else would mourn, when no one else would stop to ask for Judah's *shalom*, there remains God—Israel's source of comfort in sorrow and grief.

The theological issues and challenges remain the same for the modern readers of this text. Those who reject God choose for themselves a way of life that leads to death and destruction. When God is removed from one's life, the net effect is the removal of the true source of human comfort and peace (*shalom*). No one can bring comfort and *shalom* to a person who lives without God. Absence of comfort and *shalom* means death and destruction at work in our lives as the judgment for rejecting God. Paul viewed the ministry of Christ in terms of initiating *shalom* to those who were "far away" and those who were "near," to both Jews and Gentiles, who were "dead" in their "transgressions and sins" (Eph 2:1-18).

7. Jeremiah's Lament (15:10-21)

BEHIND THE TEXT

This section includes two sets of dialogue between Jeremiah and Yahweh (vv 10-12, 15-21) interrupted by a judgment speech (vv 13-14). Jeremiah's first speech (v 10) is a lament. Verses 11-12 contain Yahweh's response to Jeremiah. Verses 15-21 contain another lament by the prophet (vv 15-18) and Yahweh's response to the prophet (vv 19-21). Commentators consider 15:10-21 as part of the "confessions" of Jeremiah. The lack of "Yahweh said" at the beginning of v 11 in the Greek translation has led some commentators to view v 11 (and possibly vv 12-14) as a continuation of Jeremiah's lament. Verses 13-14 seem to be words of judgment spoken against the people, in response to Jeremiah's complaint that he is the object of lawsuit and ridicule of the whole nation. These words of judgment for the most part are also found in 17:3-4. Translation of v 11 is difficult (see the NIV and the NRSV as an example of divergent translations of this verse).

a. The Prophet's Complaint and Yahweh's Response (15:10-14)

IN THE TEXT

■ **10** Jeremiah's lament in v 10 indicates the despicable status of the prophet in the land. The lament begins with a cry of despair (***woe to me***) with the vocative **my mother,** which connects this verse to the bereaved "mothers" of 15:8-9. The vocative is not to be taken literally but only as a "figure of speech" (Holladay 1986, 452). He is lamenting not only about himself but also about his mother who gave him birth, who may or may not have been alive at this time. In the literary context of this verse, she joins the rest of the mothers in the land who are grieving over their children. However, emphasis here is clearly not on the mother but on her giving birth to Jeremiah as a person called by Yahweh while he was still in his mother's womb (1:5). In another lament he curses the day of his birth (20:14-18). The lament indicates the prophet's bitterness and utter despair over his call, which was actualized through the agency of his mother who gave birth to him. His birth (and thus the call) is the reason why he is ***a man of dispute*** (*rîb*) and ***contention*** (*mādôn*) with **the whole land.** Both Hebrew words mean the same; these terms indicate a person who is the subject of a lawsuit or complaints brought by others. ***A man of dispute*** may also suggest Jeremiah's role in bringing Yahweh's lawsuit against Judah (Miller 2001, 697). The plot against his life by his own family (11:21-23), and his confrontations with the religious and political leadership (20:1-6; 28:1-11; 36:26) illustrate the trouble-filled life of the prophet.

Some commentators understand the reference to lending and borrowing literally and assume that he is claiming integrity in his financial dealings with others and that he has not done any wrong by charging interest or failing to repay a debt (v 1). However, it is preferable to see here the use of a proverbial expression to make a strong claim of innocence against charges against him as a troublemaker in the land, the one who causes social disruption and disharmony. The prophet's lament concludes with the sorrowful words that though he is innocent of any crime, the whole population (***all of them***) treats him as a contemptuous individual, an object of scorn and curse in the land.

■ **11** English translations show the difficulty and disagreement over the meaning of the Hebrew text of v 11. The following is a possible rendering of the

difficult Hebrew text:
> **Yahweh said:**
> **Surely I have set you free for good,**
> **surely I have entreated for you,**
> **in time of evil, and in time of distress, with the enemy.**

Yahweh's response seems to offer comfort and encouragement to the prophet who expresses his bitterness over the miserable conditions brought upon his life by Yahweh's call. The response begins with the strong reminder that Yahweh has indeed **set** the prophet **free** or delivered him from past difficult situations. Yahweh has also **entreated** or intervened on his behalf **with the enemy** during evil and distressing times. The **enemy** here may be a reference to all those who have opposed the prophet's preaching. Another possibility is to treat "the enemy" as the direct object and thus to read the second part of v 11 as follows: "Surely I have caused the enemy to entreat (intervene) for you in time of evil and in time of distress." This reading does not make much sense in this context unless we see here a reference to the princes and the people intervening to spare the life of the prophet when the priests and the prophets wanted to put him to death for speaking about the destruction of the temple (26:1-16). In any case, the idea of Yahweh's intervention on his behalf during life-threatening times is conveyed here.

■ **12** Commentators do not agree on the interpretation of v 12. Some commentators see this verse as a word of encouragement to Jeremiah; others see this as a word about the impossibility of Judah being able to stop the power of the advancing Babylonian army. The context seems to favor the understanding of this verse as an encouragement to the prophet, and thus a continuation of v 11. Fretheim interprets the reference to **iron** to mean the "iron-willed" people of Judah, **iron from the north** to mean the Babylonians, and **bronze** to mean Jeremiah. He thinks that the verse thus is a word of assurance to Jeremiah that Judah will not be able to break the power of either Babylon or Jeremiah (2002, 236). Lundbom reaches a similar conclusion but sees the reference to iron from the north and bronze as epithets for Jeremiah (1999, 735).

Interpretation of vv 13-14 poses difficulty. The near duplication of these verses in 17:3-4, which is a judgment word against Judah, prompts us to see here another word of judgment directed against Judah. After giving the assurance to the prophet, Yahweh turns his attention to the people of Judah who abuse and mistreat the prophet. These verses describe the defeat of Judah, the plundering of its wealth by Babylon, and the nation's slavery and exile in a foreign land. Some commentators have taken vv 13-14 as a continuation of Yahweh's speech in vv 11-12. They see here a word announced to Jeremiah that he, too, will be subjected to cruel treatment when the Babylonian army comes through the land (Fretheim 2002, 236-37; Stulman 2005, 151). It is likely that these words serve the purpose of reiterating Jeremiah's words of judgment against Judah and thus vindicating the prophet as a true spokesperson of Yahweh (Miller 2001, 697).

■ **13** Verse 13 describes the judgment in terms of Yahweh giving away to the enemy the **wealth** and **treasures** of Judah as booty of the war. Yahweh will not require any payment for this transaction, but it will be a gift from Yahweh. Neither can Judah expect any compensation for the loss (Lundbom 1999, 738). Yahweh will permit the looting of the national treasures as the judgment for all the **sins** the people committed in all their **territories**. Yahweh announces that he will punish Judah's sins by making it an impoverished and economically ruined nation.

■ **14** Based on 17:4, some commentators and translations correct *I will make pass over* (*wĕhaʻăbartî*; 15:14) to "I will make you serve" (*wĕhaʻăbadtîkā*; **I will enslave you**). The Hebrew text reflects Yahweh's judgment against the enemies of the prophet (*I will make your enemies pass over*). Yahweh will make the enemies of Jeremiah go into exile in a foreign land. However, it may also be understood as a word about Judah's exile and servitude in Babylon (keeping in line with 17:4 as in the NIV). Verse 14*b* states the reason for the judgment of Judah. Yahweh's **anger** has already **kindled** the **fire** of judgment against the nation, and it will continue to burn until the destruction of the nation. Yahweh's anger is unleashed against everyone in the land (**against you** in plural). The entire population, including the prophet, will experience the effect of Yahweh's wrath. The judgment that came in 587 B.C. did not spare anyone, not even Yahweh's faithful prophet.

FROM THE TEXT

Jeremiah's lament reveals the human being behind the prophetic persona that often speaks courageously God's judgment words to Judah. He expresses his inner agony over his suffering brought upon by his faithful preaching of God's word. Here we have a prophet who has no courage or strength left in him to continue the task for which God has called him. His very life is being tormented by the call, so he could only wish that his mother had not given birth to him. We expect such words of anguish from people who suffer deep physical and emotional pain. It is possible that the exiled people would have found in Jeremiah's complaint words suitable to convey the anguish of their own tormented life in a foreign land. They would also have been reminded of the role they and the nation as a whole have played in bringing this agony to the prophet's life. In its exilic context, the text would have reminded the community the negative effect of their words on the prophet as well as on themselves (Fretheim 2002, 243); for just as the prophet suffered because of their words, they, too, are suffering because of the words spoken against them by God for bringing agony to the prophet (vv 13-14).

In a larger context, Jeremiah gives the language of lament to all who are persecuted and suffer for the sake of righteousness (Matt 5:11). The good news in this text is that God does not abandon those who are faithful to his words and calling upon their lives. God's response to Jeremiah indicates that the one who agonizes before God is seldom turned away to suffer alone. The text does not indicate an end to the prophet's conflict-filled life, but only the divine promise to continue to make him the "bronze wall to stand against the whole land" (Jer 1:18).

b. Jeremiah's Lament and Yahweh's Response (15:15-21)

IN THE TEXT

■ **15** Verses 15-21 contain the final dialogue between Jeremiah and Yahweh in 14:1—15:21. Here again, we find a lament ("confession") of the prophet (vv 15-18) and Yahweh's response (vv 19-21). The prophet's lament contains typical words and phrases found in the lament psalms.

The lament begins with the prophet's acknowledgment of Yahweh's knowledge of his condition (*you know* from yāda'), followed by an appeal to Yahweh's memory of the prophet during this period of affliction (v 15). The opening words (*you know*) could be understood as both an expression of faith and an expression of disappointment that Yahweh who knows does not act to deliver the afflicted (Brueggemann 1998, 146). **Remember me and *visit me*** together constitute a plea for deliverance. He seeks Yahweh's visitation not only to deliver him but also to punish his enemies. This is made clear in his prayer for divine retribution against those who **persecute** him. The call to **take vengeance** is best understood as a call to vindication—not only of the prophet who remained faithful to Yahweh, but also of Yahweh who sent the prophet. He does not take the matter into his own hands but leaves the matter of retribution to Yahweh. The prophet also pleads with Yahweh not to let him die (**take me away**) while he extends patience to those who persecute him. Jeremiah acknowledges the traditional faith in Yahweh as a God who is "slow to anger" (Exod 34:6). But he is also concerned that Yahweh, by keeping alive his enemies, may indeed be endangering the life of his faithful spokesperson. Verse 15 ends with his reminder to Yahweh (***know***) that his life is in danger because of Yahweh's call. This is a motivation for Yahweh to act immediately to save the one who is suffering on account of his call.

■ **16** Jeremiah's words in v 16 are aimed to further motivate Yahweh to act on his behalf. The opening words (***your words were found***) recall the experience of Yahweh putting his words in Jeremiah's mouth at the time of his call (see 1:9) as well as words that continue to come to him as part of the ongoing revelation. The prophet ingested and internalized Yahweh's words gladly without reservation or resistance (see Ezek 2:8—3:3). Lundbom views this as an indication of Jeremiah's acceptance of his call in the context of the discovery of the law-book in the temple in 622 B.C., for which there is insufficient textual or historical support (1999, 743). **Joy** and **gladness** filled the life of the prophet when he received Yahweh's words. Revelation brought an intimacy of relationship with Yahweh, and he found satisfaction with his vocation as a prophet.

Ezekiel also testifies to a sweet taste in his mouth when he ingested the scroll given him to eat (Ezek 3:3; see also Ps 119:103). Jeremiah 15:16 ends with a further statement of Yahweh's relationship with the prophet. **Your name is called upon me** indicates Yahweh's claim of ownership of the prophet (see this phrase in reference to the temple in 7:10). The One who owns the prophet is none other than **Yahweh, God of hosts,** the all-powerful Creator and sustainer of the universe.

■ **17** Following the pattern of the laments in the Psalms, Jeremiah claims his innocence in v 17a. The call set him apart for Yahweh's service. As a set-apart person, he lived his life detached from the merrymaking elements of the community. This indicates a self-imposed social isolation. However, in the second part of v 17, Jeremiah seems to suggest that Yahweh is responsible for his isolation from social and community life. The phrase **because of your hand** indicates Yahweh's total control over Jeremiah's life. Jeremiah also traces the cause of his social isolation to Yahweh's words; Yahweh has **filled** him not with words of peace and welfare but with words of **indignation.** He is an outcast in the society because he brings only words of judgment from Yahweh.

■ **18** Jeremiah's complaint continues and his accusation of Yahweh as the cause of his troubles becomes more specific in v 18. His complaint is formulated in the form of two questions; one question asks why he suffers from his endless pain and from a wound that does not heal, and the other question asks if Yahweh can be trusted. He describes his present condition utilizing the metaphors of wound and water. Unceasing **pain** and incurable **wound** most likely refer to the tormented, afflicted, and socially isolated condition of the prophet and perhaps not to any particular illness. He deals with this endless reality every day. His questions are directed to Yahweh because Yahweh is the cause of the prophet's trouble-filled life. The second metaphor raises serious questions about the trustworthiness of Yahweh. Some translations treat v 18b as a statement that makes it a bold accusation (see NRSV, for example), the opposite of his affirmation of Yahweh as a "spring of living water" in 2:13. The imagery reflects the scene of a *wadi*, a dry riverbed in the wilderness. Winter and spring rains fill a *wadi* with water, but when water is scarce and most needed in the intense heat of summer, those who look for water will find only a dry riverbed. Implied in this question is Jeremiah's assessment of the unreliable nature of Yahweh. If taken as a statement, then v 18b indicates that Yahweh has indeed failed the prophet. Jeremiah does not experience Yahweh's presence and strength at a time when he desperately needs it.

■ **19** Yahweh responds to the prophet's lament and accusation of Yahweh with a sharp rebuke and a solemn promise of help and deliverance (vv 19-21). There are two "if" clauses in v 19, the first requiring the prophet's **return** (*šûb*) and the second requiring him to speak words that are **precious.** These conditional statements indicate that even in the midst of personal suffering and questions about Yahweh's reliability, the prophet must submit himself to the demands of Yahweh. The verb *šûb* ("turn," "return," "repent") is used four times in v 19 (in Hebrew), two times in the context of the prophet's relation to Yahweh and two times in his relation to the people. Some commentators understand the first condition (**if you return**) as a call to repentance. They also understand ***I will let you return*** as Yahweh's willingness to **restore** him to his prophetic task. However, the text does not indicate any sin that he committed that required repentance. Yahweh warns Jeremiah not to let the intensity of his pain and suffering detract him from his covenantal commitment to Yahweh. He must maintain a proper perspective of his call and relationship to Yahweh. The prophet's negative assessment of Yahweh seems to be the critical issue that underlies this conditional statement (v 18). Lundbom's suggestion that the reason for the call to repent is the "false preaching . . . of peace and giving assurances of deliverance" has no support in the literary context of this text (1999, 749-50). ***I will let you return*** is a reassurance of Yahweh's covenantal fidelity to the prophet to continue to use him as his spokesperson.

The second "if" statement in v 19 makes clear what "return" involves; the prophet must **bring out** or speak that which is **precious,** words that reflect his covenantal fidelity to Yahweh and Yahweh's fidelity to him, and not words that raise questions about Yahweh's trustworthiness (see v 18). This is essential to his continued relation to Yahweh as his spokesperson (***you shall be as my mouth***). The outcome of Jeremiah's obedience to the divine demand and a new commitment to proclaim his covenant fidelity is that the people (***they***) ***will*** turn to him for guidance. **You *will*** **not turn to them** is a warning; the prophet must not follow the way of the people's thinking about Yahweh. Rather he, through his faithful speech, must bring them to his way of thinking about Yahweh and help them to turn to Yahweh for their salvation.

■ **20** The rebuke of v 20 is followed by a word of assurance from Yahweh to the disillusioned prophet (vv 20-21). Even in the midst of challenging questions, Yahweh does not abandon the prophet but reaffirms to him the promise he made at the time of his call. Verse 20 sums up the content of 1:18-19. The road ahead is not easy; the prophet can expect continued struggle with the enemy. Yahweh's promise is to continue to make the prophet a tenacious individual, unafraid of the people, and unassailable and undefeatable by the people. Yahweh also reaffirms his protective and saving presence to the prophet.

■ **21** Verse 21 adds to this promise another word about Yahweh's deliverance of the prophet from the **wicked** and the **ruthless.** This reassurance is thus an answer to the opening appeal of the prophet's lament (v 15). In the end Yahweh answers the prophet, but along with it also comes a strong reminder to remain faithful to his prophetic vocation.

FROM THE TEXT

The text presents two perspectives about being a spokesperson for God when times are difficult; one from the life experience of the one who is called and the other from God who calls people to be faithful to their calling. The prophet here expresses freely what he thinks about himself and about God, whose call puts him at odds with his audience. There is self-pity, anger, and complaint in his lament addressed to God. There is a sudden shift in this text from joy and gladness to sorrow and bitterness. The world of joy that Jeremiah found was suddenly turned into a world of pain, sorrow, suffering, and social isolation. The text indicates that prophets who confront sin and dare to announce judgment do not always find their ministry a joyous adventure with God. Loneliness, pain, despair, and doubt are only natural responses when true servants of God find themselves stuck between the compulsion to speak truthfully for God and an obstinate crowd that rejects both God and his spokesperson. If this lament is taken as a scorecard of the prophet's mission, there is no success or significance reported here; in both counts, the prophet has failed. The amazing thing about this text is that the despondent prophet does not go into a deep silence or walk away from the call but speaks with boldness to the God who called him to this dangerous mission. That tells us something about his deep convictions about his relationship with God.

Laments like these tell us volumes about the approachability of God who does not remain aloof to human concerns. Speaking from the depth of one's heart is a powerful way to communicate with God. We should add here that laments like these would have given ammunition to the exilic community to be daring in expressing its grief and complaint to God. The lament of Jeremiah in this text continues to address the concerns of those who live in exile in our world because of their faithfulness and devotion to God's powerful word.

God's response to Jeremiah brings a balance to this otherwise one-sided perspective on the prophet's personal agony. God who permits the prophet to speak his mind also has something significant to say to him. It is almost as if God is saying, "Stay focused, don't lose perspective, and remain committed to your call." Like Job, the prophet, too, was preoccupied with his world of suffering and social isolation. God's response here seems to parallel the divine response to Job (Job 38:1—42:6). In both cases, God's speech sets the record straight about himself; in both cases, there is an invitation to reorient one's thinking about God. In both cases, there is assurance of God's providential presence, strongly implied in Job, but explicit here in our text. God's covenantal fidelity is guaranteed to the prophet in this text; but to appropriate God's faithfulness the prophet must "return" to God and remain true to his covenantal commitment to God.

"I am with you" is the quintessential promise of God in the Bible. This is a trustworthy word from God. This assurance would have given the people in exile in Babylon a new perspective on their future. This is precisely the assurance the risen Christ gave to his bewildered and despondent disciples who had no idea of the world they were about to encounter (Matt 28:20). Those who struggle to remain faithful to their calling to be God's servants in the world today continue to hear this gracious promise in the midst of their trouble-filled life.

"UPROOT AND TEAR DOWN"

JUDAH'S SOCIAL WORLD (16:1-21)

Overview

This section opens with a prose sermon (vv 1-13) that begins with Yahweh's command to Jeremiah to refrain from marriage and other social practices such as mourning for the dead and feasting and celebrations. Death and exile is what awaits the nation. The prophet's life symbolically represents the end of Judah's social world. The language of judgment in vv 1-13 is harsh and severe; however, the following prose speech balances it with a word of hope (vv 14-15). In an abrupt change, another prose speech announces judgment on the nation for defiling the land with idolatry. The concluding unit is mixed with poetry and prose (vv 19-21). The confession of the nations that their idols are worthless and not gods may be linked to the theme of idolatry in vv 1-13 and 16-18. The unit ends with a brief statement from Yahweh indicating his purpose to make Judah know his power and his name (v 21).

1. Do Not Marry (16:1-13)

BEHIND THE TEXT

This unit (16:1-13), which gives us a glimpse of Jeremiah's personal life, contains three prohibitions from Yahweh: the prophet's marriage (v 2), his participation in mourning for the dead (v 5*a*), and his participation in festive celebrations (v 8). Each prohibition is followed by an oracle that explains the reason for the divine command (vv 3-4, 5*b*-7, 9). The second part of this unit, which some commentators treat as a separate unit, has a question-answer style in which Yahweh gives the theological reason for his pronouncement of calamity upon them (vv 10-13). Though these verses may be treated separately, they are not totally disconnected from the preceding section. Verse 10 sets these verses in the literary and theological context of vv 1-9.

Several literary and thematic motifs connect vv 1-13 with chs 14—15. Jeremiah suffers not only from his self-imposed social isolation (see 15:17) but also from Yahweh's command that deprives him the joy of family life through wife and children (16:2). His social isolation (15:17) is also intensified by Yahweh's command not to participate in festive occasions (16:8). He suffers from deep personal pain (15:18), but he is commanded not to share the pain and sorrow of others, which adds more agony to the prophet (16:5). The prophet who hopes for peace (14:19) is told that peace is being removed from the land (16:5). His mother gave birth to him to be a man of strife (15:10), but the destiny of sons and daughters and their mothers and fathers in the land is death by deadly diseases (16:3-4). The mothers who face death in vv 3-4 also may be linked to the bereaved and disgraced mothers of 15:8-9. The people who carry out self-righteous religious rituals (14:12) want to know the specific sin they have committed that brings upon them Yahweh's judgment (16:10). Israel's apostasy implied in 14:10 receives further elaboration in 16:11. The judgment of "sword and famine" in chs 14—15 is reiterated in 16:4. Yahweh's judgment of scattering the people (15:7) finds parallel in his decision to hurl them out of the land (16:13). The impact of the prohibitions in vv 1-9 extends beyond its immediate literary and theological landscape. The suspension of the command to "be fruitful and multiply" (Gen 1:28 NRSV) and the terrible portrait of death and destruction in Jer 16:2-4 indicates reversal of the creational order and the return to chaos (see 4:23-26; Stulman 2005, 161). Holladay assigns this text to 601/600 B.C. (1986, 468). The command not to marry may have come early in the prophet's life, perhaps in the days of Josiah (Lundbom 1999, 761). The text itself does not give any clues that permit us to assign a specific date to this oracle.

IN THE TEXT

■ **1-2** Verse 1 conveys the personal and biographical nature of the account in 16:1-13. Yahweh's command to Jeremiah that he must not marry and have children is as unorthodox as his command to Hosea to marry a woman of promiscuous character and have children of harlotry (v 2). Other instances where wives or children of the prophets are involved include the naming and birth of Isaiah's son (see Isa 8:1-4) and the command to Ezekiel that he must not mourn the death of his wife (Ezek 24:15-17). In each of these instances, the prophet's actions convey a message from Yahweh. Yahweh's command to Jeremiah that he must not **marry** (v 2) means that Yahweh is denying the prophet not only the joy of marital bliss (Deut 24:5) but also the creational and covenantal blessing (Gen 1:28; Pss 127:3-5; 128:3-4). Celibacy was virtually unknown in ancient Israel, and there is no Hebrew word for bachelor in the OT (Holladay 1986, 469). Yahweh's command also specifically denies him the privilege of having **sons or daughters** (v 2). This command projects an ominous future for the nation. Holladay sees in this divine command an indication of Yahweh's decision to bring the nation to its "extinction" (1986, 469). The mention of **this place** further indicates the utterly dangerous and life-threatening conditions of Judah that offer no hope for anyone (see Paul's recommendation of celibacy to the unmarried because of the "present crisis" [1 Cor 7:25-26]).

■ **3-4** The theological reason for the divine command is stated in vv 3-4. The message addresses **sons, daughters, mothers,** and **fathers** in the land (v 3). Entire families will perish by **deadly diseases . . . sword and famine** (v 4). The dead will not be lamented or buried. Even in death indignity will follow the people. Verse 4 portrays a land strewn with dead bodies left unburied and denied of any funeral rites. Even **the birds of the *sky*** and **the beasts of the earth** (see Gen 1:30) will participate in carrying out Yahweh's judgment of his covenant people.

■ **5** The second oracle forbids the prophet from entering the houses where people mourn and lament for the dead (vv 5-7). The precise function of the ***house of mourning*** (*bêt marzēaḥ* also could be translated "house of the mourning-feast"; Lundbom 1999, 757) is not clear (v 5). The only other occurrence of the word *marzēaḥ* is in Amos 6:7 ("feasting" in the NIV; "revelry" in the NRSV). Based on its Semitic cognates, some recent commentators have understood the word to mean a funerary association with a banquet hall for eating and drinking (see detailed analysis of this word in Lundbom 1999, 757-58). The NIV reading **house where there is a funeral meal** reflects this view (v 5). The command not to **mourn** and not to **show sympathy** indicates that perhaps mourning for the dead was the primary activity carried out in the house of mourning in this verse (see also the reference to breaking the bread and offering a cup to comfort those who mourn in v 8). Jeremiah must not engage in any activity that shows grief or sympathy for the dead in the land. The reason for this prohibition is theological. Yahweh has removed from the people his ***peace*** (*šālôm*), his ***covenant loyalty*** (*ḥesed*), and his ***compassion*** (*raḥămîm*). Jeremiah's absence from the house of mourning would symbolically represent Yahweh's withdrawal of these covenant commitments and blessings.

Verse 5*b* also directly contradicts the "lasting peace" message of the false prophets (14:13). Withdrawal of these covenant commitments and blessings does not mean that Yahweh responds to the infidelity of his people with infidelity on his part, or that, as Brueggemann argues, there is "complete absence of fidelity on God's part" (1998, 152). Rather, it is his commitment to remain faithful to the covenant that compels him to withdraw these commitments, which in turn means the curses of the covenant at work on the unfaithful people. Death and grieving in this text simply mean life lived under the curses of the covenant.

■ **6** Verses 6-7 expand the idea expressed in vv 3-4. Death will be the great leveler of all social distinctions. The rich and the famous and the poor and the destitute (***great and small***) all will suffer the same fate of death (v 6). The dead will not receive proper burial or customary funeral rites. These verses also suggest that some will survive, but these survivors will not participate in the mourning rituals, which include cutting oneself and shaving one's head. These are customs prohibited by the Law (Lev 19:28; Deut 14:1), but it seems that some people may have practiced these rituals (see Jer 41:4-7) in ancient Israel.

■ **7** Verse 7 expands the prohibition in v 5. This verse suggests that eating and drinking were perhaps part of the funeral customs. The Hebrew phrase here (*yiprĕsû lāhem*, lit. "break for them") suggests the idea of sharing food to comfort those who mourn for the dead. Bringing food to the house of mourners in this text is similar to the modern-day custom of neighbors and friends taking food to a bereaving family. Offering a ***cup of consolation*** indicates the practice of giving a cup of wine as a drink to comfort those who mourn (Lundbom 1999, 760), or perhaps to relieve them from their emotional distress (Holladay 1986, 471). The focus here is on denying any kind of consolation to those who mourn, not even for those who mourn the loss of their parents; the last part of v 7 is linked to v 3.

■ **8** The third oracle (vv 8-9) prohibits the prophet from entering the ***house of feasting*** (*bêt mišteh* is usually understood as a place of joyous celebrations such as wedding festivities (v 8); see Eccl 7:2 for this same phrase). He can show no emotions, neither sorrow nor joy, when death strikes the land. As Stulman states, "Jeremiah is to reveal in his body the woeful destruction of structured life, Judah's hour of darkness" (2005, 162).

■ **9** The reason for the prohibition is stated in v 9. Yahweh intends to ***make cease from this place*** all the joyous festivities, including wedding celebrations. The prophet will be an eyewitness to the cessation of joy in the land. Reference to the groom and the bride links this verse to the command not to marry in v 2. Jeremiah, through his celibacy and through withdrawal from any social occasion, is being called upon to demonstrate to the nation its impending death. This demand comes to the prophet at a high personal cost and sacrifice.

■ **10** Verses 10-13 contain another oracle in a question-answer format. Yahweh anticipates that Jeremiah's symbolic actions and his ominous words about the ignominious death of the nation would prompt the people to ask **why Yahweh has spoken all this great evil** (v 10). They would want to know what they have done to offend Yahweh. The questions, **What is our iniquity? What is our sin?** imply the people's claim of righteousness; they may claim that Yahweh's verdict is unmerited. These questions imply a strong denial of any sin they have committed (see 2:35). These questions also display the audacity of people who think that all is well in their relation to Yahweh.

■ **11-12** Yahweh prepares the prophet to respond to the people with a theological reason for the judgment (vv 11-12). The answer does not contain a new list of sins but a reiteration of what has already been stated previously (see, for example, 7:23-26; 9:13-14; 13:10). For generations, the nation has followed the path of apostasy and has thus violated Yahweh's *torah* (v 11; **forsaken** Yahweh, **walked after** other gods, served and worshiped them). The past and present history of the nation discloses its guilt of covenant-breaking. The present generation has committed **more evil** than its ancestors (v 12). The people are determined to follow the stubborn will of their evil hearts and pay no attention to Yahweh.

■ **13** Yahweh's judgment is upon his people who have violated his *torah* (v 13). The people who have practiced idolatry in the **land** that they have received as a gift from Yahweh will be hurled out from his land into a land where idolatry is the accepted way of life (see this curse in Deut 28:36; also Jer 10:18; 15:14). This land into which they will be expelled is a land that is totally alien and unknown to the present and the past generations. The word about worshipping **other gods day and night** perhaps means that they will be forced to worship the gods of their captors. The gods they have chosen to worship in the Promised Land will indeed become their gods in exile; moreover, in exile they will live without the experience of Yahweh's **favor**. The exiled people cannot expect to receive any favor from other gods because they can neither bless nor curse those who worship them (2:28; see Deut 32:37-38).

FROM THE TEXT

The symbolic acts in this text convey the end of Judah's social and communal life. The text also announces the suspension of all the theological claims rooted in God's covenant relationship with the people of Israel. The questions of the people and the prophet's answer in vv 10-13 indicate the instructional purpose of this text. The text clearly exposes Judah's sin, not only of the past generations but also of the present generation, and holds the nation responsible for the disruption of its social and communal life and the coming exile. The goal of the text in its original setting would have been to persuade the people to return to a relationship of fidelity and wholehearted devotion to God. Covenant fidelity is necessary for the preservation of normal social and communal life in the land, and for the enjoyment of covenant privileges. The people in exile would have found in this text the theological rationale for their expulsion to a foreign land. The tragedy of exile is God's doing, but it has happened because of the long history of Judah's recalcitrant behavior. The future of the exiled nation rests on its commitment to reestablish itself as a covenant-keeping people.

The text reminds its modern readers the dangerous consequence of infidelity to God. The thought of God withdrawing his peace, covenant loyalty, and compassion disturbs us today, as it would have shocked and surprised the ancient readers of this text. The text, however, powerfully reminds us that our personal and communal life and interactions are provisions from God and that they are sustained by his gracious gift of peace, covenant loyalty, and compassion. The text also reminds us that God's withdrawal of these gifts from those who take his grace and forgiving love for granted is a real possibility. When that happens, not only our relationship with God but also our joyful interaction and meaningful life in the community come to an end. Our exile and death begin at that moment.

We live in a world where television and other media have elevated some religious leaders into spiritual celebrity status or into prominence as political power brokers. Many young people enter into ministry with an eye on attaining fame and status in the society. The person of the prophet in this text is under the divine command to deprive himself of all the joys of personal and social life. He reminds those who are called that along with the call to speak for God comes also the call to embody the word of God, which may often bring painful and agonizing personal life experiences. For those who view ministry as an opportunity to gain acceptance and recognition, the prophetic person in this text is a discouraging figure. For those who understand ministry as total obedience to God even if the path of ministry involves difficult and painful circumstances of life, the prophet is an exemplary model, the one worthy of our attention. Jesus' words remind us of the prophetic figure of Jeremiah: "If any want to become my followers, let them deny themselves and take up their cross and follow me" (Mark 8:34 NRSV).

2. Homecoming of the Exiled (16:14-15)

BEHIND THE TEXT

These verses are a near duplication of 23:7-8, given in the context of an oracle of restoration. In ch 16 these verses are sandwiched between two harsh words of judgments (vv 1-13 and vv 16-18). The abrupt change from the harsh words of judgment (vv 1-13) to the promise of homecoming has prompted commentators to view this unit as an exilic or postexilic addition to the book. In its present context, this text softens the judgment speech in the preceding verses. These verses offer hope for those who have heard the words of judgment. Judgment is here balanced with salvation, which is a consistent feature of OT prophecies. Yahweh's plan is not to leave his people in exile, but they will be brought back to their homeland.

IN THE TEXT

■ **14-15** The opening phrase (**days are coming**) introduces Yahweh's action in the future. The oath formula *as Yahweh lives* (see also 4:2; 5:2) is attached here to two saving actions of Yahweh: one, the exodus event in which Yahweh acted decisively against the powerful and ruthless Egyptian empire to liberate the Hebrew slaves from their bondage and to give birth to the nation Israel; second, a future event that Yahweh will perform to liberate the exiled people of Israel from the lands of their exile, to bring them back to their homeland. Yahweh announces that the time will come in the future when Israel's confession of faith in Yahweh will no longer be based on the old saving event of the nation's deliverance from Egypt. Rather, this confession of faith will be replaced with a new saving event; i.e., Yahweh's deliverance of his people from **the land of the north** (Babylon) and all the lands of their exile, and their return to the land of their ancestors (v 15).

Replacement of the exodus language with a new exodus language implies that the new event will be far more glorious than the old saving event. Israel's theology will be thus rewritten and reformulated with this coming event, which will make the exodus from Egypt obsolete and the previous confessional creeds outdated. The text is extremely bold in asserting the end of the Mosaic era of salvation. Furthermore, it anticipates a new era of salvation. This theme is elaborated in the oracles of Isa 40—55 (Isa 42:9; 43:18-19).

FROM THE TEXT

The reference to the old saving event and the future saving event vividly reminds the reader of the possibility of life that God wills to create for his people. For Jeremiah's audience, the exodus from Egypt was a fixed event in their memory. It marked for them the end of slavery and death and the beginning of freedom and life in the land of promise. Nothing could supersede it or could be compared to it. Judah's covenant-breaking, however, brought an end to that era of God's salvation. The consequence was expulsion from the land of freedom to another land where the once liberated people of God would be slaves again to other gods and other political powers (16:10-13).

This text announces good news to those in exile. There will be a "new exodus," a new historical reality that would serve as the theological foundation of Israel's future relationship with God and its confession of faith. God will bring his people to their home. He will make everything new for them. The God who is portrayed in this text is not only a *God who saved* but also a *God who saves*. In Christ, God continues to make old things obsolete and create new things to bring the wayward humanity to his presence. He is indeed a God who makes "all things new" (Rev 21:5 NRSV).

3. Judgment for Defiling the Land (16:16-18)

BEHIND THE TEXT

Though the restoration is promised as a future reality, it does not take away the necessity of speaking judgment in the harshest terms possible. This unit continues the judgment theme of vv 1-13. The text is somewhat ambiguous about the identity of the agents of judgment (**fishermen, hunters**) as well as on the identity of the people being judged. One can make the argument that the reference to the people who have profaned the land in v 18 suggests the invading army of Babylon (see Fretheim 2002, 252). The overall context supports the reading of this text as an oracle of judgment against Judah. Some commentators connect the sending of **fishermen** first and then **hunters** later in v 16 to the two successive Babylonian invasions (597 B.C. and 587 B.C.). These two images also may be applied to various enemy nations, or simply to Babylon, the enemy from the north. The judgment oracle certainly anticipates the coming Babylonian invasion, and thus it most likely belongs to a context before 587 B.C. Bright places v 18 in the exilic setting because of its similarity to Isa 40:2 (1965, 111).

IN THE TEXT

■ **16** This text continues the judgment word in vv 1-13, and it does not fit well with the restoration/homecoming theme of vv 14-15. Yahweh's instruments of judgment will "fish" and "hunt" throughout the land to capture his enemies (v 16). Yahweh or the enemy as fishermen is also found in the judgment language of Ezek 29:3-5, Amos 4:2, and Hab 1:14-15. Verse 16 suggests Yahweh's intent to pursue his enemies until everyone is caught; the text gives no hope for anyone who may attempt to escape Yahweh's dragnet (see Amos 9:2-4).

■ **17** Verse 17 offers the reason for Yahweh's intense pursuit of his enemies. Yahweh's eyes are on his people whose ways of life are wicked and sinful. Neither the people nor their sins are hidden from his eyes.

■ **18** Verse 18 describes judgment in terms of Yahweh repaying the people **double for their *iniquity*.** Some commentators view **double** as excessive or massive punishment or punishment equivalent to the wrongdoing or as a reference to the successive invasions of Judah by the Babylonians in 597 and 587 B.C. The intent of v 18 seems to be that the punishment will be total and complete; it will be handed down "in the fullest sense" (Lundbom 1999, 771). The covenant people have defiled the land of Yahweh, his special **inheritance,** with "carcasses" (NRSV) of their idols, lifeless and worthless objects of worship that have taken the place of the living God of Israel. Yahweh warns here that this sin will be punished in full measure.

FROM THE TEXT

God's judgment of sin is the theme of this text. The text makes clear that the God who sees the sinful conduct and the idolatrous worship of his people is the One who brings judgment. The intensity of judgment corresponds to the systemic corruption that God sees in the land. He is determined to thoroughly cleanse his land that his people have polluted by their idolatry. The hunting and fishing imagery need not be taken too literally to project the portrait of a vindictive God who does not rest until all sinners are brought to divine justice. Judgment here and elsewhere in Jeremiah is the necessary response of God to sin, and it is always consistent with his character as a holy God. Also, here and elsewhere in the book, judgment is not the end of relationship between God and his people, but it opens the door for the experience of God's new saving action. The message of hope in chs 30—33 can be fully appreciated only if we pay careful attention to passages such as this, which seem to give no hope to Judah.

4. Confession of the Nations (16:19-21)

BEHIND THE TEXT

Jeremiah concludes the series of judgment speeches in ch 16 (with the exception of vv 14-15) with a hymn that has three parts. The first part (v 19a) consists of the prophet's statement of trust in Yahweh and his anticipation that that the nations will come to Yahweh. The second part (vv 19b-20) contains the words of confession that the nations will make when they come to Yahweh. The third part (v 21) consists of Yahweh's response to the prophet, which outlines his actions that will follow the confession of the nations. Commentators do not agree on the authenticity of this unit. Most commentators tend to see this as a later insertion. Bright sees in this text several Jeremianic expressions and argues that the idea of the nations turning to Yahweh was present during Jeremiah's day (1965, 113). The date of this text cannot be determined with any certainty.

IN THE TEXT

■ **19** The prophet's description of Yahweh as his **strength** and his **fortress** and a **refuge** *in the day of trouble* (v 19) reflects the language of several psalms (for example, Pss 27:1; 46:1) and Jer 14:8; 17:17. The prophet's anticipation of the nations coming to Yahweh is also found in 3:17. The texts of Isa 2:2-4 and Mic 4:1-3 suggest that this idea was perhaps a commonly shared perspective at least in some segments of the Israelite prophetic tradition. What is missing in v 19 is the specific mention of Zion as the destination of the nations' pilgrimage. The confession of the nations that they have inherited a **lie** or falsehood (šeqer; see 5:2) from their ancestors has no parallel in the OT (Holladay 1986, 482). The same is true of their confession that their idols are worthless things (*hebel*).

▪ **20** The prophet's anticipation of the nations' rejection of idolatry is reissued in the question the nations ask in v 20: ***Can a mortal make for himself gods, though they are not gods?*** The answer is obviously an emphatic no. How can humans who are creatures presume to make the Creator? The nations will admit the utter foolishness and futility of human beings attempting to manufacture gods that are nothing but worthless idols.

▪ **21** In v 21 Yahweh responds to the prophet's trust and his anticipation of the coming of the nations to Yahweh. Yahweh will initiate three actions toward the nations. He will **teach them;** he will ***make them know*** his **power and might;** and **they will know** Yahweh by his name. Yahweh's purpose for the nations focuses on bringing the nations to their knowledge of him as the true God. This is powerfully demonstrated by the use of the verb **know** (*yāda'*) three times in this verse. To **know** Yahweh by his name in this context essentially means confession of faith in Yahweh as the sovereign Lord of history. This knowledge of Yahweh also means their total disassociation with the idols whom they worship. They will come to know Yahweh when they see his manifestation of his power and might exercised in history. What that demonstration of Yahweh's power involves is not spelled out in the text; it perhaps indicates his power that he will demonstrate in the restoration of Israel. This is a recurring motif in Ezekiel where the prophet anticipates both Israel and the nations coming to know Yahweh through his actions in history (see Ezek 6:7, 10, 14; 25:7, 11; 37:6).

FROM THE TEXT

Jeremiah 16:19-21 seem to present an initiative on the part of the nations to come to God without the instrumentality of Israel. In other places in Jeremiah the nations' coming to God is linked to Israel's restoration (see 3:15-17; 4:2; 12:16). But in this text the nations come to God and he teaches them who he really is through the demonstration of his power and might. In other words, the nations acknowledge him as God by what they witness in history. This is in sharp contrast to Israel's stubborn resistance to acknowledge God, who is working through historical events. This coming of the nations to God and their decision to abandon their idolatry is a decisive turning point in their history. In this text there is no indication of any role that Israel would play in the coming of the nations to God. Israel has learned its idolatrous worship from the nations, and Israel is now deeply committed to that way of life. Confession of the nations and their decision to abandon idolatry could be viewed as a challenge to Israel to return to God following the example of the nations. The text thus seems to present a reversal of roles in Israel-nations relationship.

A key point in this text is the conviction of the prophet that the nations will come to Israel's God and acknowledge their faith in him. This theme is reiterated by the apostle Paul in Rom 9—10. Clarke finds in Jer 16:19-21 a "prediction of the calling of the Gentiles by the Gospel of Christ" (300). The text makes clear that God is Lord of both Jews and Gentiles and that salvation is God's gift to all who call upon his name (Rom 10:12-13).

"UPROOT AND TEAR DOWN"

JUDAH'S SELF-TRUST (17:1-27)

Overview

This section begins with a mostly poetic text that deals with the theme of Judah's idolatry and judgment (17:1-4). The following poetic oracles contrast those who trust in their own strength with those who trust in Yahweh (vv 5-8, 9-10, 11, 12-13). The outcome of trust in Yahweh is blessing, but the outcome of trust in oneself is curse and humiliation. The prophet's lament ("confession") in 17:14-18 gives specific expression to the faith of those who trust in Yahweh. The concluding prose sermon on Sabbath-keeping returns to the theme of covenant fidelity (vv 19-27). Sabbath-keeping is a clear expression of trust in Yahweh, and thus it may be linked with the overall theme of the preceding poetic oracles. The sermon with its conditional promise leaves the future of Judah as open-ended. Judah's ultimate destiny depends on its obedience/disobedience to the covenant.

1. An Indelible Writing of Sin (17:1-4)

BEHIND THE TEXT

This unit for the most part is in poetry; BHS presents v 2 and the beginning line of v 3 in prose. The NRSV prints the entire unit as prose. The Greek translation lacks these verses. The text in its present form has two parts: the first part (vv 1-3*a*) constitutes Jeremiah's assessment of Israel's moral and religious depravity; the second part (vv 3*b*-4) contains Yahweh's judgment words. Verses 3*b*-4 repeat 15:13-14 with some minor variations. The judgment words suggest a setting prior to the first Babylonian invasion (597 B.C.).

The sudden shift from the nation's coming to Yahweh in 16:19-21 to Judah's deep-rooted idolatry in this unit may be intentional. In the literary and theological setting of 16:19-21, this unit presents a rather bleak picture of Judah. Whereas there is hope for the nations in 16:19-21, this text does not seem to give any hope to Judah.

IN THE TEXT

■ **1** Jeremiah's indictment of Judah begins with a vivid portrayal of the deep-rooted character of its religious corruption. The **stylus of iron** and **flint stylus** are metal and stone engraving tools that leave permanent marks on the engraving surface (v 1). These tools and the mention of the **tablet** of Judah's heart indicate the hardened and stone-like nature of Judah's inner spiritual condition. The **horns** of the altar refer to the pointed four corners of an altar. In ancient Israel blood was smeared on the horns of the altar for atonement purposes (Exod 27:2; 29:12; 30:10; Lev 4:7; 16:18). The horns of the altar also provided refuge from the avenger of blood (1 Kgs 1:49-53; 2:28-35). Some commentators think that the reference here is to the ineradicable nature of Judah's sin; the horns of the altar cannot effect atonement for the people because Judah's sins are deeply engraved on them and they remain forever before Yahweh (Lundbom 1999, 777; Fretheim 2002, 256). The reference here may also be to the Canaanite altars where the people offered sacrifices to Baal, which remain as the public record of Judah's deep-seated sin of idolatry engraved on the tablet of its heart.

■ **2-3*a*** Verse 2 clearly links the **sin of Judah** with its idolatry. The nation is deeply committed to idolatry, which has affected past and future generations. **Children remember** and practice the idolatrous way of worship, which they have inherited from their parents. This is ironic because what the children remember is not the exodus story and the covenant making and the covenant laws, which the parents were to teach and practice before them (Deut 6:20-25), but the **altars, Asherahs, leafy trees, high hills, mountain in the field** (vv 2-3*a*), all of which represent Judah's syncretistic worship and deep involvement with Baal cult.

■ **3*b*** Yahweh's judgment (vv 3*b*-4) will result in the loss of everything (see comments on 15:13-14). Whatever Judah claimed for itself as its **wealth** and **treasures** will be plundered by the enemy. Babylon is the enemy intended here. Judah cannot expect to keep anything for itself, not even the **high places** where the people worshipped foreign gods (v 3*b*).

■ **4** The people will have to forfeit their **inheritance** from Yahweh, the land that he gave them according to his covenant promises (v 4). The people who chose to worship foreign gods will find themselves in bondage to their foreign enemies in a land that is foreign to them. This self-destruction and displacement is the inevitable outcome of covenant-breaking and idolatrous worship. The *fire* of judgment that is burning against them is the fire they themselves have started. The text makes clear that the judgment of exile is something the people themselves have brought upon them by their own sin. **Forever** indicates the intensity of Yahweh's anger; it does not mean Yahweh's permanent response to those under judgment (see Ps 30:6 for the momentary nature of Yahweh's anger). Throughout the text, we find Yahweh affirming his primary role in everything related to the history of his people. He is the One who gave the land to the people; he will be the One who will give their wealth and treasures and land to the enemy. He is the One who will make them serve the enemy. The present historical realities are inseparably linked to Yahweh, who insists on exercising his sovereign rule not only over his covenant people but also over the nations.

FROM THE TEXT

Judah's idolatry reveals the powerful impact of sin on the nation's worship and on the destiny of God's people. Sin has deeply ingrained in the heart of the people who were called to live a *torah*-obedient life by their purposeful meditation and observance of the *torah* (Deut 6:5-9). Sin manifests itself in the form of forgetfulness of God. The people live not only without any memory of God but also without the memory of their own religious traditions and value system. Instead, they remember, promote, and teach their children the cultic symbols and objects of Baal worship. Sin has taken control of the way they live and worship. The outcome is their new identity, a nation with a sin-engraved heart. The nation has rejected the offer of life that is guaranteed for *torah*-obedience; instead it has chosen for itself the curse of exile and death.

The new covenant offer we find in Jer 31:31-33 promises the possibility of a "new identity" to the people with a sin-engraved heart (Fretheim 2002, 256). The new covenant offer anticipates the gift of a new heart, a heart that is committed to single-minded devotion to God (24:7; 32:39). Instead of sin, the *torah* will be written on the heart of God's people. The promise of the new covenant is also the promise of forgiveness of sins, and thus the possibility of release from the power of sin and death, and life lived in a covenant with God. In the final analysis, what is written on our heart—sin or *torah*—determines and defines who we are: either a people sold to the power of sin or a people released from the power of sin, forgiven and free to live a life of "true righteousness and holiness" (Eph 4:24). The invitation of this text is to move from the world of sin and death to the world of covenant living through repentance and faith. This movement marks the beginning of Christian discipleship.

2. Two Ways of Life (17:5-13)

BEHIND THE TEXT

This unit, which may be subdivided into several small units (vv 5-8, 9-10, 11, 12-13), contrasts those who trust Yahweh with those who do not trust him. The Hebrew text presents vv 5-8 as an oracle (*"Thus said Yahweh"*); this introductory formula is lacking in the Greek translation. The various subsections in this unit, except perhaps vv 12-13, draw from Israel's wisdom tradition. Though vv 12-13 do not reflect the language of wisdom tradition, this text announces judgment upon those who fail to trust Yahweh. Verses 5-13 draw a sharp distinction between the righteous and the wicked and their respective destiny.

Israel's Wisdom Theology

Israel's wisdom theology promoted the view that God created all things and that there is a divinely established moral order in the universe. The universe functions according to this moral order. Wisdom tradition claimed that those who fear the Lord recognize this truth about God and the universe. Those who are righteous are thus those who fear the Lord; they trust in the Lord. The wicked, on the other hand, do not fear the Lord; they trust in themselves or in other human beings. Blessing and happiness belong to the righteous; the destiny of the wicked is death and destruction.

Verses 5-8 resemble the language of Ps 1 in that we find in both texts emphasis given to the two ways of life. The comparison of the pious to "a tree *transplanted* by water" is the most obvious connecting link between this text and Ps 1. However, there are some significant differences between the two texts. Psalm 1 begins with the statement of the blessed condition of those who meditate on the Law day and night, whereas vv 5-8 begin with the statement of the cursed condition of those who trust in human beings. This reversal in the order of the presentation is significant. In Ps 1 the wicked is compared to chaff, but here the wicked is compared to a *"destitute plant in the desert."* Also lacking in Ps 1 is the term "cursed" in reference to the wicked. Some commentators have questioned the authenticity of vv 5-8 and have assumed that this is a wisdom composition added to the book by later editors. Others have attempted to show dependence of Ps 1 to Jeremiah's words, or Jeremiah's dependence on Ps 1. Holladay treats vv 5-8 as a variation of Ps 1 (1986, 490). This issue cannot be resolved with any certainty, though the differences between the two texts seem to tip the scale in favor of the authenticity of Jeremiah's words.

We cannot assign a precise date to this unit. The theme of trust in other human beings could be related to Judah's political alliances during the days either of Jehoiakim or Zedekiah. Commentators also connect v 11 to the days of Jehoiakim. Lundbom relates vv 5-8 to the days of Josiah and his failed attempt to stop the Egyptian army at Megiddo in 609 B.C. (1999, 786).

IN THE TEXT

■ **5** Verses 5-8 are introduced as an oracle from Yahweh (***thus said Yahweh***). The opening word **cursed** (*'ārûr*; see also 11:3; 20:15) may be understood as a pronouncement of curse or as a state of being or the condition of a person. Most commentators read the text as **cursed is the *man*,** which assumes an existing condition. The cursed condition means a life totally devoid of any divine blessing. The ***man*** in Hebrew (*geber*), though it sometimes denotes a powerful and strong person, could be viewed here as a reference to any person (see the general use of *geber* in Pss 34:8; 40:4; 94:12; see also v 7 below). The cursed existence of a person is the outcome of choosing a way of life that places trust in human beings (*'ādām*). The Hebrew word *'ādām*, the general term for humanity, also indicates humans as feeble, earthly, and mortal creatures. It is clear that the alternative to this way of life is trust in Yahweh the Creator of *'ādām* (v 7). Trust denotes dependence and placing confidence and seeking security in someone or something or oneself. In military context, which this text perhaps belongs to, the reference may be to Judah's military and political alliances to save itself from the Babylonian threat. The second line (***and makes* flesh . . . his strength**) continues the thought of the effect of one's reliance on human beings for personal or national well-being. Flesh (*bāśār*) indicates human weakness and thus is similar in meaning to *'ādām*. Verse 5 also makes clear that placing trust in human beings or one's own resources is the inevitable outcome of turning one's heart away from Yahweh. Such people live under the curse of Yahweh and are deprived of his blessings.

■ **6** Verse 6 describes in detail the meaningless existence of those who trust in others for their security and well-being. Their destiny is like a ***destitute*** (*'ar'ār*, "Juniper," **bush**) plant ***in the desert*** (*bā'ărābâ*, meaning "in the Arabah"). The next line (***he/it will not see when good comes***) could be taken to mean life without the experience of anything good. In the context of the destitute plant/shrub imagery in the desert, it may mean existence without the experience of seasonal supply of rain and water (Fretheim 2002, 258). Another possible reading of this text is that ***good*** (i.e., prosperity) may come to those who put their trust in others, but they will not **see** it as blessings from Yahweh (see Stulman 2005, 169). Such individuals will live in dry and drought conditions. Their existence will be **in a salt land** where nothing grows and no one lives. The salt land is the land around the Dead Sea, which is part of the Arabah region. The focus of this text seems to be on the loneliness, lack of productivity, and lack of hope for survival for those who turn their heart away from Yahweh.

■ **7** Verses 7-8 shift attention to the person who **trusts** in Yahweh. Trust in Yahweh is an essential quality of those who have a covenant relationship with him. It is trust in the trustworthiness of Yahweh who keeps the covenant terms. Those who rely on Yahweh as a trustworthy God are **blessed** (*bārûk*); Lundbom suggests that *bārûk* has stronger implications than *'ašrê* ("happy," "blessed") of Ps 1:1 (1999, 784). In the OT, a formal priestly blessing begins with the verb form *bārak* ("bless"), which indicates Yahweh's direct activity of blessing through priestly mediation (Num 6:24). Verse 7 with its repetition of the idea of trust in Yahweh makes a direct link between blessedness and trust in Yahweh (see also Ps 40:4). Those who enjoy the state of blessedness put their confidence in Yahweh and seek their strength and security from Yahweh.

■ **8** Verse 8 introduces the analogy of a tree, which presents a sharp contrast to the "destitute" plant in v 6. In contrast to the tree that exists in a parched and salty desert land, this tree is productive, healthy, and has hope for survival even in the midst of extreme life-threatening conditions. The verb ***transplanted*** (*šātûl;* see also Ps 1:3) **by the water** conveys the idea of the tree being taken out of its previous location in a dry ground to a place of constant water supply, like an irrigation channel or a river where its roots have access to water even in the intense heat of summer and drought conditions. Verse 8 makes clear that those who trust in Yahweh have no need to **fear** or be ***anxious*** about their survival when difficult times come in their life. They will continue to **bear fruit** even in the midst of adverse conditions.

■ **9** The contrast between misplaced trust and trust in Yahweh is continued in vv 9-11. Commentators treat vv 9-10 as one unit and v 11 as a separate unit. This section contains the prophet's assessment of the human heart (v 9), Yahweh's response to Jeremiah (v 10), and a wisdom saying that illustrates the destiny of those who rely on their unjustly accumulated wealth (v 11). Verses 9-10 also reflect the language of the wisdom tradition on the human heart and divine justice (Job 11:5-6; Prov 14:10). The prophet's assessment of the human heart and Yahweh's response links this unit with Jer 17:1-4. The **heart** (*lēb*) in Hebrew thinking represents the center where thoughts, ideas, emotions, will, feeling, and decisions originate. Holladay observes that v 9 is the only place in the OT where the word appears with the definite article and therefore he considers this as a general observation about the human heart (1986, 494). The condition of the human heart is **deceitful** (*'āqob;* the same root from which the Hebrew name *ya'qob*/Jacob derives). In 9:4, the prophet uses the terms *'āqob* and *ya'qob* to describe Judah; so it is likely that this assessment of the human heart in general may have a direct application to the sinful heart of Judah (17:1) in this context. The condition of the heart is not only deceitful but also ***incurably sick.*** The rhetorical question (**who can understand it?**) implies the answer in the negative; no human being can fathom the deep and impenetrable world of the human heart. This question also seems to suggest the answer in the affirmative, "who can but Yahweh understand it," and thus sets the stage for Yahweh's response in v 10.

A Wesleyan Perspective on the Sinful Human Heart

"There is nothing so false and deceitful as the heart of man; deceitful in its apprehensions of things, in the hopes and promises which it nourishes, in the assurances that it gives us" (Wesley 1975, 2173). Clarke notes that the constant yearning of the heart is to "gratify its propensities to pride, ambition, evil desires, and corruption of all kinds" (302).

■ **10** Yahweh's response to Jeremiah is consistent with the traditional understanding of Yahweh's knowledge of the human heart (v 10; see Ps 139:23). The first person pronoun (**I**) offers a direct and emphatic answer to the question raised in v 9. Yahweh asserts that he **searches** or looks deeply into the impenetrable **heart** and **tests** the **mind** (lit. "kidneys") of humans; what is deep and hidden is visible to his probing eyes. Holladay notes that the verb form *ḥqr* (**search**; see Ps 139:1, 23) is found only here in Jeremiah (1986, 495). Yahweh's testing or assessment of the human heart and mind and thoughts is a frequent concern in Jeremiah (see 9:7; 11:20; 12:3; 20:12). The goal of Yahweh's deep probing into the human heart is to discern the core character and inner motivations of a person. A person's way of life and actions in life are a reflection of that hidden world. Yahweh assures the prophet that his judgment will be based on the actions of the individual; it will be what each person deserves.

■ **11** Using a proverbial expression, the prophet illustrates the theme of well-deserved and equitable judgment in v 11. The exact meaning of the first line (*A partridge brooded and it did not bring forth*) is not clear (compare with the NIV and the NRSV). The NIV reading, **like a partridge that hatches eggs it did not lay,** assumes a partridge robbing the nest of other birds, and thus conveys the idea of ill-gotten gains, wealth that one did not work for. The Hebrew text seems to convey the idea of incubating eggs, but not bringing forth the young (see Lundbom 1999, 790). The proverb likens a wealthy man who amasses wealth through unjust ways to a partridge that incubates eggs that do not hatch or bring forth young ones. In the context of this text, the reference to a partridge may be insignificant. The point being made here is that the wealthy cannot hope to hold onto or enjoy what they have gained unjustly. Commentators think of this verse as a censure of Jehoiakim whom the prophet sharply criticizes for his unjust practices (22:13, 17). Ill-gotten gains do not remain forever; the proverb suggests the sudden disappearance of unjust gains or the sudden death of the unjust that leaves their wealth for someone else to enjoy. Though such people may have trusted in their own self-sufficiency and resourcefulness, the world around them will know them as fools who have violated all the norms of righteousness in their life. In the wisdom tradition, contrast is often made between the fool and the wise, the wicked and the righteous. The connection between an unjust person and a fool is made in this text.

■ 12 The final segment of this unit is a praise spoken by the prophet (vv 12-13). Most commentators treat these verses together. The first part of v 13 is addressed to Yahweh, but in the second part of v 13 in Hebrew, Yahweh is the speaker (**those who turn away from *me***), though the NIV and the NRSV change "me" into "you." Brueggemann labels these verses as a "doxology of judgment" (1998, 161). The prophet not only praises Yahweh's throne but also announces judgment on those who forsake him. Lundbom regards the vocatives in v 12 (**glorious throne, exalted from the beginning, place of our sanctuary**) as three "honorific names for the Temple" (1999, 792). Holladay, however, sees here an affirmation of heaven as the throne and sanctuary of Yahweh, and thus a polemic against those who put their trust in an earthly temple (1986, 501). **Glorious throne** (*kissē' kābôd*; see 14:21) refers to Yahweh's throne, the earthly location of which in Israel's tradition is the temple in Jerusalem. The next phrase, **exalted** (or "on high") **from the beginning,** suggests the location of the throne in heaven, or the dwelling of Yahweh in heaven, which is not marked by time and space. From eternity he dwells in heaven. This suggests that the reference may not be to the Jerusalem temple. The next phrase, **the place of our sanctuary,** may refer to both the Jerusalem temple and the heavenly dwelling of Yahweh. The first person plural (**our**) in v 12 includes all who place their trust in Yahweh. Jeremiah seems to combine here Israel's theological perspectives of Yahweh, the object of Israel's praise, as the One who dwells in heaven as well as in his earthly temple in Jerusalem. His sovereign rule thus extends throughout the universe. The theological objective of this text is to extol the sovereign rule of Yahweh.

■ 13 Verse 13 begins with another vocative (**the hope of Israel, Yahweh;** *miqwēh yiśrā'ēl*; see 14:8), which is also a confession of faith. The Hebrew word *miqwēh* also means "pool," and the phrase could thus be read "pool of Israel." This imagery provides a meaningful link to the description of Yahweh as the ***fountain of living water*** at the end of this verse (see also 2:13). The unit concludes by returning to the theme of the destiny of those who turn their heart away from Yahweh (see 17:5). Those who **forsake** Yahweh are those who put their trust in themselves or other human beings or other resources such as wealth, power, or idols of the nations. **Shame** or disgrace is the destiny that awaits such people. Yahweh responds to Jeremiah with a disclosure of the shame that that awaits those who turn away from him (v 13*b*). Those who forsake him **will be written in the *earth*.** This judgment clearly presents death as the inevitable destiny of the wicked; they cannot expect to have their names written in the book of life (Exod 32:32-33; Ps 69:28). Some commentators think that "in the earth" (*bā'āreṣ*) here means Sheol or the underworld (see NRSV). Writing in dust could also indicate that the memory of those who forsake Yahweh will be easily erased from the land of the living (Fretheim 2002, 260). This is Yahweh's judgment on those who forsake ***the fountain* of living water,** the true source of life and **the hope of Israel** and the nations. The text as a whole thus treats trust or misplaced trust as a life-and-death issue.

FROM THE TEXT

Human beings' attempt to exert control over their lives is the central issue in this text. Autonomy or self-directed way of life characterized Judah's political and religious existence during Jeremiah's day, and the prophet seeks to address the negative impact of autonomy on personal and communal existence of the covenant nation. The exilic readers would have seen their life in exile as analogous to that of the shrub in the desert in this text. The metaphor of the tree transplanted by the water would have challenged them to place their trust in God in exile and thus receive strength and sustenance, the gift of life, and the ability to withstand the dark and terrible days of their life in a foreign land.

We live in a world where prosperity and good life are often seen as the result of one's ability to direct and control things to specific outcome. This kind of trust in oneself or in others values life only in terms of productivity and success. Jeremiah also lived in that kind of world, but he distances himself from that world because he sees that world as a world without God. Human sufficiency and hubris are characteristic of that world. That world takes pride in its military superiority, economic prosperity, and the scientific and technological advances. In that world, living on God's terms is not an option, because it means renunciation of self-sufficiency and self-directed ways of life. Covenantal way of life that promotes justice and righteousness in the society is seldom found in that world. Jeremiah warns his readers that death is the destiny of those who live in that world. They are like a shrub in the desert; though they may appear to have life, they bear no fruit or contribute to the well-being of the community. Those who belong to that world do not have the capacity to save themselves or others through their claim of self-sufficiency.

The clear alternative to the world of self-sufficiency is the world that embraces life through trust in God. Trust in God does not mean freedom from troubles and trials of life. Hardship and suffering, though they may come, will have no adverse effect on those who trust in God, because their strength for daily existence comes not from some internal or external resources but from the ever-present and ever-refreshing reality of God in whom they trust. They hope in the God in whom they trust. The text invites us to ponder the two ways of life portrayed here and to make a decisive step toward a life of trust in God. The promise of this text is that those who place their hope in God will never be disappointed by "the spring of living water."

The text makes a connection between human autonomy and the corrupt and devious human heart. The text also implies that what was said about Judah's heart—sin engraved on the heart—is also the condition of the human heart in general. The claim of this text is that the mystery of the heart, the deep and hidden secrets that we keep to ourselves, is not a mystery to God. He probes deep into our heart to reveal our true identity. The God who searches the heart and finds it sinful is also the One who promises to give sinners a "new heart"—a "heart of flesh"—and a "new spirit" (24:7; Ezek 36:26 NRSV). Both Jeremiah and Ezekiel indicate that this is God's gift to those who have a sin-engraved heart.

Paul's statement, "all have sinned," echoes Jeremiah's assessment of the depravity of the human heart. Paul also sees hope for the sinful humanity in God's work of justification and redemption that comes through Jesus Christ as a gift of God's grace (Rom 3:23-24 NRSV). Those in Christ, Paul calls "a new creation," a people with a heart set free from the corrupt influences of sin (2 Cor 5:17).

3. Heal Me! (17:14-18)

BEHIND THE TEXT

Commentators assign this text as one of the "confessions" of Jeremiah. This text shows several parallels to the laments in the Psalms: appeal for help (v 14); reference to the enemies (v 15); claim of innocence (v 16); expression of trust (v 17); call for divine retribution (v 18). We cannot place this lament to a precise date, though one could confidently assign this to Jeremiah's ministry during the days of Jehoiakim or Zedekiah, when he was more under attack by the false prophets (v 15).

IN THE TEXT

■ 14 The prophet's lament begins with an appeal of help and deliverance from Yahweh (v 14); the request for healing may be linked to another confession where the prophet raises the issue of his incurable wound that refuses to be healed (15:18). The appeal here is similar to that of a physically sick person in the individual laments (see Ps 41:4). The traditional faith in Yahweh as the healer of his people underlies this appeal (3:22; 30:17; 33:6; see also Exod 15:26; Ps 103:3). The appeal for salvation is also rooted in the traditional faith in Yahweh as Israel's savior (see 14:8; Exod 14:30; 15:2). Lundbom notes that **save me** is found only here in Jeremiah; this appeal is found in numerous psalms (1999, 798). This appeal for healing and salvation may be an indication of the prophet's "bitterness, despair, and spiritual defeat," rather than physical illness (McKane 1986, 408-9). **For you are *my* praise** conveys the theological motivation for Yahweh to act and respond to the prophet's appeal (see Ps 71:4-6 where the psalmist's appeal for help is followed by statements of motivation for Yahweh to act).

■ 15 Verse 15 is also another motivation for Yahweh to respond to the prophet's appeal. The false prophets, or perhaps the nation as a whole **(they)**, do not think that his words will be fulfilled. They keep challenging the power of Yahweh's word, perhaps because Jeremiah's words have not yet been fulfilled. **Let** it *come* is not only a defiant challenge but also a "taunt" aimed at both Yahweh and his spokesperson (Lundbom 1999, 798).

■ **16** Following the pattern of a typical lament, the prophet expresses his innocence in v 16. The Hebrew text translated here as *I did not press from being a shepherd after you* comes from a difficult text (**I have not run away from being your shepherd**; "I have not run away from being a shepherd in your service" NRSV). The first verb form *'aṣtî* from *'ûṣ* ("press," "be pressed," "make haste," etc.) does not convey the idea of running away from or evading a task. Another possibility is to see here the prophet's unwavering allegiance to Yahweh the shepherd of his people ("I did not waver in following as a shepherd"; McKane 1986, 410). Some have adopted the translation, "I have not pressed thee to send evil" (RSV) or something similar to this by emending *mērō'eh* ("from being a shepherd") to *lěrā'â* ("to evil"). Elsewhere in Jeremiah, the term "shepherd" is usually applied to political rulers; only here in the OT, a prophet is referred to as a shepherd (Lundbom citing S. R. Driver; 1999, 799). However, it is not unlikely that the prophet may be reflecting on his task as that of a shepherd tending Yahweh's flock. If so, the point being made here is that neither did he choose for himself this ministry, nor did he press Yahweh to enlist him to this task. He is a prophet not because of any religious and personal aspirations and dreams but because of Yahweh's call (1:4-10).

The day of despair (*yôm 'ānûš*, lit. "incurable day," meaning "the day of incurable sickness") is most likely a reference to the Day of the Lord, which the prophets anticipated as a day of terrible disaster (v 16). Jeremiah, though he has been announcing Yahweh's judgment, claims that he did not **desire** to see that day come upon the nation. The prophet also claims faithfulness to his ministry as Yahweh's spokesperson; he acknowledges that *what has gone out of* his *lips* has been *in front of* Yahweh. The claim here is that he faithfully spoke only that which was given to him to speak by Yahweh and Yahweh knows the integrity of Jeremiah's words.

■ **17** Verse 17 contains an appeal as well as a statement of trust. The prophet appeals to Yahweh not to become a source of **terror** to him; it perhaps could be understood as an appeal for protection from **the day of despair** that awaits the wicked (v 16; also see *the day of evil* in the next line). This appeal is followed by the confession that Yahweh is his *shelter in the day of evil.* Yahweh as the shelter/refuge of his people is a frequent theme in the Psalms (see 46:1, for example). *The day of evil* is the day of despair in v 16.

■ **18** The lament ends with an appeal for divine retribution, Yahweh's righteous judgment upon those who *pursue* him as his enemies (v 18). He calls for their **shame, terror,** and **double destruction.** Though the prophet did not desire **the day of despair** to come (v 16), he now urges Yahweh to bring upon his enemies *the day of evil,* from which he seeks refuge for himself. It is not clear if **the day** in vv 16, 17, and 18 are the same. It is possible that in vv 16 and 17, the reference may be to the national day of disaster, whereas in v 18 it may refer to the judgment of his personal enemies. However, we do not need to separate the two because the national judgment is also the context for Yahweh's judgment of all who are opposed to Yahweh and the prophet. **Double destruction** conveys the idea of total destruction.

FROM THE TEXT

The text is a speech directed to Yahweh. The lament of the prophet in this text echoes the cry of the righteous who, while maintaining faith in a just and righteous God, question the growth and prosperity of the wicked and the suffering of the innocent in the world.

A key emphasis of this text is God's power to heal and save those who cry out to him for help. God will heal; he will save; he will punish the wicked. In the bitterness of his spirit, the prophet cries out for help. This cry for healing and salvation is a strong affirmation of his faith in God the healer and the savior of his people.

This prayer is an open and honest sharing of the prophet's innermost emotions—his feeling of abandonment by God, the negative assessment of his effectiveness as a prophet by his enemies, and his intense desire to see God's righteous judgment upon his enemies. There is no answer from God in this text; the prophet must wait for an answer from God. We assume that waiting is precisely what Jeremiah did; however, while waiting to see what God will do, Jeremiah goes on with his life, with his call, with his trust in God, and with his prophetic ministry. God remains to him as the object of his praise. He is committed to keep his integrity and innocence as he waits for God's answer to his prayer. The prophet teaches how to pray and how to live our lives in faithful waiting for God in our moments of deep despair.

4. On Sabbath-Keeping (17:19-27)

BEHIND THE TEXT

The authenticity of this text is a key issue addressed by most commentators. Proponents of the Deuteronomistic editing of the book find in this sermon the style, structure, and theology of Deuteronomy, and they place it in the exilic or postexilic setting. The text reflects the emphasis on Sabbath-keeping in the exilic/postexilic times (Isa 56:1-8; 58:13-14; Neh 13:15-22). Scholars are puzzled by the lack of reference to Sabbath-keeping elsewhere in the book, particularly in the temple sermon, which catalogues at least five of the Ten Commandments. But we do not need to limit the emphasis on Sabbath-keeping to the exilic/postexilic period, though this was a period of renewed interest in keeping the Sabbath as holy (see Amos's indictment of the greedy businesspeople who were anxious for the Sabbath to be over to return to their deceitful practices in 8:5). The temple sermon (7:1-15) is a clear evidence of the prophet's concern for the Decalogue. The initial command (17:19) is similar to that of 7:2 and 19:1-2. Verse 19 of ch 17 also implies the existence of monarchy, and v 20 lists the kings of Judah among the addressees. An exilic or postexilic setting does not make much sense for vv 19-20. The call to obedience also contains the promise of a future that involves the Davidic kings, which rests on the people's obedience to the Sabbath commandment (vv 24-25). The parallel to Neh 13:15-22 does not necessarily mean the text originated in the postexilic period. Nehemiah's emphasis on Sabbath-keeping is tied to the perspective that failure to keep the Sabbath is what caused the destruction of the city. Destruction of the city is given by Jeremiah as a warning in this text. This text may very well belong to the preexilic setting, possibly during the days of Josianic reformation. The prophet may have spoken these words in support of the covenant renewal and centralization of worship undertaken by Josiah (Lundbom 1999, 804).

There is no good explanation for the placement of this sermon in ch 17; it does not logically follow the lament of the prophet in vv 14-18. The prose beginning after the personal lament is rather abrupt. However, if we consider the issue of Sabbath-keeping as a sign of one's trust in Yahweh, then the text has theological continuity with 17:5-8. This text has continuity with the following prose unit where the prophet is commanded by Yahweh to "go down to the potter's house" (18:1; see vv 1-12). Lundbom suggests that this unit serves as an introduction to chs 18—20 (1999, 804).

This sermon has two parts; part one, with strong imperatives demanding the Sabbath observance joined with a reminder that Israel's ancestors failed to obey the commandment (vv 19-23), and part two, which presents two options for the people that will determine the course of the future of the city (vv 24-27). Obedience to the divine command means the continuation of the political and social status of the city, and the ongoing worship in the temple (vv 24-26); disobedience will lead to the destruction of the city, which means the end of its political, social, and religious influence (v 27).

IN THE TEXT

■ **19-20** The text begins with Yahweh's command to Jeremiah to **stand in the gate of *the Sons of* the people** and in **all the . . . gates of Jerusalem** to deliver Yahweh's word to the **kings of Judah** and to ***all the inhabitants*** of **Jerusalem** (vv 19-20). The location of the gate of the ***Sons of*** **the people** (*bĕnê hā'ām*) is not known; ***the sons of*** **the people** refers to the common people or laity (see 26:23; 2 Chr 35:5, 12, 13). The reference to the kings entering through the gate of the common people is difficult to explain; **kings** may simply be a reference to members of the royal family. Commentators assume that the gate here is a temple gate through which both commoners and members of the royal family went in and out during worship times. The gates of Jerusalem were the busy places where the people gathered together to do business transactions and to engage in social interaction. Both the places of worship and common life were the target locations for the prophet to communicate Yahweh's word. He confronts here both the royal family and commoners with the message from Yahweh (v 20).

Sabbath-Keeping in Ancient Israel

The commandment to keep the Sabbath in the Decalogue in Exodus and Deuteronomy (Exod 20:8-11; Deut 5:12-15; see also Exod 34:21; Lev 19:3) specifically calls for rest from work for both humans and animals. The commandment stipulates that no work is to be performed on the seventh day. The commandment to keep the Sabbath in Exodus is based on God's rest on the seventh day after six days of his work of creation. The reason for the call to keep the Sabbath in Deuteronomy is God's deliverance of Israel from Egypt. It seems that during the days of Jeremiah the law of Sabbath was not strictly kept by the nation. Sabbath-keeping received renewed emphasis during the exilic and postexilic times in ancient Israel (Isa 56:1-8; 58:13-14; Neh 13:15-22). Strict rules for keeping the Sabbath were established during the days of Nehemiah (see Neh 13:19-22). The rules of Sabbath-keeping were expanded during the postexilic times, which included the prohibition of walking beyond a prescribed distance ("Sabbath day's journey" in Acts 1:12 NRSV).

■ **21-23** The prophet introduces Yahweh's message with the reminder that keeping Yahweh's command (**Keep the Sabbath day holy** [v 22]; Exod 20:8-11; Deut 5:12-15) is critical. Both the royal family and commoners are challenged here to *give heed* to Yahweh's command *for the sake of* their *lives*. Prohibition against carrying a **load** on the Sabbath day (vv 21-22) is not found in the Decalogue in Exod 20:8-11 and Deut 5:12-15. But this prohibition is consistent with the command to keep the sanctity of the Sabbath day and the prohibition against doing any work on the Sabbath. Bringing a load through the gates of Jerusalem may mean bringing items for sale in the marketplace in the city gates. ***From* your houses** stresses the point of keeping the sanctity of the Sabbath as a personal and family matter. Obedience/disobedience to this command is thus a life/death matter. **As I commanded your *fathers*** connects the present generation to those who received the Decalogue at Mount Sinai. The command with its added prohibition on carrying a load is not something new but is a reiteration of the covenant condition agreed upon by the ancestors of Israel. Most commentators view v 23 as a report on the rejection of the Sabbath commandment by Israel's ancestors. The various verb forms in this verse indicate active resistance to Yahweh's words and instructions by the ancestors of Israel.

■ **24-26** Verses 24-27 present a challenge to the present generation to break out of the path of stubborn refusal taken by their ancestors. The **if . . . then** statements in vv 24-27 indicate the importance of obeying the Sabbath commandment by keeping it holy. Verses 25-26 list the reward for obeying the Sabbath commandment. National, political, social, and religious life will continue in Judah and Jerusalem. The royal line will continue and the city will be permanently inhabited. The worship in the temple will continue. People from all over the land of Judah and Benjamin and from the south (**Negev**) and southwest of the land (***Shephelah***) will come to the temple in Jerusalem with their offerings and sacrifices. All the offerings and sacrifices mentioned in v 26 reflect faithful relationship with Yahweh. The people will continue to enjoy salvation from Yahweh, for which they will be thankful.

■ **27** The outcome of disobedience to Yahweh's command is stated in v 27. Yahweh will destroy the city and its citadels with a fire that will burn forever. Similar judgment language is found in Amos's judgment oracles in 1:3—2:5. The judgment of total destruction is the punishment for violating the sanctity of the Sabbath day.

FROM THE TEXT

This prose sermon is a strong reminder to the kings and the people of Judah about their covenant duty to keep the sanctity of the Sabbath day. This text would have reminded the exilic community the theological rationale for the tragic events of 587 B.C. Jeremiah's audience rejected God's word and followed the path of their disobedient ancestors. The exilic and the postexilic community would have seen in this text the critical importance of Sabbath-keeping for its restored relationship with God and for the restoration of their national, political, social, and religious life.

We may be tempted to view in this text a legalistic demand to show how faithful we are to God and to his commandments. If Sabbath-keeping is reduced to a form of legalism, then it has no meaning or value. Jeremiah would be the first to oppose such legalistic observance of the Sabbath. The text reminds us that Sabbath-keeping is more than obedience to God's law, but it is a way of life for the people of God. It is a way of life that is necessary for the life of the covenant community and for the well-being of its political and religious institutions. It is important to note that the text particularly focuses on labor and commercial activities, signs of our human capacity to produce and make profit and create our own well-being and a world for ourselves. The world of Sabbath-keeping is a world of trust (thus this text has thematic unity with 17:5-13); this world recognizes and trusts in the creative, life-giving, and life-sustaining work of God. The alternative is to live in a world of Sabbath-breaking, a world of self-sufficiency and self-reliance. The life of trust evident in Sabbath-keeping signals the faithful and regular handing over of life back to God (Brueggemann 1998, 166). It is a sign of our commitment to be faithful to the creational order—our commitment to keep relationship with our Creator in order.

JEREMIAH

17:19-27

"UPROOT AND TEAR DOWN"

JUDAH, A VESSEL FOR DESTRUCTION (18:1—20:18)

Overview

Most commentators treat chs 18—20 as a major literary unit. This section contains biographical narratives mixed with prose discourses (18:1-12; 19:1-15; 20:1-6), poetic oracles (18:13-17), and "confessions" (18:19-23; 20:7-18)—the major literary genres found in the book of Jeremiah. The prose saying in 18:18 introduces the confession that follows. Two biographical incidents (18:1-4; 19:1—20:6) provide the narrative framework for the various parts of this unit. Commentators think that at some stage in the compilation of the book, ch 18 was linked to the materials in chs 19—20 because of the potter's house (18:1-4) and potter's jar (19:1) themes of these chapters (see Bright 1965, LXXV, for other possible literary and theological links between the various sections of chs 18—20).

The introductory narrative and the prose discourse (18:1-12) set the theme of this section. Judah is a privileged but a defiant nation; it has firmly rejected Yahweh's call for repentance. The divine potter is shaping this vessel for destruction. Verses 13-17 seem to give a poetic commentary on the preceding theme of Judah's rejection of Yahweh and Yahweh's judgment on Judah. Judah responds to this prophetic word with a plot to discredit the prophet (v 18), which prompts the lament ("confession") of the prophet in vv 19-23. The narrative of Jeremiah's symbolic act of destroying a flask signals the destruction of Judah/Jerusalem (19:1-13). The plot to discredit the prophet is executed by Pashhur, who imprisons him and thus attempts to silence the prophetic word (19:14—20:6). The prophet's lament ("confession") that follows (20:7-12) is prompted by the plot to discredit the prophetic word. The section ends with an agonizing lament ("confession") of the prophet (vv 14-18). The fate of the prophet, as he sees it, is not unlike the fate of Judah, a vessel being shaped for destruction by Yahweh's irrevocable decree of destruction.

1. Yahweh the Potter (18:1-12)

BEHIND THE TEXT

Verses 1-12 have several distinct components. The text begins with a narrative (vv 1-4) that is often described as a symbolic act; however, Jeremiah simply observes an act and does not participate in the act. Holladay describes these verses as "the narrative of a symbolic event" (1986, 513). Verses 6-10 contain an oracle from Yahweh to Jeremiah. Verse 11 is a messenger-style speech addressed to the people of Judah and Jerusalem. Verse 12 conveys the response of the people to his message.

The authenticity of vv 1-12 has been questioned by some commentators. Some have thought of vv 1-6 as authentic to Jeremiah and vv 7-11 as an expansion by Deuteronomistic editors. Others view vv 7-11 as an integral part of vv 1-6 and regard the whole unit as original to Jeremiah (see Holladay 1986, 514). It is difficult to assign a specific date to this text. Verse 11 clearly indicates the pre-587 B.C. setting of this text. Lundbom associates vv 1-12 with the Josianic reformation (1999, 817). Holladay suggests a period between 609 and 605/604 B.C. (1986, 514). Bright also dates this event to the early years of Jehoiakim (1965, 126).

IN THE TEXT

■ **1-2** Following the customary introduction (v 1), the narrative section (vv 2-4) conveys the account of Yahweh's command to Jeremiah to go down to the potter's house to receive Yahweh's word and his observation of the work of the potter. This is followed by a messenger-style oracle, the word that contains Yahweh's word to Jeremiah (vv 5-6). The command to **go down** (v 2) suggests the destination of his journey in the lower part of the city where the potter would have access to water supply, such as the Gihon Spring or the Pool of Siloam (Lundbom 1999, 813). The Hebrew word commonly translated as **potter** (*yôṣēr*, from the verb *yāṣar*, meaning "to form" or "to fashion") refers to someone who forms or gives shape to an object using materials such as metal, wood, or clay. **Potter** is appropriate here since the individual whom the prophet observes is a shaper of a vessel from clay. Yahweh chooses the place and the method of revelation. Positive response to this command is necessary for the prophet to receive the revelation from Yahweh.

■ **3** Jeremiah obeyed the command (compare with the response of the people to Yahweh's urgent appeal in vv 11-12) and made his way down to the potter's house and there he observed the potter **at the wheel** (v 3; lit. "on the two stones"). The wheel consisted of two disks, an upper one made of wood or stone where the clay was shaped into a vessel by the potter's hands, and a lower one made of stone, which the potter turned with his feet. The upper disk pivoted on the lower one and revolved with the rotation of the lower disk.

■ **4** Jeremiah saw the potter reworking the clay to make another vessel, when the vessel he was making from the clay was spoiled in his hand (v 4). Some commentators and translations read the perfect forms of the verb in v 4 as conveying more than one incident (thus, "whenever a vessel that he was working on . . ." "he would begin again . . ." [Bright 1965, 121; Lundbom 1999, 814]), and thus assume more than one failed attempt on the part of the potter to shape the vessel. The making of **another *vessel*** indicates that the potter discarded his original plan/design for the vessel because of some material defect in the clay. Instead of discarding the defective clay, the potter reworked it and shaped it into another vessel. The final phrase of v 4 (***as it seemed right in the eyes of the potter to do***) shows the potter's best judgment as to what kind of vessel he would make out of the clay that thwarted his original plan and purpose for it.

■ **5-6** Jeremiah's obedience to the divine command is the context for the revelation—the coming of Yahweh's word to his prophet (v 5). Yahweh compares himself in v 6 to the **potter** and the **house of Israel** to the **clay in the hand of the potter** and announces to Israel that he has the freedom to reshape Israel according to his sovereign will. Israel is in the hand of Yahweh very much like the clay in the hand of the potter. Just as the potter has reworked the clay that thwarted his plans into another vessel, Yahweh plans to rework and reshape Israel, who frustrated his plans for that nation. Implied here is the idea that Israel's future is now in the hands of Yahweh and that he has the sovereign freedom to do whatever he wishes to do with it.

God the Potter

In the creation tradition of Israel (Gen 2:7), Yahweh "formed" (verb form here is *yāṣar*, the same verb from which potter/*yôṣēr* is derived) humanity from the ground. He also "formed" out of the ground the animals and birds (Gen 2:19). The confession of Yahweh as potter is explicitly stated in Isa 64:8 (see also Isa 29:16; 45:9). Jeremiah himself was "formed" by Yahweh in his mother's womb (Jer 1:5).

■ **7-8** Verses 7-10 give theological expression to the work of the potter narrated in v 4. These verses indicate that though Yahweh is free to pronounce judgments or to determine the destiny of any nation in the world, his actions toward that nation will be controlled by that nation's response to the divine pronouncement. There is a shift from the attention given to Israel in v 6 to nations and kingdoms in the world in vv 7-10. What is said about Israel is stated as a general principle of Yahweh's actions in the world. Verses 7 and 9 begin with the Hebrew word *regaʻ* ("in a moment" or "suddenly"), which conveys the idea of a sudden speech of Yahweh requiring an action or response from the people; Yahweh will then act according to the response of the people. Judgment and salvation words in these verses reflect the language of 1:10. When Yahweh speaks the words of judgment (***pluck up and overthrow and destroy***) against a nation or a kingdom, that is not a final word (v 7). The implementation of that judgment word is shaped by the response of that nation or kingdom. If that nation **repents of its evil,** then Yahweh will *repent* of the evil he had planned against it and will cancel his judgment word (v 8).

■ **9-10** Conversely, when Yahweh speaks words of salvation to a nation or a kingdom (*to build and to plant*), that is not a final word (v 9). The implementation of that word is shaped by the obedient and faithful response of that nation. If that nation follows an evil path by disobeying Yahweh's word, then he will *repent* of the promised welfare of that nation (v 10). The conditional nature of the implementation of Yahweh's words is made clear in these verses. The human response of repentance or disobedience shapes the course of action taken by Yahweh.

■ **11** Verse 11 is an application of the action of the potter (v 4), which is here made directly to the people of Judah and Jerusalem through a messenger-style speech. Just as the potter reworked the clay into another vessel as it seemed good to him, Yahweh is reshaping the destiny of Judah. The nation that he intended to shape as his elect and holy people in the world are now being told that they are being shaped into another vessel. This is not because of some arbitrary decision on the part of Yahweh but is necessitated by the recalcitrant behavior of Judah. Yahweh the potter is **shaping** (*yôṣēr*) evil against Judah (v 11). Yahweh's new plan for the nation is not to rework it into another vessel that can be useful to him, but to a vessel destined for destruction. This is a word spoken "in a moment" that requires positive response from Judah. Judah's welfare depends on the commitment of the nation to **turn** (*šûbû* from *šûb*, meaning "repent") from its **evil way** and to **make good** their **ways** and their **actions** (v 11). However, the text also clearly presents the opportunity to avoid judgment. Responding to this urgent call will lead to the experience of Yahweh's blessing; rejection of this word will lead to its destruction.

■ **12** Verse 12 seems to be a report from Jeremiah to Yahweh; this verse conveys (**But they say**) what the people have been saying in response to Yahweh's past and present calls for repentance (see Lundbom 1999, 816; Holladay 1986, 517). They are determined to pursue in their self-centered ways; they do not have any intention to conform to Yahweh's plan for them or to repent of their evil. Their decision is to continue in their path of evil, to follow the **stubbornness of** their **evil heart.**

FROM THE TEXT

This text clearly conveys the perilous condition of the elect people of God. The text presents Judah as a vessel in the making; at this stage in its history, God is shaping it into a vessel for destruction. This shift in God's plan for his elect nation happened because of its corruption and stubborn refusal to live in conformity to God's will. However, God offers the nation yet another opportunity to repent and escape the disaster he is planning against it. The calamity of 587 B.C. came upon Judah because of its final no to God's call for repentance.

The image of God as the potter would have conveyed to the exilic community the message of hope that its future remains open in God's hand. God will work again with his people to bring about his good purpose for them; however, their future still depends on how they will respond to God's new, gracious initiative for them.

The text maintains a balanced perspective of God's sovereignty and his gracious freedom, as well as human freedom and destiny. Like a potter who works with the clay, he has control over the history of the nations and the destiny of individual human beings. In his sovereignty he determines what he may or may not do with the nations and peoples in the world (vv 7, 9). However, the text also makes clear that God's plans and purposes are not static and rigid, but they are open to the possibilities of change. They are not some predetermined decrees that he is bound to keep to maintain his sovereignty and integrity. This is alluded to in the potter's decision to rework the marred clay into another vessel rather than discarding the clay because the vessel he was making was spoiled in his hand. This idea of God's freedom is made clear in vv 8 and 10, which speak of God changing his mind according to human beings' response to God. The text also indicates the human freedom to respond to God's intentions through repentance and obedience or through sin and disobedience. Our response, while we are in the shaping and molding hands of the potter, will determine our future—a vessel for his good and gracious purpose or a vessel for destruction.

Paul seems to be alluding to this text in Rom 9:21-24. "The objects of wrath that are made for destruction" (v 22 NRSV) most likely is a reference to the unrepentant Judah that is faced with the judgment of destruction (Jer 18:4, 11). God "endured with much patience the objects of wrath" (Rom 9:22 NRSV) or the unbelieving Jews, according to Paul, to reveal his glory to the "objects of mercy" (v 23 NRSV); i.e., both believing Jews and Gentiles—whom he refers to as the recipients of the abundance of God's mercy (vv 23-24). Both Jeremiah and Paul portray God as a merciful God who will respond with mercy and salvation to all who repent and turn from their evil.

2. My People Have Forgotten Me (18:13-17)

BEHIND THE TEXT

The first part of this poetic oracle (vv 13-15) shows a thematic similarity to 2:10-13. As in the latter case, 18:13-15 present the idea that Yahweh's people have committed an act that is unheard of among the nations in the world. Yahweh's complaint in 2:13 is that his people have "forsaken" him; here the complaint is that they have "forgotten" him (18:15). The oracle begins with a messenger-style introduction (***therefore thus said Yahweh***). Verses 13-16 constitute Yahweh's accusation; v 17 conveys Yahweh's judgment word.

IN THE TEXT

■ **13** The opening word (**therefore**, v 13) connects this oracle to the preceding text (vv 1-12). Yahweh's accusation begins with a rhetorical question that suggests that what is happening among Yahweh's people is unique and unheard of among the nations in the world (see 2:10). The reference to the **nations** links the passage to the nations and kingdoms in 18:7-9. **A most horrible thing** (*ša'ărûrit*, v 13) could be a wordplay on the claim of the people that they will follow the "stubbornness" (*šĕrirût*) of their "evil heart" (v 12). It is not clear whether the reference is to the stubborn rejection of the people (v 12) or to their idolatry and forgetting of Yahweh (v 15). **Virgin Israel** (see also 31:4, 21; Amos 5:2) seems to be a designation for the whole nation, not just the people of Judah or the city of Jerusalem.

■ **14** The two rhetorical questions in v 14 indicate what is naturally expected to be found in the mountains of Lebanon. It is a place where one will find **snow** and *cold flowing streams.* The Hebrew text of v 14 is difficult, but the sense of this text is clear. One would not think of snow and water leaving the mountains of Lebanon. The constancy of snow and cold water in the mountains of Lebanon (possibly Mount Hermon is intended here) conveys faithfulness and stability in the natural world.

■ **15** Using the natural order of things as illustrations, Yahweh proceeds to show that reliability and constancy of relationship are qualities lacking in his covenant people (v 15). Yahweh's complaint against his people is that they have **forgotten** him (see also 2:32; 3:21; 13:25; 23:27). The covenant with God meant that the people were to remain in the presence of Yahweh, their "natural habitat," just as snow and water remain in their "natural habitat" in the mountains of Lebanon (Brueggemann 1998, 170). Forgetting Yahweh is tantamount to the breaking of the covenant and leaving his presence. This is not an accidental loss of memory but an intentional violation of the command "do not forget" but "remember" Yahweh (Deut 8:11, 18).

Judah's idolatry—burning **incense *to nothing*** or idols (v 15)—is the clear evidence of its forgetfulness of Yahweh the covenant maker. The outcome of idolatry is that the idols have made the covenant people who have forgotten Yahweh **stumble in their ways.** Covenant-keeping and fidelity in relationship mean living under the providential care and guidance of Yahweh. Idols cannot lead and guide those who worship them; worshipping idols did not lead Judah anywhere, except its detour from the ***eternal*** or **ancient paths** that Yahweh had designed for its walk (see 6:16). The covenant way of life has set up for the people markers and signposts for safe travel along the path that Yahweh has designed for them to walk. Following the path of idolatry has taken them on dangerous ***paths*** or highways that are **not built up** for good travel (v 15). The imagery of this verse describes Judah as a nation lost on its path without proper guidance because of its idolatry (McKane 1996, 433).

■ **16** Verse 16 conveys the dangerous consequence of Judah's idolatry. What makes the land a ***desolation*** and a ***hissing forever*** is Yahweh's judgment upon the people who have forgotten him and worshipped idols. Those who pass by the land will be shocked at its devastation. Hissing and shaking of head seems to indicate external physical expressions of shock and horror; Lundbom explains these as gestures of contempt (1999, 823).

■ **17** Yahweh's judgment is stated explicitly in v 17. The imagery of the ***east wind*** (see also 4:11; 13:24; Isa 27:8; Ezek 17:10; 19:12; 27:26) conveys the destructive power of Yahweh's judgment. Judah will be defeated and carried into exile by the enemy. On the day of disaster, the people will see Yahweh's **back,** and not his **face,** turned toward them. Instead of his grace and compassion, they will experience the wrath of their God whom they have forgotten.

FROM THE TEXT

This text makes clear the tragic consequence of forsaking and forgetting God. Jeremiah reminds his audience that they were meant to be a part of the life of God just as the snow is very much a part of the mountains of Lebanon. Now they have risked that relationship with God. They no longer have a part in the life of God; neither do they have God's life in them. The reason for this is their abandonment of God. The people have forgotten their God. They have by their own choice left God and thus now remain as a people who no longer have an identity in the world as God's people. They have chosen for themselves the identity as an idolatrous people by following the ways and worship of the nations in the world. God's judgment will scatter them among the nations where they belong.

This text would have reminded the post-587 B.C. community that its future as God's people rests on its decision to return to their God whom they have forgotten and abandoned. The text reminds its modern readers that forsaking and forgetting God means rejecting grace and saying no to God's presence in our lives. Rejection of God's presence means exile or homelessness, a life where God's presence is no longer a source of comfort but is experienced only as judgment. The text challenges the faithful to remain at home with God; it also invites those in exile to return to God, our home, where we rightfully belong (see Ps 90:1).

3. The People's Plot and Jeremiah's Lament (18:18-23)

BEHIND THE TEXT

The lament of Jeremiah in vv 19-23 is the fourth "confession" of the book. Most translations treat v 18 as prose; Lundbom treats it as a self-standing poetic-prose (1999, 824). The question of the relationship of v 18 to vv 19-23 does not have a good answer. It is possible that it may have once existed as a separate piece, although the likelihood of it as an original part of vv 19-23 cannot be ruled out (see Holladay 1986, 529). In the literary context of the present unit, v 18 serves as the context for the lament of the prophet. Lundbom suggests a date between 609 and 605 B.C. for this text (1999, 834); Holladay places this text around 601-600 B.C. (1986, 530).

Opposition to Jeremiah's Message

Opposition to and persecution of Jeremiah is a theme throughout the book (see 11:18-23; 12:6; 15:10, 15, 19-21; 17:18; 20:2, 10; 26:8, 24; 28:1-11; 36:26; 37:11-21; 38:1-16). The book clearly portrays the prophet as a persecuted, harassed, rejected, and ostracized member of the community. From Jeremiah's own perspective, he suffers this tragedy because of Yahweh's call on his life to be a prophet.

IN THE TEXT

■ **18** Verse 18 is a summary of the opposition against Jeremiah. It is likely that **they** in v 18 includes the priests, the wise, and the (false) prophets whose religious authority was threatened by the message of the prophet. The **priest** is the official custodian of the Torah, the interpreter and the teacher of Yahweh's laws and ordinances. The **wise** or the wise men are the source of wisdom and counselors to kings and commoners. The **prophet** is the official recipient and communicator of divine revelation. In their thinking, they are the source of knowledge of Yahweh in the land, and they see Jeremiah as an outsider to their establishment. They would have found Jeremiah's accusations (see 2:8; 6:16; 8:8; 14:13-16) as offensive and a direct challenge to their authority over the people. Their plot is to *strike* the prophet with their **tongues,** and to **pay no attention** to his words (see Pss 12:4; 64:3). Their plan is to discredit the authentic voice of Yahweh through slander and verbal attack. Their decision to pay no attention to his words indicates their rejection of Yahweh's words to the nation. Ironically, the response of the leaders to the prophetic voice is the same as the response of the people to Yahweh's voice (see v 12).

■ **19** Verses 19-23 constitute the prophet's response to the conspiracy against him and his preaching. This confession begins with an appeal to Yahweh to **give heed** or **listen,** a typical appeal found in the lament psalms (v 19; see Ps 5:2, for example). Jeremiah appeals to Yahweh to listen not only to his voice but also to the voice of his **accusers,** or the plot of the enemies.

■ **20** Jeremiah's confession continues in v 20 with a rhetorical question, which indicates that evil is the reward he is getting from the people for whom he has interceded with Yahweh for their good. In spite of the good he has done for the people, they have **dug a pit** for his *life.* The goal of the opposition is not only to verbally attack him but also to put him to death (see v 23). The prophet appeals to Yahweh to remember how he interceded and prayed for his enemies.

Perhaps he is recalling here his repeated attempts to intercede for the people in spite of Yahweh's repeated commands to the prophet not to intercede for them. Though he faithfully fulfilled his duties as a prophet, he is now the target of attack and evil plots. This is the reason why he is seeking Yahweh to send his judgment upon those who plot against his life (vv 21-23).

Verses 21-23 echo Yahweh's judgment words in 6:11*b*-12; 11:22-23; 14:15-16; 15:2, 7-9; 16:4; 21:9; 27:8, 13. The language of Jeremiah here is very harsh and is typical of the laments in the Psalms (see Pss 28:4; 35:4-6; 40:14-15; 58:6-10; 109:2-20; 137:7-9). Jeremiah's appropriation of Yahweh's judgment words conveys the prophet's conviction that judgment belongs to Yahweh. He is calling on Yahweh to fulfill his judgment words on his enemies who are also the enemies of Yahweh.

■ **21** Verse 21 describe the effects of a military invasion of the land. The prophet seems to be urging Yahweh to go ahead with his plan to bring the enemy nation against Judah. The prophet who persistently interceded to spare the nation from famine and sword is now in full agreement with Yahweh's judgment of the nation. He calls upon Yahweh to begin the process of judgment—the death of children, young men, and husbands, which would make the women of the land childless and widows (v 21). **Famine** and **sword** are what they should receive from Yahweh's hand.

■ **22** Verse 22*a* continues the imagery of the military invasion; v 22*b* gives the reason for the prophet's appeal for Yahweh's judgment. What the prophet wishes to hear is the **cry** of despair that rises from the houses of those who are his enemies when Yahweh brings **invaders against them** (v 22). The people who have **dug a pit to capture** the prophet and have **hidden snares for** his **feet** do not deserve any compassion, but their sudden destruction by the invading army.

■ **23** The prophet concludes his lament with a final appeal to Yahweh (v 23). The prophet implies that Yahweh's knowledge of the plot requires him to take action. This is not the time for Yahweh to show compassion and forgiveness. His enemies do not deserve to have their iniquities atoned for or their sins blotted out by the mercy of Yahweh. What is significant and unusual here is the prayer not to ***cover their iniquity*** (**forgive**); Lundbom notes that this form of prayer using the verb form *kpr* ("to atone, cover, forgive") is found only here in the OT (1999, 833; see Ps 109:14 and Neh 4:5 for similar prayers). This is time for Yahweh to show his wrath toward those who are enemies of both Yahweh and his faithful spokesperson. What they deserve is not mercy, but stumbling—the very same fate they have planned against Jeremiah's life.

FROM THE TEXT

Jeremiah's lament in this text is prompted by the intense opposition to the message he proclaimed in the name of God. Opposition to Jeremiah comes from those who are committed to preserving the status quo—the established ways of communicating the knowledge of God in the land (see similar opposition to Jesus in Mark 3:6). The hostility is not simply against the prophet but also against God. The rejection of Jeremiah as a prophet by the religious leaders indicates the nation's rejection of both God and the prophet. The opposition's plan to silence the prophet is in a sense an attempt to silence God's word. At this point Jeremiah recognizes the reality that only God's righteous judgment can put an end to the disastrous path that Judah has decided to take (18:12). Though we see here an attempt on the part of the prophet to see God's judgment to come upon his personal enemies, the text as a whole is about his decision to agree with God about the necessity of judgment. The time of intercession has come to an end. It is now time for the judgment to work. In that sense he is urging God to go ahead with his plans to bring the Babylonians against the land of Judah.

Jeremiah's lament is the voice of an individual in despair, but also that of a person who trusts in a moral order that guarantees the punishment of the wicked and the deliverance of the righteous. Even though he raises questions about the way good is repaid with evil by his opponents, he continues to trust in the power of God to restore the covenant way of life among his people. He perceives the necessity of judgment to rebuild the collapsed moral order and the social disintegration of the covenant community. Ironically, the exilic community appropriated similar imprecatory language in their prayers to God for the judgment of the Babylonians (Ps 137:7-9). Both Jeremiah and the exilic community leave the matter of judgment in the hands of God. Both Jeremiah and the exilic community that cries out for vengeance in Ps 137 hope for an orderly and structured world under the governance of God.

Curse Language in Jeremiah's Laments

Jeremiah's lament in this text and laments like these in the Psalms dominated by imprecatory language and call for vengeance reflect an attitude contrary to the love commandment in the teachings of Jesus (Matt 5:44). This should not, however, lead us to conclude that grace and forgiveness are uniquely NT perspectives. We need to take the following perspectives into consideration when trying to make sense of the language of imprecation in the OT.

First, lament as a genre in the OT belongs to extremely hostile and life-threatening situations in the life of God's people. The raw human emotions of rage and anger in the laments display the intensity of the situation. As the lament of Jeremiah shows, he is appropriating the language he has learned from God's own judgment words. The lament psalms show that Israel's religious faith has nurtured such language when speaking against the enemies. Jeremiah here stands in the tradition of the righteous who cry out to God for his intervention on their behalf. We should also note that the cry for vengeance is something that we hear even from the mouth of the martyrs (Rev 6:9-10).

Second, a possible goal of laments like these is to remind God of his promise to deliver his people from their enemies. Jeremiah himself has received assurances of personal protection and safety from his enemies (see 1:8, 19; 15:20-21). The prophet is now demanding God to deliver what he has promised. He recognizes that only through the judgment of the enemy can his deliverance become a reality.

Third, the command to love and pray for the enemies in the NT does not exclude the reality of judgment upon those who stand in opposition to God and his faithful messengers (see Jesus' woe statements in Matt 23:13-36; also his lament over Jerusalem in vv 37-39).

Fourth, the language of Jeremiah in this lament or the language of the psalmists where imprecation is found or even the language of the martyrs in Revelation does not promote or give license to its indiscriminate use by the readers of the Bible. When such outburst of anger could be made is difficult to determine. Fretheim suggests that this language could be placed in a "rare-use category," to be used with proper discernment of the given situation by those who face or witness horrible abuse of human life (2002, 279). Even when a particular situation of outrageous and cruel mistreatment could be a legitimate context for the use of this biblical language, the gospel invites us to consider the alternative first—that is, to pray for the enemy who persecutes us (Matt 5:43-44).

4. The Valley of Slaughter (19:1-13)

BEHIND THE TEXT

Most commentators treat 19:1—20:6 as a larger narrative unit because of the continuity and the sequence of events described in these verses. However, a shift in the setting from the Valley of Ben Hinnom (19:2) to the court of the temple (v 14) offers a natural break in the text. We treat this larger unit as two narrative units (19:1-13 and 19:14—20:6). The Valley of Ben Hinnom is the setting of a symbolic act (19:10) that is preceded by two short messenger speeches (vv 3-5, 6-9) and followed by two more messenger speeches (v 11, vv 12-13). These oracles all deal with the theme of judgment for Judah's idolatry and child sacrifice in the Valley of Ben Hinnom. This unit is connected to the narrative of ch 18 through reference to the work of a "potter" (18:1; 19:1). Proponents of the Deuteronomistic redaction of the book view vv 2*b*-9 and 11*b*-13 as secondary insertions by Deuteronomistic editors. Address to the kings of Judah (v 4; also v 13) suggests a date before 587 B.C. for this text. Both Holladay and Lundbom place this text during the reign of Jehoiakim (Holladay 1986, 539; Lundbom 1999, 842).

IN THE TEXT

■ **1-2** This unit begins with the usual introductory words (***Thus said Yahweh***); this introduction and the command that follows (**go and buy**) closely parallel the opening words of 13:1. Yahweh's command instructs the prophet to buy a ***potter's earthenware jar*** (v 1), perhaps a jar for carrying water, and take with him certain elders of the people and of the priests, and **go out to the Valley of**

Ben Hinnom (see comments on 7:31) at the **entrance of the Potsherd Gate** (v 2). **Elders of the people** suggest respected members of the community. **Elders . . . of the priests** were senior priests (see 2 Kgs 19:2). The text suggests that the **Potsherd Gate** may have been the gate through which the people went out of the city into the valley. Its location is not clear, though some scholars associate it with the Dung Gate (see Neh 2:13; 3:13-14; 12:31). People in the city may have taken their trash, including broken pottery, through this gate into the valley. This was an appropriate place for the prophet to perform the symbolic act of breaking the jar (see v 10). Yahweh's command in v 2 is not explicit about the symbolic act; here Yahweh simply tells the prophet to speak his words. The command to break the jar is given later (v 10).

■ **3** Yahweh's message is addressed to the **kings of Judah** and the **people of Jerusalem** (v 3). The message begins with a judgment word (v 3*b*) followed by the reason for the judgment (vv 4-5). **Kings** here may be a general reference to the members of the royal family (see also 17:19-20) and not to any particular king, though Jehoiakim may have been the king of Judah at the time of this incident. This could also be an indictment against all the kings of Judah who would have participated and promoted the Valley of Ben Hinnom as a cultic place. The judgment word announces Yahweh's plan to bring *evil* **on this place** (i.e., the city of Jerusalem). The idea of Yahweh bringing evil (*rā'â*) is frequently found in Jeremiah. As in other similar contexts in Jeremiah (6:19; 11:11; 19:15; 23:12; 35:17, etc.), evil here is not something immoral, but his actions of judgment in response to the evil committed by the people. The NIV/NRSV "disaster" reflects the idea of judgment. The phrase **the ears of everyone who hears of it tingle** is not a common expression in the OT (see also 1 Sam 3:11; 2 Kgs 21:12). The expression seems to convey the disorienting effect of the news of Yahweh's judgment of his city.

■ **4-5** Verses 4-5 list a catalog of the sins of Judah that have prompted Yahweh to take this action. The people have **forsaken** him (v 4); they have *profaned* or made foreign this place (v 4); they have **burned** in this place *incense to other gods* (v 4); they have **filled this place with the blood of the innocent** (v 4); they have **built the high places of Baal** to offer child sacrifice (v 5). The essence of Yahweh's complaint is twofold: the covenant people have rejected Yahweh and his chosen place of worship and have chosen for themselves a place of worship and a religious system of their choosing in direct violation of the command that prohibited the worship of other gods. The land that was holy has now become profane. Shedding the blood of the innocent in this context is most likely a reference to child sacrifice in the Valley of Ben Hinnom. Elsewhere in the OT, this refers to the miscarriage of justice and violence against the poor in the land (see 2:34; 7:6; 22:3, 17; also Deut 19:10; 27:25). High places of Baal are perhaps the same as the "high places of Topheth" in 7:31. Lundbom suggests the possibility that Baal is a title here and that the reference may be to the sacrifice of children to Molech (1999, 839).

■ **6-9** Verses 6-9 announce Yahweh's judgment. Just as there is a catalog of Judah's sins in vv 4-5, here we find a catalog of Yahweh's actions. Yahweh will: make the Valley of Ben Hinnom **the Valley of Slaughter** (v 6); annul the plans of the nation (v 7); let the sword of the enemy wield its power (v 7); give the dead bodies of the people as food for birds and animals (v 7); make the city a desolate place (v 8); make the people eat human flesh during the enemy siege of the city (v 9). These actions reflect the unleashing of Yahweh's covenant curses (Deut 28:36-37, 53-57). The place where the people have slaughtered their innocent children will become the place of their own slaughter. Annulling or making void the plans of Judah refers to Yahweh's plan to carry out his plans for the nation though the Jerusalem leadership is busy with their own plans and policies for the survival of their state. The enemy nation (Babylon) will serve as the instrument of Yahweh's judgment. These verses clearly express the wartime destruction and devastation of the city and the distress it will bring upon the people. The people who have incorporated into their worship the most merciless act of child sacrifice will pay the price for their sin in an equally horrific manner—by engaging in cannibalism during the most distressing times of their life.

■ **10-12** In v 10 Yahweh commands Jeremiah to **break the jar** in the presence of the elders who accompanied the prophet to the Valley of Ben Hinnom. This command is followed by a message from Yahweh that interprets the symbolic act (vv 11-13). Bright suggests that in the cultural setting of that day, this act would have been perceived by the audience as "the actual setting in motion of Yahweh's destroying word" (1965, 133). Perhaps the significance of this symbolic act is not in the inevitability of the destruction of the nation and the city because it symbolizes some predetermined divine action, as some commentators seem to think (see, for example, McKane 1986, 458), but in the effect of the destruction this act intended to convey. The effect of the breaking of the jar is that *it cannot be mended again* (i.e., the irreparable destruction of the jar). The pieces of the broken jar cannot be put together to remake the vessel to its original shape. The **nation and this city** (i.e., Jerusalem) will suffer a similar fate (v 11).

This symbolic act reiterates the theme of 18:1-12; there the potter is reshaping the vessel as "seemed good to him," a vessel for destruction (18:4, 11 NRSV). The possibility of Yahweh sparing the nation from destruction is lacking here because the nation rejected the call for repentance (18:11-12). In 18:12 the people seal their own fate by their callous rejection of Yahweh's call for repentance. In 19:11-12, Yahweh seals the fate of Jerusalem and its inhabitants.

Topheth, the place of their Baal worship, will become the burial site (v 11; see 7:31 for more on Topheth). The place the people have made unclean by their idolatry will be made unclean by Yahweh by making it their burial ground. Yahweh's intent is to destroy the city of Jerusalem and make it unclean like Topheth (v 12).

■ **13** Verse 13 conveys a judgment word against the houses of the ordinary citizens and the kings of Judah; the people have profaned the holy city of Yahweh by burning **incense** and pouring **drink offerings** to ***all the host of heaven*** and to **other gods.** The preference is to the practice of idolatry on the flat roofs of the houses in Jerusalem (see 32:29; Zeph 1:5). The ***host of heaven*** **(starry hosts)** indicates the worship of astral deities (see the "Queen of Heaven" cult in 7:18).

FROM THE TEXT

This symbolic act and the accompanying message communicate in the most forceful way the reality of God's judgment upon Judah and Jerusalem. God's covenant commitment to Jerusalem ends here, at least for the present time in Judah's history. The future of Jerusalem is yet another undertaking on the part of God; but for now, it is no longer a protected place because of the outrageous breaking of the covenant by the citizens of the city. This should not have surprised the audience of Jeremiah because the text here simply conveys precisely what is anticipated in the covenant tradition for Israel's disobedience to God. However, the story of Jeremiah's beating and imprisonment by Pashhur (20:1-6) indicates that the response to this message was not repentance and appeal to God for his mercy by a people on the verge of destruction, but a continued defiant stance on the invincibility of Jerusalem as God's city that enjoys his unconditional guarantee of protection. Only the historical reality of the events of 587 B.C. would finally shatter their complacency and false confidence.

The text conveys judgment on a people who have failed to distinguish the holy from the profane. The people of Jerusalem could not tell the difference between Jerusalem and Topheth. The people rejected the holy God, the outcome of which was the merging of the sphere of God's holiness with the sphere of the profane. This happens in our day not only in the strange mixing of the Christian faith with non-Christian religious ideas but also in the strange mixing of our faith with self-serving and self-assertive political, economic, and cultural ideologies of our day.

Jeremiah in this text is a paradigm of faithful preaching and faithful interpretation of God's actions in human history. We see here a courageous and highly imaginative preacher, unafraid to tackle the most sacred theological belief of his day promoted by the powerful political and religious establishment. He utilizes a forceful symbolic act and harsh language to confront the idolatry of the covenant nation and to shatter their complacent religious attitudes. How one hears and communicates the judgment word against idolatry in the church is a critical challenge of this text. This text does not sugarcoat the judgment word; neither does it make it disappear from Scripture because of the character of God as a merciful and compassionate God. The faithful preaching of this text would mean faithful proclamation of judgment against all forms of idolatry in the harshest language possible.

5. A Beaten but Bold Messenger (19:14—20:6)

BEHIND THE TEXT

The setting of 19:14—20:6 is the court of the Jerusalem temple. Verse 14 is a report of his return from Topheth and the delivery of a message in the court of the temple. We assume that Jeremiah broke the jar and proclaimed the message that Yahweh had given him. The text does not contain an actual report of the breaking of the jar and Jeremiah's proclamation of the message at Topheth. Verse 15 is a rather brief message to the people in the court of temple. This message is followed by another narrative that reports the outcome of Jeremiah's judgment words against the city (20:1-3). The encounter between Pashhur the priest and Jeremiah is somewhat similar to the encounter between Amos and Amaziah the priest at Bethel, but without the physical violence (Amos 7:10-17). The unit ends with a judgment message that Jeremiah prophesied against Pashhur, a top-level priest in the temple who beat the prophet and put him in the stocks for speaking against the city (20:4-6). This text belongs to the same period as that of 19:1-13. A date prior to 605 B.C. could be assigned to this text based on the report about the debarment of the prophet from the temple (see 36:1, 5).

IN THE TEXT

■ **14** According to 19:14, Jeremiah's mission in the Valley of Ben Hinnom was to **prophesy** or to speak Yahweh's authentic words. There the prophet's task was to expose the sin of the people in the valley. His next stop is the **court** of the temple where there are worshippers assembled for daily worship or for other special occasions.

■ **15** The prophet announces in the court of Yahweh's house the destruction of Jerusalem and its surrounding cities (v 15). This message may have been a summary of the prophecy given in the Valley of Ben Hinnom. The message lacks the details of the prophecy given in the valley. There is no reference to Topheth or the idolatry in the Valley of Ben Hinnom. This word of judgment given in the court of the temple confirms the prophetic words announced at Topheth. The people have committed evil by refusing to pay attention to Yahweh; they have pursued a path of stubborn resistance to his words. Therefore what they can expect from Yahweh is *evil*, which will come in the form of enemy invasion and the destruction of Jerusalem and its surrounding cities.

■ **20:1** The narrative in 20:1-3 sums up the consequence of Jeremiah's sermon in the temple courtyard. **Pashhur son of Immer, the chief officer in the temple** heard Jeremiah prophesying the destruction of Jerusalem and the surrounding cities. He belonged to a priestly family that had a long history (see 1 Chr 24:14). Pashhur's title indicates that he was a high-ranking priest with major administrative responsibility, which most likely included keeping law and order in the temple area.

■ **2** Verse 2 sums up the action Pashhur undertook to discipline Jeremiah for prophesying against the city. We cannot be certain if Jeremiah was beaten severely by Pashhur; the verb in Hebrew (*nkh*) suggests violent or deadly assault (v 2). Some commentators think that Pashhur himself may not have struck the prophet, but had him beaten. Acts 23:2 indicates a parallel to this action where the high priest Ananias had given orders to those who stood nearby to strike Paul on his mouth.

After striking the prophet, Pashhur put Jeremiah in **stocks,** which would have been some kind of instrument of confinement. Stocks usually are devices made of two pieces of wood to confine the neck, legs, or arms to immobilize a prisoner. Some commentators think that stocks here simply may refer to his confinement in a prison (see 2 Chr 16:10). The location of Jeremiah's confinement was in the **Upper Gate of Benjamin** in the temple court area. This is not the same as the Benjamin Gate of the city of Jerusalem (see Jer 37:13; 38:7). This may have been the entrance into the temple court at the north end of the city (Lundbom 1999, 847).

■ **3** The text does not say what prompted Pashhur to release Jeremiah from the stocks on the next day or what threats he may have made to silence the prophet (v 3). The one who speaks with courage here is the prophet. Jeremiah announces Yahweh's renaming of Pashhur to **Magor-Missabib,** or ***Terror on every side***. This phrase, also found in 6:25; 20:10; 46:5; 49:29 (see also Ps 31:13), seems to be a favorite of Jeremiah. The Septuagint lacks "on every side" and assumes the meaning of *māgôr* as "alien" or "sojourner" (from the verb *gûr*, "to sojourn"), which fits with the word about Pashhur's exile in vv 4 and 6. Just as the Valley of Ben Hinnom is renamed, Pashhur is also renamed (see 19:6). Both the valley where the people carried out idolatry and the priest who mistreated Yahweh's spokesperson are now symbols of the coming judgment. The phrase ***on every side*** indicates that judgment will be intense, comprehensive, and all-encompassing.

■ **4** Verses 4-6 describe how intense fear will overtake not only Pashhur and his **friends** but also the whole nation. The phrase **terror to yourself** perhaps means that he will be frightened by his own shadow. Panic and fear will follow his friends wherever they go. They will be killed by the sword of Babylon in his own presence. The same fate will come upon the entire population of Judah. The divine instrument of terror on Judah is the **king of Babylon,** who will take the population into exile in Babylon where he will ***strike*** them down with the sword. Now it is Yahweh's turn to *strike* the nation for its complicity to Pashhur's striking of his prophet. The enemy from the north is clearly identified here for the first time in the book.

■ **5** Yahweh's judgment also includes his handing over to the Babylonians the wealth of the city of Jerusalem (v 5). The wealth of the city includes its **products**, its valuable assets, and the **treasures of the kings of Judah.** The Babylonian army will carry the wealth of the city of Jerusalem to Babylon as booty; this is

Yahweh's gift to the enemies of Judah for carrying out his judgment on the city.
■ **6** Verse 6 returns to the fate of Pashhur and his family and his friends; captivity and death and burial in Babylon is what they can expect as their end. Verse 6 ends with the mention of Pashhur as a false prophet. This indicates that he may have given prophetic oracles in the temple. Jeremiah accuses him of prophesying falsehood or prophesying by the "lie" (*baššāqer*). Lundbom associates it with prophesying by the Baal (1999, 849).

FROM THE TEXT

The text presents to us two contrasting figures of religious authority—one concerned with self-preservation and the other concerned with faithful proclamation of God's word. Pashhur in this text is the representative of a secure priestly establishment that claims to have its authority derived directly from God and passed on through hereditary privilege. Jeremiah also claims his authority, but it comes through God's personal encounter with him. Though his antagonist has power, Jeremiah demonstrates perseverance, courage, and a strong determination not to be intimidated by his opponent. Pashhur's rejection of the reality of God's judgment and failure to remain true to his priestly vocation serves as a warning to contemporary readers of this text. The one who was given the privilege to mediate God's grace to his people became the enemy of God's word. Neither he nor his followers could recognize the lonely, nonetheless the true voice of God; neither could they discern the truth proclaimed by the true prophet because of their deep commitment to a false political-religious ideology that refused to recognize the fact that sometimes God may confront his people with words that are difficult and disturbing. When the claims of God's word are surrendered to a particular political and/or religious ideology, we lose our capacity to hear the authentic voice of God; we hear only what we want to hear.

Jeremiah's boldness to remain faithful to his calling and the opposition he suffered from religious leadership have parallel in the stories of the arrest of the apostles and their trial (Acts 5:17-32), the arrest and imprisonment of Paul and Silas in Philippi (16:22-39), and Paul's trial before Ananias (22:30—23:5). All of these instances show that in the end it is the voice of truth, though persecuted and oppressed by the powerful establishment, that triumphed and gave direction to God's people who were "like sheep without a shepherd" (Matt 9:36).

6. Jeremiah: A Broken Vessel (20:7-18)

BEHIND THE TEXT

This is the final collection of confessions in Jeremiah. There are two confessional poems in this unit. The first confession (vv 7-10) is clearly a complaint. The second confession (vv 14-18) utilizes the curse language similar to that of

Job 3. The shift from complaint to curse suggests the possibility that these confessions may have originated on separate occasions. In the middle part of this unit (vv 11-13) the prophet expresses his trust and confidence, which concludes with a song of praise. Some commentators have taken these verses, either in part or as a whole, as a later addition; others see continuity between vv 7-10 and vv 11-12 and possibly v 13. In the present arrangement, this middle part serves a critical function. These verses provide the prophet's proper perspective of God in the midst of his disorientation and deep despair. Such expressions of hope and trust and praise are typical of laments in the Psalms. Confessions in Jeremiah generally lack expressions of trust and praise. The pattern we see here is similar to that of most of the lament psalms where expressions of confidence and trust usually follow complaint and statements of despair (see Ps 13, for example). The present unit is connected to Jer 19:14—20:6 by the phrase "terror . . . all around" (20:10 NRSV; see v 3). It is difficult to give a precise date for this text; the occurrence of the phrase "terror . . . all around" suggests the possibility of a setting not too long after the incident with Pashhur.

IN THE TEXT

■ **7** Jeremiah's complaint begins with a strong accusation against Yahweh (v 7). The twice occurring verb **enticed** (*piel* and *niphâl* forms of *pātâ*) conveys the sense of sexual seduction (see Exod 22:15) and deception (see 1 Kgs 22:20-22). You have **overpowered me** (from *ḥzq*) also can have sexual connotation of a man sexually overpowering a woman (2 Sam 13:14). **You have overcome** (from *yākōl*) conveys the idea of someone much stronger prevailing over a weaker individual. Commentators all agree that the prophet is here reflecting on the call. There is no consensus on the precise meaning intended by the verb forms, whether to take the meaning from the field of sexual seduction or from the field of deception. The situation for the prophet is highly precarious; he feels terribly betrayed by his God who encountered him at a tender age. The prophet utilizes here the imagery of sexual violence and rape and/or deception to convey his raw emotion. This highly charged emotional reminiscing of his call reflects the prophet's present state of mind about Yahweh's call that came when he was a young boy and his ongoing personal struggle with the call. He accuses Yahweh of exercising his superior, overpowering, and dominating strength over an innocent and helpless young boy. Jeremiah also sees himself as a victim of mistreatment and abuse by the people. He claims that Yahweh has made him an object of ridicule and contempt to everyone in the land; such mistreatment is usually reserved for false prophets.

■ **8** Verse 8 indicates that every time Jeremiah proclaimed Yahweh's message, the subject of his preaching has been **violence and destruction;** this pair of words presents ambiguity with regard to its meaning and purpose. Commentators are not certain whether these words refer to the sins of the nation or Yahweh's judgment that will lead to destruction or the enemies' mistreatment of the prophet or Yahweh's mistreatment of the prophet (see Holladay 1986, 554). Verse 8*b* deals with the consequence of preaching Yahweh's word; it has made him an object of ridicule. The people ridicule not only Yahweh's words but also his spokesperson. Based on v 8*b*, we may interpret violence and destruction in v 8*a* as an indication of the abuse of the prophet by his opponents.

■ **9** Verse 9 deals with the only real option available to the prophet as he reflects on the current situation. Every time he thinks of the possibility of not mentioning (lit. "remember") Yahweh or not speaking ever again in his name, it becomes clear to him that it is futile and impossible to remain silent. The prophet would rather forget about the mission that Yahweh had given him and go on with his life without any association with Yahweh (see "I will forget him"; Bright 1965, 129). However, that thought does not bring any comfort, but only more misery to the prophet. When he decides to remain silent, then Yahweh's **word *becomes* in** his **heart like a *burning* fire**, fire that remains **shut up** in his **bones.** He comes to the conclusion that he does not have the strength to hold it within him. Jeremiah knows that the words of judgment are too powerful and have the capacity to destroy him if he attempts to contain them. Verse 9 "emphasizes the strong sense of the prophetic burden, an inner compulsion that will not allow him to give up the enterprise" (Miller 2001, 727). Here we find Jeremiah's resolve to continue his task; he prefers death by the hands of the angry mob to death by the fire that burns within his bones—the fire of Yahweh's words. The former would be more bearable than the latter.

■ **10** Verse 10 indicates that there is a "whisper campaign" against the prophet in the land (Brueggemann 1998, 182). Verse 10*a* is also found in Ps 31:13. **Whispering** conveys the idea of "deliberate talk calculated to hurt someone's reputation" (Holladay 1986, 555). ***Terror all around*** (*Magor-Missabib*) was a contemptuous name that Yahweh has given to Pashhur (20:3; also a theme of Jeremiah's preaching; see 6:25; 46:5; 49:29). Bright suggests that the prophet's enemies have taken this phrase, which was perhaps frequently used by him as a "nickname" for him (1965, 132-33). When the prophet passed by, the people might have whispered: "There goes old *Magor-Missabib*!" (Thompson 1980, 460). Jeremiah's opponents now use this phrase against him to show that he is the object of national contempt, because he is disturbing the nation's *shalom* through his terror-filled message.

There are two possible ways to interpret the phrase ***report, let us report him*** (v 10). This could mean the enemies' plan to report him to authorities who would then bring him to trial on charges of treason (Lundbom 1999, 857). Holladay, however, reads "report him" as "announce it" and sees here a "mock proclamation" of the enemies or a "mimicking" of Jeremiah's words "terror . . . all around," so that the prophet could be provoked to speak words that could be used to bring charges against him (1986, 556). The rest of v 10 seems to support the former interpretation. His opposition comes from people whom he had ***trusted*** and counted as his **friends.** His neighbors and friends have turned against him and are treating him as their enemy. What they wish to see happen is Jeremiah's stumbling or fall as a disgraceful person. The last two lines of v 10 seem to be coming from his former friends and neighbors. They hope that he can be **deceived** or enticed (*pātâ* as in v 7) to speak words that by his own admission were Yahweh's enticing words, and they further hope that his message will in turn prove false; then they will be able to **prevail over him** (*yākōl* as in v 7) because he could then be charged as a false prophet, not under the protection of Yahweh. Verse 10 concludes with the plan of the opposition to carry out their **revenge** on Jeremiah for discrediting them and speaking false words of judgment and condemnation against them.

■ 11 It seems that the plans of the opposition to discredit and destroy the prophet (vv 10-11) gave him a renewed perspective and confidence in who he is in relation to Yahweh and who Yahweh is in relation to him (v 11). The transition from accusation in vv 7-8 to trust and confidence and praise in vv 11-13 is striking. Laments usually begin with a strong complaint and description of distress and conclude with expression of confidence and trust. Trust in God and confidence in his power to save is the theological basis of strong words of accusation and complaint in lament psalms. Jeremiah follows that theological tradition in this text. His claim that Yahweh is with him like a **mighty warrior** (*gibbôr*) has its basis in Yahweh's assurances to the prophet (v 11; see 1:8, 19; 15:20-21). Previously, in a prayer the prophet offered on behalf of the people, he asked if Yahweh would be like a "warrior" (*gibbôr*) who cannot save or help his people. This verse replaces that sentiment of doubt and skepticism with a contrary perspective about Yahweh's ability to save the prophet from his troubles.

Those who **persecute** the prophet (or "pursue" him) and watch for his fall and demise in turn will **stumble,** and they will not be able to **prevail** against him (v 11). They intended to bring dishonor to the prophet, but now the tables are turned; the enemies are faced with disgrace because **they will not succeed** in their plans to dishonor the prophet. Compared to the prophet's present disgrace, the disgrace of the enemies will be **eternal.** His opponents schemed to "cut him off from the land of the living, so that his name will no longer be remembered" (11:19 NRSV). Here the prophet is confident that their shame and dishonor will be remembered forever because of the lasting effect of Yahweh's judgment upon them.

■ 12 Verse 12 is a near duplicate of 11:20. In 11:20 the prophet appeals to Yahweh the righteous Judge, who tests the heart and the mind; here the appeal is to **Yahweh of Hosts** (*Yahweh Sebaoth*), the One who **examines** or tests (*bōḥēn*) the **righteous** and **sees** their **inner being** (*kĕlāyôt*; lit. "kidneys") and **heart** (*lēb*). Lundbom interprets v 12*a* as the prophet's thinking of his recent trials as testing from Yahweh (1999, 862; also, Fretheim 2002, 294). Yahweh's testing here is perhaps to establish the innocence of his prophet. He is confident that Yahweh's searching eyes will confirm his innocence. The prophet also appeals to Yahweh, who *sees* the innocent, to let him *see* his righteous judgment (**ven-**

geance) against the evildoers. The prophet who presents his ***complaint*** (*rib*) to Yahweh is confident that Yahweh will act to defend and vindicate the innocent and punish the wicked.

■ **13** Jeremiah's lament ends with praise (v 13); praise and trust in God's deliverance is usually found at the conclusion of lament psalms (see Ps 13:6). The plural imperatives (**sing** and **praise**) invite all the faithful to join with him in Yahweh's deliverance of the prophet's life (see Exod 15:21; Ps 149:1). The prophet identifies himself as the ***poor*** and his opponents as the **wicked**. The use of these labels is also consistent with the lament psalms. Jeremiah counts himself among the oppressed and the powerless in the land; their cry for help and God's deliverance of them from **the hands of the wicked** is also a frequent theme in the lament psalms (Pss 9:18; 12:5; 35:10, etc.).

The text concludes with a bitter lament (vv 14-18), a cry of deep despair, which silences the bold and confident voice of praise in v 13. However, as stated earlier, vv 11-13 give us the proper theological orientation of the prophet necessary for us to evaluate his emotional distress and its positive or negative impact on his relationship with Yahweh. The voice in 20:7-10, 14-18 is the voice of disorientation, pain, protest, accusation, and utter despair. The voice of vv 11-13 is that of trust, confidence, and praise. Taken together, vv 7-18 suggest the complexity of Jeremiah's life that is lived to please Yahweh and to do his will in the midst of enormous struggle, both internal turmoil and external opposition.

■ **14** The language of this lament is very similar to that of Job's opening monologue (Job 3). It is not clear whether this text borrows from Job or vice versa. This poem suggests a massive assault on the life of the prophet by the opposition, heightened by the apparent inattentiveness of Yahweh to the prophet's predicament. This lament begins with a pronouncement of curse on the **day** of his birth (v 14). Though it is a soliloquy, the lament is indirectly addressed to Yahweh. The prophet pronounces curse on the day of his birth because his birth on that day initiated him to a life of misery and hardship. Since Yahweh is responsible for creating that day and creating the prophet as his messenger of judgment words, one could conclude, as Lundbom does, that the prophet "borders on blasphemy" (1999, 869). The second line of v 14 repeats the same idea. The day of his birth (**the day my mother bore me**) is the day that brought happiness and blessedness to his mother. The curse calls for the withdrawal of all blessing and joy that day has brought to his **mother**. The prophet wishes for the obliteration of that day and all memories associated with that day.

20:12-16

■ **15-16** The focus of attention in vv 15-16 is **the man who brought** Jeremiah's father the news of the birth of a son to him. The intent of the curse on **the man** who was a messenger of good news to his father is not clear (v 15). The curse is harsh, particularly Jeremiah's wish for his destruction like that of the cities that Yahweh destroyed without showing pity (v 16). Commentators assume that the reference here is to Sodom and Gomorrah (Gen 19:24-25). What is being wished for is the death and destruction of the messenger when Yahweh's judgment falls upon Jerusalem and Judah. Verse 16*b* perhaps implies the sudden invasion of Judah by the Babylonians and the cry of panic and the sound of alarm that will be heard throughout the land all day long. He and the nation will see, hear, and experience the realities of judgment proclaimed by Jeremiah.

■ **17** *Because* **he did not kill me in the womb** is difficult to make sense of (v 17). Commentators generally agree that the messenger mentioned in the previous verses is not the subject intended here. **He** in this line is most likely Yahweh. The complaint here is against Yahweh, who kept Jeremiah alive in his mother's **womb** rather than making it his **grave.** Yahweh could have made his mother's womb his grave and thus spared not only the prophet from a miserable existence but also Judah from suffering the calamitous effects of his preaching.

■ **18** The concluding verse of this lament questions the very purpose of his trouble and sorrow-filled existence (v 18). If Yahweh had a special purpose for Jeremiah, the prophet fails to see it. Should Yahweh have entrusted Jeremiah with his word and destined him to a life of suffering and shame? What did Jeremiah do to deserve such mistreatment from Yahweh? The poem ends in deep despair over his call, his life, and the prospect of no end to his suffering.

FROM THE TEXT

The elements of despair and trust in this text invite us to consider both as critical to our hearing of this text today. The fundamental issue that the prophet is dealing with here is the burden of the call. He is caught between the call of God that appointed him to a specific task and the kind of life he is forced to live because of the call. He speaks of God's deception and betrayal because of God's overpowering word that continues its demand upon the prophet. There is deep despair in this text because he has not yet seen the promised deliverance from God. Life has become unbearable for the prophet because the message has been difficult.

The question that remains for us to answer is this: "Why did he choose to live with the tension between God's overpowering word and the persistent rejection of that word by the people?" The answer is clear. He opted to live a miserable, wretched, and even cursed life because he understood and embraced God's word as the truth that needs to be proclaimed though there were other compelling and conflicting voices heard in the land. Giving up on the call would be tantamount to giving up on the truth of God's message. The prophet refuses to do so but resigns to a life of misery and despair. The only thing he could do is commit his cause to God and offer praise to the One who promises to rescue the needy from the power of the wicked. Trust and praise provide not an end to despair but only some relief. Life would continue to be troublesome, but trust and praise would keep him oriented to God as the source of his strength and salvation.

Laments like these are difficult for modern readers to deal with and make sense of because they violate all the rules of modern expressions of piety and spirituality. Parallel expressions in Job 3 and Ps 31:13 and other lament psalms indicate the following about prayers like these in the Bible:

i. Laments like these come from those who are in deep darkness and find no way out; in the midst of intense pain, loneliness, and utter misery, prayers like these offer an appropriate language to express the anguish of the soul.

ii. Laments like these sustain and comfort those who are persecuted for their faithfulness to God. Faithfulness to God means staying committed to his word of truth and proclaiming the truth found in his word. This text indicates that proclaiming God's truth may mean exposure to attacks and slander and isolation from the community. The biblical tradition and the history of Christianity are filled with the stories of faithful people who have been persecuted for their faithfulness to God. We are reminded here of the words of Jesus, "Blessed are you when people revile you and persecute you and utter all kinds of evil against you falsely on my account. Rejoice and be glad, for your reward is great in heaven, for in the same way they persecuted the prophets who were before you" (Matt 5:11-12 NRSV).

"UPROOT AND TEAR DOWN"

JUDAH'S POLITICAL AND RELIGIOUS LEADERS (21:1—23:40)

Overview

The royal family and false prophets receive focused attention in chs 21—23 as those who are culpable for the impending destruction of the nation. Chapter 21 begins with Zedekiah's desperate wish for Yahweh's miraculous intervention to save his people from the grips of Nebuchadnezzar of Babylon (21:1-2). However, he receives a rather ominous word that Yahweh himself is about to deliver him and his people into the hands of Nebuchadnezzar (vv 3-7). Yahweh is depicted in this text not as the divine deliverer but as the divine warrior who is waging a holy war against Judah, Jerusalem, and against the royal house. The time has run out; neither Zedekiah nor the nation can expect any mercy from Yahweh. Most of the rest of the oracles and discourses in chs 21—23 give the theological rationale for Yahweh's judgment on Judah and Jerusalem.

There is some discernable literary structure to chs 21—23. Following the prose discourses addressed to Zedekiah (21:1-7) and to the people (vv 8-10), we find a mixture of poetic oracles and prose discourses concerning the Davidic house and the three immediate predecessors of Zedekiah in 21:11—23:8. This section begins with a call to the royal house to perform justice to its people (21:11-12) and ends with a prose discourse in which Yahweh promises to bring home his flock scattered by the unfaithful shepherds/Davidic kings (23:1-8). Verses 9-40 constitute a series of poetic oracles and prose discourses concerning the false prophets and their role in the downfall of Judah.

Chapters 21—23 provide specific chronological data that are lacking in chs 1—20. The message to Zedekiah in 21:1-7 belongs to the period of the Babylonian siege of Jerusalem around 588/587 B.C. Oracles against the Davidic kings in 22:10-30 indicate chronological order, beginning with the oracle against Jehoahaz (vv 10-12), followed by Jehoiakim (vv 13-19), and Jehoiachin (vv 24-30).

1. Death and Life Decisions (21:1-10)

BEHIND THE TEXT

This section contains a narrative introduction (vv 1-2) that establishes the setting of the two prose discourses, the first one addressed to Zedekiah (vv 3-7) and the second addressed to the people (vv 8-10). The message to Zedekiah in vv 1-7 has some parallel to 34:1-7 and 37:3-10. In 21:1-2 and 37:3-10, King Zedekiah sends messengers to the prophet to inquire of Yahweh (see 21:2; 37:7). The messengers are Pashhur and Zephaniah the priest in 21:1-2; in 37:3 the messengers are Jehucal and Zephaniah the priest. Common names and themes have prompted some scholars to see 21:1-7 and 37:3-10 as variant accounts of the same event. However, in 21:1-7, the context of this appeal to the prophet is the siege of Jerusalem by the Babylonian army (see 52:4). In 37:3-10, the context is the withdrawal of the Babylonian army from Jerusalem because of the news that the Egyptian army is on its way to Jerusalem. The siege of Jerusalem by the Babylonian army (21:1-7) may have taken place in January 588 B.C. and the withdrawal of the Babylonian army that summer (Bright 2000, 330). In 21:1-7, the fate of Zedekiah is vividly described (see also 34:1-7); in 37:3-10, the focus is on the fate of the city. The message to Zedekiah is firm and harsh in 21:1-7; no hope is given to the king and to the inhabitants of the city. In 21:8-10, Yahweh offers an alternative to death that faces the inhabitants of Jerusalem. Though Yahweh reiterates his threat, he offers life to those who surrender to Babylon, which in turn means surrender to Yahweh's will, his judgment on Judah by the agency of Babylon.

IN THE TEXT

■ 1 The narrative introduction reports the coming of Yahweh's word to Jeremiah when messengers from **King Zedekiah** came to the prophet seeking a word from Yahweh on behalf of the king (v 1). Zedekiah is the throne name given to Mattaniah, a son of Josiah, by Nebuchadnezzar in 597 B.C. (2 Kgs 24:17). Nebuchadnezzar placed Zedekiah on the throne after the deportation of Jehoaichin and the prominent citizens of Jerusalem to Babylon. Though Zedekiah remained a loyal vassal of Babylon, in 588 B.C. he rebelled against Nebuchadnezzar (Jer 37:7; 2 Kgs 24:20).

One of the messengers that Zedekiah sent to the prophet seeking a word from Yahweh was **Pashhur son of Malkijah,** who most likely was a member of the royal family (see reference to Malkijah as Zedekiah's son in 38:1-6). Ironically it was another Pashhur, an officer of the temple, who punished Jeremiah for prophesying on behalf of Yahweh (see 20:1-6). Pashhur is mentioned in 38:1-6 as one of the four officials who attempted to persuade Zedekiah that Jeremiah deserved the death sentence because of his subversive and unpatriotic words. The priest **Zephaniah** (see also 29:24-32; 37:3; 52:24-27) seems to have been a temple official responsible for law and order in the temple (see 29:24-32). Zephaniah was "the second priest" (52:24 NRSV), and thus the next in rank to the chief priest in the temple. In a letter sent from Babylon, Shemaiah criticized Zephaniah for not restraining or putting Jeremiah in the stocks for playing the role of a prophet (29:24-32). Perhaps he, unlike his predecessor Pashhur the priest (20:1-2), was sympathetic to the prophet. Zephaniah and Seriah the chief priest and other prominent officials were executed by the Babylonians at Riblah (52:24-27).

■ **2** Zedekiah's request to the prophet to **inquire** of Yahweh (v 2; *dāraš* implies seeking or consulting or praying to God for counsel and guidance and help) is consistent with the practice of kings seeking a word from God during critical times, particularly during wartimes (1 Kgs 22:5; 2 Kgs 3:11). Jeremiah noted before that the kings have not prospered and that their flock have scattered because of the failure of foolish kings to inquire of Yahweh (Jer 10:21). Unlike his predecessors, in desperate conditions Zedekiah showed interest in consulting Jeremiah for a word from God (see also 37:3-10, 17-21; 38:14-28). The crisis here is the invasion of the land by **Nebuchadnezzar, king of Babylon**. This is the first reference to Nebuchadnezzar in the book of Jeremiah.

Nebuchadnezzar/Nebuchadrezzar

In the book of Jeremiah, the name of the Babylonian king is often spelled as Nebuchadrezzar (with an "r") except in chs 27—29 where the name is spelled Nebuchadnezzar (with an "n"). Scholars think that the name spelled with "r" corresponds more closely to the Babylonian form of the name *Nabū-kudurri-uṣur*, which means "Nabu, protect the (eldest) son" (Lundbom 2004a, 100). In this commentary, we follow the spelling with "n," the form adopted by the NIV and most English versions.

Zedekiah's request may actually have been for the prophet's intercession on behalf of the nation (*on our behalf*). This request expresses his hope that Yahweh would deliver the nation once again by his ***marvelous deeds*** "as he has often done" (21:2 NRSV) in the past history of the covenant nation. This request stems from the traditional notion of Yahweh as a God who performs wonders for his people, the history of which goes back to the days of Israel's deliverance from Egypt, the wilderness journey, and the conquest of the land. In Judah's recent history, Yahweh miraculously delivered Jerusalem from the Assyrian king Sennacherib and his army during the days of Hezekiah in 701 B.C. (Isa 37). Only a similar intervention on the part of Yahweh would force Nebuchadnezzar to **withdraw** from Jerusalem and leave Judah alone. This appeal does not necessarily reflect the piety of Zedekiah, who acted more often under political pressure than in consultation with Yahweh or his prophet for the nation's future.

■ **3-4** There is no report of the prophet's intercession or inquiring of Yahweh on behalf of Zedekiah. Verses 3-7 simply report Yahweh's response. The king hoped for Yahweh's miraculous deeds, perhaps his demonstration of himself as the divine warrior fighting against the Babylonian army. Yahweh responds with the word that he will indeed fight, not against Judah's enemy, but rather against Judah on the side of the enemy. Yahweh will turn back Judah's weapons and direct them toward the city (v 4). Christensen describes 21:1-5 as "the most explicit text in Jeremiah which portrays judgment as holy war against Judah" (1975, 186). The **king of Babylon** and the ***Chaldeans*** (or Babylonians) who have laid a siege of the city are not going to withdraw and go away. **I will gather them inside this city** is ambiguous (v 4). **Them** could be understood as either the weapons of war with which Judah is fighting the Babylonians or the Babylonian army, though commentators prefer to see here Yahweh bringing the Babylonians who have besieged the city from outside into the city and thus delivering the city into their hands.

Chaldeans

Chaldeans is a general term for the people who lived in Chaldea, a region in the southern part of Babylon. This term is also applied to the last dynasty that ruled Babylon from 626 to 539 B.C. Nabopolassar was the founder of the Chaldean dynasty, and Nebuchadnezzar was its most powerful king. This dynasty was so powerful that the whole region of Babylon began to be known as Chaldea. Chaldeans and Babylonians are thus interchangeable terms.

■ **5** The theme of Yahweh's direct involvement in this holy war against Judah continues in vv 5-7. Verse 5 contains phrases usually associated with Yahweh's actions to bring deliverance to his people. This verse makes clear that Yahweh himself is personally involved in this war against Judah. The phrase **outstretched hand and a mighty arm** is found in reverse order ("mighty hand and outstretched arm") in Deuteronomy (4:34; 5:15; 7:19; 11:2; 26:8) to indicate Yahweh's miraculous intervention to deliver the people of Israel from their Egyptian bondage. Elsewhere in Jeremiah, Yahweh's stretched out hand conveys the idea of judgment (see 6:12; 15:6). At this time in history, Judah can expect nothing but what Egypt experienced when Yahweh brought his judgment on that nation. Yahweh who fought against Egypt to bring his people out of their bondage will now fight against them to send them back to slavery and death. This judgment is a clear indication of Yahweh's **anger and fury and great wrath** upon a people who have broken their covenant with him. This chain of words indicates the intensity of Yahweh's resolve to destroy Judah (Stulman 2005, 208).

■ **6** Verse 6 continues the holy war ideology and the Exodus tradition. Yahweh who struck down (*nākah*) both humans and animals in Egypt with plagues (Exod 12:12) will strike down (*nākah*) the inhabitants of Jerusalem by "a great pestilence" (NRSV). The reference to both humans and animals in v 6 is another indication of how Yahweh plans to treat his covenant people the same way he treated Egypt during the Exodus days. Judah has become like Egypt, stubborn and resistant to Yahweh's divine demands, and so it is now faced with the same calamity that came upon Egypt.

■ **7** Verse 7 utilizes a series or chain of words to show the decisiveness of Yahweh's words, the final fate of the Davidic king and the Judean population, and the end of divine mercy. Using a group of four words (**Zedekiah, his *servants*, *and the people*, *and those who survive*** in this city) the prophet announces Yahweh's decision to hand the entire nation over to the king of Babylon. The text identifies the last group as those who survive from **the plague, sword and famine,** again another string of words to show that no one in the city will be spared from the coming destruction. The survivors of judgment will become victims of a greater calamity. Using another string of three terms the prophet describes the agency of judgment as **Nebuchadnezzar king of Babylon,** the **enemies** of Judah, and as **those who seek** the life of Zedekiah and the people of Judah. There is no question about the identity of the real enemy of Yahweh. Neither is there any question about the identity of Yahweh's instrument of judgment. Here we have another reversal of the Exodus tradition. Verse 7 also shatters the hope that Judah held in the presumed stability and fixed status of the Davidic royal house. The royal house that Yahweh had brought into existence by a covenant with David (2 Sam 7:14-16) is now under the threat of extinction. The king of Babylon will strike down (*nākah*) Zedekiah and his people with the sword. This is parallel to Yahweh striking down the firstborn of the Egyptians (Exod 12:29). Again using another string of three words, the prophet announces that Nebuchadnezzar will show no **mercy or pity or compassion** to Zedekiah and his people. The prophet proclaimed at another time that Yahweh will show no mercy, pity, or compassion when he destroys Judah (13:14). The text thus makes clear the role that Babylon will play in carrying out his judgment word.

■ **8-9** Verses 8-10 contain a word of warning and exhortation announced to the people of Judah. **The way of life and the way of death** (v 8) that Yahweh sets before his people reflects the life-and-death choices in Deut 30:15-19. It is important to note that this offer is made to the people, and the king is excluded. Whereas in Deuteronomy, obedience/disobedience to the Torah determined life-and-death issues, here life is offered to those who surrender to the Chaldeans. Those who are determined to remain in the city will die **by sword, by famine and by pestilence.** But anyone who **goes out and surrenders to the Chaldeans** who are besieging the city will live (v 9). The verb **goes out** (from *yāṣā'*) is frequently found in the exodus language where it is used in connection with Israel's "going out" of Egypt. The verb here may be taken to mean that the nation's only hope is in its "exodus away from the 'bondage' of Jerusalem to an odd 'freedom' under Babylon" (Brueggemann 1998, 191). This exodus is an act of surrender to the enemy; nonetheless, it is a way of escape from the impending death and destruction that is about to befall the city.

■ **10** Verse 10 makes clear the fate of the city; ***I have set my face against this***

city for evil and not for good indicates Yahweh's strong determination to destroy the city. The city can expect nothing but evil from him. He will hand his beloved city over to Nebuchadnezzar, who will burn it down. The offer of life in vv 8-9 needs to be understood in light of this severe judgment word in v 10. In the midst of this harsh word of judgment, those under judgment hear yet another way to stay alive. Obeying Yahweh and his word, though this word runs against the very core of the nation's political ideology and foreign policy, is the only way of escape for the people. The royal policy makers who are determined to resist the enemy are not given any hope (see 38:17-18 for a similar offer of life to Zedekiah if he would surrender to Babylon). Here again, there is a reversal of the ancient covenantal traditions and the Deuteronomic alternatives of life and death. Life offered here is not life in the land of promise but life in an alien land. The Deuteronomic notion of exile from the land of promise as death is reversed here, and the land of exile becomes indeed the place where life will be a possibility for the exiled people of God. On the other hand, the choice of life in the city (in the land of promise) will mean death for those who reject this offer. Just as the Davidic royal house promise is suspended in the previous verses, the judgment here suspends the ideology of the land. Ultimately what counts is life, and this life is promised as the "prize of war" (NRSV) for those who give heed to Yahweh's final word. The promise here is thus life as the only reward for obedience to Yahweh's word.

FROM THE TEXT

There is a hidden recognition in this text, though this comes belatedly to Zedekiah, that only God has the answers to the political crisis of Judah. God does not remain on the sidelines as a spectator in the affairs of the world waiting for a human appeal for his help, but rather he is at the center of the historical processes guiding and determining the course of events as the sovereign Lord of history. This text challenges and critiques the tendency to seek God's help as a last alternative when all of our human efforts have failed.

Most readers of this text would be surprised at the response of God to Zedekiah. Where is grace in this text? To be sure, there is no grace in vv 3-7. We do not see here the picture of a merciful, compassionate, and gracious God. We do not see here a God who answers our prayer for deliverance and help. Instead of deliverance, God threatens the praying community with death and destruction. This portrait of God is counter to the testimony of the faithful people of God who have experienced God during their trouble. The text, however, challenges us to think that there is a relationship between ineffective prayer and consistent disobedience to God. Zedekiah is a prime example of a long history of disobedience and rejection of God's word. In his case, the judgment has already begun and therefore his prayer for deliverance had no effect.

The reversal of Israel's covenant history and covenant traditions in this text is disturbing. The judgment in this text suspends or reverses all the sacred notions of Israel—the Exodus, the land, the city of Jerusalem, the Davidic royal house. But these are temporary reversals. Israel, a nation that once trusted and found security in its sacred traditions, must now learn to find security in the graciousness of God and his power to reverse the conditions of judgment. Elsewhere in the book we find promises of a return and reestablishment of the people in the land and the restoration of the Davidic kingship (see chs 30—31). These promises indicate that this judgment at this point in Israel's history was a temporary measure, and that Israel needs to trust in the graciousness of God to reverse his judgment and to fulfill his promises for its future.

The offer of the way of life to those who surrender to the Babylonians is indeed the "gospel" in this text. Life is offered to those who are willing to surrender their religious claims and political ideologies and embrace God's will, which at this point in history is the judgment of exile and death. It is a severe judgment on the one hand, but on the other hand a remarkable expression of grace bestowed upon a people who have reneged on their covenantal commitments to God. God wills life in the midst of death. Grace expressed in this text is grace that comes through judgment. It is in dying—separating oneself from the land of promise—that one would find life. Those who cling to their old way of life and old traditions and ideologies will perish. Those who are courageous to embrace God's hidden plans for their future will live, though this plan includes loss of home, religious and political ideology, statehood, and freedom.

This text would have reminded the exilic community of God's plans and purposes for them beyond the days of the destruction of their beloved city and their exile in a foreign land. The text also affirms the biblical idea of finding life through self-denial and total surrender to God's will. Relinquishing freedom and privileges, dislocation and displacement, and life as exiles in an alien environment are not easy and are less preferable to life in safe and secure surroundings. However, this is precisely the demand of the gospel that confronts anyone who seeks to be a disciple of Jesus. Jesus said to his disciples: "If any want to become my followers, let them deny themselves and take up their cross and follow me. For those who want to save their life will lose it, and those who lose their life for my sake, and for the sake of the gospel, will save it" (Mark 8:34-35 NRSV).

2. Covenantal Duty of the Royal Family (21:11-14)

BEHIND THE TEXT

This poetic oracle may be understood as a third part of Yahweh's response to Zedekiah's appeal to the prophet (21:1-2). The judgment theme of vv 3-7 and vv 8-10 is continued here. The oracle itself is addressed to the house of the king of Judah, the Davidic royal house, but no particular king is mentioned. The key issue here is the covenantal responsibility of the Davidic house to its subjects. This theme is continued in the next series of oracles addressed to the royal family in 22:1—23:8. So it is also possible to view 21:11-14 as the preface to the collection of oracles against the royal family. In this preface the prophet outlines the royal duty and issues a stern warning and threat to the royal family that the consequence of its failure to fulfill its covenantal obligation to the nation will be disastrous.

This oracle has two parts: vv 11-12 contain an admonition to the royal house to perform justice. This admonition is accompanied by a warning of judgment. Verses 13-14 contain a judgment word against the pride and evil of the city of Jerusalem. Commentators think that the words of vv 11-14 were originally spoken during the reign of Jehoiakim (609-598 B.C.) who paid no attention to the covenantal duty to administer justice in the land.

IN THE TEXT

■ **11-12** Verse 11 identifies *the house of the king of Judah* or the entire royal family as the addressee of the oracle in vv 12-14. The house of the king of Judah is specifically identified as the **house of David** in v 12. This is a reminder to the ruling family that its existence and authority derive from the covenant that Yahweh had made with David (2 Sam 7:12-16). The ruling Davidic family receives two stern commands from Yahweh in v 12. The first command, *execute justice in the morning,* is a clear call to the most basic responsibility of the Davidic kings. Before they engage in any other royal duty, as a priority, they must begin their day (*in the morning*) with a commitment to carry out justice for their people. Justice (*mišpāṭ*) here and elsewhere in the OT refers to the fulfillment of the covenantal obligations to others who are members of the covenant community. This act has both legal and moral implications. The primary obligation of kings is to guarantee the legal rights of their subjects as stipulated in the Sinai covenant. They are reminded here that the social and community life will break down without their commitment to be the guarantors of *mišpāṭ* to their people. A specific example of carrying out justice is mentioned in the next line—*deliver the robbed from the hand of the oppressor* (see also 22:3). This command is followed by the warning and threat that if the royal house failed in this duty and permitted oppressors to go unpunished, then that miscarriage of justice will ignite Yahweh's wrath that will burn like an unquenchable fire. Verse 12 ends with the reminder that the specific reason for the unleashing of Yahweh's wrath is the evil deeds of both the kings and the people (*their evil deeds;* **the evil you have done**).

■ **13** The addressee of v 13 is in feminine, and it is generally understood as an address to the city of Jerusalem. The city that Yahweh has chosen for his royal residence hears the word that he is **against it**. *Inhabitant of the valley* and *the rock of the plain* are ambiguous terms. The reference may be to the general geographical location of the city in the hill country of Judah, surrounded on three sides by valleys. Whatever is said of the royal family is also true of the city in which the royal residences are located. The identity of the royal family is wrapped up in the identity of the city. The second part of v 13 may be taken as prideful boasting of the royal family that dwelt in palaces protected by strong fortifications. The city and its first citizens are arrogant and complacent in their thinking that their palaces are safe and secure from the enemy's attack.

■ 14 Verse 14 returns to the theme of Yahweh's judgment by fire, already introduced in v 12. He is determined to punish the city and the royal family for their evil deeds. The fruit of their deeds was evil, and evil is what is therefore in store for them as Yahweh's punishment. **In your forests** may be a reference to the palaces built by the wood from the forests of Lebanon (see 1 Kgs 7:2; 10:17). The mighty and beautiful palace complex will be burned and consumed by the fire of Yahweh's judgment.

3. Another Sermon on Covenantal Duty (22:1-9)

BEHIND THE TEXT

There are three distinct literary units in 22:1-9: a prose speech in vv 1-5, a poetic in vv 6-7, and another prose speech in a question-answer form in vv 8-9.

In the first speech (vv 3-5), the addressee is the king of Judah, but no specific king is identified here. The speech could have been directed to any king who sat on the throne of David during the final years of Judah. The emphasis on social justice supports the placement of this speech during the days of Jehoiakim (see 22:13-19). Verses 1-5 are similar to 21:11-12, which also has an emphasis on social justice. The language and theme of 22:3-5 is parallel to 7:5-7. The speech begins with a covenant exhortation, followed by positive and negative covenant conditions (22:3-5). Obedience to Yahweh's demands means guarantee of the survival of the royal house; disobedience to Yahweh's words means ruin and destruction. The threat of destruction is couched in the form of an oath formula.

The second unit (vv 6-7) implies that the royal house has already made its choice and has followed the path of disobedience and thus it is faced with the disastrous consequences of covenant-breaking. Through a question-answer dialogue, the theological rationale for the city's destruction is given in the third unit (vv 8-9), which imagines a setting after the 587 B.C. catastrophe. This prose unit may have been composed before the fall of Jerusalem, though it reflects the realities of the exilic period.

IN THE TEXT

■ 1 The first unit begins with a command from Yahweh to Jeremiah to **go down to the *house* of the king of Judah** and speak Yahweh's words to the king (v 1). The command to **go down** indicates that the prophet may have been in the temple area when this directive came from Yahweh. The divine directive includes the command to speak Yahweh's word at the royal palace.

■ **2** Verse 2 implies that the prophet delivered his message in the gate of the palace (**through these gates**). The message from Yahweh begins with a command to **hear Yahweh's word.** Members of the royal family are the general addressees of this message; however, the message here is directly addressed to the **king of Judah** who sits **on David's throne.** The secondary audience is the **servants** of the king and his **people. Servants** are those who are employed by the king to serve him at his pleasure as his officers. **Your people** may mean those who are members of the royal family and those who have a privileged relationship with the palace, those who can freely come in and go through the palace gates without special permission. The command to **hear** is a call to listen and obey the word that Yahweh is about to proclaim through his prophet.

■ **3** Verse 3 states the covenantal responsibility of the Davidic king and his royal court—*do justice and righteousness*. The rest of this verse elaborates the practical expressions of justice and righteousness. Doing *justice* (*mišpāṭ*) and *righteousness* (*ṣĕdāqâ*) is the covenantal responsibility of all the members of the covenant community (see Amos 5:24; also Jer 5:1; 7:5; 21:12). Faithful kings like Josiah modeled this way of life for the people (see v 15). *Mišpāṭ* in the context of this text involves the royal duty in the judicial process to decide what is right and delivering impartial judgments by the king. That meant the king was to deliver the innocent and pronounce the guilty verdict on the criminal.

Mays on *Mišpāṭ* and *Ṣĕdāqâ* the OT

Mays describes *mišpāṭ* and *ṣĕdāqâ* as the "quintessence" of Yahweh's will for his people, "qualities which ought to be present in the social order" (1969, 92, 108). He also describes *ṣĕdāqâ* as the "source" of *mišpāṭ* and the latter as the "fruit" of the former. *Ṣĕdāqâ* in the OT is not "righteousness that is oriented to an absolute ethical norm . . . but a relational concept whose content and meaning is determined by the particular social context in which it is used" (Mays 1969, 92).

In Israel, monarchy was an institution established by Yahweh, and as his representative, it was the solemn business of the king to execute justice and righteousness in the nation (see 1 Kgs 10:9; Ps 72:1-4, 12-14; Isa 9:7). Yahweh reminds the king and the royal court their covenantal obligation to maintain social order and to promote the welfare of those who could become victims of ruthless and oppressive powers. They should take the lead in delivering the poor, the oppressed, the marginal, and the powerless in the community—the sojourner, the orphan, the widow, and the innocent (v 3).

■ **4** In vv 4-5, using both positive and negative conditional statements, Yahweh sets before the royal house two alternatives—the continuation of Yahweh's covenant promise to David concerning an eternal dynasty and eternal throne

(2 Sam 7:16) or the ruin of the Davidic house. In essence these are life-or-death choices, patterned after the Deuteronomic life-or-death choices (Deut 30:15-20). In v 4 the king and his people are reminded that doing justice and righteousness (*if you indeed do this word*) is the prerequisite for the continuation of the Davidic dynasty. Riding in chariots and on horses is a symbol of the royal power and here perhaps implies a royal procession such as the one during coronation. Verse 4 guarantees the continuation of the royal power and privileges of the kings who sit on the throne of David. The gates of the palace will remain open for the royal entourage as Yahweh's reward for the king's faithful execution of his covenantal duty.

■ **5** The negative conditional statement in v 5 utilizes an oath formula that indicates that Yahweh will remain true to himself by acting on his word about the destruction of **this house** (*habbayit hazzeh*), most likely the palace. However, it is not just the palace building that is being threatened with destruction, but this threat is made also against the royal house. The ruin of **this house** is thus also the ruin of the house of David. The continuation of the royal line and the royal palace depends on the faithful performances of the covenantal obligations. The Davidic covenant promises in 2 Sam 7:16 are suspended here, at least temporarily.

■ **6** The brief poetic oracle in vv 6-7 announces the fate of the royal house. The oracle begins with Yahweh's relationship to the royal house; it is to Yahweh like **Gilead** and the top of **Lebanon** (v 6). The meaning of these metaphors in their relation to the palace is not clear. Gilead is a mountain region in the Transjordan area. Lebanon is another mountain region north-northwest of Israel. Both of these areas are known for their luxurious forests. The metaphors perhaps suggest the building of the palace complex in Jerusalem with choice woods from these regions. Solomon is said to have built "the House of the Forest of the Lebanon" with pillars, beams, and roof made of cedar (1 Kgs 7:2 NRSV). The second part of v 6 announces the reversal of Yahweh's relationship to the royal house. Holladay suggests that **I will surely** has the force of an oath (1986, 583). Yahweh's decision is to make the royal palace an uninhabitable place; it will lie in ruins like a desert and uninhabited cities.

■ **7** Verse 7 continues the metaphor of the forest applied to the palace. Using the holy war imagery and vocabulary, Yahweh announces that he is **consecrating** (*wĕqiddaštî*) **destroyers** against the palace (Holladay 1986, 584). **Destroyers** (*mašḥîtîm*) here are the forces of the Babylon army; the same word in singular appears in Exod 12:23 where the destroyer is the angel of death. This enemy will come with its **weapons** and cut down the choice cedars with which the kings of Judah have built for themselves palaces, and they will be destroyed in fire.

■ **8** The prose narrative in vv 8-9 follows a question-and-answer form; the text is very similar to Deut 29:24-26, where the question is about the tragic devastation of the land as a result of Yahweh's unleashing of the covenant curses on those who break the covenant with him. Some commentators place this text in the exilic period, though it is likely that this is an imagined situation and thus this dialogue could have been formulated prior to the events of 587 B.C. This text assumes that the destruction has taken place, and thus it attempts to provide a theological rationale for the destruction of Jerusalem. In Deuteronomy, the question comes from the mouth of the next generation as well as foreigners/nations. Here also the question comes from the mouth of **many nations** that will **pass by** the ruined Jerusalem (v 8). Those who pass by will ask each other why Yahweh has brought this disaster to the city. The phrase this "great city" (NRSV) implies that the nations had some knowledge of Yahweh's special relationship to Jerusalem.

■ **9** The answer comes from the mouth of the nations who ask the "why" question (***they will say***). The nations know the answer. The question-and-answer form of this text implies an "apologetic agenda," a clear attempt to release Yahweh of any evil plans against his beloved city (Miller 2001, 741) and to place the responsibility squarely on the kings of Judah. This tragic fate has come upon the city because **they have forsaken the covenant of Yahweh their God and have worshiped and served other gods** (v 9). In the context of this text, **they** seems to refer to the kings, but it could also be taken to mean both the kings and the people. The fate of the city will be a stark reminder to those who pass by it that Yahweh has forsaken the Davidic kings and their capital city because they have forsaken their covenant with him.

In 22:2-5, the basis of judging the kings is the neglect of their duty to provide justice and righteousness; in vv 8-9 they are being judged for their covenantal infidelity. These two issues are not mutually exclusive. Covenant commitment means loyalty to Yahweh not only in worship but also in ethical and moral conduct. Violation of ethical obligations is the direct outcome of covenant-breaking and worship of other gods. The text warns that such infidelity to the covenant will be met with serious repercussions.

FROM THE TEXT

This text as well as 21:11-14 reminds those in authority that proper administration of justice and righteousness and commitment to show care and concern for the most disadvantaged and marginalized in the society are an integral part of their responsibility. Justice and righteousness are most clearly manifested through compassion and sensitivity to human needs. However, we cannot limit the application of this text to those in positions of power and authority. In the temple sermon (7:1-15), Jeremiah clearly indicated that meeting this most fundamental need is the responsibility of all who are part of a worshipping community. The conditions that God set for the well-being of our community life apply to all who participate in the community life. The text reminds the modern readers that they, too, stand under judgment for violating or attempting to circumvent the call to social justice. The text also reminds us that our neglect of the poor is the direct outcome of our passionate pursuit of other gods—gods that we seek to enhance our own personal welfare. When we become too preoccupied with our own self, others and their need become less and less important. The text does not guarantee a future to those who are preoccupied with their own personal well-being.

The judgment scene in Matt 25:31-46 clearly sets forth God's nonnegotiable conditions for social well-being and the punishment of eternal fire for those who violate the most fundamental requirements of human compassion and concern for others. The Gospel writer defines for us what justice and righteousness mean in the world in which we live—giving food to the hungry, drink to the thirsty, welcoming the stranger, clothing to the naked, caring for the sick, and visiting those in prison. To this we may add the admonition of John the Baptist to "bear fruits worthy of repentance" and his warning that "every tree . . . that does not bear good fruit is cut down and thrown into the fire" (Luke 3:8*a*, 9*b*; see vv 7-14).

4. Kings Under Judgment (22:10-30)

There are four separate literary units in this section. The section begins with a poetic lament spoken for Shallum followed by a prose speech concerning this king (vv 10-12). This is followed by a woe oracle addressed to Jehoiakim (vv 13-19). The oracles against the royal family are interrupted by a judgment oracle that announces the fate of Jerusalem (vv 20-23). The oracles against the royal family continue in vv 24-30, where the subject is **Coniah** (NIV margin). There is a chronological sequence to vv 10-12, 13-19, and vv 24-30 since the subjects of these oracles (Shallum, Jehoiakim, Coniah) have ruled Judah in descending order from 609 to 597 B.C.

a. Shallum Shall Not Return (22:10-12)

BEHIND THE TEXT

This short unit includes a poetic lament (v 10) followed by a prose oracle, which is a judgment speech addressed to **Shallum son of Josiah** (vv 11-12). Shallum ruled for only three months, after the tragic death of his father Josiah in 609 B.C. This unit can be dated to a period shortly after Shallum's removal from the throne by Pharaoh Neco in 609 B.C. The prose oracle is a judgment speech that announces the fate of Shallum in the land of his captivity.

IN THE TEXT

■ **10-12** The poetic lament mentions two individuals, one who is **dead** and another who **goes away** (v 10). The one who is dead is not clearly identified; v 11 identifies the dead king as Josiah who was killed in 609 B.C., and the **one who goes away** as Shallum. The Chronicler mentions that Jeremiah uttered a lament for Josiah and that lamenting for Josiah has become a "custom in Israel" (2 Chr 35:25 NRSV). The text here seems to admonish the people that they should cease their mourning for Josiah the dead king. It is now time to mourn for the next king—Shallum (also known by his throne name Jehoahaz) who was deposed by Neco after being on the throne for only three months and was exiled to Egypt (2 Kgs 23:34). Lundbom sees here an "idiom of exaggerated contrast" in which the prophet is saying to the people that they should "weep more for Jehoahaz" who is alive and in exile than for their dead king (2004a, 129). Death in the Promised Land is preferable to exile and death in a foreign land. Josiah died a valiant death in battle against Egypt, where as Jehoahaz' fate is to die in the land of Israel's bondage. The **one who goes away** and does not return to **the land of his birth** remains as the symbol of the hopelessness of the nation and its own coming exile (v 10). The text does not indicate the reason for the judgment on Jehoahaz. Verse 12 reiterates the judgment that Jehoahaz will not return and see the land of his birth, but that he will die in the land of his exile. Lamenting for the exiled king in that sense is a lamenting over the nation's impending exile.

FROM THE TEXT

What is disconcerting in this text is the repetition of the point that the exiled king will "never" see his homeland again. This is a final word about the king's expulsion from the land of promise. This is also a stern word to Judah that God is suspending whatever promises he had made about the eternal Davidic dynasty. The exile of the king portends the fate of the nation. The text powerfully and emphatically rejects any claim of an undisturbed and secure future for the nation. There is no hope given to those who think that they can "continue in sin in order that grace may abound" (Rom 6:1 NRSV). Judgment of the wicked and the unfaithful indeed is a reality and when it comes, the result will be a "forever" exile from God's presence.

b. Woe to the Oppressive and Unjust King (22:13-19)

BEHIND THE TEXT

The first part of this unit is a woe oracle (vv 13-17) that does not identify the subject; vv 18-19 make clear that this is a judgment pronounced on Jehoiakim, who was placed on the throne of Judah by the Egyptians after deposing Shallum in 609 B.C. Verses 18-19 announce the dishonorable burial of Jehoiakim (vv 18-19). Some commentators treat these two oracles separately, but the beginning of v 18 (**therefore**) indicates continuity. This oracle belongs to the period of Jehoiakim's reign, perhaps at the heights of his power around 605-604 B.C., by which time he would have built a new palace for himself with slave labor and unjust practices (vv 13-14).

Verse 13 begins with the pronouncement of **woe** (*hōy*), but it quickly moves on to a bold accusation of the subject as an unjust and greedy monarch who was preoccupied with building a spacious palace for himself through slave labor (vv 13-14). Verses 15-17 contrast Jehoiakim who was greedy and oppressive with his father Josiah, who was concerned about justice and righteousness in the land. This indictment and accusation is followed by the verdict of judgment in vv 18-19.

IN THE TEXT

■ **13-14** Jeremiah strongly denounces Jehoiakim with a pronouncement of **woe**, which in this context is an announcement of the doom and gloom days that await the king (v 13). This same interjection is also found in v 18, where the assumed setting is that of a funeral. Holladay suggests that though the oracle begins with an accusation, it anticipates a funeral of the one being indicted (1986, 594). Jeremiah stands here in the tradition of Samuel (1 Sam 15:10-23), Nathan (2 Sam 12:7-15), and Elijah (1 Kgs 21:17-19) who have boldly and courageously confronted political authorities without the fear of retaliation. The prophet is the king's chief antagonist and prosecutor. He brings charges against the king for failing to do **righteousness** and **justice**, the very principles that the Davidic monarchy was responsible to uphold in the land. The violation of this royal duty is evident in the building project undertaken by the king. The text suggests that the king undertook either a large and spacious palace building project (**house of measurements,** v 14a) or the expansion of the palace complex with spacious **upper rooms, windows, panels** of **cedar,** and **red** paint (vv 13-14). Upper rooms were roof chambers with latticed windows (Lundbom 2004a, 135). He did all these without paying attention to **righteousness** and **justice** (see v 3).

Verse 13 lists the violation of the principles of righteousness and justice—forced labor and withholding of **wages** from the workers who are his **neighbors** or fellow members of the covenant community. Violation of the Deuteronomic law is the charge here (see Deut 24:14). The policy of forced labor goes back to the earliest days of monarchy in Israel (see 2 Sam 20:24; 1 Kgs 5:13-18). Jehoiakim continued this practice at a time when he was also collecting gold and silver from the people of the land to pay tribute to Pharaoh Neco to keep his kingship (2 Kgs 23:35).

■ **15** Verse 15 begins with a rhetorical question aimed to establish the defining qualities of Davidic monarchy. The answer to the bold and probing question, **Are you a king because you compete in cedar?** is clear (v 15a). This question asserts the truth that vast building projects are not the criteria that determine the essence of kingship. The phrase **compete in cedar** indicates that Jehoiakim may have been trying to outdo his predecessors or perhaps may have been trying to elevate himself to the status of Solomon who had undertaken massive palace building projects. The second rhetorical question in v 15 reminds Jehoiakim that his father (Josiah) also lived the life of a king by eating and drinking like royal figures do, but his kingship was defined by his commitment to do *justice* and **righteousness.** **All went well** (vv 15*b*, 16*a*) with Josiah because of his commitment to do justice and righteousness. This remark is most likely about his kingship in general without any reference to Josiah's untimely death in the battle of Megiddo.

■ **16** In v 16, Jeremiah describes the essence of kingship practiced by Josiah; **he defended the cause of the poor and needy.** Josiah kept the Deuteronomic command to care for the widows, orphans, and aliens in the land, who depended on the king for proper judicial process. The prophet instructs the king that social justice is the fundamental duty of Davidic kings. Ironically, the son had not learned that lesson from his father but presumed that building palaces was what kingship was all about. This lesson on kingship ends with another rhetorical question: *Is not that* **to know me?** The essence of kingship illustrated through the just and righteous actions of Josiah is equated in v 16*b* as the knowledge of Yahweh. **To know me** also implies the covenantal duty of the king before Yahweh who established monarchy for his people. The king rules as the agent of Yahweh, and the king lives and rules by the covenant laws. In this context **to know** Yahweh means to do justice and righteousness (v 16*b*).

■ **17** In v 17 the prophet makes a direct accusation against Jehoiakim as a dishonest, cheating, unjust, unrighteous, violent, and oppressive ruler. The king has only one goal in mind—personal profit through violent and oppressive actions. The phrase **your eyes and your heart** indicates his perceptions and thoughts and the preoccupation of his life. He is not concerned with anyone else. He considers this self-aggrandizement as his royal prerogative. **Shedding innocent blood** is a direct violation of Yahweh's command to the Davidic kings (see 22:3).

■ **18** Verses 18-19 announce Yahweh's judgment on Jehoiakim; this is an oracle from Yahweh addressed directly to the king, and it is placed here as Yahweh's response to the prophet's indictment of the king in the preceding verses. The text begins with a clear identity of the unnamed king in vv 13-17 as **Jehoiakim son of Josiah king of Judah** (v 18). In contrast to the call to "weep bitterly" for Jehoahaz, Yahweh announces that no one in the nation shall lament for Jehoiakim, a line repeated again later in this verse. The death of Jehoiakim is anticipated here. Four times the word *woe* (*hōy*) appears in v 18, which clearly presents this verse as a lament. The usual words of lament at the time of the death of a beloved king are presented here as words that will not be spoken about Jehoiakim. No one will utter words of lament such as **my brother, sister, lord, majesty** at the time of Jehoiakim's death. The meaning of the lament word **my sister** is not clear. Fretheim suggests that all of these designations indicate "symbolic roles" a king would have assumed in the lives of the people (2002, 320). The prophet may be using here stereotypical lament words heard in funeral processions in the ancient times without any reference to the gender identity of the deceased individual. No one will miss this selfish and ruthless king when he dies.

■ **19** Verse 19 expands on the disgraceful end of the king. The text seems to convey a contradictory message. Does the text mean that he will be buried like a donkey (***with the burial of a donkey he will be buried***) or that he will be left unburied—**dragged away and thrown *out beyond* the gates of Jerusalem**? The force of this text seems to be on his dishonorable fate of receiving no burial at all. He will be treated like a dead donkey and will thus suffer the curses of breaking the covenant (Deut 28:26). His corpse will be food for birds and wild animals. The manner in which Jehoiakim met his death is not known to us. Commentators speculate on various possibilities, such as assassination during a palace revolt or natural death prior to the arrival of the Babylonians in 598 B.C. or death on the way to Babylon as a prisoner. At any rate, it is difficult to determine whether this prediction was literally fulfilled (see 2 Kgs 24:6; 2 Chr 36:5-6).

FROM THE TEXT

This text presents the most daring criticism of the abuse of political and social power, economic exploitation, and social injustice committed by the wealthy and the powerful against the disadvantaged and the marginalized in the society. Those in power exist to preserve and protect the society, not to destroy it. A preoccupation with self-preservation and self-aggrandizement of the powerful elements in the society often leads to social injustice and lack of care and concern for the poor in the society. In this text, those who live this way of life are members of the ruling class, those charged with the responsibility to maintain and lead in the covenant way of life. The text reminds us that in any society, whether religious or secular, God expects the practice of social justice and equity. There is no indictment against wealth or living a rich and prosperous life in this text, but rather the indictment is against those who do so at the expense of the poor and those who show no concern to the needs of the poor. A society and government that promote programs and policies that benefit the rich and shortchange the poor do not find any comfort in this text.

Is that not what it means to know me? (v 16). This powerful question raises an important issue then and now. Knowledge of God is more than mental acquiescence to God; it is more than belief and experience of personal salvation. Knowledge of God is putting faith and experience into action, particularly actions of social concerns for the benefit of the poor in the community. We cannot separate personal piety from personal involvement in social and community life. Jeremiah is not alone in this understanding of the relation between spirituality and social concerns (see Amos 5:14-15; Mic 6:8; Isa 1:17). Israel had no shortage of spirituality and worship. What it lacked was social concern. This is precisely what brought the demise of the northern kingdom. This is one of the compelling reasons of judgment on Judah, according to Jeremiah. We hear in this text a pattern for practicing faith as well as a strong warning of the consequences of our failure to truly "know" God through actions of obedience.

c. The Fate of the Defiant City (22:20-23)

BEHIND THE TEXT

The connection of vv 20-23 to the preceding and following oracles that deal with the royal family is not clear. One possible aim is to show that the fate of the royal family is to have a devastating effect on the capital city. The placement of this oracle between oracles against Jehoiakim (vv 13-19) and Coniah (vv 24-30) has prompted some commentators to date it to 597 B.C. (Lundbom 2004a, 153).

This poetic oracle interrupts the judgment speeches against the Judean kings and returns to the judgment of the city of Jerusalem. Yahweh is the speaker of this oracle (v 21). Verses 20-22 are clearly addressed to a woman; commentators agree that Jerusalem personified as an adulterous woman is the addressee of these verses.

IN THE TEXT

■ **20** The oracle begins with a call to **go up to Lebanon** (v 20); v 23 is addressed to **you who live in "Lebanon"** "nested among the cedars" (NRSV). Lebanon in v 20 refers to the mountains of Lebanon, north of Israel; in v 23 the reference is most likely to the royal family that dwells in houses in Jerusalem built of cedar from the mountains of Lebanon. The people of Jerusalem are being asked to go up to Lebanon and the mountains of **Bashan** and **Abarim** and **cry out** or lift their voice in lament. Bashan, located northeast of Jerusalem, is a high mountain area north of Gilead in the Transjordan. Abarim is a general designation for the entire Moabite region, located southeast of Jerusalem. The lament from these mountain ranges will be heard throughout the north, northeast, and southeast regions surrounding Jerusalem. Jerusalem is being asked here to **cry out** or to raise a loud cry of lament because all her *lovers* are **crushed**. The crying out (*ṣaʿāq*) indicates not only helplessness but also a cry for help. "Your lovers" (NRSV) may be those nations with whom Judah entered into political alliances and the gods of these nations that Judah worshipped to show loyalty and allegiance in return for military help. These nations and their gods are being crushed by the Babylonians. Jerusalem can do nothing but lament over her helpless situation. The main objective of this divine directive is to show that Jerusalem cannot expect to receive any help from any of her human or divine allies. The crushing defeat of her allies is also her fate that awaits her.

■ **21** Yahweh reminds Jerusalem that he has spoken to her in her *prosperity*, her prosperous and peaceful days (v 21). *I spoke to you* here refers to his messages given through the prophets. Jerusalem's response to Yahweh in the past has been **I will not listen** (see 6:17). This defiant refusal to listen to Yahweh's words has been a consistent feature of Judah's relationship with Yahweh (see 2:20, 23, 35). Yahweh further reminds Jerusalem that this has been her **way** of life, her conduct toward Yahweh since the days of her **youth,** from the earliest days of her relationship with him. This is in sharp contrast to the highly romanticized picture of Yahweh-Israel relationship portrayed in 2:2, when there was devotion and love on the part of Israel toward Yahweh. The portrait here is that of a consistently disobedient and rebellious people. **You have not obeyed me** corresponds to **I will not listen.** Both the people and Yahweh agree on one thing: obedience to Yahweh, which is a prerequisite to the covenant relationship, has been missing in the Yahweh-Jerusalem relationship since the beginning days of their relationship (see Exod 19:5).

■ **22** Verse 22 announces Yahweh's judgment on Jerusalem, who consistently disobeyed his voice. Judgment will come upon the **shepherds** of Jerusalem; **shepherds** refer to the kings of Judah. Using a wordplay, Yahweh announces that judgment will come as a **wind** that ***will shepherd*** (verb *rā'â*, meaning "tend," "graze") **all your shepherds** (*rō'ayik*, from *rō'eh*, meaning "shepherd"). The shepherds who have neglected their duty to gather Yahweh's sheep will face **the wind;** the hot and destructive east wind is the image of judgment here (see 4:11-12; 13:24; 18:17). It will destroy and scatter the unfaithful shepherds of Yahweh. **Your shepherds** in the first line is parallel to ***your lovers*** (*mĕ'ahăbayik*); most commentators think that reference to shepherds and lovers in v 22 is to Judah's kings, though "your lovers" (*mĕ'ahăbayik*) in v 20 (NRSV) seems to refer to foreign nations and foreign gods. ***Your lovers shall go into captivity*** makes clear what is meant by **the wind will *shepherd* all your shepherds** in the previous line. The coming exile of the kings of Judah is clearly the judgment of Yahweh for their failure to be his faithful shepherds. If *your lovers* in v 22 refers to foreign nations and foreign gods, then the text may mean the exile of both Jerusalem's kings and her foreign political and religious allies. When this happens (***indeed then***), the city will be ashamed and disgraced because there will be no one to give leadership to the city. The leaders in whom the city trusted will be taken into captivity. Using another wordplay, the judgment announces **all your wickedness** (*rā'ātēk*, from *rā'â*, meaning "evil," "wickedness") as the root cause of the exile of **your shepherds** (*rō'ayik*) and the shame and disgrace that will be experienced by the inhabitants of the city.

■ **23** Verse 23 addresses those who **live** in buildings constructed of wood from the forest of **Lebanon.** It is likely that the intended addressees are members of the royal family who live in palace buildings paneled with cedars of Lebanon. The phrase **you who nested among cedars** is parallel to **you who live in "Lebanon"** (see 21:13). The imagery in the second line is that of birds situated safely in their nests. The rest of 22:23 indicates that the luxury and comfort enjoyed by the royal family will soon be replaced with intense pain like that of a woman in labor. The NIV reading **how you will groan** could also be read as ***how you will be pitied.*** The idea seems to be that there will be no one to pity or comfort the royal family when it experiences **pain like that of a woman** giving birth. All protection and comfort will be removed from Jerusalem when she comes under the attack of the Babylonian army.

FROM THE TEXT

Jerusalem's response to God ("I will not listen") is a defiant no to the One who is the source of its prosperity and life. This rebellious attitude reflects an outright rejection of the covenant way of life that calls for submission, obedience, and faithfulness to God. The text shows that the Jerusalem community, particularly the leadership, has replaced trust and humility before God with values of the world that promoted wealth, affluence, other gods, and political powers. The covenant community ceased to obey the voice of God and followed other gods who have become its "lovers." Palace buildings of the covenant community that were to be symbols of justice and righteousness in the land have become symbols of power and pride. The text announces shame, disgrace, exile, and death to those who reject the covenant way of life and pursue a covenant-breaking way of life.

d. Coniah: A Despised, Broken Vessel (22:24-30)

BEHIND THE TEXT

22:24-30

The last unit (vv 24-30) has two parts; the first part is a prose speech that announces the captivity of Coniah (vv 24-27). This part belongs to a period immediately before his exile to Babylon in 597 B.C. This is followed by a poetic speech that laments the fate of the exiled king (vv 28-30). This lament assumes that Coniah is on the way to the land of his exile or has already arrived there. The date of this part would also be 597 B.C., but sometime after he left Judah to begin his exile in Babylon.

Coniah (or Jeconiah), also known by his throne name Jehoiachin, assumed kingship in 597 B.C. Three months later the Babylonians took control of Jerusalem and exiled him to Babylon along with his mother and other prominent citizens of Jerusalem (2 Kgs 24:8-17). Hananiah announced the false message that Yahweh will bring Jehoiachin and the temple vessels and the exiled people back to the land within two years (Jer 28:2-4). These oracles do not give any hope in the continuation of the Davidic monarchy through the line of Jehoiachin. As in the case of Jehoahaz, there is no reason given here for the judgment on Jehoiachin.

IN THE TEXT

■ **24** Verse 24 begins with Yahweh's oath, *as I live,* to indicate his commitment to stand behind the word that he is about to proclaim; Yahweh takes this oath by invoking his own existence. The rest of v 24 indicates the divine decision to "tear . . . off" (NRSV) Coniah **son of Jehoiakim** from the throne. This decision is announced directly to the king (**you, your** in vv 24-26). The text indicates violent action, a forceful removal of a ring from one's finger. **Even if** (or "although") Jehoiachin were a **signet ring** on Yahweh's **right hand,** he would remove him from that position of authority. Signet ring is the symbol of royal authority; the seal on the ring is the seal of the owner of the ring, which is the signature of the person, or the stamp of authority. The Davidic kings were Yahweh's official representatives who ruled with authority granted to them by Yahweh (see Hag 2:23, which announces Yahweh's plan to make Zerubbabel, Jehoiachin's grandson, his signet ring). The text is not clear whether Yahweh's decision is to remove the king who rules without divine authority or to deprive the king of his authority, though he rules with authority from Yahweh. Some commentators see in the Hebrew conjunction (*'im*) a negative emphasis and thus they render the text as "Coniah . . . shall not be the signet ring" (Thompson 1980, 482; see also Holladay 1986, 604). The emphasis seems to be on the removal of royal authority from Jehoaichin.

■ **25** Verse 25 elaborates the fate of the deposed king. Using the phrase *into the hand of* four times in v 25, Yahweh announces his resolve to hand Jehoiachin over to his enemies. He will be removed from Yahweh's hand, and he will be delivered into the hands of those who are seeking to destroy his life. His enemies in general are the **Chaldeans,** and **Nebuchadnezzar** in particular. The enemies **seek** his **life,** and he is *afraid* of them. From the place of protection, security, and authority, he will be removed and he will live his life in fear and uncertainty.

■ **26-27** Yahweh's judgment on Jehoiachin is continued in vv 26-27. He will **hurl** the king and his **mother . . . into another country** (v 26). His mother, Nehushta, was among those who were taken to Babylon in 597 B.C. (2 Kgs 24:15). **There you . . . will die** is the divine pronouncement of Jehoiachin's fate. Though the exiled royal family may deeply *desire* **to return** to their homeland, *they shall not return* to that land (v 27; see a similar word to the Jewish exiles in Egypt in 44:14). Jehoiachin will die without comfort and without ever seeing his homeland again. Death in exile in another land means withdrawal of all the blessings promised to the covenant community; no ancestral promises, no covenant life in the land of promise, but only the harsh consequences of covenant-breaking.

■ **28** The poetic oracle in vv 28-30 reflects a situation already in exile, and thus it could have been delivered after Jehoiachin was taken to Babylon in 597 B.C. Verse 28 is a lament that is formulated in the form of a number of rhetorical questions. It is not clear who is asking these questions. Commentators suggest supporters of Jehoiachin or the people or the prophet or Yahweh as the possible speaker of v 28. It is possible that Yahweh is the presumed speaker of this verse. The questions convey Yahweh's grief over his decision to discard Jehoiachin like a **despised, broken pot,** though that is not what he was meant to be. He was born to be the heir to the divine promises, to continue the dynastic promises Yahweh had made to David. The Hebrew word *'eṣeb* (**pot**), found only here in the OT, is understood by most commentators as a pottery vessel, parallel to *kĕlî* (***vessel;* object**) in the next line. His destiny was not to be like that of an unwanted vessel or a jar that has no value. The broken vessel imagery here is parallel to the shattered flask narrative in 19:1-13. Why would the legitimate heir to the Davidic throne become a despised human being? The answer is obvious. The royal house has broken the covenant, and therefore Yahweh terminates his promise with grief. The second question also reflects Yahweh's grief over his decision to send Jehoiachin and his children into exile in a foreign land. The text assumes that Jehoiachin had children at the time of his exile, though no mention of this is found in 2 Kgs 24:15 (see 2 Kgs 24:8 and 2 Chr 36:9 for variant accounts on the age of Jehoiachin when he was taken into exile).

■ **29** Yahweh's lament continues in v 29. Yahweh invites the **land** to hear **the word of *Yahweh*.** The three times repeated address (**land, land, land**) indicates emphasis and urgency to hear the word (see Brueggemann for the view that the repeated words express Yahweh's grief over the death and forfeiture of the land and over the king; 1998, 204-5). Calling upon heavens and earth to hear Yahweh's solemn words or witness covenant oaths is a custom attested elsewhere in the OT (Isa 1:2; Mic 6:1-2). Which land is addressed here? Is it the land from which Jehoiachin was taken away or the land into which he was exiled? It is likely that the message is addressed to the covenant community in both lands—those in the homeland and those taken into exile in the land of Babylon.

■ **30** In v 30, Yahweh continues to address the tragic destiny of Jehoiachin. The command ***write*** is presumably given to the scribes who create census lists of the tribes of Israel. Though he had children, his fate will be like that of a **childless** person. By a divine decree, he will be recorded in Israel's genealogical list as a man without children. As a childless king, he **will not prosper** or have anyone to succeed him. This judgment is not only on Jehoiachin but also on his children; there will be no one from his **offspring** that will continue the royal line, to sit on the **throne of David,** to **rule** the people of Judah. The judgment on Jehoiakim has begun to take its effect on his son Jehoaichin (see 36:30-31). Yahweh's promise to David is suspended here; at this point, the text does not seem to give any hope to Judah for the continuation of the Davidic throne through the legitimate royal line of descendants. However, this is not an announcement of the termination of the Davidic covenant in 2 Sam 7:13-16. Other texts indicate that the Davidic line will continue through a promised descendant of David who will rule with justice and righteousness (23:5-6; 33:17).

FROM THE TEXT

This text conveys God's profound sadness and grief over the death of his land and his king. Judgment is never pronounced by God without passion, pity, and sorrow. God of the Bible is not an impassionate and fickle deity who would make promises arbitrarily and cancel them whimsically. In this text he annuls his promises of the land and the royal dynasty, although temporarily, not without passion and grief. He is grieved at the terrible reality of sin that compels him to move and to take action against sinners. At the same time, his grief does not dissipate with the pronouncement of judgment. His grief continues over the pain of those who are sentenced to judgment. The exile of Jehoiachin from the land is in a real sense God's exile from the land. He can be comforted only when his exiled people come to the land of their promise. The oracles of consolation in chs 30—33 convey this comfort for both God and Judah.

This text and the preceding texts challenge the notion of a permanent royal house with kings from the house of David ruling the nation for eternity. The suspension of God's promises was necessary because his promises were hijacked by the nation to create a theological rationale for political ideologies that promoted corruption, injustice, oppression, and aggrandizement of wealth and power. The royal family may have thought of its existence as an indispensable God-ordained necessity for the nation. But God recalls it out of necessity for the welfare of the future of his people. This text powerfully speaks about God's freedom to suspend and even terminate what he intended to do, if and when his plans are diverted to create ideologies that have a self-serving purpose. Moreover, the prophetic voice in these texts challenges us to critique and raise questions about the legitimacy of self-serving political or religious ideologies that claim to have theological support.

5. Woe to the Shepherds (23:1-8)

BEHIND THE TEXT

The collection of oracles addressed to the kings of Judah concludes in 23:1-8. The theme of Yahweh's judgment on the Davidic kings is continued here. There are three distinct oracles within vv 1-8. The first oracle (vv 1-4) is in prose, and it begins with a woe announcement addressed to the shepherds but ends with hope given to Yahweh's scattered flock. The second oracle (vv 5-6) is in poetry and it announces salvation for Judah in the future days. The third oracle (vv 7-8) is in prose, and it announces a new exodus for the house of Israel and its settlement in the land.

All three oracles contain a promise from Yahweh and each of these promises begins with **look** (vv 2*b*, 5, 7). The second and the third oracles also begin with **days are coming,** which indicate that these promises are to be realized sometime in the future. The promise of restoration in the first oracle is also for the future. These oracles have considerable similarity to the judgment, restoration, and promised future statements in Ezek 34. The second oracle (23:5-6) shows continuity with the judgment pronounced on Jehoiachin; here the oracle focuses on the reversal of the judgment on the Davidic house. This oracle also shows that 22:30 was not the announcement of the final termination of the royal line. The third oracle (23:7-8) is for the most part a duplication of 16:14-15a. The second and the third oracle indicate the scattering of Yahweh's flock. In the second oracle, this scattering is brought about by the shepherds, whereas in the third oracle it is Yahweh's judgment. These oracles (23:1-8) were given after Jehoiachin and the prominent citizens of Jerusalem were taken into exile in 597 B.C. or toward the end of Zedekiah's reign in 587 B.C.

Some commentators treat 23:1-8 as a unit; others treat vv 1-4, 5-6, and 7-8 separately. These oracles are treated here together as one unit because of the thematic and theological continuity of these verses (indictment, judgment, and promise issues).

IN THE TEXT

The first section (vv 1-4) contains three prophetic oracles, perhaps spoken at different times (see ***oracle of Yahweh*** at the end of vv 1, 2, and 4). The shepherd-flock theme connects these oracles together in the present arrangement. Verses 1-2 announce what the shepherds have done to the flock and Yahweh's judgment on the shepherds (indictment and judgment) and vv 3-4 describe what Yahweh plans to do for the flock.

■ **1** The unit begins with a **woe** announced to the **shepherds,** a strong denunciation of the shepherds that also implies their impending destruction (v 1). Shepherds here and in most instances in Jeremiah are the political rulers, kings who belonged to the Davidic house. The text does not identify particular kings of Judah. Rather, they are described by what they have done to their flock. Does it include all the kings who were unfaithful in the history of Davidic monarchy, or is the reference limited to the more recent kings? It is likely that the prophet had in mind Jehoiakim and Zedekiah as the more specific targets of this general indictment.

The shepherd imagery naturally evokes the picture of pastoral setting with shepherds attending to the needs and welfare of their flock. The Davidic kings in a similar way as Yahweh's appointed rulers were to faithfully lead and guide Yahweh's flock. Verse 1 denounces the shepherds who are **destroying and scattering the sheep of** Yahweh's **(my) pasture.** How the kings destroyed and scattered the flock is not stated. **Sheep of my pasture** affirms the tradition of the covenant people as the sheep of Yahweh's pasture (see Pss 74:1; 100:3, etc.).

■ **2** In v 2, using a play on words, Yahweh announces his judgment on the **shepherds *who shepherd*** (*hārō'îm hārō'îm*) **my** (Yahweh's) **people.** The reason for the judgment is the same as that of the woe pronouncement in v 1. The charges are made directly to the kings (**you**) that they have **scattered the flock, driven them away,** and "not attended [*pāqad*] to" (NRSV) the needs of the flock. **You** in plural includes more than one king or even the entire royal family. The judgment is that Yahweh will ***attend to*** the shepherds for the **evil** they have done (*pāqad* here clearly conveys the idea of Yahweh's visitation to punish the shepherds). What they have done as evil to their flock will be their punishment. They have scattered Yahweh's flock, so they, too, will be scattered or sent into exile.

■ **3** Verses 3-4 convey what Yahweh will do on behalf of his scattered flock (v 3 is similar to the promises in 29:14). These verses contain three specific promises from Yahweh to his flock:

(a) Yahweh will **gather the remnant of** his **flock** (v 3). Gathering is the beginning of the reversal of judgment of scattering. **Remnant** indicates what is left of the flock and its destruction and scattering. **My flock** indicates the special relationship that continues to exist between Yahweh and his people even in the midst of judgment and exile. The promise of gathering is given not only to those who are in Babylon but also to those who live in exile in "all the lands" (NRSV). In v 2, the kings were the ones who scattered the flock; here Yahweh admits that it was he who scattered the flock (see also 9:16; 13:24; 18:17; 30:11). We should not regard these as contradictory statements, as Holladay does (1986, 615), but see here both human and divine agency in the exile of Judah. On the one hand, it happened because of the sin of failed leadership; on the other hand, it happened as Yahweh's judgment on both the leaders who failed and the flock that followed failed leadership.

Remnant Idea in Jeremiah

The "remnant" of Israel is a common idea in the OT; it is most often found in the book of Isaiah. In Jer 6:9 the Judean people that remained as the survivors of Israel after the Assyrians destroyed the northern tribes in 722 B.C. are called the "remnant of Israel." The designation "a remnant of Judah" is given to the Judeans who remained in the land after the Babylonian destruction of Judah in 587 B.C. Most of this group eventually went to Egypt, but the prophet did not give much hope to them (40:11; 42:15; 44:14). Clearly he favored the exiled population in Babylon as the true remnant; they received the word about their eventual return to their homeland (24:4-7; 50:19-20).

(b) Yahweh will **bring them back to their pasture** (v 3). Here Yahweh reverses the judgment of scattering and dispersion of his flock. **Pasture** is the land of promise, the land from which the people were driven out. Yahweh who scattered his people will bring them back to their homeland. Attached to this promise is the promise that **they will be fruitful and increase** (see 3:16). This is God's promise to the whole creation, which is reiterated in the promises to

Abraham (Gen 1:22, 28; 17:2-8).

■ **4** (c) Yahweh will raise up faithful shepherds over his people. After they are settled in the land, Yahweh will once again place over his people ***shepherds who will shepherd them*** (v 4). Shepherds (plural) suggest a line of kings, presumably the restoration of the Davidic monarchy. The rest of v 4 indicates that these shepherds will faithfully perform their duties and their flock will not be driven away. They will live without "fear" (NRSV) of foreign invasions; neither will they be "dismayed" (NRSV), because these new rulers will care for and protect the flock. The text here envisions a future for the exiled people in which there will be orderly and peaceful political existence. The meaning of the phrase **nor will any be missing** (*wĕlō' yippāqēdû*, from *pāqad*) is not clear; the phrase also could be translated as "they will not be visited" since *pāqad* also conveys the idea of Yahweh's visitation to punish the wicked. Does the text mean that under the faithful leadership of shepherds, the remnant will be protected and accounted for? Or, does it mean that the exile was the punishment for wickedness and that the remnant will not be subjected to another punishment by Yahweh? Both are possible readings and the exact meaning remains uncertain. Most translations prefer the former reading, though some commentators see here the latter meaning (Fretheim 2002, 326; Lundbom 2004a, 169).

■ **5** The second oracle (vv 5-6) focuses on yet another activity of Yahweh on behalf of his people (see the near parallel in 33:14-16). **The days are coming** (v 5) clearly indicates an eschatological event; the time of this activity is not known (33:14 indicates a time after the fulfillment of Yahweh's promise to the house of Israel and the house of Judah). Verses 5-6 constitute a solemn promise that clearly conveys the idea that Yahweh has not abandoned the Davidic house. Yahweh will **raise up** a Davidic king to continue the line of David. Through a divine action, Yahweh will make it possible for Davidic kingship to be restored in Israel (see Amos 9:11; Mic 5:2; Isa 9:6-7; 11:1 for similar expressions). This is especially significant in light of the words spoken concerning the end of the succession of kings in Jer 22:30.

The focus of v 5 is on a **righteous Branch**—an individual king, in contrast to shepherds in v 4. The relation of a single individual in v 5 to shepherds in v 4 is not clear. Though the text has continuity with the preceding verses, the text here focuses on a unique individual, a shepherd from among the shepherds of the people, whom Yahweh will raise up.

Righteous Branch (*ṣemaḥ ṣaddîq*; see 33:15) is generally considered as a messianic designation (see *ṣemaḥ* [branch] in Zech 3:8; 6:12). Isaiah 11:1 also conveys a similar idea of a Davidic king though the terms used there are "shoot" (*ḥōṭer*) and "Branch" (*nēṣer*). The actual meaning of *ṣaddîq* is not clear; most translations follow the meaning "righteous," but Holladay, based on parallel Phoenician and Ugaritic expressions, argues for the translation "rightful," which conveys the idea of this individual's legitimate claim to the Davidic throne (1989, 618).

Two possible meanings can be applied to this designation: (1) the coming king will indeed be the real righteous king in contrast to Zedekiah, whose name means "Yahweh is righteousness"), or (2) Yahweh will raise up in the future the real rightful/legitimate heir to the throne of David, since the dynastic line will not continue through the sons of Jehoiachin. The emphasis on righteousness in vv 5-6 supports the former meaning. The designation contrasts the future Davidic king with Zedekiah, the present Davidic king who sits on the throne of David. This coming king indeed will follow the rules of kingship and perform the duties of Davidic kings. Unlike the previous kings who have not acted wisely, this king will act **wisely** and ***perform justice and righteousness*** **in the land** (v 5). He would fulfill the demands of Yahweh on the Davidic kings (see 22:3), and thus be a true shepherd over Yahweh's flock.

Messianic Idea in Jeremiah

Jeremiah 23:5 clearly presents the idea of God raising up for his people an ideal king from the Davidic house (see also 33:14-26). The hope he gives to the people is very similar to the hope found in Isa 11:1-9. The idea of a restored Davidic kingdom is also found in other OT prophets (see Amos 9:11; Mic 5:2). This hope has its theological root in God's covenant with David, which clearly speaks of an eternal throne and an everlasting kingdom (2 Sam 7:12-16).

■ **6** Verse 6 continues the description of this future king. Whereas in the former days Judah experienced destructive invasions and exile, the future king will usher in days of salvation for Judah. **Judah will be saved** from the spiritual and political forces that dominate Yahweh's people (v 6). **Israel** (northern kingdom) also will experience security during the reign of this king. The text conveys the idea that the people will dwell in their homeland in freedom, security, prosperity, and in the enjoyment of all the covenantal blessing. The text also keeps alive the hope in a united Israel under one Davidic king (see 3:18; 30:1-9; 31:27; 33:23-26; also Hos 1:11; Ezek 37:15-28).

This coming king will be called by a special name—***Yahweh*** (***is***) **Our Righteousness** (*yhwh ṣidqēnu*, v 6). The text assumes that it will be a name given to the king by the people who will see in his kingship the righteous rule of Yahweh over his people. This name seems to be an intentional wordplay on Zedekiah (*ṣidqîyāhû*, meaning "Yahweh is my righteousness"), the last king to sit on the throne of David. Ironically, it was Nebuchadnezzar who gave Mattaniah, the young son of Josiah, the throne name Zedekiah (2 Kgs 24:17), presumably to give legitimacy to his kingship and hope to the people that he will rule with righteousness. The text clearly suggests a future ruler who will rule wisely and with righteousness and thus be totally unlike the present king who has failed to live up to the qualities of kingship represented by his name. Zedekiah is a symbol of failed leadership and shattered hope. In name and actions, the coming king will be the true embodiment of Yahweh's righteous rule. Whereas the policies of Zedekiah have led the nation to its destruction, the coming king will bring salvation and security to Yahweh's people. The people will have to wait for "the days [that] are coming" to see the fulfillment of this promise.

■ **7-8** Verses 7-8 are closely parallel to 16:14-15; see the discussion and commentary on 16:14-15. What is missing here, but present in 16:15, is reference to the land as the land that Yahweh gave to the ancestors of Israel. Also, 16:15 has the divine promise, "I will restore them." **They will live in their own land** (v 8) is missing in 16:15. Clearly the text anticipates a period after the exile; the word is given as a promise and hope for the nation that has heard the word of exile prior to the events of 587 B.C. This word would have been more meaningful to the exilic community, and it would have given them hope in their return to their land in **the days** that **are coming.** This future deliverance is contrasted with the exodus from Egypt, which hitherto has served as the center of Israel's confessional creed. No longer will Israel confess the exodus as the center of its faith, but it will replace it with a new confession of faith in Yahweh who reunited them with their land from the lands of their exile. This confession will include the recognition that it is Yahweh who **banished** them to their exile to **the land of the north** (Babylon) and all other lands (v 8). It will also include the confession that it is Yahweh who brought them out of their lands of exile. This new confession thus acknowledges Yahweh as the One who makes possible for Israel a new beginning. For that new beginning to happen, there had to be the judgment of exile, the total loss of the land before it was given back again.

FROM THE TEXT

The text, though it begins with judgment, quickly moves to the future possibilities that God is preparing for his people. The flock that is being scattered and destroyed is God's people. God's covenant relationship with his people is emphasized again and again in this text. Failure of the Davidic kings to provide faithful leadership does not lead God to nullify his covenant. He remains faithful to his covenant. The future of God's people rests not on an uninterrupted Davidic dynasty but on God's covenant faithfulness.

Scattering of God's people in this text is on the one hand brought upon by failed human leadership; yet, on the other hand, it is God's judgment on both the leaders and the people. God acts in judgment not because of some predetermined plans on the part of God but precisely because of failed human leadership. It is clear in this text that God holds the leadership accountable for their mistreatment and mismanagement of his flock.

The text also makes clear God's commitment to make things right for his people. In judgment he scattered his flock, but in grace and mercy he will gather them. The promise here concerns the ending of the exile and the beginning of a new history for God's people. God will act in a new way to bring deliverance and a new exodus for his people that will be far more dramatic than the old exodus experienced by the ancestors. This text is emphatic in its assertion of God's intent to bring about newness though present historical realities do not seem to give much hope.

The promise "be fruitful and multiply" (NRSV) conveys the idea of a fresh beginning for God's people. The end of their exile and their homecoming will usher in for Judah the opportunity to fully participate in God's covenantal blessing to their ancestor Abraham, the most fundamental blessing that God bestowed upon all creation. God's promise here is thus closely linked to his creational intentions.

The promise of a "righteous Branch" reveals God's plan to establish righteousness for his people—a condition of proper social order and community welfare, where everyone will live without fear and anxiety. This condition does not exist for God's people, but Jeremiah foresees this as a concrete reality. The "righteous Branch" signals hope for the community that lives in despair and hopelessness.

God as the caring and faithful shepherd of his people is a powerful theme in the OT that conveys his relation to his people (Isa 40:11; Ezek 34:11-16). The good shepherd of this text is a Davidic king who will practice righteousness. The hope expressed in this text is what the church found fulfilled in Jesus of Nazareth, the embodiment of God's righteousness. God continues to gather his lost and scattered sheep with the promise of newness of life and of the possibility for righteous living through Jesus "the good shepherd" who laid down his life for the sheep (John 10:1-18).

6. Judgment on False Prophets (23:9-40)

This section contains a number of literary units (vv 9-12, 13-15, 16-22, 23-32, 33-40); poetic pieces (vv 9-15, 18-22) alternate with prose speeches (vv 16-17, 23-40). This section begins with an introductory heading **Concerning the prophets** (v 9). Throughout this section we find indictment and judgment words pronounced against false prophets. No particular prophet is named here; this is a group indictment. The section begins with an indictment of prophets and priests (vv 9-12). Another indictment and judgment follows in vv 13-15. Verses 16-22 contain Yahweh's warning and condemnation of false prophets. Condemnation of false prophets continues in vv 23-32. The section concludes with a prose discourse on "the burden of the Lord" (v 33 NRSV; see vv 33-40).

There is no clear indication of the date of these oracles. It is very likely that they were given at various times during the reign of Jehoiakim and Zedekiah, and they have been collected and placed here as an appendix to the collection of oracles against the royal family to show that the people have been led astray not only by unfaithful kings but also by fraudulent spiritual leaders.

Verses 9-40 indicate Jeremiah's intense conflict with those who claimed to be Yahweh's spokespersons, who were proclaiming a message of peace at a time when political, social, and religious conditions in Judah were deteriorating rapidly. Jeremiah's encounter with Hananiah (ch 28) in 594 B.C. shows the intensity of this conflict during the reign of Zedekiah.

a. Indictment and Judgment (23:9-12)

BEHIND THE TEXT

Yahweh's indictment and judgment of prophets and priests in vv 10-12 is a response to Jeremiah's lament (v 9). The **oracle of Yahweh** formula in v 11 and v 12 indicate the divine origin of vv 10-12. The dialogue style of these verses (Jeremiah's lament followed by Yahweh's response) is typical of Jeremiah's book (Lundbom 2004a, 180). Verses 10-11 indicate national apostasy and evil that was found even in the temple. Both Holladay (1986, 625) and Lundbom (2004a, 180) place this oracle during the reign of Jehoiakim.

IN THE TEXT

■ **9** Commentators understand **concerning the prophets** (*lannĕbi'îm*) of v 9 as a superscription to the entire section (vv 9-40), similar to the introductory heading given to the oracles against the royal house (see 21:11). The rest of 23:9 reflects the deep anguish of the prophet and his weak physical and mental state **because of Yahweh and his holy words.** Fretheim entertains the possibility that Jeremiah may be describing here a state of ecstasy in which he received Yahweh's words, similar to the experience of ecstatic prophets in ancient Israel (2002, 332). This may not be the case here. Yahweh's words (presumably the words of judgment on Judah) have caused his heart to be broken or to be "deeply disturbed" in his mind (Thompson 1980, 492). He has lost his physical strength and become unstable like a person under the influence of strong, intoxicating drinks. The setting of the reception of the words of Yahweh may have been the divine council (see vv 18, 22). **Holy words** are words that originate with Yahweh; in this context they are his powerful words of indictment and judgment.

■ **10** Verses 10-11 contain the holy words of Yahweh. Yahweh's charges are specific. The indictment begins with the charge that **the land is full of adulterers** (v 10; see 9:2). **Adulterers** refer to an unidentified group; in the context of this larger unit (23:9-40), the reference is most likely to the false prophets. Adultery, then, would be falsehood promoted by these religious leaders (see v 14). However, it may also refer to the real act of illicit sexual relationship (see 29:23). An alternate interpretation of **adulterers** would include all who practice religious apostasy and sexual immorality in the land (see the indictment in 5:7-8). This is the pervasive condition in the **land,** which is Yahweh's land. Because of this perversion, the land suffers the **curse** of covenant-breaking and the land *mourns* because of the curse (v 10). The next line **(the pastures in the desert are *dried up*)** connects the curse with a drought in the land. The phrase

pastures in the desert (v 10; also in 9:10) refers to "uncultivated meadows in the open country" of Judah (Lundbom 2004a, 183) or "uninhabited pasturage out on the steppes" (Thompson 1980, 494). The impact of covenant-breaking on the environment is emphasized here. The subject of ***their course*** is not clear. The NIV supplies **the prophets** as the subject (v 10). "Adulterers" in the previous line is intended here. The adulterers have chosen a **course** (lit. "running") or a way of life that has been **evil** (it could thus mean that they are running after evil). They do not use their **power** in a just and right manner; instead, they use it to promote their own way of life.

Covenant-Breaking and Its Effect on Creation

Jeremiah frequently spoke about the negative and destructive effect of covenant-breaking on the world that God created. He clearly saw a connection between drought or mourning/withering of creation and the covenant-breaking committed by God's people (3:2-3; 4:28; 9:10; 12:4; 14:1-6; 23:10; see also Lev 26:18-19; Deut 28:23-24; 2 Chr 7:13-14; Hos 4:3). These biblical texts show that the effect of sin is not just on those who commit sin, but on the whole creation.

■ **11** Verse 11 specifically charges **prophet and priest** with ungodliness and evil. Though the focus is on false prophets, priests are included here perhaps because these two groups appear together elsewhere in the book as objects of Jeremiah's attack (see 5:31; 6:13; 14:18). These religious leaders are **godless** people (lit. "defiled" or "polluted") or leaders who have "lost their holiness" (Lundbom 2004a, 183). Their **evil** is found not only in the land but even in Yahweh's **house,** the Jerusalem temple.

■ **12** Verse 12 announces the judgment. What is in store for these unfaithful religious leaders is a dangerous and unpredictable path that is in **thick darkness.** Those who have self-directed their way of life will find themselves not only lost but also in grave danger. Yahweh will push them down in this **slippery** path, and they will fall to their destruction (see Ps 35:6). They have pursued *evil* (*rā'â* in vv 10 and 11) and their punishment will therefore be *evil* (*rā'â*) from Yahweh. They shall reap what they have sown when Yahweh will visit them to bring his punishment upon them. ***The year of their visitation*** (in the year they are punished; see also 11:23) indicates that Yahweh's punishment of the wicked is an inescapable reality.

FROM THE TEXT

What is the distinguishing mark of those who speak God's word truthfully? Jeremiah is a prophet of courage who speaks with passion, but at the same time with deep grief and pain. He is brokenhearted as a messenger of God's powerful words of judgment; he is also brokenhearted because corrupt religious leaders who have influence in the house of God speak falsehood in the name of God and thus betray not only God but also the community they serve.

They bring death not only to the people but also to the land. Those who bring anguish to the prophet are part of a religious system that is more committed to the dominant political ideologies of the day than to God's call for faithful covenant life. They go on with their easygoing way of life whereas the true prophet suffers beyond words because he must truthfully speak the words that God has given to him.

Who speaks truthfully and authoritatively for God? The text suggests that such voices are seldom found in powerful and politically influenced ecclesiastical structures that claim to speak authoritatively for God but in lonely and hurting places like the world of Jeremiah that holds truth-telling, even if it hurts and brings intense grief, as imperative for community survival. Such voices always speak against sin and wickedness in the world; such voices call the people to account for their actions that bring destruction and death to an already death-filled world.

b. Prophets of Samaria and Jerusalem (23:13-15)

BEHIND THE TEXT

Verses 13-15 contain indictment and judgment on the prophets of Samaria and Jerusalem. Verses 13-14 contain the charges; v 15 announces the judgment. Yahweh is the speaker in vv 13-14; v 15 has the messenger formula ("therefore thus says [Yahweh] of hosts" NRSV). Charges of adultery and evil in vv 10-11 are continued here; vv 13-15 may have been delivered about the same time as that of vv 9-12.

IN THE TEXT

■ **13** The divine speech begins with a reference to what Yahweh has seen in **the prophets of Samaria** (v 13), and then contrasts it with what he has seen among **the prophets of Jerusalem** (v 14). Both verses begin with a conjunction (*waw*), which Lundbom describes as *waws* that "set up a contrast and not a comparison" (2004a, 186). Samaria and Jerusalem, the capital cities, represent Israel and Judah respectively. The indictment against the prophets of Israel is that they have done a **repulsive thing** (*tiplâ* has a moral connotation, and it means something "unseemly" or "unsavory"). Their repulsive (or "disgusting" NRSV) behavior is that they **prophesied** in the name of **Baal** and led **my** (Yahweh's) **people Israel astray** from their covenant relationship with Yahweh (v 13). The text recalls here the widespread influence of Baal religion and the syncretistic activities of Israel's prophets throughout the history of the northern kingdom. Elijah counted himself as the only true prophet of Yahweh against four hundred and fifty Baal prophets (1 Kgs 18:22).

■ **14** Verse 14 describes the activities of the prophets of Jerusalem as **something horrible** (*ša'ărûrâ*), in contrast to the repulsive behavior of the prophets of Samaria. The purpose of this contrast is to indicate that the prophets of Jerusalem are involved in more serious offenses than their counterparts in Israel. Commentators agree that the Hebrew term *ša'ărûrâ* (also 5:30 and 18:13; see "a more shocking thing" in NRSV) is a stronger term than *tiplâ* ("repulsive thing"). This verse lists three specific sins of the prophets of Jerusalem: (1) they commit adultery; (2) they walk by the lie; and (3) they empower the wicked. Charges of committing adultery and following an evil path are already stated in v 10. As in v 10, **adultery** here is most likely religious apostasy as well as illicit sexual conduct (v 14). **Live a lie** (lit. "walking by the lie"; *šeqer* with the definite article here means "the lie," which some commentators understand as a reference to Baal; see also 3:23 and 5:31) means a life wrapped up in the falsehood they promote in the land through false prophecy. Moreover, they are on the side of those who do evil; **strengthen the hands of evildoers** implies complicity and support given to the wicked (v 14); instead of prophetic condemnation of evil, and calling evildoers to turn from evil, they encourage and empower evildoers to commit more evil. Verse 14 ends with a comparison of the population of Judah and the inhabitants of Jerusalem with the cities of **Sodom** and **Gomorrah** (see Gen 18—19). These cities were condemned and destroyed because of their wickedness. Verse 14 implies that a similar fate awaits the people because of false prophets.

■ **15** Verse 15 is a messenger-style speech that announces Yahweh's judgment on the prophets of Jerusalem (the prophets of Samaria have already suffered judgment in 722 B.C.). **Therefore** refers to the indictment in v 14. Feeding **wormwood** and making the prophets **drink poisoned water** convey the idea of judgment (see 9:15 for the same judgment on the people). Wormwood and poisonous water suggest an extremely unpleasant and bitter end to the prophets. The prophets of Jerusalem, instead of being the examples of godliness in Judah, have become the source of **ungodliness** (*ḥănuppâ* also means "profaneness," "pollution") in the land. They have polluted the land through their ungodly activities; therefore Yahweh's judgment is on them.

FROM THE TEXT

Jeremiah's indictment of the prophets of Jerusalem as a despicable group that belongs to the company of Sodom and Gomorrah shows the deep moral and spiritual corruption of the religious leaders of Judah. Their sins are worse than the sins of the Baal prophets of the northern kingdom prophets who have brought about the collapse of Yahwism and the eventual destruction of the nation itself. The text makes clear God's intent to bring punishment upon the religious leaders who destroy the moral and social fabric of the covenant community. This contrast between the two groups also suggests that Judah's fate will be worse than that of the northern kingdom. Reference to Sodom and Gomorrah indicates the intensity and inevitability of judgment.

Prophets who speak for God have the sacred responsibility to stand for God against all the forces that attempt to remove him from the community. Prophets of Samaria sold Yahwism out to the Canaanite religion and led the people away from their ancestral faith. Jerusalem's prophets stood by the side of those who exploited the weaker members of the community. In both cases, the prophets failed to act as the covenant community's conscience and to remind both the people and the leaders God's covenant requirements. In both kingdoms, (false) prophets supported state programs and policies that violated the Sinai covenant and effectively removed God from community life. As a result, in both kingdoms, injustice and violence ruled and the poor were denied basic principles of justice. This text cautions against any uncritical support for state programs and policies that violate God's call to covenant life, a key requirement of which is the practice of justice and righteousness in the community. Religious support of policies that benefit only the wealthy or the privileged members of the society inevitably means disregard for the "least of these" in the society. The text challenges the church to be the voice of God, the conscience of our national and political existence that constantly reminds our leaders to shape programs and policies that lead to the well-being of all members of the community.

c. True and False Prophets (23:16-22)

BEHIND THE TEXT

Most commentators treat vv 16-22 as a poetic unit (NRSV prints vv 16-17 as prose). Lundbom divides these verses into two units (vv 16-17 and vv 18-22) (2004a, 189, 193). Holladay also divides vv 16-22 into two units (vv 16-20 and vv 21-22) (1986, 633, 637). Verses 16-18 and 21-22 clearly address the issue of false prophecy and bring an indictment against false prophets. Verses 19-20 insert a judgment word. Yahweh is the speaker in vv 16-18 and 21-22. Jeremiah seems to be the speaker in vv 19-20, though some commentators treat these verses as Yahweh's words. The unit begins with a warning to the people concerning the false prophets and their message (vv 16-17). Verse 18 establishes the illegitimacy of these prophets and their words. Verses 19-20 convey Yahweh's judgment of the wicked. The unit ends with a clear and emphatic announcement of Yahweh that the false prophets are not his messengers.

IN THE TEXT

■ **16** Through a messenger-style speech, Yahweh warns the people concerning the false prophets and their message (v 16). **Do not listen** is a clear warning that implies at the outset that the prophets who prophesy to the people are not legitimate spokespersons of Yahweh. This warning is followed by an indictment of false prophets and their message. What they prophesy to the people is ***nothing*** or **false hopes** (*mahbilim*, from *hebel*, meaning "vanity," "nothingness"). The words of these prophets do not have any content because they do not proceed from the **mouth of Yahweh.** Rather, what they speak in the name of Yahweh are words that originate in their own **minds. Visions,** here and in 14:14, are false revelation or messages made up by the prophets.

■ 17 Another charge against the false prophets is that they keep making false promises to the people who **despise** Yahweh and continue to give them assurances of Yahweh's favorable words (v 17). The false prophets offer **peace** (*šālôm*) or total well-being to the wicked, but the true prophets announce Yahweh's judgment (see 6:14; 8:11; 14:13; 28:9). They assure those who stubbornly resist Yahweh's word that no *evil* (*rā'â*) will come upon them. When the nation as a whole is faced with the imminent danger of Yahweh's judgment through the agency of Babylon, these prophets announce to the people the message that all is well. When Jeremiah announces disaster and destruction, these prophets assure the people that evil will not come. They promote complacency in the land and give religious sanction to the people to continue to pursue the path of evil.

Divine Council in the OT

The council of Yahweh in the OT is a heavenly council or the assembly of divine beings where Yahweh makes decisions concerning matters on earth (see 1 Kgs 22:19-23; Job 1—2; Ps 82; Isa 6:1-8). Those who stand in the council of Yahweh not only have the privilege of seeing and hearing Yahweh's word but also have the responsibility to take that word from the heavenly realm to the people on earth. They also function as intercessors for the people (see Jer 18:20). The underlying assumption is that only those who are privileged to stand in the council of Yahweh have the true message.

■ 18 Verse 18 poses two rhetorical questions, and the implied answer affirms that the false prophets have not **stood in the council of Yahweh** or have listened or heard Yahweh's word. Lundbom suggests that the term council (*sôd*) assumes the idea of "confidentiality or secrecy" (2004a, 195). True prophets are the legitimate messengers of Yahweh because they receive their message directly from Yahweh and truthfully proclaim that message. If the false prophets had stood in the divine council, they would not have promoted the message of peace in the land because judgment on Judah is the decree that Yahweh announced in his divine council.

■ 19 As a true prophet and as the one who was privileged to stand in the council of Yahweh, Jeremiah announces what he has seen and heard in the divine council (vv 19-20). The intent here is to intentionally contradict false prophecy and replace it with true prophecy. Unlike the soothing words of the false prophets, what Jeremiah declares is the **storm of Yahweh** (v 19), a tornado-like whirling wind (*sa'ar*) that brings the destruction of the wicked [see 25:32 where Jeremiah describes the Babylonian army as a "mighty storm" (*sa'ar*) that is "rising from the ends of the earth"]. The storm imagery conveys the **wrath** of Yahweh against the wicked. Jeremiah's authenticity and legitimacy rests on the fact that he is not afraid to speak the truth of Yahweh's judgment of the wicked.

■ **20** Verse 20 announces that the **anger of *Yahweh*** that is bursting out like a destructive storm will complete its purpose. It is already unleashed against the wicked, and it will bring about their destruction. The statement that it will **not turn back until he fully accomplishes the purposes of his heart** indicates the certainty of Yahweh's plans and his intention to carry out his words of judgment (see a similar statement about the power and efficacy of Yahweh's word in Isa 55:10-11). At the time when Jeremiah proclaimed these words of judgment, the people would not have fully grasped the purposes of Yahweh's heart or his will. The prophet announces that **in days to come** the people who act foolishly now will gain some wisdom from the events of judgment. The phrase **days to come** means a later time, the days after the judgment. The last line, **you will understand it clearly,** suggests that the people will recognize their exile as Yahweh's anger against their wickedness. This would also be the time of their recognition of Jeremiah as Yahweh's true prophet.

■ **21** Yahweh is the speaker in vv 21-22. The divine speech here picks up the theme of Yahweh's council introduced in v 18. Verse 21 implies that only those who stand in Yahweh's council are sent as Yahweh's messengers; only those who see and hear Yahweh's word are authorized to speak for him. Though Yahweh **did not send** them, false prophets ran as if they were his messengers; though he **did not speak to them,** they prophesied words they did not hear from him. This verse also identifies Yahweh's sending of his messengers and his speaking a message to be delivered as two essential elements of authorized prophecy (see also Isa 6:8-9).

■ **22** Verse 22 continues the portrayal of the false prophets as unauthorized individuals. The conditional beginning of this verse indicates that they have not **stood in** Yahweh's **(my) council** and that they have not ***caused*** Yahweh's **(my) people *to hear*** his **(my) words.** If they had stood in Yahweh's council, they would have heard Yahweh's words of judgment. If they had proclaimed words of judgment instead of words of peace, then the effect would have been different. Words of judgment would have prompted the people to turn **from their evil ways and from their evil deeds** rather than continuing in "the stubbornness of their hearts" and believing that they will have "peace" and that "no harm will come" to them (v 17). The present crisis is due to the preaching of the false prophets "visions from their own minds" (v 16).

FROM THE TEXT

The question of "Who speaks for God?" does not have an easy answer. This was a difficult issue for the people of Judah during Jeremiah's day, and it remains a difficult issue even today. This text, however, gives guidance to God's people with two key criteria for making assessment of who speaks God's word truthfully.

First, those who speak God's word truthfully do so from their perspective of God's work in human history. Their religious ideology is not wedded to local or national or world politics, but it centers on God's sovereignty over the world and his active work to bring the world into conformity to his plans and purposes. They refuse to give legitimacy to any voice other than the voice of God and are particularly suspicious of those who speak "visions from their own minds" (v 16). They see hope when there is no hope, but they also see ill-health and calamity when people confidently think that all is well with them. They refuse to say *shalom* when there is no *shalom* and announce judgment to those who "stubbornly follow their own stubborn hearts" (v 17 NRSV). They see *shalom* as God's gift to his people that practice justice and righteousness in the community, and not some unconditional guarantee of well-being. True prophets, like Jeremiah in this text, refuse to make the people comfortable with words they want to hear but challenge them with words that call for repentance, faithfulness, obedience, and transformation.

Second, this text speaks of the divine council as the source of origin for a true prophetic word. This OT religious idea simply points to the fact that we cannot make claim of divine authority to words that originate in our hearts and minds. Our thoughts, however noble and good, are still human thoughts, limited to human perceptions of realities. The text cautions against our tendency to hastily claim divine authority to our human words, and our penchant to speak without being sent by God. In the absence of an established canon in the OT times, the divine council idea served to authenticate and distinguish between true and false prophecy. The Bible, the canon of the Christian community, now serves as the source of authority for words spoken on behalf of God. Those who proclaim God's word truthfully today are those who faithfully hear God's word, who make diligent attempt to discern God's word, and are obedient to proclaiming that word without distorting it with the visions of their human minds. Such modern-day prophets are the ones who are sent by God, who stand "in the council of the LORD" (v 18).

d. Lying Prophets and Their Lying Dreams (23:23-32)

BEHIND THE TEXT

Jeremiah 23:23-32 is a discourse by Yahweh, the main focus of which is false prophecy and false prophets. Yahweh's emphatic statement that he did not send the prophets (v 32) connects this oracle with the preceding unit (see v 21). The unit has three parts: the first part, which is in poetry (vv 23-24), is Yahweh's claim of his transcendence and immanence; the second part (vv 25-29) is a strong censure of the false prophets who claim to have dreams through which they receive communications from Yahweh; the third part (vv 30-32) clearly states Yahweh's opposition to false prophets. Verses 25-32 are for the most part in prose, with the exception of a brief poem in vv 28*b*-29. Beginning with v 28b, there are six brief oracles, marked by the **oracle of *Yahweh*** formula. Verses 30, 31, and 32 begin with Yahweh's statement, "I am against the prophets/those who prophesy." The NIV and the NRSV treat vv 25-32 as prose.

Commentators are divided on the issue of the relationship of vv 23-24 to vv 25-32. Verses 23-24 do not make any specific mention of the false prophets. Therefore, they treat these verses as a separate unit. In vv 23-24, Yahweh establishes himself as the God who is both near and far off and from whom nothing is hidden, and then proceeds to reveal in vv 25-32 what he hears and what he knows about the false prophets. Verses 23-24 thus seem to function as a preface to the discourse in vv 25-32. This oracle, like the preceding oracles, most likely belongs to the period of Jeremiah's intense confrontation with the false prophets during the days of Jehoiakim or Zedekiah.

IN THE TEXT

■ **23** Yahweh's rhetorical question, *Am I a God nearby . . . and not a God far off*, affirms the fact that Yahweh is both near and far off (v 23). The first part of the question, *Am I a God nearby*, expects the answer no. Brueggemann sees here a theological assertion of the distance of Yahweh from the temple cult; he sees here a claim that Yahweh is "not near and available" (1998, 213). Emphasis on the distance of Yahweh does not, however, negate the nearness of Yahweh. The expected negative answer simply shows that Yahweh is not, and cannot be, confined to earthly times and locations. He is near and available, but at the same time he is sovereign and free from human attempt to control him or manipulate his presence.

■ **24** Verse 24 expands the idea of Yahweh's nearness and distance. The answer to the first rhetorical question is clear. No one can **hide in secret places** and assume to escape from Yahweh's judgment. Nothing is hidden from the all-seeing eye of Yahweh. The second rhetorical question asserts the fact that Yahweh fills ***the heavens and the earth.*** This reiterates the claim of Yahweh's nearness and distance in v 23. He owns and occupies the world he created (see Isa 66:1; Amos 9:2-4).

■ **25** Yahweh's discourse continues in vv 25-32. The speech is a strong censure of the false prophets who **prophesy *falsehood*** in Yahweh's **name** (v 25). Yahweh charges that the prophets speak a lie and take his name in vain. The words they speak are a lie because they are words of peace and well-being. Their words contradict the words of judgment spoken by his authorized spokespersons. Yahweh who fills the heavens and the earth, who is near and far, makes it known that he not only sees (v 24) but also hears everything in creation (**I have heard**). What he is hearing from the mouth of the false prophets is their boastful claim **"I had a dream! I had a dream!"** which implies that they are authentic recipients of revelation (v 25). Dreams are a traditionally recognized means of receiving communication from Yahweh in ancient Israel (see Gen 28:10-22; Num 12:6).

■ **26** Yahweh discredits the claims of the false prophets and describes them as **lying prophets** (v 26) and their dreams as "lying dreams" (v 32 NRSV). Verse 26 begins with a rhetorical question for which the answer is negative. The opening phrase of the question (**how long**) is found in a number of lament psalms, an expression of despair by the lamenting individual or the community (see Pss 6:3; 74:10; 80:4; also Jer 4:21; 12:4; 13:27). This question from the mouth of Yahweh indicates his agony over the continued activity of the false prophets who prophesy ***falsehood*** and ***the deceit of their heart.*** Some commentators see here a negative answer to the question whether the false prophets can ever turn back to Yahweh (see Holladay 1986, 642; Fretheim 2002, 339). Their falsehood originates in their deceitful ***heart*** (v 26), the seat of their human thoughts and will.

■ **27** Verse 27 is a continuation of Yahweh's lament; he agonizes over the deliberate plans of the false prophets to make the people forget Yahweh's **name** (v 27). This verse also implies a scheme among the false prophets to authenticate each other as legitimate prophets by telling their dreams to each other, and to pass their dreams on to the people as true revelation from Yahweh. Yahweh also laments that what is taking place here is parallel to Israel's ancestors forgetting Yahweh through **Baal** (see 2:5-8). Prophesying falsehood is tantamount to Baal worship. Both lead Yahweh's people to forsake and forget him.

■ **28** Verse 28 indicates a contest that Yahweh initiates to establish the true criterion of prophecy. The **dream** of a false prophet (v 28) is a passing phenomenon that has no actual content; it cannot be considered true prophecy. In the context of this verse, it is not a rejection of dreams as a means of revelation but rather a rejection of the dreams of false prophets. True prophecy is speaking Yahweh's word that is given to a prophet. The true prophet is a person who has Yahweh's **word *with him.*** The intent of this verse is also to show that true prophecy is speaking Yahweh's word truthfully. ***Let him speak my word truthfully*** (v 28) can also be translated as "let him speak my word of truth" (Holladay 1986, 644). The contrast between false prophecy and true prophecy is made clear in the rhetorical question, ***what is the straw to the wheat?*** False prophecy is like straw, which has nothing in common with wheat—Yahweh's words spoken truthfully.

■ **29** Verse 29 shows why the dreams of false prophets cannot be compared with the genuine words of Yahweh. Yahweh's word spoken truthfully has the effect of a **fire** that burns and a **hammer** that ***shatters rock.*** The effect of dreams is not mentioned but is implied in v 29. They have no content or power; they result in nothing. The imageries of burning fire and hammer that shatters rock convey the idea of judgment (see 4:4; 5:14; 20:9; 51:20). The dreams of the false prophets are nothing compared to the dynamic power of Yahweh's word.

■ **30** Verses 30-32 contain three **I am against** statements pronounced by Yahweh against false prophets. The opening word (**therefore**) indicates that what follows is a judgment speech. **I am against** implies Yahweh's intense opposition to the false prophets. Yahweh's spoken opposition to the prophets also conveys the idea of judgment, though specific form of judgment is not mentioned here. Each **I am against** statement is followed by the description of a specific activity of the false prophets. In v 30, Yahweh is against the prophets **who steal *my words from one another.*** Commentators are not certain on the meaning of this accusation. ***My words*** seem to imply authentic words of Yahweh spoken by the true prophets. If this is so, the accusation is that the false prophets have taken Yahweh's true words and have reshaped them to fit their own agenda. It may also mean that the false prophets repeat each others' words and claim that these are Yahweh's words that they themselves have received by means of dreams (see Bright 1965, 153). Stealing here reflects the activity of not only taking Yahweh's name in vain but also claiming revelation they have not received.

■ 31 The second **I am against** sentence describes the false prophets as those who ***take their*** tongue to ***utter an oracle*** (v 31). ***They utter an oracle*** (*yin'ămû nĕ'ūm*, lit. "they oracle an oracle," a wordplay in Hebrew) is a rare phrase in the OT; the verb form is found only here in the OT. These prophets are engaged in creating an oracle, whereas Yahweh's true prophets proclaim words that originate with Yahweh as **an oracle of Yahweh** (*nĕ'ūm yhwh*), a frequent expression in Jeremiah (six times in vv 28-32). The false prophets use their tongue to convey their words, which they claim as words from Yahweh.

■ 32 The third **I am against** sentence sums up all the accusations in the preceding oracles against the false prophets (v 32). The charges of lying dreams (see vv 16, 25-26), recounting the dreams (see v 27), leading the people astray with falsehood (see v 13), and Yahweh's statement that he did not send or command the prophets to speak (see v 21) are repeated in v 32. Yahweh accuses the prophets that they have misled and misguided the people with their falsehood and **reckless** talk (*paḥăzût* may mean "loose talk," "exaggerated tales," etc.; Bright 1965, 153). The final conclusion is that the prophets who are not sent by Yahweh ***do not profit*** or generate any good to the people. They would have profited the people had they communicated the true words of Yahweh. Then the people would have had an opportunity to repent of their unfaithfulness to Yahweh.

FROM THE TEXT

The peace and well-being message of the false prophets was rooted in a distorted view of the character of God as a God who is confined to his temple, who could always be counted on for protection and prosperity. The temptation to characterize God this way and to confine him locally is very much alive in our day. The peace and prosperity message we often hear is evidence of this one-sided view of God. It is this kind of theology that often leads to the distorted view of "God on our side" that is played out in politics and national policies, and particularly on matters of foreign affairs. The text invites us to see God as both "near" and "far off" (v 23 NRSV)—near to us by his gracious presence, but sovereign and free, too majestic to be confined by human thoughts and plans, and too mysterious to be fully known by feeble human beings.

God who fills the heavens and the earth is in contact with every part of creation. He sees and hears everything that takes place in his world. What we say or do not say in his name and what we do or do not do in his name is in the sphere of his knowledge. This is a warning to the unfaithful, but the knowledge of God's presence comforts the faithful. God who is present in our lives is also present in the lives of people everywhere in the world. This text also cautions us against making any theological claim about how and where God works in the world, or making any claims about God's exclusive relationship to this or that group of people.

This text makes a sharp distinction between false visions and dreams that mislead people and faithful proclamation of God's word that consumes like fire and breaks rocks like a hammer. Dreams have no lasting effect; they produce only forgetfulness of God. Dreams have no content; they are effective only in turning the people away from the true and living God to gods (Baals) that offer false promises of security and well-being. God's word spoken faithfully, on the other hand, has the power to penetrate deep, destroy and shatter, but at the same time, to effect change and transformation—it destroys, but it builds up; it uproots, but it plants. It is "living and active, sharper than any two-edged sword, piercing until it divides soul from spirit, joints from marrow; it is able to judge the thoughts and intentions of the heart" (Heb 4:12 NRSV). The text is an indictment against preaching that serves the purpose of making people feel good and secure in their self-serving and self-centered existence. "I am against" is God's word not only to those who mislead the people with lies but also to those who expect to hear from their preachers messages that do not bring discomfort to them.

e. The Burden of Yahweh (23:33-40)

BEHIND THE TEXT

The final segment of the collection of oracles that deal with the false prophets is a long discourse (vv 33-40) centered on the expression **the burden of Yahweh** (*maśśā' yhwh*). This discourse has two discernible sections. The first section (vv 33-34) is Yahweh's word to Jeremiah in which Yahweh gives a message of judgment to those who seek an oracle of Yahweh. Verse 34 follows the question-answer style. It is difficult to determine the speaker of the second section (vv 35-40). Jeremiah seems to be the speaker in vv 35-36, giving a word of instruction to the people who ask for Yahweh's word ("you" is plural in vv 35-36 but singular in v 37). The addressee of v 38 is also the people ("you" in plural). Verses 38-40 clearly contain a judgment word from Yahweh given by the prophet.

Commentators generally agree that only v 33 belongs to Jeremiah and that vv 34-40 are a "midrashic extension" or an extended commentary of v 33 by later contributors to the book (see Holladay 1986, 648). Lundbom, however, shows several verbal similarities and language expressions between vv 34-40 and the rest of the book and convincingly argues that these verses are original to Jeremiah and not the product of a later period (2004a, 213-14).

Those who see vv 34-40 as the product of a later period place these verses in the postexilic period. Lundbom places the entire section (vv 33-40) in the early part of Zedekiah's reign (2004a, 221). The whole discussion here reflects the misuse and abuse of the traditional oracle-giving formula (**oracle of Yahweh**) by the false prophets, and its fits well with the issue of lying prophecy in the preceding section. Thus it is more likely that this unit belongs to the period of Jeremiah's conflict with the false prophets during the reign of Jehoiakim or Zedekiah.

IN THE TEXT

■ **33** In v 33, Yahweh announces to Jeremiah what he should say to anyone in the community who asks him the question, **What is the oracle/burden of Yahweh?** This question may come from the **people, a prophet,** or **a priest.** The context of this question is not clear; the text implies an urgent situation such as an external threat when the community would be frantically seeking a word from Yahweh (see 21:1-2; 37:1-10, 17). This also suggests a situation when oracle-giving would have been a popular activity in the land (see v 34). Yahweh's speech assumes that the people would recognize Jeremiah as a prophet among other prophets in the land who were speaking in Yahweh's name, and that they would come and ask him for the **oracle/burden of Yahweh** (*maśśā' yhwh*), just as they would ask for an oracle from the false prophets in the land.

Oracle/Burden (*maśśā'*)

A key hermeneutical issue in vv 33-40 is the meaning of the word *maśśā'* (from the verb *nāśā'*, meaning "to lift," "to carry," etc.). Hebrew lexicons identify two nouns with the same sound and spelling (*maśśā'*) but with two different meanings (homonym). *Maśśā'* in its literal sense means something "lifted up," and thus a "burden" or a load. The other meaning derives from the technical use of this noun for an utterance or an oracle given by the prophets. Scholars think that the technical sense derives from the idea of lifting up the voice by the prophets. Its technical use as a term for a divine oracle is attested in 2 Kgs 9:25. Other prophetic books use this word (e.g., Isaiah, Nahum, Habakkuk, Zechariah, Malachi) as the title of a prophetic utterance. Though Jeremiah uses this word in its literal sense (17:21-27, for example), it is not found in its technical meaning ("oracle") in Jeremiah except in this text. The NIV translates this word as "oracle" in vv 33-40, which guides a reader to the interpretation that this text as a whole is Yahweh's ban against seeking an oracle or giving an oracle, even by Jeremiah. However, the general consensus of commentators is that the text utilizes here a wordplay on *maśśā'*. The word here seems to have a double meaning; "burden" in a literal sense, and "burden" or "oracle" in a technical sense.

Yahweh tells Jeremiah that **you are the burden** should be his response when anyone in the community asks for a burden/oracle from Yahweh (v 33). The response in Hebrew literally is **what burden/oracle?** (*'et-mah-maśśā'*). Most commentators and modern translations follow the Septuagint reading here and reconstruct the Hebrew to read **you are the burden** (*'attem hammaśśā'*), which fits better with the next phrase **I will cast you off** [I will forsake you (v 33); the Hebrew verb *nāṭaš* conveys here the idea of casting off or throwing off (Holladay 1986, 650)]. This oracle-seeking people have become a **burden** to Yahweh. Yahweh's word to them is that he will throw them off like an unwanted load.

■ **34** Verse 34 implies that oracle-giving had become a common activity in the land. It is no longer the **prophet** who claims to have an oracle; even the **priest** and **the people** also make this claim. This verse is a strong denunciation of anyone using the phrase **the burden of Yahweh** and thus claiming revelation from Yahweh. This verse implies that Yahweh has banned the use of this phrase in the land, which has lost its meaning through its unauthorized use by the people. He also threatens to punish those who violate this ban. Yahweh announces his judgment not only on the individual who makes this claim but also on his entire house.

■ **35** In vv 35-36 Jeremiah seems to be instructing the people (***Thus you shall say each man to his neighbor and each man to his brother;*** v 35) what should be the proper question they should ask among themselves since Yahweh has banned their claim of receiving oracles of Yahweh. The people should no longer say to each other **the oracle of Yahweh** but ask among themselves ***what has Yahweh answered*** or ***spoken*** (v 35). The emphasis here is thus on seeking Yahweh's answer or his spoken word, or true revelation from Yahweh. The point of this verse (v 35) is that a genuine oracle of Yahweh is a word that Yahweh reveals as answer to a request or as his spoken word. This is what the people should seek.

■ **36** Verse 36 again prohibits the **mention** of the **burden of Yahweh**. The reason given here is that the burden/oracle they claim to have received from Yahweh is actually their own words and not words from Yahweh. Only Yahweh's words can be called a burden/oracle of Yahweh. All other words are words that originate in the hearts of those who make the claim that they have an oracle from Yahweh. They actually **distort the words of the living God** when they make their words an oracle from Yahweh. There is no truth-telling in false prophecy, but only a total distortion or perversion of truth.

■ **37** Verse 37 is a near parallel to v 35. This verse also begins with the instruction ***Thus you shall say . . .*** Here the second person (**you**) is in singular; it is difficult to explain the shift from plural in the previous verses to singular in v 37.

Jeremiah seems to be continuing his speech to the people. Lundbom thinks that the singular here is an "impersonal directive"; he supports the translation "one shall say" (2004a, 218). The alternative is to change the singular to the plural and assume here scribal carelessness (Holladay 1986, 648). The instruction to the people here is that they should ask **the prophet** the same questions they have been instructed to ask among themselves (see v 35). Does the prophet mean a specific individual? Jeremiah might be saying to the people that they should ask him, the true prophet, what Yahweh has answered or said.

■ **38-40** Verses 38-40 is a judgment word, an expansion of the judgment stated in v 33. If the people reject the instruction given above and continue to **claim** or seek *the burden of Yahweh* (v 38), then they are faced with the judgment of expulsion from the city that Yahweh gave to them and their ancestors, and from his presence. The NIV follows the Hebrew text of v 39 (**I will surely forget you** from the verb root *nš'*, meaning "to forget"); most commentators and versions translate this phrase as "I will surely lift you up" (reading the verb as *nś'*, meaning "to lift up"). *I will surely lift you up* seems to connect better with the next phrase (**cast you out**). The destiny of those who follow false prophecy is exile. Yahweh will cast them out of the city that they and their ancestors have received from Yahweh as a gift. That means they will be expelled from the **presence** or the nearness of Yahweh (v 39). The nearness of Yahweh to his people has been the theological basis for the false prophets' message of peace and well-being (see discussion of v 23). Moreover, the **disgrace** and **shame** that will come upon them will be **everlasting**; the effect of Yahweh's judgment on those who follow false prophecy will be eternal (v 40).

FROM THE TEXT

Can God's word lose its meaning and significance? In this text, God forbids oracle-seeking and oracle-giving because oracle as God's word has lost its significance. Everyone in the land claimed to have an oracle of God. The proliferation of oracle-seeking and oracle-giving undermined the authenticity of God's word. The preceding text (vv 23-32) indicates that oracles that the people sought were oracles that promised them peace and well-being—good things and good life. The true and authentic words of God spoken by Jeremiah were for the most part words that challenged, confronted, and even threatened the future. This text indicates that giving heed to the authentic voice of God was not an option that the people preferred. Such people have become a burden to God.

In the Christian world, Scripture is readily available in print and in the TV/electronic media. In world areas where Christianity has limited access, Scripture is rarely available to most believers. In both of these contexts, determination of who truly speaks God's word remains a difficult challenge for God's people. In both of these contexts, this task is made more difficult by the proliferation of those who claim to have God's word. Another issue compounds this problem. On the one hand, we have the Scriptures. This is clearly an advantage that we have over the audience of Jeremiah. On the other hand, we, like the people of Judah, are faced with the difficulty of determining what God is doing in our day and how God is fulfilling his eschatological purposes for his creation. So, what do we do, and how do we know what God is saying to us these days? This text instructs with the following guidelines for proper discernment of God's word:

    i. The canonical scripture is the word of God to us today. God who speaks through the Bible is the God who speaks to us. His words are authentic and reliable. The text instructs us to be cautious about those who claim to have God's word but distort his word with their own words.

    ii. Any human voice that claims to speak for God must be tested by the standards set forth by authentic spokespersons of God in the Bible. The criteria that distinguished true prophets from the false prophets in the Bible are still valid today. A significant issue for Jeremiah was to speak God's word faithfully even if that meant disturbing the comfortable life of Judah. Words we hear today that affirm our personal agenda of well-being can certainly be taken as words that do not originate with God.

"UPROOT AND TEAR DOWN"

JUDAH'S CLAIM OF THE LAND (24:1-10)

The Good and the Bad Figs (24:1-10)

Overview

Scholarly discussion on ch 24 focuses primarily on two key questions. The first question is about its authenticity. Some commentators have taken this chapter as the work of Deuteronomistic redactors in the exilic period. They see this chapter as a literary work aimed to place the Babylonian exiles in a more favorable light than those who have remained in the land and those who have escaped to Egypt after 587 B.C. They assume an exilic date by relating the reference to the Jews in Egypt (v 8) to the Jewish emigration to Egypt following the destruction of Jerusalem in 587 B.C. Some scholars also see in this text a theological conflict that developed after 587 B.C. among the various Jewish communities (Babylon, Palestine, Egypt), and the claim of the exiles in Babylon that they are the ones destined to shape the future of Judah. Others recognize some later expansions in this chapter, but consider the chapter for the most part as original to Jeremiah. These scholars think that the reference to the Jews in Egypt pertains to those who have already settled in Egypt prior to 587 B.C.

The text in its present form clearly conveys a situation between 597 and 587 B.C. Those who were left in Jerusalem and Judah after 597 were eventually deported to Babylon in 587. The text gives preferential treatment only to those who were deported in 597 and gives a negative picture of those who were left in the land after 597. If the text belongs to the exilic setting, why would it leave out the deportees of 587 from Yahweh's promised restoration? The exilic setting also raises serious questions about the function of v 8 in this unit.

The second question is on the relationship of this chapter to the rest of the book. Commentators often treat ch 24 as the conclusion of the oracles against the royal family that begin in ch 21 because of the judgment words against Zedekiah and his officials in 24:8 (see 21:7). Some connect this chapter with ch 25 because both chs 24 and 25 deal with the future of Judah and the future of Babylon and all the other nations including Judah. Lundbom argues that in "form, content, and location," this chapter functions as the "beginning" of a new section (chs 24—36) in the book (2004a, 223, 253-54). He includes in the content of chs 24—36 "the Zedekiah Cluster" (chs 24, 27—29), "the Jehoiakim Cluster" (chs 25—26, 35—36), and "the Book of Consolation" (chs 30—33).

The historical introduction together with the vision account (24:1-3) gives this chapter the appearance of a new section in the book. The preceding oracles against the prophets (23:9-40) clearly disconnect ch 24 from the oracles against the royal family. Though the judgment theme in vv 8-10 is reiterated in ch 25, ch 24 has no other literary or theological linkage to ch 25. The hope message of ch 24 receives further expansion in chs 30—33. In the present arrangement of the book, ch 24 thus seems to stand alone without any direct linkage to the preceding and following sections. It primarily serves the purpose of giving a detailed theological commentary on the issue of life in the land vs. life in exile (perhaps a commentary on 21:8-10). Those who are exiled to Babylon receive Yahweh's favor. Those who remain in the land of promise are destined for death and destruction. The ideology presented in this chapter effectively dispels any hope the people have maintained about life in the land as a sign of Yahweh's favor and blessings.

BEHIND THE TEXT

Chapter 24 narrates a prophetic vision of two baskets of figs, one basket with good figs and the other with bad figs, followed by Yahweh's interpretation of the vision. Verses 1-2 describe the setting of the vision and the vision itself. Verse 3 is a dialogue between Yahweh and the prophet. Verses 4-10 contain the interpretation of the vision; the first part of the interpretation (vv 4-7) deals with the good figs. The second part (vv 8-10) deals with the bad figs. The setting of the vision is the temple. It took place after the exile of Jehoiachin in 597 B.C. No specific date is given; it might have taken place anytime between 597 and 587 B.C.

There are some obvious parallels between ch 24 and chs 1 and 21. Yahweh's question and Jeremiah's answer in 24:3 follows the literary pattern of 1:11 and 13. Verse 6 reiterates the theme of 1:10. Lundbom suggests that the vision account together with Yahweh's dialogue with Jeremiah in ch 24 gives it a unique place in the book, similar to that of ch 1 (2004a, 223).

There is also a parallel between vv 6-10 and 21:6-10; in both passages those who remain in the land are given no hope, whereas those who go to Babylon are given the prospect of a future. The judgment on Zedekiah, his officials, and the people of Jerusalem in 21:7 is reiterated in 24:8. Verses 8-10 describe the fate of those who refuse Yahweh's offer of the "way of life" (21:8-10).

IN THE TEXT

■ **1** Verses 1-2 describe the vision and its setting. The text begins with the phrase **Yahweh showed me** (v 1), a typical introduction to vision narratives (see Amos 7:1, 4, 7; 8:1). Yahweh shows Jeremiah in a vision **two baskets of figs**. Some commentators have assumed that this was an objective physical seeing of two real baskets of figs. It is possible that this vision was an inner vision and not real baskets that were physically seen by the prophet. The baskets of figs were set **in front of the temple** (v 1). The text does not indicate a specific location; the ritual in Deut 26:1-4 describes the priest placing the basket of firstfruits "in front of the altar" (v 4). Lundbom suggests that these baskets were offerings of firstfruits placed in the temple for the priest to determine their worthiness (2004a, 228). However, it is difficult to make a clear connection between these baskets and the offering of firstfruits since it is not clear who is bringing these baskets as offering. The rest of this text does not elaborate on any ritualistic aspect of firstfruit offering. The baskets are treated in vv 4-10 as symbolic representation of two groups of people.

The description of the vision is interrupted by a parenthetical statement that places the vision in a historical setting. The vision took place **after** the exile of **Jeconiah** (Jehoiachin), the **officials** of Judah, the **artisans**, and smiths into Babylon by king **Nebuchadnezzar** (v 1). This would place it after 597 B.C. The statement does not give a specific year or month; the vision could have taken place anytime between 597 and 587 B.C. **Officials** is a general term that includes both royal and nonroyal and high-ranking members of the administration (Lundbom 2004a, 229). Artisans and smiths were highly skilled people and a valuable asset to Babylon. Nebuchadnezzar's strategy was to remove from the land its influential political leaders and skilled workers and thus to weaken the nation and reduce the chances of a revolt against Babylon.

■ **2** Verse 2 describes the quality of the figs placed in the baskets. This is what Jeremiah observed in the vision. In one basket he saw **very good** figs; they looked **like the early figs,** or figs that were picked during the first season of harvest in May. The second fig harvest season is in August. The first ripe fig receives several references in the OT as a specially desired fruit (Isa 28:4; Hos 9:10; Mic 7:1). The figs in the other basket were **very . . . bad** or so rotten that **they could not be eaten.** The figs in the two baskets are thus compared and an assessment has been made by the prophet with regard to its usefulness.

■ **3** Verse 3 reports the dialogue between Yahweh and Jeremiah. Yahweh's question is similar to the question in 1:11, 13. **What do you see** is not a casual question but an intentional question that seeks an informed response based on careful observation. Jeremiah gives his careful analysis of what he observes as his answer to Yahweh's question. The good figs are good and useful; the bad figs are bad and unusable.

■ **4-5** Verse 4 introduces Yahweh's word in response to Jeremiah's answer. **Yahweh the God of Israel** announces his plans and purpose for the covenant nation (v 5). The interpretation of the vision in vv 5-10 makes clear that the two types of figs represent two groups of the Judean population. The good figs represent the people whom Yahweh **sent away** from Judah to Babylon (v 5). The text makes clear that the Babylonian exile was not some unfortunate outcome of a military conquest by an imperial power but rather Yahweh's judgment on his own people. He **sent** them **away from this place,** the place he has given to Israel as a gift, to **the land of *the Chaldeans*,** the place from where their ancestor came (v 5). However, Yahweh who sent his people away into exile announces that he will regard the exiles *for* good (*lĕṭôbâ*). The NIV **as good** implies the assessment of moral character. The text does not necessarily mean that Yahweh will consider the exiles as morally superior but that he will regard them with favor and look after their welfare and well-being. His intent is to bestow upon them his blessing.

■ **6** Verses 6-7 continue Yahweh's plan for the exiles of Judah. Throughout these verses the emphasis is on what Yahweh has done or will do (see the repeated "I" in these verses). *I will set my eye upon them for good* means that he will show favor toward the people whom he sent away (v 6). Yahweh's plan is **for their good,** their well-being. He will reverse the judgment and will **bring** the exiles **back to this land.** The exile did not mean the end of the covenantal promises; neither did it cause a permanent relocation of the people from the land of promise. What is being described here is Yahweh's gracious activity and his faithfulness to the covenant promises to Israel's ancestors. **Build, tear . . . down, plant,** and **uproot** are actions found in the call of the prophet (1:10). Yahweh's plan for the exiles is to build them up and plant them and not to tear down or to uproot them. The announcement thus focuses on Yahweh's activity of re-creating and reestablishing his people in the land. Judah's future is not in Babylon but in the land that Yahweh promised to give to the descendants of Abraham, Isaac, and Jacob.

■ **7** Yahweh's plan for the exiled Judah does not end with their return and settlement in the land of promise. He promises to **give them a heart to know** him (v 7). This promise together with the promise of the covenant is further elaborated in 31:31-34. The promise of the gift of a heart (**I will give them a heart**) is reiterated in 32:39 and in Ezek 11:19 and 36:26. **To know** Yahweh means to enter into a personal and covenantal relationship with him. The people who have refused to live in faithfulness to the covenant because of their stubborn heart (7:24; 11:8) are promised here the gift of a new heart. Heart is the center of human thoughts, emotions, and will. The gift of a heart suggests a radical reorientation of the people from their self-centered ways to an obedient and faithful response to Yahweh. **I am *Yahweh*** expresses his sovereign grace and freedom to bestow the gift of a new heart to the people with a stubborn heart.

The gift of a heart will further reestablish the covenant relationship between Yahweh and his people (v 7). The reiteration of the ancient covenant formula (**they will be my people, and I will be their God**), also found in 7:23; 11:4; 30:22; 31:1, 33; 32:38), indicates that Yahweh's commitment to Israel made long ago at Mount Sinai has not changed in spite of Israel's sin and Yahweh's judgment. The people broke the covenant, but Yahweh offers to mend it. Yahweh anticipates that the promise of the gift of a heart and the promise of reestablishing the covenant will prompt the people to **return** to Yahweh ***with their whole* heart** (v 7). **Return** (*šûb*) is a total turnabout from a self-directed way to the way of living life under the instructions of Yahweh. Repentance in this verse is the total and unreserved response of the heart to Yahweh's promises to his people.

■ **8** Verses 8-10 identify the bad figs with **Zedekiah**, **his officials**, those who **remain in this land** and those who have escaped to **Egypt** (v 8). Their future is described in vivid details. Unlike the Judeans exiled to Babylon, these people do not receive any promises, but they are threatened with shame, banishment, and destruction. The fate of these people will be like that of the **bad** figs that cannot be eaten, but thrown away (v 8). The reason for Yahweh's unfavorable treatment of these people is not clear. It is possible that this judgment is pronounced because of the refusal of Zedekiah and his supporters to surrender to the king of Babylon (chs 27—28), the instrument of Yahweh's judgment. Judgment is also pronounced on those who have attempted to escape the judgment, either by remaining **in this land** or by escaping to **Egypt**. Migdol and Memphis were places of Jewish settlement before Jeremiah arrived at Tahpanhes with Johanan and his group (44:1). Bright thinks that the pro-Egyptian Jews settled in Egypt when Jehoiakim became an ally of Babylon (603 B.C.) or when Babylon invaded Judah in 597 B.C. (1965, 193).

■ **9-10** Those who have refused to acknowledge Babylon as the instrument of Yahweh's judgment are faced with a more serious calamity. Using a series of words that convey Yahweh's curse upon this group (***horror, evil, reproach, byword, taunt, curse***), v 9 announces Yahweh's banishment of this people from the land. Verse 10 uses another familiar series of words (**sword, famine, *pestilence***) to announce the total destruction of this group of people from the land that they and their ancestors have received from Yahweh.

FROM THE TEXT

This vision and its interpretation make clear God's direct and intimate involvement in the history of Judah. It was he who sent Judah into exile; Babylon was his designated place where Judah should spend its days of judgment. Those who have escaped to Egypt and whoever was left in the land by the Babylonians live outside of that world. They may have considered themselves as those who have escaped God's judgment or who are unaffected by it. But the text makes it known to them that in reality, they, too, live in a world of judgment, a world in which the judgment will be far more severe and a world out of which there is no escape. This is the destiny of those who attempt to circumvent God's judgment.

This text is mostly about what God is planning to do for those whom he has sent into exile. Though they are under his judgment, they hear words of God's loving care and gracious concern. They are part of his plans for the nation. The future belongs to them because God is with them. They receive words of hope for their future, their return to the land, and the rebuilding of their relationship with God. He offers to reverse their misfortune and do for them what they themselves are unable to do. They did not do anything in particular to deserve this promise of future. This promise comes as a surprise to them and to all who read this text. What this text announces is the surprising grace of God. He gives hope to those who live without hope. The God who speaks in this text is the God who does for us what we are unable to do for ourselves. We find in the New Testament the story of this God who showed his surprising grace and love through Jesus Christ to the helpless and sinful humanity (Rom 5:6-8). The God who gives hope in this text is a God who will not disappoint those who trust in his promises.

God promises in this text the gift of a heart that knows God and the re-establishment of his covenant relationship with his people. What we see here is the lavish display of God's love and grace to those who have rejected his love and grace. This is God's gift to his people who have squandered their blessings and reneged on their covenant relationship with him. This is a gift that they do not deserve; yet God offers this gift without conditions. This gift is "pure grace" (Miller 2001, 759). This gift is offered to those are characterized in this book as a people with a stubborn and rebellious heart, people with a sin-engraved heart. As such, they are unable to respond to God or return to him. And so, what is offered here is a *new* heart. It is this *new* heart that motivates faithful response—the return to God with "their whole heart" (v 7 NRSV). Hearts that are touched by the work of God's grace are the hearts that are able to respond to God's grace. Returning to God with one's whole heart means repentance of sin and commitment to loving God with one's whole heart, soul, and strength (Deut 6:5). The gift of a heart thus anticipates from its recipients love and devotion. As John puts it, "We love because he first loved us" (1 John 4:19).

"UPROOT AND TEAR DOWN"

JUDAH AND THE NATIONS (25:1-38)

Overview

Chapter 25 concludes the first half of the book of Jeremiah. Yahweh's judgment on Judah and the nations is the major theme in these chapters. Babylon is clearly identified here as the enemy from the north mentioned in the previous chapters. Chapter 25 signals the rise of Nebuchadnezzar to power, which in turn indicates that Yahweh's judgment of Judah has already begun. However, Babylon itself will be judged when Yahweh brings his judgment on the nations.

Most commentators think chs 1—25 contain the oracles that Jeremiah dictated to Baruch in 605 B.C. (see 36:1-32). The original scroll that Baruch made was destroyed by King Jehoiakim. The prophet dictated his words a second time to Baruch, which he wrote down on another scroll. This second scroll contained the prophet's words that were part of the original scroll as well as other words of the prophet (36:32). Based on 25:1-3, 13 commentators assume that the words that Jeremiah dictated to Baruch constitute his message to Judah during the first twenty-three years of his preaching (627-605 B.C.). Commentators also think that ch 25 concludes the judgment oracles in the book.

The content of ch 25 can be divided into two sections. The first section (vv 1-14) is an announcement of Yahweh's judgment of Judah for its disobedience. Nebuchadnezzar is Yahweh's servant-agent; but he and Babylon will in the end be punished. The second section (vv 15-38) has two parts. In vv 15-29, the prophet gives Yahweh's wrath to all nations to drink. In vv 30-38, Yahweh's judgment is announced to the whole world.

A summary of the judgment message of chs 2—24 is given in 25:1-14. This section thus serves as a fitting conclusion to chs 1—24. The second section (25:15-38) with its introductory "cup of wrath" theme anticipates Yahweh's judgment word against Judah (see chs 27—29; 34—45) and the nations (see chs 46—51). Yahweh's judgment on Judah is thus linked to his judgment on the nations (for a different perspective on ch 25, see Lundbom 2004a, 238). In the Septuagint (LXX), the Oracles Against the Foreign Nations are placed after 25:13*a* (after "all that are written in this book"). These oracles are found in chs 46—51 in the Hebrew Bible (MT) and English versions.

The introductory statement (v 1) places 25:1-14 in the fourth year of Jehoiakim (605 B.C.). The cup of Yahweh's wrath given to the nations to drink (vv 15-29) indicates the beginning of Yahweh's judgment on the nations. Though Babylon itself is among the nations judged in this text (v 26), the text seems to indicate the Babylonian army advancing against the nations in the Syria-Palestine area following the Babylonian victory over Egypt in the Battle of Carchemish in 605 B.C. Verses 30-38, which deal with Yahweh's universal judgment, also could be placed in this general setting of 605 B.C.

1. Because You Have Not Obeyed (25:1-14)

BEHIND THE TEXT

Verses 1-2 constitute the introduction and the setting of the message. Jeremiah is the speaker in vv 3-4. These verses present Jeremiah and other prophets as Yahweh's messengers. Verses 5-7 are a summary of the message from Yahweh that Jeremiah preached for twenty-three years. Verses 8-11 contain the judgment word against Judah. The unit ends with a judgment word against Babylon (vv 12-14).

IN THE TEXT

■ **1-2** Verses 1-2 indicate that the message that follows is Yahweh's word that he received **concerning . . . the people of Judah,** which he related to them and to the citizens of Jerusalem. He received this word in **the fourth year of Jehoiakim** (605 B.C.), which is also identified as **the first year of Nebuchadnezzar king of Babylon** (v 1). These historical references are intentionally placed in this text. The rise of Nebuchadnezzar to the throne of Babylon in 605 B.C. signaled a critical shift in the balance of world power in the ancient Near East. The Babylonian victory over

Egypt in the Battle of Carchemish opened the way for Nebuchadnezzar to expand his conquest into the Syria-Palestine region (Bright 2000, 326-27). Judah's fate is now firmly in the hands of Nebuchadnezzar.

■ **3** Verse 3 states that Jeremiah received Yahweh's word and preached persistently **for twenty-three years,** from the thirteenth year of Josiah (627 B.C.) *until this day,* the fourth year of Jehoiakim (605 B.C.). Verse 3 ends with the indictment that in spite of the prophet's unrelenting preaching, the nation has not listened or responded to Yahweh's word.

■ **4** Verse 4 is another summary statement. It asserts that Yahweh repeatedly **sent all his servants the prophets** to Judah with his word (see also 7:25; it also asserts the failure of Judah to pay attention to their words. Jeremiah thus stands among a multitude of prophets that Judah had rejected.

■ **5** Verses 5-7 sum up Yahweh's message that the prophets conveyed to Judah. Yahweh demanded his covenant people to *return*/repent of their *evil way and their evil doings* (v 5). *Return* or repent (*šûb*) of evil has been Jeremiah's consistent message to Judah (3:12, 14; 4:1, etc.). This is the same demand Yahweh placed upon the people through other prophets. *Evil way* and *evil doings* are actions and lifestyle contrary to the covenant way of life. Yahweh repeatedly reminded the nation that repentance and covenant faithfulness are essential conditions for the nation's continued existence **in the land** (v 5). Life in the land that Yahweh has given to the people and their forefathers **for ever and ever** can continue only if the people lived in obedience to Yahweh's call to repentance. The land is a gift from Yahweh, but that gift comes with conditions.

■ **6** Yahweh's message through the prophets included the prohibition of worshipping **other gods,** the work of human hands (v 6). Through the prophets Yahweh also gave both warning and promise to his people: the warning not to **provoke** Yahweh **to anger** by worshipping the work of their hands, and the promise that if they obey his demands, he would do them no **harm** or evil (*ra'*).

■ **7** Verse 7 is the indictment that the people did not listen to Yahweh; they did exactly the opposite of what Yahweh commanded them not to do and worshipped the work of their hands. Consequently, Yahweh was provoked to anger.

■ **8-9** The judgment word (vv 8-14) deals with Judah first (vv 8-11) and then with Babylon (vv 12-14). **Therefore** . . . "**because you have not listened to my words** . . ." (v 8) implies that the people have done what they were commanded not to do. The judgment that is being announced is thus the consequence of the sins of the people. Verses 9-10 utilize a number of first person pronouncements. Verse 9 makes clear the political nature of the judgment and Yahweh's direct control of contemporary political events. *I am sending and I will take all the tribes of the north* (v 9) reflects the language of 1:14-15. A coalition of forces from the north will come against Judah as Yahweh's agent of judgment. Yahweh will also bring against Judah and its inhabitants and against all the neighboring nations **Nebuchadnezzar king of Babylon, my** (Yahweh's) **servant.** Second Kings 24:2 mentions an attack on Judah by bands of Chaldeans, Syrians, Moabites, and

Ammonites. Bright suggests that these guerrilla groups were dispatched by Nebuchadnezzar around 600-599 B.C. to keep Judah off-balance in retaliation against Jehoiakim's rebellion (2 Kgs 24:1) in 601 B.C. (2000, 327). This was followed by the arrival of the Babylonian army in 597 B.C.

The reference to Nebuchadnezzar as **my servant** (v 9; also in 27:6 and 43:10) is unusual; this designation is usually applied to Yahweh's faithful prophets and others like Jacob and David in the book of Jeremiah. The term here has limited application; the Babylonian king is Yahweh's servant only in the sense that he will fulfill a particular purpose of Yahweh. The first person verbs in vv 9-10 indicate that Yahweh is the One who is acting in and through these events. Nebuchadnezzar is simply a human agency that Yahweh has chosen to execute his judgment. At a later time he chose Cyrus the Persian king as his agent ("shepherd," "anointed," in Isa 44:28; 45:1) through whom he brought salvation to the exiled Judah.

Yahweh's intent is to use the tribes of the north and Nebuchadnezzar to destroy Judah (**this land**) and its inhabitants as well as all the neighboring nations (v 9). **I will completely destroy them** (*haḥăramtîm*, from *ḥāram*, lit. "I will devote them to destruction") conveys the holy war idea (Lundbom 2004a, 247). This action is similar to the ban (*ḥērem* or dedicating the captured cities and the people and their properties for destruction) that Israel practiced during the conquest period (Deut 2:34-35). Holladay sees here a connection between Yahweh's plan to destroy the idolatrous Judah and the command to destroy idolatrous cities in Deut 13:12-18 (1986, 668). Judah and the neighboring nations will become desolate lands, places that are cursed as objects of utter disgrace and horror. The desolation will be such that these lands will remain in **ruins for ever**.

■ **10** Verse 10 shows that Yahweh's judgment will bring an end to all joyous occasions and daily life in the land that will be made desolate by the Babylonian army. The end to the **sounds of joy and gladness** and the **voices of bride and bridegroom** are stereotypical expressions found in judgment speeches (see also 7:34; 16:9). The land that will be made desolate is a land where no expression of joy will be heard. **The sound of millstones** reflects the daily activity of grinding grain to make bread, done most likely in the morning. **The light of the lamp** indicates the beginning of evening and the night life. Desolation of the land will also mean the end to all normal human life and activities, both day and night. Judah will suffer the consequences of covenant-breaking; the blessings of life that the covenant guaranteed will be taken away from the land that has become idolatrous.

Seventy Years

In 25:11 ("these nations will serve the king of Babylon seventy years") and in 29:10 ("When seventy years are completed for Babylon") Jeremiah makes reference to "seventy years." Later traditions of Judaism interpreted the "seventy years" of Jeremiah as the period that God had allotted for the desolation of Jerusalem and the temple (see Dan 9:2; Zech 1:12; 7:5; 2 Chr 36:21). It is difficult to precisely date the "seventy years" of Babylon. This seems to correspond to the seventy-year period that spans from the end of the Assyrian power in 609 B.C. and the defeat of Babylon by Persia in 539 B.C. However, there were only sixty-six years from the rise of Nebuchadnezzar to power (605 B.C.) to the defeat of Babylon in 539 B.C. "Seventy years" in the Hebrew thinking indicates the full length of a set period of time (see "seventy years" as the full life-span in Ps 90:10). This number in Jeremiah thus may simply mean that Babylon will exercise its control over the nations the full length of time that God had set for it to do so, rather than a literal seventy years.

■ **11** Verse 11 begins with another word about the ruin and desolation that will come upon *this land* or Judah. The second part of v 11 announces the servitude of Judah and the surrounding nations (**these nations**) to Babylon for **seventy years**.

■ **12** Verse 12 also seems to connect seventy years to the Babylonian hegemony over Judah and other nations. This verse focuses on Yahweh's judgment on Babylon after its dominion over other nations for seventy years. The rest of v 12 clearly shows that Babylon, though it acted as Yahweh's agent of judgment, is not exempt from his judgment on the nations. He will **punish** (*pāqad* meaning "visit," "punish," etc.) **the king of Babylon,** the Babylonians, and *the land of the Chaldeans* (Babylon) **for their guilt.** The guilt of Babylon is not specifically stated here. Yahweh calls for the punishment of Babylon for its pride and defying Yahweh the Holy One of Israel (50:29). The judgment word in 51:24 refers to all the evil the Babylonians have done in Zion as the reason for Yahweh's punitive action against that nation. The nation that has devastated Judah and made it a desolate land forever itself will be devastated and made **desolate forever.**

■ **13** Verse 13 continues the theme of judgment on Babylon. Yahweh will bring upon **that land** (Babylon) the fulfillment of all the words he has spoken against it. The phrase *everything* written in this book *which Jeremiah prophesied against all the nations* is unclear. This part of v 13 may be an editorial insertion. If this assumption is correct, its function may have been to authenticate Jeremiah as a "prophet to the nations" (1:5, 10). Verse 13 continues the focus on Babylon and then it shifts to all the nations, which may very well include Judah. The oracles of judgment in vv 15-38 include Judah and the nations, including Babylon. The identity of **this book** is a widely debated issue among scholars. Does this mean a scroll that contained oracles against Babylon and other nations, that is presently found in chs 46—51? Or, does it refer to the book in its present form with 52 chapters? Or, does it refer to the scroll that Baruch made at the dictation of Jeremiah (36:32). Though a definitive answer cannot be given, **this book** indicates the existence of a scroll of Jeremiah at some point in the history of its formation in some form other than the present

25:10-13

form of the book.

■ **14** The judgment on Babylon is continued in v 14. Just as the Babylonians have made other nations their slaves, they themselves will become slaves to **many nations and great kings.** Moreover, Yahweh will **repay** the Babylonians for their **deeds,** which are evil, and for its idolatry or worshipping **the work of their hands. Repay** (from the verb *šālēm*, meaning "be complete") conveys the idea of "coming full circle" (Fretheim 2002, 356). No one is exempt from judgment, not even Yahweh's chosen servants! The evil they have committed will indeed be their own experience when Yahweh brings his judgment on them.

FROM THE TEXT

This text is bold in its claim of God's lordship over human history. God is not simply the God of Israel; he is the God of the world. The sovereign God of the world is fully engaged in the affairs of the world. Judah is about to experience his sovereignty as judgment. What is shocking about this word of judgment is that God will use a ruthless pagan king as his servant to carry out his judgment. The Babylonian takeover of Judah is another display of God's sovereignty. The text also makes clear that the agents of God's judgment themselves will ultimately be brought under judgment. They, too, will experience God's sovereignty as judgment. The sin of Judah is its persistent rejection of God's persistent word. The sin of Babylon is its evil deeds, idolatry, pride, and arrogance. No one is exempt from the judgment of the sovereign God.

God using an evil power to accomplish his sovereign purposes is an unsettling issue for the modern readers of this text. Modern history of the world also has its share of brutal and evil world powers and rulers. It is difficult for us to assume that God would use an evil person like Adolph Hitler to accomplish his purposes in the world. It is equally difficult for us to speculate on the good purposes of God every time we see evil leaders or evil people causing ruthless destruction in the world. Ironically, in Isaiah, Cyrus the Persian is the agent of God's salvation to the exiled people of Judah (Isa 44:28—45:7). What Nebuchadnezzar the pagan king destroyed, Cyrus the pagan king will rebuild! Texts like these leave us perplexed about God's ways of working out his sovereignty in the world, even wondering about the morality of God's sovereignty. What the text asserts here is that he will not let Babylon, an evil empire, reign forever. Babylon's end is certain. "Seventy years" thus portend God's commitment to let justice prevail over evil in the end, even over evil that he has used for his good purposes.

Total destruction is the verdict on Judah. Life as Judah has known it will terminate. This is because of God's holy war against Judah. This war would result in the "everlasting" ruin of everything in the land. The good news in this text is that even that word of the end of everything is not final. This condition will last only for "seventy years." The "seventy years" thus portend for Judah a future; that future is not specified here but only hinted. God's judgment on Babylon will be the end of desolation and destruction for Judah. Beyond the days of desolation wait the days of reconstruction, restoration, renewal, and transformation. Judah will again experience God's sovereignty—this time as restoration and renewal. The text thus speaks about an end that is really the beginning of new life for God's people.

2. The Cup of Wrath and Yahweh's Universal Judgment (25:15-38)

BEHIND THE TEXT

In the first part of this unit (vv 15-29), the cup of wrath given to the nations is the main theme. In vv 15-16, Yahweh speaks to Jeremiah to take the cup of wrath from his hand and make the nations drink from it. In vv 17-29, the prophet executes this command. In the present arrangement of these verses, vv 27-29 interrupt the flow of thought. In verse 17 the prophet obeys the command and makes the nations drink the cup; this is followed by a list of the nations that drank the cup (vv 18-26). In vv 27-29, there is another speech from Yahweh; here the prophet is asked to speak to the nations to drink the cup and vomit (v 27). Verses 28-29 report Yahweh's words that the prophet must speak to the nations that may refuse to drink the cup. Commentators have attempted to resolve the awkwardness of the narrative by suggesting either vv 17-26 or vv 27-29 as later additions to the text. Taken together, this unit illustrates how Jeremiah carried out his commission by Yahweh to be a prophet to the nations (1:5, 10). This narrative seems to describe a symbolic act; however, it does not state how the prophet carried out the act of making the nations drink from the cup or what represented the nations listed in the narrative. Commentators think that symbolic act may have been part of a vision experience in which the prophet receives a command from Yahweh and fulfills it.

The second part of vv 15-38 announces Yahweh's judgment against all humanity (vv 30-38). This section continues the theme of the cup of Yahweh's wrath on all nations. This section is in poetry except for v 33. Verses 30-31 announce Yahweh's lawsuit against humanity. Verses 32-33 speak of the dead bodies of those slain by Yahweh's storm covering the surface of the earth. The unit ends with an oracle that calls the shepherds to wail because Yahweh is about to destroy their pasture (vv 34-38).

IN THE TEXT

■ **15** Yahweh's speech to Jeremiah begins with two imperatives: **take from my hand this cup . . . make all the nations . . . drink . . .** The cup is already in Yahweh's hand; the prophet is simply the human agency. The content of the cup is **the wine of** Yahweh's **wrath** (v 15). The cup in the Bible is a symbol of divine wrath, as is the case here (see also 49:12; 51:7; Pss 11:6 [NRSV]; 75:8; Lam 4:21; Rev 14:10; 16:19; 18:6), or of blessing and salvation (Pss 16:5; 23:5). Jeremiah is Yahweh's cupbearer who is being commanded here to force the nations to drink the wine of Yahweh's wrath from the cup. The picture is not that of a friendly dinner table but a hostile setting in which the guests may not refuse what is offered them to drink. Even those who may resist must ultimately comply with the demand of the host (see vv 28-29). The text is parallel to 13:12-14 where the whole nation of Judah is forced to drink from the wine jar filled with wine.

■ **16** As the divinely sent messenger, the prophet's function is to make the nations drink the cup; i.e., deliver to them the powerful word of judgment that will make the nations **stagger and go mad** (v 16). The imagery here is that of a person who had too much to drink and had thus become physically unstable and lost mental capacity. However, the quantity of wine consumed is not the issue here but rather the effectiveness of the potent and lethal words of judgment. Yahweh's judgment will make those being judged totally powerless and ineffective. The judgment will be carried out by Yahweh's **sword** that he is sending among the nations (v 16). The sword here is most likely Nebuchadnezzar and his army that is marching against the nations (see v 9).

■ **17** Verse 17 reports the obedient response of the prophet. In the vision, the prophet carried out the commission and made all the nations to whom Yahweh sent him drink from the cup of Yahweh's wrath.

■ **18** The nations to whom the prophet is sent by Yahweh (see 1:5, 7, 10) with his cup of wrath are identified in vv 18-26. The first in the list of the nations to drink the cup of Yahweh's wrath is **Jerusalem** and **the towns of Judah** and its **kings** and **officials** (v 18). Yahweh's covenant people are placed first in the list to drink his cup of wrath. The outcome of this will be the ruin and desolation of the land, which will make it an object of total contempt and cursing. **As they are today** may be an editorial addition to indicate that the judgment word had been fulfilled.

■ **19-26** Verses 19-26 list the non-Israelite nations that are given Yahweh's cup of wrath; the list begins with Egypt and ends with Babylon. Egypt is the old enemy of Yahweh who resisted his sovereign plans. It is also the first nation listed in the oracles against the nations (46:1-26; see also 43:10-13). It is important to note that vv 18-26 specifically mention **all the kings** of the nations as the recipients of Yahweh's cup of wrath. Yahweh establishes his sovereignty and lordship over the nations by bringing his judgment on the sovereign rulers of the nations. The judgment on the kings is also judgment on the nations. The

mixed people of Egypt (v 20) refer most likely to the people of foreign origin (**foreign people**).

The specific location of the land of **Uz** (v 20) is not known. Uz is not among the nations listed in the oracles against the nations. This land mentioned in Job 1:1 is associated with Edom in Gen 36:28 and with Aram/Syria in Gen 10:23. Some scholars think it refers to a location in northwest Arabia. The listing of the cities of the Philistines includes **Ashkelon, Gaza, Ekron,** and **Ashdod,** four of the five major cities of the Philistines located in the coastal plain southwest of Judah (v 20). **Edom, Moab,** and **Ammon** (v 21) are located south, southeast, and east of the land of Judah. **Tyre** and **Sidon** (v 22) are located northwest of Israel. **Dedan, Tema,** and **Buz** (v 23) are locations probably in the Arabian Desert. ***All who have shaven temples*** (v 23; see NIV footnote) probably refers to some particular desert inhabitants in Arabia. Verse 24 includes all the inhabitants of the Arabian Desert. **Zimri** (v 25) is an unidentifiable location. **Elam,** located east of lower Tigris, and **Media** (v 25), located in the northwest part of modern Iran, were powerful nations in the late seventh and early sixth centuries B.C. **All the kings of the north, near and far** (v 26) include any nation in the northern region not listed in the previous verses. **All the kingdoms on the face of the earth** will drink from the cup of Yahweh's wrath. No nation is left out; no nation is immune to judgment. The last part of v 26 makes this clear. After all the nations have drunk from the cup of Yahweh's wrath, it would be the turn of **the king of Sheshach** or Babylon (v 26).

25:26-27

Sheshach

Scholars recognize Sheshach (ššk) as a cipher for Babylon (bbl), and an example of the device called atbash (also found in 51:41), the substitution of Hebrew consonants in reverse alphabetical order (the last letter tāv substituted for the first letter ālef, the next to the last letter šîn for the second letter bêt and so on). The purpose of the use of this cipher is not clear. It may be a cryptic device or simply a wordplay.

Babylon, the agent of Yahweh's judgment on the nations, itself will drink the cup of Yahweh's wrath (v 26). Babylon is an evil nation though Yahweh has used it to carry out his judgment. Its mention at the end shows the plan of Yahweh to fulfill his purpose. The destroyer of Judah itself will be destroyed. This must have been a comforting message to the Judean population to whom Yahweh's elevation of Nebuchadnezzar as his servant posed a theological dilemma.

■ **27** The flow of thought in vv 15-29 can be better understood if we place vv 27-29 between v 16 and v 17. In vv 27-29, the prophet is commanded again by Yahweh to speak to the nations. The One who gives this command is ***Yahweh of hosts the God of Israel***, who is sovereign over the nations and to whom all the armies of heaven and earth belong. Jeremiah is to command the kings of the nations to **drink, get drunk and vomit, and fall to rise no more** (v 27). The imperatives **drink, get drunk,** and **vomit** indicate total intoxication with the wine of Yahweh's wrath. The second part of v 27 makes clear that the **sword** (the army of Babylon) that Yahweh is sending will effectively and completely destroy the nations; the nations are given no hope of ever rising up again.

■ **28** Verse 28 implies the possibility that some nations may resist this command and refuse to drink the cup of Yahweh's wrath. Yahweh instructs Jeremiah to speak to these defiant nations in the name of **Yahweh of hosts** and demand them to drink the cup of Yahweh's wrath **(You must drink it!** v 28). No one can resist Yahweh's judgment; no one is exempt from it.

■ **29** The prophet is then to tell these nations that they cannot expect to **go unpunished** given the fact that Yahweh's judgment is already coming upon Jerusalem, the city that is called by his name (v 29). The *evil* that is coming upon Yahweh's beloved city signals the beginning of his judgment on all the inhabitants on the earth. There is no escaping from the **sword,** the army of Babylon that Yahweh is summoning to carry out his judgment of the nations. The text does not indicate the specific sins of these nations. The announcement of judgment means that they have been found guilty of violating the standards of proper human conduct.

■ **30** The final section of ch 25 is introduced as an oracle from Yahweh (vv 30-38). Yahweh commissions the prophet to **prophesy . . . against them** (v 30); i.e., the nations that have been given his cup of wrath to drink. The oracle begins with the image of Yahweh as a roaring lion and then moves to the image of those who tread grapes (v 30). The unit also ends with the image of Yahweh as a roaring lion (v 38). The heavenly dwelling of Yahweh **(on high . . . holy dwelling)** is the place from where he roars against his *pasture* (see Amos 1:2, where he roars from Zion/Jerusalem). His *pasture* (not **his land** as in the NIV, which implies the land of Judah) is the whole earth. The last line of v 30 makes this clear. The whole earth belongs to Yahweh, and now he is coming to destroy it like a hungry lion. The roar of the lion is compared to the **shout** of **those tread the grapes** (v 30). At the harvesttime those who tread the grapes will shout and sing for everyone to hear their joy at the season of harvest. Yahweh's shout, however, is the expression of his fury against his pasture, **against all who live on the earth.**

■ **31** Yahweh's shout will be so loud, like the **tumult** or the "battle shout" (Lundbom 2004a, 271) of a great marching army, that it will be heard throughout the earth (v 31). The image changes in v 31 to that of a prosecutor who is bringing a *case* (*rîb* has a legal connotation, meaning "case," "dispute," "controversy") **against the nations,** and seeking **judgment** *against all flesh.* **He has given the wicked over to the sword** (v 31) indicates that the nations have been found guilty and have received the judgment from Yahweh who is not only the prosecutor but also the judge. **The sword** is the Babylonian army, the instrument of Yahweh's judgment.

■ **32-33** In vv 32-33, the image of judgment changes to evil (*rā'â*) that goes forth **from nation to nation** and a **mighty storm** that is ***stirring from the farthest part of the earth*** (v 32). The intent of v 32 is to show that Yahweh's judgment will destroy the nations from the entire earth. The evil or disaster that Yahweh is sending will spread from one nation to another like a fierce storm that blows everything away until all the nations are destroyed. The result of this evil that Yahweh is sending is that **from one end of the earth to the other** there will be dead bodies, those who are slain by Yahweh, scattered like *dung* on the ground (v 33). There will be none left to gather the dead or make lamentations for them or to bury them because the judgment will be extensive and will include all humanity. The march of the Babylonian army conquering the nations on its way is the evil/storm intended by these verses. Babylon will be the instrument with which Yahweh will bring about his judgment on the nations.

■ **34-35** The last part of this unit begins with a call to the shepherds to lament, but then moves on to describe the shepherds as helpless and lamenting because of the desolation that is being caused by the wrath of Yahweh (vv 34-38). It is not clear if this oracle is addressed to the shepherds/rulers of Judah. There is no reference to the nations in these verses, so some commentators think the oracle is addressed to the rulers of Judah. In the present context, it is likely that the shepherds are kings of the nations addressed in vv 17-26.

The text announces the arrival of the days of the **slaughter, scattering**, and the **fall** of the rulers of Judah (v 34). The only thing the shepherds can do in the face of their impending doom is to **weep and wail** and **roll in the dust** (v 34), rituals that people perform when tragedy comes. The ominous phrase, *fulfilled are your days for slaughter,* conveys the idea that verdict of death has been given and the day of execution has come (v 34). Verse 34 also indicates the *scattering* of the rulers (*your scattering,* omitted in the NIV). They all will **fall** and become like the broken pieces of a **fine pottery** that cannot be mended or repaired (v 34). This verse thus conveys the usual ideas of death, exile, and fall from glory found in judgment oracles. When the day of slaughter comes, the shepherds and leaders will find themselves at a loss, without any place for escape (v 35).

■ **36-37** Verses 36-37 portray two realities; Yahweh's burning anger that wreaks havoc on the peaceful pasture of the shepherds, and the cry and wailing that rise from the shepherds because of the devastation of their pasture. The shepherds are doing precisely what the prophet has called them to do ("weep and wail"; v 34). There is nothing left for the shepherds; their flock has been destroyed and their land has been devastated. This has been brought about by Yahweh's **fierce anger** that is raging against them (v 37).

■ **38** The text returns to the lion image in v 38. Yahweh, like a young lion, has left his lair/abode to make waste the peaceful abodes of the shepherds of the nations. Commentators are not clear on the meaning of *mippĕnê ḥărôn hayyônâ* (lit. "before the oppressive burning"); see the NIV **because of the sword of the oppressor.** The NIV follows the reading of *ḥereb* ("sword") in the place of the MT *ḥărôn* ("burning"), based on some Hebrew manuscripts and the Septuagint. The text makes clear that it is the ***burning anger*** of Yahweh (vv 37, 38) that is causing the massive devastation of the land.

FROM THE TEXT

God's sovereignty over the world is clearly the issue here. Judah and the nations in the world will experience God's sovereignty as judgment. The judgment begins with Judah, in the "household of God" (1 Pet 4:17 NRSV). Judgment then moves in to the sphere of the nations in the world. No nation in the world is exempt from the experience of God's judgment. Chapters 1—25 make it clear that God's judgment came upon his elect people for their failure to keep his *torah*, for their failure to listen and obey and fulfill their covenantal obligations. Though issues like idolatry and pride and arrogance of the nations are mentioned here and there in chs 1—25, here we do not have any specific list of the crimes committed by the nations. The specific references to kings in vv 18-26 suggest that these nations, including Judah, refused to submit themselves to the sovereign rule of God. So, the judgment here may not necessarily be judgment for a particular crime committed by these nations, but for their claim of autonomy and freedom from God's sovereignty over the world. Kings of these nations ruled their people with their own laws and refused to acknowledge the truth that they stand under the transcendent authority of God who created the universe. The text clearly conveys the intent of God who rules the world to call everyone in God's creation to accountability to the Creator. In a world where kings, presidents, prime ministers, or some ruthless dictators rule, this text asserts that "God has not abdicated God's governance" (Brueggemann 1998, 227). The theme of final judgment in the NT clearly reflects this perspective.

This text's claim of God's sovereignty is what brings comfort to God's people, then and now. Judah in exile would have found hope for its future in the assertion of this truth in this text. The God of Israel who raises kings and kingdoms is also the God who brings them down. What the community in exile can hope for is another display of God's sovereignty in the historical processes that would create for it a context for its deliverance. The prophet hints at this in his announcement of "building and planting" in several places in chs 1—25 (see 12:14-16; 18:7-9; 24:6). The second part of Jeremiah (chs 26—52) fully develops this hope for the community in exile. The Christian community finds this hope fully realized in Jesus Christ. In the Christian thinking, God displays his sovereignty on the cross both as judgment and salvation of the sinful world. The cross announces the "wrath of God . . . revealed from heaven" (Rom 1:18), but it also symbolizes the justification of sinners by "grace" through their faith in "the redemption that is in Christ Jesus" (Rom 3:24 NRSV). To those who have been given the "cup of wrath" to drink, the cross offers the "cup" that "is the new covenant" in the blood of Christ (1 Cor 11:25). This is the good news of the gospel of Jesus Christ.

www.ingramcontent.com/pod-product-compliance
Lightning Source LLC
Chambersburg PA
CBHW070300240426
43661CB00057B/2601